D1707000

RENEWALS 458-4574
DATE DUE

WITHDRAWN
UTSA LIBRARIES

Histories of
the Modern Middle East

Histories of the Modern Middle East

NEW DIRECTIONS

EDITED BY

Israel Gershoni
Hakan Erdem
Ursula Woköck

LYNNE RIENNER PUBLISHERS
BOULDER
LONDON

Published in the United States of America in 2002 by
Lynne Rienner Publishers, Inc.
1800 30th Street, Boulder, Colorado 80301
www.rienner.com

and in the United Kingdom by
Lynne Rienner Publishers, Inc.
3 Henrietta Street, Covent Garden, London WC2E 8LU

© 2002 by Lynne Rienner Publishers, Inc. All rights reserved

Library of Congress Cataloging-in-Publication Data
Histories of the modern Middle East : new directions / [edited by] Israel Gershoni, Hakan Erdem, and Ursula Wokoeck.
p. cm.
Includes bibliographical references and index.
ISBN 1-58826-049-6 (alk. paper)
1. Middle East—Historiography. 2. Nationalism—Middle East. 3. National state. 4. Globalization. 5. Historiography—Middle East. I. Gershoni, I. II. Erdem, Y. Hakan. III. Wokoeck, Ursula.
DS61.6.H57 2002
956'.007'2—dc21
2002017815

British Cataloguing in Publication Data
A Cataloguing in Publication record for this book
is available from the British Library.

Printed and bound in the United States of America

The paper used in this publication meets the requirements of the American National Standard for Permanence of Paper for Printed Library Materials Z39.48-1984.

5 4 3 2 1

Library
University of Texas
at San Antonio

Contents

Part 4   Constructing Identities, Defining Nations

Part 5   Conclusion

Tables and Figures

Table

Figures

Acknowledgments

This book developed from a collaborative project sponsored by the Institute for Advanced Studies at the Hebrew University of Jerusalem, Boğaziçi University, and the Haim Herzog Center for Middle East Studies and Diplomacy at Ben Gurion University of the Negev. We are most grateful to these institutions for their financial support and encouragement. Special thanks goes to the Boğaziçi University Foundation for its support during the days that a workshop, "New Approaches to the Study of Ottoman and Arab Societies," was held at the university. In addition, we would like to thank the Irene Young Endowment Fund for Scientific Publications and the Lester and Sally Entin Faculty of Humanities at Tel Aviv University for its support during the publication process.

We are particularly appreciative of Ariel Weiss's generous support throughout the various stages of the project. David Shulman, former head of the Institute for Advanced Studies at the Hebrew University of Jerusalem, played a crucial role in developing the idea for the workshop; his many productive suggestions helped the project come to life. Alex Levitzki, head of the Institute for Advanced Studies in 1999, offered valuable support and collaboration. At Boğaziçi University, Selçuk Esenbel, the History Department chair, and Üstün Ergüder, the former rector, and the organizing team invested great effort to make the environment of the workshop both pleasant and welcoming.

We thank also the other workshop participants for their insightful observations and input during that event: Iris Agmon, Faruk Birtek, Selim Deringil, Allen Douglas, Mine Ener, Selçuk Esenbel, Jane Hathaway, Samuel W. Kaplan, Fedwa Malti-Douglas, Adel Manna', Yoram Meital, Gabriel Piterberg, Eugene Rogan, Lawrence Rosen, Amy Singer, Ilkay Sunar, Binnaz Toprak, and Dror Ze'evi.

We received additional help from many colleagues and friends. Liba Maimon of the Institute for Advanced Studies provided administrative assistance, without which the Istanbul workshop would not have proceeded so smoothly. The efforts of Shani Freiman, also of the Institute, are most appreciated. Dvora Kremer of the Haim Herzog Center for Middle East Studies and Diplomacy most willingly donated her time to assist the project. Susynne M. McElrone and Avi Mor provided valuable editorial and administrative assistance. Lynne Rienner, Sally Glover, Lesli Athanasoulis, and Jody Berman of Lynne Rienner Publishers gave splendid editorial advice and suggestions for improving the structure and content of this volume. To all, our most sincere thanks.

—Israel Gershoni
—Hakan Erdem
—Ursula Woköck

1

Doing History: Modern Middle Eastern Studies Today

Israel Gershoni & Ursula Woköck

Broad Perspectives

Middle Eastern studies, as any academic profession, from time to time needs to re-examine the nature of its discipline and vocation. Since the 1970s, some substantial developments have occurred in the field, in particular the expansion of the scope of inquiry into new areas, an openness to interdisciplinary endeavors, and the digestion of new methods and paradigms suggested by the humanities in general. Still, it is crucial for scholars working on the Middle East—historians, sociologists, and anthropologists—to meet in order to rethink their profession.

A gathering in Istanbul in May 1999 seemed to be an appropriate location for such self-re-examination. The vantage point of fin de siècle—as well as the close of the millennium—provides a site of memory for some major historical events and processes that the region experienced beginning in the early modern era and throughout the modern era, in which the capital of the Ottoman Empire and, later, a major city in the Turkish Republic, played both direct and indirect roles. Suffice it to recall that 1999 commemorated, among other events:

- The 700th anniversary of the Ottoman Empire
- The 300th anniversary of Carlowitz
- Approximately 200 years after Napoleon's invasion of Egypt
- 160 years after the Hatt-ı Şerif of Gülhane
- 80 years after the 1919 national revolution in Egypt
- 75 years after the establishment of the Turkish Republic

- 70 years after the Wailing Wall revolt in Palestine
- Some 20 years after Edward Said's *Orientalism*

We thought that this time and place created an ideal setting for a scholarly rethinking of Middle Eastern studies.

We view this volume as a part of a general effort to re-examine our profession, as an intermediate report on the "state of the art."[1] The intention was modest: We convened a group of scholars for the exchange of ideas, attitudes, and thoughts, checking one another and critically examining various dimensions of the field and of the scholarly profession. In spite of the diversity of the approaches and methods suggested by the various chapters presented here, the common thread is a commitment to rewrite specific areas of the discipline. This, we should stress, is neither an abstract, a theoretical exercise, nor a purely methodological discussion; rather it is a historical inquiry into specific case studies that attempt to implement new insights within real historical experiences and environments. Indeed, the overall aim of this volume is to rethink Middle Eastern studies by "doing history."[2]

Because the forces and processes that shaped and continue to shape Middle Eastern societies and cultures are not exclusive to the region, a serious study of the Middle East should be part of an ongoing dialogue with studies on European and other, non-European, cultures and societies. Hence, the chapters contained in this work attempt to relate to some of the more essential issues concerning the discipline of history at large and beyond it to the humanities in general. Over the second half of the twentieth century, the general study of history was dramatically reshuffled while emulating a whole system of new theories, models, and approaches:

- The "new" social history, with its attention to the symbolic cultural dimensions of social realities.
- The "history from below" and the "history of everyday life," which strive to recover experiences and voices of the ordinary, the subaltern, the outcast, and the marginal.
- Developments in political economy and dependency theories and the study of world economic systems.
- New cultural history, with its emphasis on social and cultural ethnographies and their strong tendency toward anthropological interpretation and the decoding of meanings, and in association with them, the history of *mentalités,* which originated in the Annales school.
- The study of the history of the family.
- Feminist theory, women's studies, and the study of gender relations.

- Intellectual history, focused on the social history of ideas, discourse analysis, and the history of representation.
- The study of collective memory and the complex relationships between history and memory.
- The postmodernist paradigm, with its narrativism and textualism associated with literary criticism and the question of the relations between knowledge and representation and between power and wealth.
- Colonialism and postcolonialism studies.

Put forward in the field of humanities, these new theories and paradigms have had an impact on Middle Eastern studies. The chapters in the volume, and the discussions that helped to develop them, critically relate to these theories and methods in various dimensions while re-examining their applications to political, social, and cultural Middle Eastern cases. We first attempt to highlight some of the general issues that served as an inspiration for the themes presented in these chapters. These issues, we believe, are indicative of theoretical and practical challenges with which the profession is coping, or with which it should attempt to cope.

First, the impact of the "linguistic turn" on the study of history was so considerable that it became common to speak about social, political, cultural, and intellectual history after the linguistic turn. Although perhaps a little late, Middle Eastern scholars learned that language does not reflect reality but rather, constitutes it. Language is not transparent; it is a record, or store, of representations of reality that we attempt to grasp, interpret, and describe. External reality is comprehended through mediated linguistic categories or images of our own, of the historical actors in whom we are interested, of the experiences they undergo, and of the culture in which they live.

A more radical approach considers the language expressed in the text to be the "reality," or in Jacques Derrida's words, "*Il n'y a pas de hors-texte*" (There is nothing outside the text).[3] Many years earlier, Ludwig Wittgenstein had already expressed the notion that the borders of the real world are linguistic boundaries, or, "a [linguistic] picture is a fact."[4] Thus, tangible historical units such as a social group, a nation, a state, and even a class or a family have become discursive formations that are constituted and organized by language. Accordingly, human communities are not only social, political, imagined, or "textual communities,"[5] they are also "discursive communities." The question that arises immediately is: To what extent does the linguistic turn shape or change the field; that is, does it really help to reach a better understanding of the historical material and processes? Now that scholars have become somewhat disenchanted with this method, the question that remains to be asked is: To what extent can material entities like cotton, currency, statistics, demography, inflation, trade, or even family, class, and slavery be treated as merely linguistic phenomena, or can human conditions such as poverty, hunger, violence, or crisis be accurately described through linguistic constructs alone? It appears that historical events have been reduced to the status of literary tropes, verbal structures, and rhetorical devices.

In spite of the constructive inspiration of the linguistic turn and the new sensitivities it contributed to the profession, there remains a need to distinguish between language and the world, between evidence and the interpretation of evidence, between reality and its representation, between experience and its meaning. A return to a clear differentiation between text and context—a context that is not merely another textual frame—is essential since a context also contains stable extra-representative physical elements that can be identified and described. An illustration of the limits of the impact of the linguistic turn can be found in the histories written about the Arab-Jewish conflict in Palestine. On the one hand, there have unquestionably been enormous efforts invested since the 1970s to gain a better understanding of both Ottoman and mandatory Palestine; on the other hand, one of the results is the emergence of two supposedly equivalent narratives—the story of the Palestinians and the story of the Zionists. In light of this, then, it must be asked how much has actually been achieved in the profession at all. It certainly appears that scholars have missed an opportunity to contribute to the effort to provide a more realistic and balanced historical view of the topic to the public discourse being conducted in the context of this ongoing, heated political dispute.

The second general issue is the study of elites—the ideas, policies, and practices produced by elites, their experiences, and identities—on which Middle Eastern studies has traditionally been focused. It was assumed that this form of enquiry would give a clue to wider society, culture, or politics in general. This proved misleading, however, as the outcome was a description of the life of the elites alone. Then came the reaction: Scholars became enthusiastically caught up in the history of nonelites, termed "history from below" and "popular culture." Now, scholars are seeking the social and cultural middle ground, the middle discourse, somewhere between the "high learned culture" and the "low illiterate culture." There is an attempt to explore the relative social role of both elite and nonelite groups in shaping what Dominick LaCapra has defined as "common culture."[6] Yet we still know very little about interactions and the mutual feedback between different layers of culture. It is easy enough to isolate a specific cultural layer or trait, a discourse, intellectuals, and secondary intellectuals, and to discuss each of them as defined units. It is far more difficult, however, to identify systems of interaction, negotiation, and agents of mediation operating between these units and the layers of the various levels of culture, society, and politics. Scholars need to ask where, in the space between high and low cultures, are the lost voices and experiences that were never given attention. It is questionable whether the suppressed, "missing" discourses have indeed been extricated and, if so, what their significance is to the entire cultural field.

Third, for many years the tendency of the profession was to identify broad social structures and processes, or large ideological units, leaning toward structural history. The aim was to identify and analyze the overall structural historical change, to reconstruct processes of *longue durée*. The Annales provided us with one example of such a structural history in society, culture, *mentalités*, and even in politics. At the end of the 1970s it appeared as if Lawrence Stone's call for a "revival of the narrative"[7]—though not in the sense expressed by postmodernism[8]—was bringing about a healthy return to common sense, to more human and less impersonal stories and descriptions. The process of breaking away from the structure was more rapid and more aggressive, however. Now, the tendency is toward the small, the personal, the low-key story, the ethnography of the pastoral, the exotic, the anecdotal, or the episodic, and toward the marginal voices of the oppressed and the inarticulate. There is less attention paid to the big picture, somehow a neglect of the mainstream, and a withdrawal from generalized statements. The danger exists, though, that in limiting our interests to narrower fields of research, we will offer merely small answers to small questions.

Fourth, after having dealt with production and producers, scholars have more recently moved on to deal with the issue of the history of reception and consumers. From the authors we moved to the readers, or at least attempted to. Today, some effort is also directed to the discussion on disseminating and transmitting agents. The field of cultural production has become complex and problematic. Here, too, it is easier to identify the luminary planners and producers of culture but much more difficult to ascertain precisely who are the agents of transmission and what are the communities of reception, particularly now that more recent research has taught us that the consumer of culture is not a passive bystander in the dynamics of cultural dissemination but is also a producer or reproducer of cultural products. Even more complicated is to describe how patterns of consumption and assimilation change a culture's modes of production, as well as its content and symbols. Hence, in the tension between production, transmission, and reception, there remain some key questions:

- Who produces the repertoire of cultural models?
- What are the forces that enforce and reinforce this repertoire?
- How is the cultural canon constructed?
- Who is pushed to the sidelines and becomes noncanonic?

- What is the nature of reciprocal negotiation, exchange, and appropriation between the various forces and agents operating in the cultural field?

Fifth, current trends in the profession seem to indicate a shift toward what may be termed the "ethnic turn" in the study of history, what Edward Said has critically defined as the "politics of identity."[9] This trend can also rightfully be called the "politics of me/we" or the "poetics of self/us." David A. Hollinger insightfully defined this trend: "[T]his 'ethnicization' of all discourse through the 'decentering' strategies of postmodernism is thus a culmination of the process by which the term 'ethnic' has lost its connotations of marginality—originally, 'ethnic' meant 'outsider,' 'pagan,' or 'gentile'—and has come to stand for situatedness within virtually any bounded community, regardless of its relation to other communities."[10] In other words, the fashion is to contrapose local culture and multiculturalism with the uniformity and universality of the Enlightenment project, which assumes total hegemony for one assimilatory civilization, fusing all cultures into one civilizational melting pot. The large, universal, supposedly canonic narrative is being deconstructed in favor of innumerable local and particularistic narratives. Each narrative, it has been repeatedly claimed, expresses a unique cultural environment; it means different things to different people in different contexts.

Obviously, once the ethnos of the grand narrative—the Eurocentricism, essentialism, male chauvinism, Orientalism, imperialism, and racism inherent in it—had been identified, it became essential to deconstruct it. There is a universal, humanistic justification for enabling many other legitimate voices and narratives to be heard. Hence, a further turn, to the accent on the "*differénce*": an emphasis on heterogeneity as opposed to homogeneity, pluralism as opposed to hegemony, to decentering as opposed to centralization, to the many voices of non-European societies as opposed to the solipsistic voice of the "universalist Enlightenment." The narratives and stories of women, minorities, subalterns, deviants, and outcasts were recognized and defended.

But to what extent is there an awareness of the price that this ethnic turn demands? With all the charm of multiculturalism, it would still be difficult to deny that color, race, nation, religion and other ethnos-centered particularisms are antithetical to reason, humanism, and social justice. Politics of identity may operate against the universality and globalism of the real problems of class tensions, gender discrimination, child abuse, economic poverty, and political oppression. From a broader view, the ethnic turn seems to have reproduced the opposition between the eighteenth-century Enlightenment and the counter-Enlightenment.[11] In the struggle against objective, empiricist positivism, there is a danger to be trapped in subjective, romantic historicism. To be sure, in contrast to the culturalism of the nineteenth-century classical Romanticism, society today is more aware that culture is invented ("invention" in the Eric Hobsbawm and Terence Ranger connotation of "the invention of tradition"[12]) and that the self is dissolving in intersubjective and intertextual language. Since Giovanni Battista Vico and Johann Gottfried von Herder, however, language has also been strongly linked to cultural identity, ethnic roots, the irrational and the mystic, and to "ethno-centered discourse" as opposed to "species-centered discourse."[13] In other words, by fostering the politics of identity, a door is opened to a new form of historicist Romanticism.

For Middle Eastern studies, a return to the old universalist enthusiasm may be naive or impossible, since a suspicion will always remain that "universalism" means Western-imposed universalism. However, the postethnic perspective suggested by Hollinger should still be seriously considered; it is a perspective that "tries to remain alert to features of any given ethnos common to one or more other ethnoi that see each other as opposed. When communities are construed as 'localities' to which a norm, an aspiration, or a condition may be 'historically particular,' it remains true that these localities can be sites for the display of traits and conditions also found in other localities."[14]

Sixth, the fixation on the study of literate, or print, culture has been undermined by a growing interest in oral culture, and nonwritten, visual culture—illustrated, photographed, televised, and filmed materials. Until fairly recently, the dominant presumption was that written texts were the key to our historical understanding of social reality. There now exists, however, a growing awareness that these reflect only a portion of the human experience. The relationship between written, printed texts and diverse, visual texts in the process of building culture and in its changes, has been realized to be more complex than once thought. The fascination with film as representing key dimensions of modern culture is particularly striking. But here, too, there exists a feeling that the "visual revolution" is closing in on itself. It is vital to Middle Eastern studies to consider cinema and television as visual media that represent Middle Eastern realities. Nevertheless, it is also crucial to study the essential negotiations and exchanges between the visual and written texts and other nonvisual texts operating in the field of cultural production in print capitalism. There is also a need to locate the visual text in the overall cultural system of society and to weigh its relative role in creating that society's cultural meanings, experiences, and social practices.

Middle Eastern Perspectives

Focusing on specific case studies, each of the chapters in this volume, in its own way, attempts to appropriate or negotiate these broader issues, offering reappraisals and new perspectives on modern Middle Eastern history. The topics range from the material world of economic history to the visual arts studied by cultural historians. Covering the period from the late eighteenth century to the contemporary Middle East, the studies deal with territories of the Ottoman Empire, the Arab Middle East, and Iran. Despite the wide scope, some basic elements are shared, allowing for a fruitful academic exchange among the various approaches. All the contributions are concerned with major trends in historical developments, while they adapt their approaches to individual case studies. Most important, they raise methodological questions concerning possible conceptualizations of the interrelation between the micro and the macro levels in the context of Middle Eastern history.

The present collection approaches modern Middle Eastern history via the study of specific local developments situated within a global, international framework. Part 1 focuses on aspects of nineteenth-century history against the background of a developing colonial setting. Part 2 brings into focus particular Middle Eastern aspects of globalization—seen once from the turn of the nineteenth to the twentieth centuries and once from the end of the twentieth century. Attempting to recover "lost voices" in the pre–World War I period, Part 3 addresses issues in the field of intellectual history within the colonial age proper. Part 4 deals with what may be seen as essentially anti- or postcolonial phenomena, namely, processes of formation of national discourse and identity. Finally, Part 5 reviews the various chapters of this volume in light of a more general perspective.

In Chapter 2, Şevket Pamuk offers a study in political economy (traditionally reserved for the approach to modern societies), which stands out for its subject and period under investigation, the great Ottoman debasements of 1808–1844. Debasement, that is, the reduction of the specie content of the currency by the monetary authority—which provided temporary relief from shortages of species and coinage—has widely been considered the result of a haphazard process and, ultimately, an exercise in futility. By contrast, Pamuk argues that the persistence of debasement throughout the medieval and early modern periods suggests that these interventions could not simply be futile efforts. He sees the appeal of debasements in the fact that they provided fiscal relief for the state with regard to its obligations to soldiers, bureaucrats, and suppliers that were expressed in monetary units of account and thus functioned often as an alternative to additional taxation. Moreover, the issue of debasement was not determined by the government alone but often depended upon the struggle between it and various social groups. Pamuk argues further that the spectrum of social groups involved was a rather wide one, since—contrary to the traditional assumption that the use of money was limited to long-distance trade and parts of the urban economy—the monetary economy went well beyond these limits and, consequently, debasements affected virtually all groups of Ottoman society. On the basis of this analytical framework, Pamuk's investigation of the great debasements of 1808–1844 shows that government policies follow a clear cost-benefit rationale and that Mahmud II (1808–1839) appears to have used debasement as a tool for centralization. Later on, that instrument of fiscal policy was abandoned not for lack of effectiveness but due to European pressure.

In Chapter 3, as in Chapter 11, modern themes are found in contexts that are usually considered distinctly premodern with regard to the themes in question. Seen within the wider debate on the beginnings of the modern period, within which the "baseline" was first moved from 1798 into the second half of the eighteenth century and is now about to be relocated to the midnineteenth century (and, at times, beyond), the two chapters do not call for a shift in paradigm. Rather their contributions highlight the complexity of the developments, thus questioning the seemingly clear-cut dichotomy between premodern and modern.

In Chapter 3, the findings of Wael B. Hallaq's investigation of the potential for legal change in the late 1820s may point in a similar direction as Pamuk's, namely, that the Islamic legal tradition was abandoned not for its lack of ability to modernize but due to European pressure, which drew on the enduring scholarly paradigm according to which Islamic law suffered from a rigidity that ultimately led to paralysis. In his chapter, Hallaq aims at showing three major points: (1) The mechanisms of legal change constituted a structural feature of the law; (2) the discourse of the author-jurist—as a manipulator of the discursive tradition (a hitherto overlooked category or role)—was necessarily an integral part of these structural mechanisms; and (3) through the discursive strategies of the author-jurist, a fundamental reformation of legal methodology and theory was effected. Specifically, Hallaq investigates the treatment of the issue of custom as a source of law by the last major Hanafite jurist, the Damascene al-Sayyid Amin Ibn ʻĀbidīn (1783–1836). He begins with an overview of the debate on custom as a legal source within Islamic law, in particular in the Hanafite tradition. Against the background of that outline, the detailed analysis of Ibn ʻĀbidīn's writings on the issue can place him firmly within the Hanafite tradition, while he introduces a major change: the acceptance of custom as a legal source. Ibn ʻĀbidīn may thus be seen as having taken the first step paving the way to modern legal reform, which would seem quite different from the one chosen by later modernist reformers such as Muhammad Rashid Rida.

In Chapter 4, while drawing on a micro-historical approach within a global framework, Mary Wilson is able to change perspectives on, and the understanding of, one specific episode: a ritual murder trial in Damascus. Whereas it has traditionally been seen in the lineage of an enduring theme in European Jewish history since the twelfth century, Wilson relocates the episode within the French colonial context. Wilson's investigation of the ritual murder trial in Damascus in 1840 is a highly fascinating example of micro-history. She uses a judicial proceeding to explore the connection between individual lives and the outlines of known history. In the case in point, fourteen Jews were found guilty of killing a Capuchin missionary and his assistant for ritual purposes. It is exceptional for at least two reasons: First, the trial is not exemplary, because it is the only such case in the Arabic-speaking lands; and second, there is an exceptionally rich body of literature on the subject. Despite fundamentally different evaluations of the verdict, the event is commonly seen as a chapter in Jewish history. Using the tools of micro-history, Wilson identifies the French consul as a central actor on the scene. By investigating him and his context, the trace leads to Paris and the broad scheme of French colonial aspirations in the Middle East (including North Africa). From that perspective, the 1840 trial in Damascus would appear as a function of the attempt to bring the Maronites in Lebanon, as Catholics, under French protection.

In the long tradition of art history, the focus was most exclusively on aesthetics and products of high culture. More often than not, art provided merely fancy decorations for historical works; it did not figure into historical research. In the general field of art history, this paradigm has been successfully challenged. Research has moved deep into the exploration of popular culture, and great methodological efforts have been made to utilize products from the field of visual arts as sources for historical research, to "read" them in conjunction with other available texts.

In comparison with this general development in historiography, Middle Eastern studies seem to be lagging behind. Although there are truly outstanding scholars pursuing such directions, the mainstream has not yet fully realized the vast potential opened by these new research perspectives. Afsaneh Najmabadi's and Walter Armburst's chapters illustrate the significance of visual arts as a valuable source providing new insights and perspectives on culture and history.

In Chapter 5, Najmabadi provides a fascinating example of two approaches that have still not been sufficiently explored in Middle Eastern history. One is based on the notion of gender—distinct from women's studies, where separate sections or departments are established for women's issues, thus keeping them excluded from the overall historical narrative—as an analytical category, whereby sources about men can also become sources about women or, more precisely, they become sources about how "man" and "woman" are constructed. The second approach draws on the visual arts as a source for historical research, rather than as mere illustrations. Commonly, written texts are seen to have a self-sufficiency that visual texts are assumed to lack. By contrast, Najmabadi intends to read visual texts historically and to use methods of visual interpretation to craft historical arguments. Her case study takes up Qajar art, which in the nineteenth century stands out for the abundance of its representations of women. These pictures mostly lack any social information, however; thus, they cannot be approached as mere reflections of reality. Instead, Najmabadi suggests considering them as constitutive of meaning. Within this framework, Najmabadi proceeds to contextualize the pictures, both with regard to potential viewers and to the nineteenth-century Iranian-European controversy on male homoeroticism versus heteroeroticism.

Part 2 takes up the issue of globalization. Research on economic history of the modern Middle East has traditionally focused on the process of the region's integration into the world market—mapping and investigating the various stages of market orientation, peripheralization, colonialism, imperialism, and globalization. Within that framework, the analytical concept of political economy has been utilized to approach the study of the nexus between the economic, political, and social spheres in the modern complex societies that emerged in the course of the integration process. Accepting the importance of these lines of investigation for the understanding of the modern Middle East, Roger Owen and Joel Beinin set out to suggest new perspectives and reappraisals by expanding the scope of investigation, that is, the study of concrete local conditions as a precondition for understanding processes of globalization.

In Chapter 6, Owen takes up the issues of globalization and imperialism during a first wave at the end of the nineteenth century. Despite the difference in period, Owen's approach shares with Beinin's the assumption that the macro perspective is insufficient. He suggests using the medium of biography as the basis for an alternative perspective, specifically Lord Cromer's transition from liberalism to liberal imperialism in the course of his Egyptian experience under the impact of globalization. The process of transition can be seen as moving toward defining the state interest in the context of an open economy dependent on foreign capital for further development. At the same time, Cromer's perception is flawed by his total lack of comprehension for Egyptian nationalist aspirations and for self-government. The chapter focuses on the experience of Cromer as a central figure in his encounter with, and attempts to manage, the interplay of powerful global forces in one central, contested space. Thus, it illustrates the importance of global or international components in the study of the pre-1914 Middle East.

Whereas Owen traces an early wave of globalization, in Chapter 7 Beinin investigates developments of globalization in the Middle East since the early 1970s. Usually processes of globalization tend to be seen with an almost exclusive focus on the international arena, transcending the framework of the nation-state. At the same time, research on political economy turned away from the conceptual category of class in the course of the

1990s.[15] By contrast, Beinin takes *class* as a central category for his research, which investigates the social reorganization of the working classes and the discursive reconfiguration of their political salience in conjunction with a general transition from various forms of economic nationalism, comprising state-led development, import-substitution industrialization, and populist politics, toward a neoliberalism that is based on integration into the world economy, favors private enterprise, and entails the upward redistribution of the national income. While not denying the importance of the international/global settings, which he critically identifies as the "Washington consensus" in conjunction with the effects of labor migration, Beinin's study, similar to Owen's, requires a concrete national framework for class analysis; specifically the socioeconomical and political developments in Tunisia, Egypt, and Turkey are investigated. He is therefore able to show that globalization is not, as is often assumed, a one-way process that can be understood in merely general terms but rather needs to be studied under concrete local conditions. Only on the basis of such case studies, some regional (Middle Eastern) generalizations may become possible. His contribution provides both detailed country studies in political economy in which class is a central category, and a critical analysis of the dominant research trend, which can be shown to share the basic assumptions underlying the current political rationale of globalization (the Washington consensus).

Though following somewhat different lines of investigation, the three chapters in Part 3 attempt to redress major deficiencies in the research of intellectual history in the pre-1914, colonial era. Since the 1970s, there have been major new research trends in the study of modern Egyptian history going well beyond the traditional focus on political and diplomatic history. The interwar period, in particular, and, although after some delay, also the post–World War II period, have been subject to intense research efforts encompassing political, social, economic, institutional, intellectual, and cultural history. A second major current in historiography has focused on the re-evaluation of the nineteenth century, often in conjunction with the eighteenth century. In relation to these two major eras, the period spanning the last decades of the nineteenth century up to World War I is somewhat understudied, most often appearing either as merely the "tail" of the long nineteenth century, or as the precursor to the full-fledged developments of the interwar period.

Chapter 8, by Zachary Lockman, and Chapter 9, by Eve M. Troutt Powell (as well as Chapter 6, by Owen, in Part 2), aim at showing that the period merits research from new perspectives. By recovering secondary intellectual voices, Lockman and Troutt Powell try to add to and/or replace a more traditional method that highlights elite ideas and luminary intellectuals such as Jamal al-Din al-Afghani, Muhammad 'Abduh, and Ahmad

Lutfi al-Sayyid. Second-tier intellectual activities were greatly facilitated by the expansion of the print culture as a major agent of cultural production.

In comparison to Egypt, Ottoman-Turkish history seems to have taken a slightly different turn, namely, the recent, intense interest in the period of Abdülhamid II (1876–1909). This effort has led to major re-evaluations of the period and includes a variety of new approaches and research themes. Since the traditional historiography had approached that stage of Ottoman history in its relation to Western powers and the context of Westernization/modernization, the new current has adopted a dominantly internal perspective. Despite the clear benefits of such an addition for the understanding of historical developments, one aspect has thus far remained excluded from consideration: the Iranian dimensions. Juan R. I. Cole shows in Chapter 10 that this is a highly fascinating and important field for investigation.

Lockman suggests a new perspective on historical research about the 1882–1914 period in Egypt. The literature has traditionally been dominated by diplomatic and political history, with an emphasis on Anglo-Egyptian relations. Intellectual history of the period has almost exclusively focused on the elite, in their relations to ideas and concepts coming from Western Europe. Therefore, history of the period has tended to be written "from above" and to follow a narrative of modernization. To redress that deficiency, Lockman suggests new venues for systematic investigation, the large number of second- and third-tier writers, journalists, thinkers, and other intellectuals operating within the cultural-political field. Ideally, such an approach should not adopt the traditional methods of intellectual history but rather shift the focus from ideas to practices. Such a procedure is ultimately thought to enable us to move from the elite perspective to the study of the cultural expectations of broader sectors of society. Lockman adds three illustrations to his programmatic outline: the recovery of lost voices (two almost-forgotten intellectuals); practices combining the concepts of youth and nationalism; and those of nationalism and Islam.

Troutt Powell recovers what may, according to Lockman's outline, be considered a lost voice, Abdallah al-Nadim's contributions (1892) on the issues of women and Sudanese slaves. The setting is similar to that in Cole's chapter: The position of an exceptional individual is juxtaposed with a controversial, highly politicized discursive field, the debate on family and slavery within the framework of the well-established British occupation. The images of the family encompassed a wide range from a symbol of timeless stability via a cultural buffer against British occupation to a target of cultural reform. British officials tended to focus on the family as a framework for women's seclusion, veiling, and lack of education, thus linking the question with the controversies over slavery and the abolition movement/policy. Within these debates, al-Nadim's formulations were quite outstanding; he introduced the perspective of (manumitted) Sudanese slaves; he envisaged equality between Egyptians and former (male) slaves; and he saw women's equality to men as a function of the amount of work they performed for the family: The harder women work, the more equal they are.

Cole follows similar lines, as does Owen, insofar as they both focus on the biography and writings of one person as an approach to understanding major historical developments. Cole takes up the case of the pan-Islamic movement under Sultan Abdülhamid II. The person in question, Abu al-Hasan Mirza "Shaikh al-Ra'is" (1848–1921), a Qajar prince, poet, Shiite clergyman, political activist, and secret member of the heterodox Baha'i religion, was less prominent in the political field of action and not as well known as Cromer. Cole's study recovers the story of this intellectual who had an important part in the pan-Islamic movement. His addition is particularly valuable, for it brings into focus a (nongovernmental) Iranian dimension that has been widely overlooked in research on the pan-Islamic project. Moreover, the conceptual framework of his study emphasizes complexity and dynamics, both with regard to the individual, based on the concept of multiple identity, and to intellectual-political movements, such as anti-imperialism that easily shifted between absolutism, elite reformism, and parliamentarism.

Research on nationalism, national imagination, and national narratives has been an important subject in recent decades. The field has seen far-reaching sophistication and refinement of approaches and conceptualizations as is, for example, reflected in the collection *Rethinking Nationalism in the Arab Middle East.*[16] Despite these achievements, there is still room for additional research and new perspectives as the chapters in Part 4 (as well as those by Beinin and Lockman) show.

Similar to Hallaq's chapter in Part 1, Hakan Erdem's chapter in Part 4 on the composition of the regular Ottoman army in the nineteenth century uncovers what is considered to be a modern theme, namely, ethnic nationalism in a rather unexpected place. Founded in 1826, the Asakir-i Mansure was conceived as a new regular army based on conscription. Contrary to what might be expected of the imperial army in light of Ottoman history, this new army was almost exclusively Turkish. This ethnic exclusivity had far-reaching consequences: It promoted both Ottoman-Turkish nationalism—on the ground that it was the Turks who bore the greatest burden of the defense of the empire—and local nationalisms—for a regular Ottoman army that excluded non-Turkish Muslims came to be increasingly perceived as a foreign army of occupation. In Chapter 11, Erdem investigates the possible roots of this ethnic exclusivity. The preference for Anatolian peasants can be traced back to the recruitment of the Nizam-ı Cedid (1792–1807); this bias increased in the course of the Greek war of independence. As for the Asakir-i Mansure, Erdem finds an explicit policy of exclusion with regard to converts, attributable to Sultan Mahmud's distrust. With regard to non-Turkish Muslims, his study of the provinces of Damascus and Aleppo indicates that the process of exclusion may be attributable to factors of expedience, a side effect of centralizing efforts. By identifying developments and practices that made the nation and nationalism thinkable, Erdem can thus be seen to follow in the footsteps of Benedict Anderson's *Imagined Communities*.

Chapter 12, by Fatma Müge Göçek, and Chapter 13, by Rashid Khalidi, focus on national narratives in two somewhat extraordinary cases, both in the post-1920 Middle East era, when nationalism became a hegemonic force. In the Palestinian case, it is a national narrative that still has no place (or rather state) "of its own," a situation that impedes multivocal narration, but, as Khalidi shows, certainly calls for multiple comparative perspectives. By contrast, the Turkish narrative had a place of its own relatively early on. Here, those controlling the dominant narrative took rather extraordinary steps to ensure its hegemony by making, for example, criticism a criminal offense. Göçek is able to show the lineage of two opposing narratives that nonetheless run from the Lausanne Peace Conference (1922–1923) to the present.

Göçek takes up the issue of the importance of remembering significant historical events for the construction of nations and national identity and the ensuing politics of history and memory when political challenges are expressed in oppositional narratives. To investigate such competing narratives, she suggests a shift from a strictly historical perspective to that of historical sociology, which entails a shift in emphasis from the narrative to its societal context, especially the power relations involved. Moreover, she employs a multidimensional approach that combines past events with their reconstructions in the present. Both these elements are brought together in her analysis of the Lausanne conference, a historical event of central importance for the establishment of the Turkish nation-state. Historical research about the conference largely relies on memoirs, for post-1914 archives are not freely accessible, and it is further hindered by penal legislation prohibiting critical perspectives on Atatürk. At the Lausanne conference, two positions emerged within the Turkish delegation that were then transformed into two separate narratives in Ankara. The official one was crystallized in a long speech that Atatürk gave in 1927, whereas the oppositional one was formulated in reaction to, and along the lines of, that speech. These two narratives still form the basis for the contemporary political confrontation between secularists and Islamicists.

Khalidi investigates a historical issue of similarly constitutive importance to national identity, that is, the question of Arab society in mandatory Palestine culminating in the events of 1948 that did not lead to what should have occurred: the establishment of a Palestinian state. Khalidi argues that there are two possible comparative perspectives. One is the very widely employed comparison between the Palestinian Arab society and the Zionist *yishuv* (burgeoning Jewish community). Though it might be misleading inasmuch as it does not stress crucial external factors, such a comparison is surely called for because the two communities shared the country until 1948 and were in competition with one another. The second comparative perspective relates to societies of neighboring Arab countries, in particular the other parts of Greater Syria. Khalidi argues that this second perspective is needed for a clearer understanding of Palestinian Arab society per se, especially since it is often held that Palestinian society before 1948 was incomplete or distinctively flawed, thus explaining the rapid collapse in 1948 and implying that the Palestinians did not have the necessary preconditions for a successful national effort. Such a comparison has to differentiate between two levels. On the first level, contrary to the Palestinian case, both other Arab national movements and the *yishuv* operated within the framework of a state or a para-state. On the second level, contrary to often-expressed assumptions with regards to the sense of identity or the vibrancy of civil society, Khalidi shows that Palestinian society before 1948 was in comparative terms relatively coherent and reasonably developed.

By putting the spotlight on the cinema and its cultural environment, Walter Armbrust opens a new venue for the study of the formation of national identity in Egypt. In Chapter 14, he sets out to challenge one of the prevailing assumptions about Egyptian cinema—that the dominance of commercially marketed stars makes it imitative and uninteresting. To this end, his chapter examines the career of Farid Shauqi, an Egyptian actor who entered the business in the 1940s and blossomed during the 1950s. Shauqi was notable both for the image of masculinity he promoted on the screen and for his ability to embody national identity. Armbrust analyzes Shauqi-the-nationalist as a figure closely tied to Shauqi-the-traditionalist, a manly man. His masculinity is constructed in several contexts. In life, Shauqi was portrayed as not just an actor but as a businessman capable of influencing his chosen profession; on screen, he was cast as an icon of masculine honor in a traditional sense; in fan magazine portrayals of Shauqi and his relationship with his actress/singer wife Hoda Sultan, she is presented—paradoxically, given his hypermasculine screen image—as an equal partner in a companionate marriage rather than as the feminine element of a stereotypical "honor-shame" relationship; and most important for Armbrust's study, Shauqi's image was closely tied, in both films and related media discourse, to the ongoing construction of Egyptian nationalism in the first decade of independence from colonial rule. Shauqi's emergence as a star by the end of the 1950s cannot be understood apart from his capacity to embody a gendered nationalism. The image of a star is inherently unfixed, always a mixture of his or her real life, constructed through publicity, with fantasy constructed on the screen. In Shauqi's case the creative ambiguity of stardom made him a powerful vehicle for synthesizing a conservative nationalist vision—symbolized in his on-screen image embodying fiercely protective honor—with a progressive modernist image suggested by his companionate marriage to actress/business partner Sultan. In the end not only is our understanding of the cinema enriched by examining it in light of nationalist history, but the history of Egyptian nationalism is flawed and incomplete without consideration of figures such as Shauqi and of the influence of new media such as the cinema.

In sum, the chapters in this volume share an effort to reappraise and add new perspectives to the study of the modern Middle East. Clearly, they cannot and do not encompass all the important issues and topics now being treated by Middle Eastern scholars, and the many others still awaiting treatment. The case studies offered, however, cover a broad range across time and space and theories and approaches, and they demonstrate the urgent need to tighten the link between our professional pursuits and new theories and insights already implemented in the study of European and other, non-European, societies and cultures. The chapters herein also recognize the value of applying interdisciplinary, cross-regional, and cross-cultural dimensions to sharpen our understanding of the Middle East and beyond. We hope that this collection will provide a modest contribution to the improvement of the agenda of modern Middle Eastern studies.

Notes

1. Other efforts along similar lines in the 1990s can be found in Tareq Y. Ismael (ed.), *Middle East Studies: International Perspectives on the State of the Art* (New York: Praeger, 1990); Hisham Sharabi (ed.), *Theory, Politics, and the Arab World: Critical Responses* (New York: Routledge, 1990); Albert Hourani, "How Should We Write the History of the Middle East?" *International Journal of Middle East Studies* 23 (1991): 125–136; Jacqueline S. Ismael and Earl L. Sullivan (eds.), *The Contemporary Study of the Arab World* (Edmonton: University of Alberta Press, 1991); Albert Hourani, Philip S. Khoury, and Mary C. Wilson (eds.), *The Modern Middle East: A Reader* (London: I. B. Tauris, 1993); Israel Gershoni and Ehud R. Toledano, "Editors' Introduction," *Poetics Today*, special issue on *Cultural Processes in Muslim and Arab Societies* 14 (1993): 241–245. See also Israel Gershoni and Ehud R. Toledano (eds.), *Cultural Processes in Muslim and Arab Societies,* special issues of *Poetics Today* 14, no. 3 (1993), and 15, no. 2 (1994); Thomas Naff (ed.), *Paths to the Middle East: Ten Scholars Look Back* (Albany: State University of New York Press, 1993); Edmund Burke III (ed.), *Struggle and Survival in the Modern Middle East* (London: I. B. Tauris, 1993); Nancy Elizabeth Gallagher, *Approaches to the History of the Middle East: Interviews with Leading Middle East Historians* (Reading, UK: Ithaca Press, 1994).

2. For the "doing history" concept, see J. H. Hexter, *Doing History* (Bloomington: Indiana University Press, 1971).

3. Jacques Derrida, *Of Grammatology*, trans. by Gayatri Chakrvorty Spivak (Baltimore: Johns Hopkins University Press, 1976), p. 156. The French original was published in 1967.

4. Ludwig Wittgenstein, *Tractatus Logico-Philosophicus* (London: Routledge and Kegan Paul, 1933), p. 39.

5. For the concept of textual communities, see Brian Stock, *The Implication of Literacy: Written Language and Models of Interpretation in the Eleventh and Twelfth Centuries* (Princeton, N.J.: Princeton University Press, 1983), pp. 88–240, and his *Listening for the Text: On the Uses of the Past* (Baltimore: John Hopkins University, 1990), pp. 22–24, 140–158.

6. See Dominick LaCapra, *History and Criticism* (Ithaca: Cornell University Press, 1985), pp. 45–94.

7. Lawrence Stone, "The Revival of Narrative: Reflections on a New Old History," *Past and Present* 85 (1979): 3–24.

8. Some of the most visible voices to express this position were Roland Barthes, Paul de Man, Hayden White, Jacques Derrida, and Jean-François Lyotard. See Art Berman, *From the New Criticism to Deconstruction: The Reception of Structuralism and Post-Structuralism* (Urbana: University of Illinois Press, 1988).

9. Jacqueline Rose, "Edward Said Talks to Jacqueline Rose," in Paul A. Bové (ed.), *Edward Said and the Work of the Critic: Speaking Truth to Power* (Durhan, N.C.: Duke University Press, 2000), pp. 9–30.

10. David Hollinger, "How Wide the Circle of the 'We'? American Intellectuals and the Problem of the Ethnos Since World War II," *American Historical Review* 98 (1993): 317–337; quotation from p. 322.

11. Isaiah Berlin, *Against the Current* (New York: Penguin Books, 1982).

12. Eric Hobsbawm and Terence Ranger (eds.), *The Invention of Tradition,* Canto ed. (Cambridge, UK: Cambridge University Press, 1992).

13. Hollinger, "How Wide the Circle?" pp. 321–322.

14. Ibid., p. 330. For further elaboration on this topic, albeit a different view, see Richard Rorty, *Objectivity, Relativism, and Truth* (Cambridge, UK: Cambridge University Press, 1991), pp. 1–7, 203–210.

15. See, for example, Alan Richards and John Waterbury, *A Political Economy of the Middle East: State, Class, and Economic Development* (Boulder, Colo.: Westview Press, 1990); and Richards and Waterbury, *A Political Economy of the Middle East*, 2nd ed. (Boulder, Colo.: Westview Press, 1996).

16. Edited by James Jankowski and Israel Gershoni (New York: Columbia University Press, 1997).

Part 1

New Dimensions of Modernizing Processes

2

The Great Ottoman Debasement, 1808–1844: A Political Economy Framework

Şevket Pamuk

At the threshold of the modern era, from the 1770s until the 1840s, Ottoman state finances frequently experienced large budget deficits arising mostly from wars and, to a lesser extent, from costs of military reform. These deficits reached their peak during the 1820s and 1830s. In response, the government attempted to increase its control over revenue sources and made use of various forms of internal borrowing. However, the state's demand for funds in relation to both the size of the economy and the ability of the fragile domestic institutions to handle them was too large.[1] As a result, when short-term fiscal pressures mounted, the government resorted to debasements. The highest rates of debasement in Ottoman history took place during the reign of the reformist and centralizing Sultan Mahmud II (1808–1839). This chapter will argue that debasements were not the result of a haphazard process but were undertaken or not undertaken by the government after the weighing of associated benefits and costs. In other words, far from being an exercise in futility, debasements are viewed here as a potentially effective instrument of fiscal policy, especially in the short term. In fact, one may even argue that debasements were used as an instrument of centralization by Mahmud II. The timing and magnitude of the debasements also suggest, however, that the government was quite sensitive to the political opposition they generated among the janissaries and other urban groups.

Toward a Political Economy Framework

The causes and consequences of premodern debasements, that is, the reduction of the specie content of the currency by the monetary authority, have been the focus of much debate.[2] Some of the causes, such as the wear on the existing stock of coins in circulation or the mismanagement of the mints, appear technical or administrative in nature. Another possible cause was the increase in the economy's demand for money and the need to increase the money stock in circulation. In the short term, debasements provided relief from shortages of specie and coinage in circulation by increasing the nominal value of coinage in circulation. However, the alteration and expansion of the money supply through debasements could provide only temporary relief because prices tended to adjust upward sooner or later, and the volume of coinage in circulation adjusted for the price level tended to return to its earlier level. For this reason, the efforts of premodern states to offset the detrimental effects of a bullion shortage by means of debasement were doomed to frustration.

The persistence of debasements throughout the medieval and early modern periods suggests that these interventions were not simply futile efforts. Although they did not solve the problems of specie shortages, debasements did provide fiscal relief for the states, and there lay their appeal. Because the obligations of the state to the soldiers, bureaucrats, and suppliers are expressed in terms of the monetary unit of account, a reduction in the silver content of the currency enabled the state to increase the amount it could mint from or the payments it could make with a given amount of silver. As a result, debasements were frequently utilized as an alternative to additional taxation.

Prices almost always rose in the aftermath of debasements because a debasement typically increased the nominal value of coinage in circulation. Even if the prices did not rise quickly because of the shortages of specie or for some other reason, long-distance trade acted as the ultimate equalizer in the long term. If prices expressed in grams of silver in a given region became less expensive vis-à-vis the neighboring areas, increased demand for the lower-priced commodities attracted large quantities of silver, thus raising prices. Price adjustments after a debasement tended to be more rapid, the more open the economy and the more frequently debasements were used.[3]

Another possible cause of debasements was the pressure from some social groups in favor of inflation. Even if a social group did not always benefit from debasements and inflation, it could still prefer debasements to additional taxation. For example, merchants sometimes preferred debasements to increased taxation whenever the government faced fiscal difficulties. This is because the prices of goods held by the merchants typically rose together with other prices after a debasement. On the other side of the coin were social groups who stood to lose from debasements and the accompanying inflation and therefore opposed them. Under these circumstances, the fate of the currency was not determined solely by the government but often depended upon the struggle between it and various social groups. Before we begin an examination of Ottoman debasements in the early decades of the nineteenth century, let us examine how different groups in Ottoman society fared in the face of such debasements.

For a long time it has been assumed that the use of money in the Ottoman Empire was limited to long-distance trade and parts of the urban sector.[4] Yet recent research has shown that the urban population and some segments of the countryside were already part of the monetary economy by the end of the fifteenth century. Even more significant, there occurred a substantial increase in the use of money during the sixteenth century, both because of the increased availability of specie and increasing commercialization of the rural economy. There also emerged an intensive pattern of periodic markets and market fairs where peasants and larger landholders sold parts of their produce to urban residents. These markets also provided an important opportunity for the nomads to come into contact with both peasants and the urban population. Large sectors of the rural population came to use coinage, especially the small denominations of silver akçe and the copper mangır, through their participation in these markets.[5]

Second, small-scale but intensive networks of credit relations developed in and around the urban centers. Evidence from thousands of court cases in these towns and cities involving lenders and borrowers leave no doubt that the use of credit, small and large, was widespread among all segments of urban as well as parts of rural society. It is clear that neither the Islamic prohibitions against interest and usury nor the absence of formal banking institutions prevented the expansion of credit in Ottoman society.[6] As a result, debasements had an impact on virtually all groups in Ottoman society, and in turn, each group took a position. Most men and women, both urban and rural, were clear about the consequences of different ways of dealing with the coinage, and who gained and who lost. In general, all those who had future obligations expressed in terms of the unit of account—mainly borrowers and tenants paying fixed rents in cash—stood to gain from debasements. Conversely, those who expected to be paid fixed amounts in terms of the unit of account stood to lose from debasements.[7]

In the rural areas, taxes and rents on both public and privately held lands were paid almost entirely in kind during the eighteenth and nineteenth centuries. Moreover, those producers who sold part of their crop in local markets received higher prices during periods of inflation. As a result, debasements and inflation did not have a major impact on rural producers. The significant exception, of course, were the lenders and borrowers in the countryside. Local court records indicate that numbers of court cases involving lending and borrowing by rural as well as urban residents typically showed sharp increases during periods of frequent debasement and rapid inflation.

In the urban areas there existed a dense network of credit relations, most of which involved small-scale lenders and small-cash *vakıf*s (pious foundations) that lent on interest. The local *sarraf*s (money changers), with their expert knowledge of the markets, often benefited from the uncertainty and fluctuations in exchange rates as well as the requirements to surrender old coins in the aftermath of debasements. Most of them were net lenders, though, and they stood to lose from the inflation that followed debasements.

As the fiscal problems of the Ottoman state intensified in the second half of the eighteenth century, the *sarraf*s of Istanbul began to provide increasingly larger loans to the state, utilizing their connections to the financial markets in Europe. This lucrative process soon transformed the traditional money changers into the so-called Galata bankers, named after the financial district in the capital city. The Galata bankers also held considerable amounts of *esham* (long-term government bonds). As a result, they were in favor of monetary stability.[8]

It would be interesting to explore the attitudes of the *ayan* (notables) of the provinces toward money and inflation during the eighteenth and early nineteenth centuries. Many *ayan* were the holders of various types of tax farms, both short-term and long-term. To the extent that the tax farmers were expected to make fixed payments to the state each year, they tended to benefit from debasements and inflation. At the same time, however, many *ayan* were engaged in trade, especially long-distance trade. In their role as long-distance merchants, they must have favored monetary stability.

Merchants and shopkeepers in the urban areas did not appear to lose from debasements, as the prices of goods they sold tended to rise during periods of inflation. There was always the risk, though, that the government would impose price ceilings on essential goods sold in the urban markets whenever prices rose too fast. As a result, they were also wary of debasements.

The groups that stood to lose the most from debasements were those who were paid fixed amounts in terms of the unit of account. The most important groups in this category were the employees of the state, the bureaucracy, the ulema, and especially the janissaries. There existed a large overlap between the guild members and the janissaries after the latter began to moonlight as artisans and shopkeepers in the seventeenth century.

The Great Debasement, 1808–1844

When Mahmud II ascended the throne in 1808, the standard kuruş or piaster contained 6.90 grams of silver, unchanged since the debasement of 1789. During the next three decades, the silver content of the Ottoman currency declined at times sharply, at times more slowly. The lowest point was reached in 1831–1832 at 0.5 grams of silver, although the kuruş subsequently rose to 0.9 grams in 1832 and then to 1.0 gram in 1844, where it stayed until World War I. All in all, the kuruş lost more than 83 percent of its silver content from 1808 to 1844.[9] (See Table 2.1.)

Table 2.1 The Silver Kuruş and Its Exchange Rate, 1780–1914

Year	Weight (grams)	Fineness (percent)	Pure Silver Content (grams)	Exchange Rate of the British Pound (in kuruş)
1780	18.50	54.0	10.00	11.0
1789	12.80	54.0	6.90	15.0
1800	12.60	54.0	6.90	15.0
1808	12.80	46.5	5.90	19.0
1809	9.60	46.5	4.42	20.5
1810	5.13	73.0	3.74	19.8
1818	9.60	46.5	4.42	29.0
1820	6.41	46.0	2.95	35.0
1822	4.28	54.0	2.32	37.0
1828	3.20	46.0	1.47	59.0
1829	3.10	22.0	0.72	69.0
1831	3.00	17.5	0.53	80.0
1832	2.14	44.0	0.94	88.0
1839	2.14	44.0	0.94	104.0
1844	1.20	83.3	1.00	110.0
1914	1.20	83.3	1.00	110.0

Sources: Chester L. Krause and Clifford Mishler, with Colin R. Bruce II, *Standard Catalog of World Coins,* 21st edition, (Iola, Wisc.: Krause Publications, 1994); Benjamin Sass, "The Silver and Billon Coins Minted at Constantinople Under Sultan Mahmud II (1223–1255 H ["Hegira/Hijra"])," *The American Numismatic Society Notes* 18 (1972): 167–175; Çüneyt Ölçer, *Sultan II. Mahmud Zamanında Darp Edilen Osmanlı Madeni Paraları,* (Istanbul: Yenilik Basımevi, 1970); Jem Sultan, *Coins of the Ottoman Empire and the Turkish Republic: A Detailed Catalogue of the Jem Sultan Collection,* 2 vols. (Thousand Oaks, Calif.: B&R Publishers, 1977), pp. 213–297; İsmail Galib, *Takvim-i Meskukat-ı Osmaniye* (Istanbul, H. 1307/1889–1890); Daniel Panzac, "La Piastre et le Cyclotron: Essai sur les Monnaies Ottomanes, 1687–1844," paper presented to the Conference on *Money and Currencies in the Ottoman Empire, 1690–1850* (Istanbul, November 1997); and Charles Issawi, *The Economic History of Turkey, 1800–1914* (Chicago: University of Chicago Press, 1980), pp. 327–331.

Note: The Tashih-i Sikke (correction of coinage) operation of 1844 introduced the new gold lira, which equaled 100 silver kuruş and fixed the gold-silver ratio at 15:09. The standards of Ottoman silver and gold coinage did not change after that date.

Closely paralleling the debasement of the currency was the sharp fall in its exchange rate and the rapid rise in the general price level, both of which were equally dramatic. In 1808, one Venetian gold ducat exchanged for 8 kuruş and one British pound sterling for 19 kuruş. By 1844 one ducat equaled 50 to 52 kuruş and the British pound exchanged for 110 kuruş. In other words, the Ottoman unit also lost about 83 percent of its value against the leading European currencies during these thirty-five years. Indices recently constructed from data obtained from the account books of *vakıfs*, their soup kitchens, and the account books of the imperial kitchen at Istanbul show that food prices increased by about fourfold between 1808 and 1844 and about tenfold between 1789 and 1844.[10] It is possible to follow the silver content of the kuruş on an annual basis from the available numismatic evidence. During his thirty-two-year reign, Mahmud II issued ten different series of silver coins each with different standards. Most of these series covered the full range of coins from the small one, or five para, to the two, five, and even six kuruş pieces. Each of these series remained in circulation anywhere from one to eight or more years. Mahmud II ended up issuing forty-seven different types of silver coins, more than any other Ottoman ruler. Detailed information is available about the standards of each coin for each of these series. In addition, a limited number of coins have been subjected to content analysis to establish their specie and alloy content (Table 2.1).

The government continued to issue varieties of gold coins such as zeri mahbub, rumi, adli, hayriye, and mahmudiye, each with different and changing standards during the reign of Mahmud II. These gold coins were not subjected to such rapid rates of debasement, however. The overall decline in the specie content of the gold coins during these three decades remained below 20 percent.[11] It is clear that the government did not view the gold coins with the same fiscal logic that was applied to the silver kuruş. This was because the obligations of the state were expressed in terms of the silver kuruş and not linked to any gold coin. As a result, the government did not stand to gain much from debasing the gold coins.[12]

An examination of the timing and magnitudes of the debasements provides important insights into the motives of the government. On the basis of the available evidence presented in Table 2.1, the debasements during the reign of Mahmud II can be divided into two subperiods. The first subperiod covers the early years of his reign, from 1808 until 1822. Six separate series, or sets, of silver coins were issued during this period. By the sixth series, the silver content of the kuruş had been reduced to 2.32 grams, by a total of 60 percent in comparison to 1808. The fiscal difficulties created by the wars against Russia, Iran, and the Greek revolution figured prominently in the decline of the currency during the first subperiod.[13] In fact, the third series of silver coins issued by Mahmud II in 1810 with lower silver were called cihadiyye, in reference to the ongoing war with Russia and the need to raise fiscal revenue for that effort. These coins remained in circulation for eight years.[14] The government also issued special cihadiyye eshamı during this period, which can be considered the first example of Ottoman war bonds.[15]

The second and even more rapid subperiod of debasement took place during and after the war of 1828–1829 with Russia. In addition to wartime expenditures, the large, 400-million kuruş indemnity the Ottomans agreed to pay at the end of the war weighed heavily on Ottoman finances and the currency for a number of years.[16] Between 1828 and 1831, the silver content of the kuruş was thus reduced sharply from 2.32 grams to 0.53 grams, a decline of 79 percent in four years. As financial conditions began to improve after 1832, the silver content of the currency was raised to 0.94 grams.[17]

We can now examine the attitudes and behavior of the Ottoman government toward debasement during the reign of Mahmud II. In this framework the government is viewed as weighing the short-term fiscal benefits accruing from debasements against both the short-term and long-term costs of such action. If the government perceives these costs to be less than the expected fiscal benefits, then a debasement or a series of debasements may be adopted. In other words, far from being an exercise in futility, the debasements are seen as a potentially effective instrument of fiscal policy, especially in the short term. At the same time, this framework will emphasize the economic and political constraints on the state's ability to take advantage of debasements.

The fiscal benefits of a debasement are not difficult to establish. The government was able to issue a larger amount of coinage in nominal terms with the same amount of specie and meet a larger fraction of its obligations.[18] One related measure often adopted by the government in the aftermath of a debasement was to prohibit the use and sale of gold and silver in local markets and order that these be surrendered to the imperial mint at below-market prices.[19] Finally, the state also obtained revenue from the old coins brought to the mint by the public.

On the other side, there are a number of costs that may be borne by the state as a result of debasements. As prices rose, including those paid by the state in the aftermath of a debasement, many of the state revenues, fixed in nominal terms, declined in real terms. In other words, debasements generated an initial surge in revenues followed by their decline in real terms due to the inflation they created. In the longer term, a debasement might even lead to a real decline in revenues if the government did not adjust upward the taxes and other revenues that had been fixed in nominal terms.[20]

Second, if the public loses confidence in the currency and begins to anticipate further debasements, it will become increasingly difficult for the government to take advantage of further reductions in the specie content of coinage. In the open-mint system, for example, the public may begin holding another currency and stay away from the mints. A large degree of currency substitution must have taken place during the reign of Mahmud II, as varieties of foreign coinage were free to circulate.[21]

A third cost of Ottoman debasements was the spread of counterfeiting.

When the government issued new coins with a lower specie content, counterfeiters immediately began to mint the new coins with the same or even higher silver content in order to share the seigniorage revenues of the state. This opportunity declined, however, when precious metal prices adjusted upward along with other prices. Price ceilings on the specie and government attempts to obtain the specie at those official prices also encouraged counterfeiting.[22]

Another cost was the adverse implications of debasements for the ability of the state to borrow domestically. As the government began to make use of debasements, the public began to anticipate more, and it became more difficult to borrow from the public at large. There is evidence that with the acceleration of debasements after 1808, rates of interest increased even further and it became even more difficult for the government to sell the esham. For example, it appears that the ratio between the initial sale price of esham and the annual payments declined after 1808 when the government began to use debasements more frequently.[23]

Yet the most important cost of Ottoman debasements was the political opposition they generated among the urban groups, especially in the capital city. One group that disliked debasements consisted of the guild members, shopkeepers, small merchants, and the wage-earning artisans. Another group that stood to lose from debasements were those who were paid fixed salaries by the state, the bureaucracy, the ulema, and especially the janissaries stationed permanently in the capital. There existed a large overlap between the guild members and the janissaries because the latter began to moonlight as artisans and shopkeepers. This broad opposition acted as a major deterrent against the more frequent use of debasements by the government not only in the capital but also in the provincial centers. It would be interesting to explore the causal linkages between the debasements and the urban rebellions of the late eighteenth and early nineteenth centuries in Syria, Iraq, and elsewhere in the empire.[24]

The effectiveness of this urban opposition against debasements should not be measured in terms of the frequency of their rebellions, however. Just as E. P. Thompson had argued in his study of the moral economy of the English crowd in the eighteenth century, that the effectiveness of the bread riots should not be measured in terms of their frequency, it was the threat of rebellions that proved just as effective in the longer term;[25] it ensured that the governments would refrain from debasements, at least during periods of peace.

Into this framework of costs and benefits and interaction between the state and society, wars enter as exogenous shocks, events that raised both the need for short-term revenues for the state and the willingness of the public to accept extraordinary measures such as debasements. As the urgency of generating revenues increased, the state often invoked references to holy wars and even linked the new coinage explicitly to the ongoing wars, calling the new issues of coins and bonds cihadiyye, for example.

During the reigns of both Selim III and Mahmud II, the governments were well aware of the limitations imposed by the janissaries and related urban groups. From the very beginning of his reign, Mahmud II wanted to replace the janissaries with a Western-style army. But during the early years of his long reign, he did not have the political support to make this critical move. After the janissaries were finally defeated and the order was abolished in 1826—in what is usually considered one of the most important political events of this period, known as Vaka-i Hayriye, or the Auspicious Event—a major constraint in the way of debasements was lifted. Only two years later, the government began the largest debasement of Ottoman history, reducing the specie content of the kuruş by 79 percent within a period of four years.

In terms of revenues for the state, the debasements of 1828–1831 were considered a major success by the contemporaries. The credit for this accomplishment was given to Artin Kazaz, an Armenian financier who had risen through the ranks of the *sarraf* guild to head the imperial mint in the 1820s. Kazaz was actually only one in a long chain of Armenian financiers to administer the imperial mint from the late eighteenth century until the 1840s. One of his biographies relates that during the war of 1828–1829 with Russia, the grand vizier considered issuing copper coinage. However, Kazaz convinced the sultan that there should be at least some silver in the new coinage. He then went on to produce a very large volume of five kuruş pieces.[26] His rationale was that the presence of some silver would help the state raise more revenue by making the coins more acceptable to the public and helping the state retain the opportunity to raise additional revenues by lowering the silver content in the future.[27]

One unique aspect of this debasement episode was that the contemporaries calculated the seigniorage revenues of the state from the mint records. According to these calculations, during the regnal years of 22 to 25 (approximately 1828–1831), the imperial mint produced 23 million units of the large five kuruş pieces as the eighth series of Mahmud II after lowering the silver content of the coins. The net seigniorage revenues of the state were estimated at 39.7 million kuruş. During the regnal years 25 and 26 (1831–1832), an additional 245 million kuruş worth of new coinage with even lower silver content was issued as the ninth series. This operation is estimated to have provided the state with net revenues of 119 million kuruş. After the end of the war, during the regnal years 26 through 32 (1832–1838), the mint issued a variety of new coins with a total value of 137.8 million kuruş as the tenth series. The silver content of these coins, however, was higher than both the eighth and the ninth series, and the state did not obtain any seigniorage revenue from them. The purpose of this last phase was to bring back price stability and renew confidence in the currency.[28]

These were large magnitudes in relation to the size of total state revenues and expenditures at the time. Since the various revenues and expenditures were not yet incorporated into a single budget, it is difficult to estimate total annual revenues, but the sum of 250 to 300 million kuruş appears as a reasonable figure for these years. Yavuz Cezar provides an estimate of 300 million kuruş for the budget of 1838.[29] In other words, the debasements of 1828–1832 provided the state with total revenues associated with the debasements amounting to more than one-half of one year's total revenues, or an average of more than 10 percent of annual revenues for these five troubled years.

The debasements provided another, and somewhat unexpected, benefit to the treasury by reducing the borrowing requirements of the state and bringing down interest rates. The decline in interest rates then provided fiscal relief through its impact on the tax-farming system as well. Tax farmers who entered state auctions for the right to collect specific tax revenues were required to make a certain fraction of these payments in advance for which they typically borrowed from private financiers. When the domestic interest rates declined, therefore, the auction prices of tax farms tended to rise.

Bimetallism and External Borrowing

Monetary conditions had assumed crisis proportions by the end of the 1830s. While the government had succeeded in raising short-term revenue from frequent debasements, the resulting inflation created serious political problems. In addition, the production of a large variety of coins since the beginning of the century and the inability of the government to retire the earlier series from circulation had added to the difficulties. These conditions created difficulties both for daily transactions and international trade. At the same time, the appeal and use of European coinage had increased, especially in international trade and for store-of-wealth purposes.[30]

For European governments and especially the British, who were concerned about Russian expansionism to the south, the success of Ottoman reforms was considered essential for the territorial integrity of the empire. European governments also believed that rapid expansion of commercial ties with Europe based on the principle of comparative advantage and European direct investment were essential for the development of the Ottoman economy. As a result, they began to exert considerable pressure on the Ottoman government to abandon debasements and establish a more stable monetary system. Bimetallism was proposed as a monetary regime that would bring the Ottoman Empire more in line with the prevailing international trends and help expand both trade and European investment. The

European governments also linked Ottoman access to European financial markets to fiscal reform and monetary stability. They made clear that they were ready to provide the technical expertise necessary for this purpose.

After the death of Sultan Mahmud II in 1839, the new government openly expressed the intention to carry out such an operation. New machines and technology were imported from England. Mint technicians and other specialists were invited from England and France to install the machines and advise the Ottoman government about the new standards of coinage.[31] After some delay, the government finally decided to adopt the bimetallic standard in which the silver kuruş and the new gold lira were both accepted as legal tender, freely convertible at the fixed rate of 100 kuruş for one gold lira and obtainable at the government mint. The new gold coins began to be produced in 1843, and the new silver coins were issued the following year along with an official declaration from the imperial mint, setting out the reasons for the reform. The gold-silver ratio was fixed at 15:9. The open mint system was to be continued. All silver and gold coinage minted until 1922 adhered to the standards established in 1844.

In the early part of the nineteenth century, governments in Cairo and Tunis, facing very similar constraints and pressures, also abandoned fiscally motivated debasements in favor of bimetallism and stable coinage.[32] It was not so much the interaction between these governments that brought about the monetary regime shift. In addition to the growing domestic costs of debasements, it was the rising forces of globalization, the rapid increase in trade with Europe, and the growing interaction with European merchants and governments as well as their advice and pressure that led these governments to embrace those monetary institutions that conformed to the requirements of international trade.

The decision to abandon debasements as a means of raising fiscal revenue without the elimination of the budget deficits proved very costly in the long term. All three governments began to borrow in the European financial markets during the 1850s in order to meet their short-term budgetary needs. By the middle of the 1870s, with their annual debt payments far in excess of their ability to pay, they were all forced to declare moratoriums on their outstanding debt. The establishment of the European Public Debt Administration in Istanbul (1881) and, even more dramatically, the occupation of Tunis (1881) and Egypt (1882) by the European powers were directly linked to these moratoriums.[33]

Notes

1. For state attempts to increase its control over revenue sources and the evolution of the domestic institutions for credit during the late eighteenth and early

nineteenth centuries, see Şevket Pamuk, *A Monetary History of the Ottoman Empire* (Cambridge, UK: Cambridge University Press, 1999), pp. 188–192.

2. Carlo. M. Cipolla, "Currency Depreciation in Medieval Europe," *Economic History Review* 15 (1963): 413–415, provides a useful list of the causes of debasements and a good starting point. Also see Harry A. Miskimin, *Money and Power in Fifteenth-Century France* (New Haven, Conn.: Yale University Press, 1984); Michael D. Bordo, "Money, Deflation, and Seigniorage in the Fifteenth Century," *Journal of Monetary Economics* 18 (1986): 337–346; and Nathan Sussman, "Debasements, Royal Revenues, and Inflation in France During the Hundred Years' War, 1415–1422," *The Journal of Economic History* 53 (1993): 44–70.

3. Bordo, "Money, Deflation, and Seigniorage."

4. F. Braudel, *Civilization and Capitalism, 15th–18th Century,* Vol. III: *The Perspective of the World* (New York: Harper and Row Publishers, 1984), pp. 471–473.

5. R. C. Jennings, "Loans and Credit in Early 17th-Century Ottoman Judicial Records," *Journal of the Economic and Social History of the Orient* 16 (1973): 168–216; Suraiya Faroqhi, "The Early History of Balkan Fairs," *Südost-Forschungen* 37 (1978): 50–68; Suraiya Faroqhi, "Sixteenth Century Periodic Markets in Various Anatolian Sancaks," *Journal of the Economic and Social History of the Orient* 22 (1979): 32–80; Suraiya Faroqhi, "Rural Society in Anatolia and the Balkans During the Sixteenth Century," *Turcica* 9 (1977):161–196, and vol. 11 (1979):103–153; and Halil İnalcık, "Osmanlı İdare, Sosyal ve Ekonomik Tarihiyle İlgili Belgeler: Bursa Kadı Sicillerinden Seçmeler," *Türk Tarih Kurumu, Belgeler* 14 (1981): 1–91. See also the studies on the rural economy by these authors that appeared in two collections: Halil İnalcık, *The Middle East and the Balkans Under the Ottoman Empire: Essays on Economy and Society* (Bloomington: Indiana University Turkish Studies and Turkish Ministry of Culture Joint Series, 1993); and Suraiya Faroqhi, *Coping with the State, Political Conflict, and Crime in the Ottoman Economy, 1550–1720* (Istanbul: ISIS Press, 1995).

6. Pamuk, *Monetary History*, pp. 77–87.

7. For greater detail on the responses of different social groups to Ottoman debasements during the fifteenth, sixteenth, and seventeenth centuries, see ibid., pp. 55–58, 138–142.

8. Araks Şahiner, "The Sarrafs of Istanbul: Financiers of the Empire" (M.A. thesis, Department of History, Boğaziçi University, 1995); Mehmet Genç, "Esham," in *Islam Ansiklopedisi*, Vol. XI (Istanbul: Diyanet Vakfı, 1995), pp. 376–380.

9. The overall rate of debasement is even higher if 1789 is taken as the beginning point. Until that year, the kuruş contained approximately 8.4 grams of silver. The Ottoman unit lost 88 percent of its silver content between 1789 and 1844. For both the 1808–1844 and 1789–1844 periods, these represent the highest rates of debasement in Ottoman history. There is no other period in which the Ottoman currency was subjected to such a high rate of debasement in such a short period of time.

10. Şevket Pamuk, *Five Hundred Years of Prices and Wages in Istanbul and Other Ottoman Cities, 1469–1998* (Ankara: Turkey State Institute of Statistics, Historical Statistics Series, forthcoming).

11. Chester L. Krause and Clifford Mishler, *Standard Catalog of World Coins,* 21st ed. (Iola, Wisc.: Krause Publications, 1994); also Remzi Kocaer, *Osmanlı Altın Paraları* (Istanbul: Güzel Sanatlar Matbaası, 1967).

12. In a different context Akira Motomura has argued that the Spanish government of the seventeenth century made a similar distinction between copper coinage on the one hand and silver and gold on the other. The government obtained large revenues from the minting and international circulation of silver coinage and, in order to maintain worldwide confidence in the currency, did not want to change the standards of these coins. However, the copper coinage used in the domestic economy was subjected to a policy of regular debasements. See Akira Motomura, "The Best and Worst of Currencies: Seigniorage and Currency Policy in Spain, 1597–1650," *The Journal of Economic History* 54 (1994):104–127.

13. Stanford J. Shaw and Ezel Kuran Shaw, *History of the Ottoman Empire and Modern Turkey*, Vol. II, *1809–1975* (London: Cambridge University Press, 1977), pp. 12–19.

14. BOA (Başbakanlık Osmanlı Arşivleri/ Prime Ministry, Ottoman Archives), Cevdet Darphane, 158, 3220, 1964, 1656, and 1632.

15. Çüneyt Ölçer, *Sultan II. Mahmud Zamanında Darp Edilen Osmanlı Madeni Paraları* (Istanbul: Yenilik Basımevi, 1970); Benjamin Sass, "The Silver and Billon Coins Minted at Constantinople Under Sultan Mahmud II (1223–1255 H.)," *American Numismatic Society Notes* 18 (1972): 167–175; Krause and Mishler, *Standard Catalog of World Coins*.

16. The Ottomans were expected to make this payment over a period of ten years. This sum amounted to approximately 150 percent of the annual revenues of the Ottoman state. It was subsequently reduced after territorial concessions by the Ottomans. Shaw and Shaw, *History of the Ottoman Empire*, Vol. II, p. 32; Yavuz Cezar, *Osmanlı Maliyesinde Bunalım ve Değişim Dönemi: XVIII. yy.dan Tanzimat'a Mali Tarih* (Istanbul: Alan Yayıncılık, 1986), pp. 244–301.

17. The exchange rate of the kuruş followed its silver content closely during these decades, with two exceptions. First, the decline in exchange rate of the kuruş slowed and even stopped during the Napoleonic wars as the European currencies also depreciated. Second, the link between the silver content of the Ottoman currency and its exchange rate was severed and the kuruş became a fiat currency during the rapid debasements of 1828–1833 (see Table 2.1).

18. Contemporary Ottoman commentators have argued that debasements were not useful for the state because the prices rose and the state revenues, which were fixed in nominal terms, declined in real terms after each debasement (Cezar, *Osmanlı Maliyesinde Bunalım*, p. 147). This argument, however, does not take into account the revenue obtained by the state during the first round by issuing additional coinage. With the time horizon shortened under the pressure of war and severe financial crises, it thus made sense to pursue debasements for short-term fiscal gains.

19. This measure was used during the debasement of 1789 and later during some of the debasements of Mahmud II (Cezar, *Osmanlı Maliyesinde Bunalım*, pp. 99, 139). For government attempts to bring in more silver to the Istanbul mint during this period, also see BOA, Cevdet Darphane 823, 13, and Hatt-ı Hümayun, 16505.

20. When the public can immediately observe or learn of the rate of debasement, prices adjust more quickly and the fiscal benefits of the debasement are exhausted sooner. If, on the other hand, both the size and the degree of fineness of the coins are constantly changed, as was the case during this period, the public might underestimate the extent of the debasement and adjust to the actual rate of debasement with a lag. In that case, the government's revenues will be higher. Sussman ("Debasements," pp. 44–70) argues that manipulating the monetary stan-

dard in this fashion offers the government the same kind of opportunity to raise revenues as with fiat money.

21. For an earlier episode of currency substitution in the Ottoman Empire arising from the instability of the akçe during the seventeenth century, see Şevket Pamuk, "In the Absence of Domestic Currency: Debased European Coinage in the Seventeenth-Century Ottoman Empire," *Journal of Economic History* 57 (1997): 345–366; and Pamuk, *Monetary History*, pp. 138–158.

22. For examples of counterfeiting and the circulation of counterfeit coinage during this period, see BOA, Hatt-ı Hümayun, 52541/A, 52563, 27644, 48486, 48487, 48488, 24243, and Cevdet Darphane, 1816, 1472, 1818.

23. Cezar, *Osmanlı Maliyesinde Bunalım*, pp. 79–89, 133–135, 239–241.

24. I am indebted to Dina Rizk Khoury for information on the urban uprisings in Syria and Iraq during the period 1770 to 1830.

25. E. P. Thompson, "The Moral Economy of the British Crowd in the Eighteenth Century," *Past and Present* 50 (1971): 76–135; also Charles Tilly, "Food Supply and Public Order in Modern Europe," in C. Tilly (ed.), *The Formation of Nation States in Western Europe* (Princeton, N.J.: Princeton University Press, 1975), pp. 35–151.

26. Haydar Kazgan, "İkinci Sultan Mahmut devrinde enflasyon ve darphane amiri Kazaz Artin," *Toplum ve Bilim* 11 (1980): 115–130; Diran Kelekyan, "Kazaz Artin," *Tarihi Osmani Encümeni Mecmuası,* 26 and 27 (June and August H.1330/1912).

27. According to a story still being told among the Armenian community of Istanbul, the Russian government demanded and obtained a large payment of indemnity after the war ended with the defeat of the Ottomans. Aware that the Ottoman government frequently debased the currency, however, the Russians demanded that the sum be paid in old kuruş, not new and debased currency. The Ottoman government produced new and debased coinage anyway but soon realized they had a problem on their hands. The coins were obviously new, very bright, and shiny. So, the story goes, they lined up the new reform soldiers on the Asian side of the Bosphorus for several miles and instructed them to hold out their hands. The new coinage was then passed on from hand to hand. By the time they reached the other end, they all looked just like the old kuruş. I am indebted to Dr. Nurhan Davutyan for this story. For the negotiations with the Russian government regarding the indemnity payment and the Ottoman request to pay the indemnity in silver kuruş rather than Hungarian gold coins, see BOA, Hatt-ı Hümayun, 42935, 46216, 20194.

28. A. du Velay, *Essai sur l'Histoire Financière de la Turquie* (Paris: Arthur Rousseau, 1903), pp. 28–32.

29. Cezar, *Osmanlı Maliyesinde Bunalım*, pp. 244–301.

30. For a detailed list of Ottoman and foreign coinage circulating in the Balkans, see David Cohen, "La circulation monétaire entre les Principautés Roumaines et les terres Bulgares (1840–1878)," *Bulgarian Historical Review* 4, no. 2 (1976): 55–71. For the different varieties of coinage in circulation in Baghdad in the 1830s and their exchange rates, see Hatt-ı Hümayun, 27815/D, 52490.

31. Ölçer, *Sultan II. Mahmud*, p. 17.

32. It is interesting that even during the 1820s and 1830s when Governor Muhammad Ali successfully fought and defeated the Ottoman armies for the independence of Egypt, he chose to keep the two currencies linked. The strength of commercial linkages between the two regions must have played an important role in the persistence of the monetary linkage. It is also likely that in the rapid deprecia-

tion of the kuruş in Istanbul, Muhammad Ali saw an opportunity for his own government to generate additional fiscal revenue and thus went along with the debasements. As a result, the timing of the overall decline of the para and kuruş of Egypt was remarkably similar to those in Istanbul. For the rapid decline in the exchange rate of the para of Egypt during this period, see Kenneth Cuno, *The Pasha's Peasants: Land, Society, and Economy in Lower Egypt, 1740–1858* (Cambridge, UK: Cambridge University Press, 1992), Appendix 2, pp. 211–215. Muhammad Ali was the first to invite European monetary specialists. With the monetary reforms of 1834, Egypt embraced the bimetallic system ten years ahead of the Ottomans in Istanbul. The standards adopted for gold and silver Egyptian coinage remained unchanged until World War I.

33. David Landes, *Bankers and Pashas: International Finance and Economic Imperialism in Egypt* (London: Heinemann, 1958); Roger Owen, *The Middle East in the World Economy, 1800–1914* (London: Methuen, 1981), pp. 122–135; and Abdelhamid Fenina, "Les Monnaies de la Régence de Tunis sous les Husaynides, Études de Numismatiques et d'Histoire Monétaire (1705–1891)" (Thèse de Doctorat, Nouveau Régime, Université de Paris-Sorbonne, 1993).

3

A Prelude to Ottoman Reform: Ibn 'Ābidīn on Custom and Legal Change

Wael B. Hallaq

The State of the Art

With the zenith of European colonialism, Western legal scholarship on Islam constructed a paradigm according to which Islamic law suffered from a rigidity that ultimately led to a sort of paralysis. This paradigm, which was put to the service of colonialist doctrine and practice, was a necessary step in occidentalizing the East and, effectively, in vindicating a structural demolition of traditional Near Eastern legal systems. Structural dismantling was, in turn, a prerequisite for constructing Western-like national legal systems that were instrumental for the realization of colonialist policies. Unfortunately, this paradigm continues to prevail to a large degree, although increasingly attempts are being made to dislodge it. A characteristic feature of these attempts has been the effort to show that at certain times and in certain places the law did undergo change.

This chapter represents a product of a larger study that aims to go beyond these emerging themes. Ibn 'Ābidīn's discourse is identified here as the work of the author-jurist, a hitherto overlooked juristic category or role that was conducive to legal change as a structural function. In other words, while showing that episodic change in the law is, in and of itself, a worthy quest, this chapter aims, in part, to demonstrate not only that the mechanisms of legal change constituted a *structural feature* of the law but that the discourse of the author-jurist—as a manipulator of the discursive tradition—was necessarily an integral part of these structural mechanisms. More specifically, and within the parameters set by the present volume, this chapter attempts to show that through these mechanisms—of which one tool was the discursive strategies of the author-jurist—a fundamental reformulation of legal methodology and theory was effected.

The Problem

At the heart of Islamic legal philosophy lies the fundamental conception that law and juridical norms, whether obliquely inferred or descending directly from the revealed texts, were created in the interest of believers.[1] Taken in reverse order, the same elements amount to the valid proposition that the interest of believers lies in a law that originated with God, the point being that human interest and public good have always been seen as divinely preordained. The mutual complementary nature and substance of the formal sources of the law precisely reflect this conception: The Quran and prophetic Sunna provide the material sources of the law; *qiyās* (method of legal interference) affords the jurist a set of logical methods for legal reasoning on the basis of these sources; and consensus projects the agreement of jurists on a legal matter,[2] be it explicitly stipulated in, or otherwise inferred from, the texts of revelation. This articulated quartet undeniably constitutes the discursive and theoretical core of the legal sources and methodology.

Yet such a synopsis may be charged with being reductionist and even crude, and to a certain extent the charge is justifiable. After all, no account is taken of the detail, qualifications, and variables that intrude upon the major components of this conception. We know, for instance, that at nearly every juncture of its developmental history, law and legal theory had to deal with the imperatives of mundane reality and social exigency, for these could not have been, and indeed were not, dismissed out of hand. We also know that under the rubric of *ta'līl* (causation), disguised as it may have been by layers of theological and logical discourse, legal theory, even in its highest form of theorizing, recognized the social dimensions of the law and its worldly imperatives.[3] The very recognition of the so-called supplementary or informal sources of the law—*istiḥsān* (juristic preference), *istiṣlāḥ* (public welfare/interest), and so on[4]—is highly indicative of the attention that social reality and its requirements commanded from the jurists. A recently published study has shown how these informal sources, together with the prophetic Sunna and consensus, have long accommodated social custom, usually regarded as independent of the revealed sources.[5] Admittedly, however, this mode of accommodation was more common in the early history of Islam, when law was undergoing a process of formation whereby even the Sunna of the Prophet, a presumably divine source, was able to allow, quite readily and extensively, the absorption of social customs, practices, and values that had lain, until then, outside the realm of Islamic norms.

Nonetheless, such sources as *istiḥsān* and *istiṣlāḥ* may have quite likely continued to serve the interests of this accommodation, albeit in a highly circumscribed fashion: Both methods were, toward the end of and after the formative period, gradually redefined and brought under a controlled methodology that was as systematically rigorous as that which underlies *qiyās*.[6] It is even likely that these two informal sources were no more open to serve this accommodation than *qiyās* itself, which allowed, also in a restricted fashion, the absorption of extra-legal customs and social practices through the theory of causation, particularly the recondite method of *munāsaba* (suitability).[7]

It remains true, however, that whatever the means or methods that legal theory allowed for the accommodation of custom and humanistic considerations—areas that effectively lay outside the province of the law—these same means and methods remained strained and largely inauspicious. As formal methods dictating modes of legal reasoning, they continued to be not only narrow in scope but also limited in quantitative application. This is particularly true since the operation of the law did not, strictly speaking, demand in each case a fresh interpretation of the sources through reference to legal methodology and legal theory. Rather, the application of the law presupposed a body of authoritative legal doctrine that afforded the jurist not only the positive stipulations of the law but also the *uṣūl* (principles) that described the limits of legal interpretation, principles that in effect defined the hermeneutical contours of his school.[8] In other words, custom, social reality, and humanistic considerations were allowed to trickle into religious law through the narrow definitions of legal theory and through the existing perforations in the authoritative, cumulative tradition of the school.

In Ḥanafism, for instance, the limits of hermeneutical activity were set by the imposition of a hierarchical taxonomy of legal authority that only the *mujtahid* (jurisprudent, highly qualified jurist) might, in certain instances, be allowed to transgress.[9] At the top of this hierarchy stood the doctrines of the three founding masters: Abū Ḥanīfa, Abū Yūsuf, and Muḥammad b. al-Ḥasan al-Shaybānī. Preserved in written form, these doctrines, known as *ẓāhir al-riwāya*, were transmitted via many channels by trustworthy and highly qualified jurists. A relatively few cases qualifying as *ẓāhir al-riwāya* were also attributed to Zufar and al-Ḥasan b. Ziyād, two of Abū Ḥanīfa's most outstanding pupils.[10] The second rank of this hierarchy came to be known as *masā'il al-nawādir*, consisting of legal works and cases attributed to these same founding masters but with neither the sanctioning authority of highly qualified transmitters nor a large number of channels of transmission.[11] The third rank consisted of what were termed *wāqi'āt* or *nawāzil*, namely, cases of law that were not addressed by the early masters but that were solved by later jurists who flourished in the H. fourth/tenth century and thereafter.[12]

This taxonomy represents the boundaries within which the mufti, or jurist, and *qāḍī* (judge) operated, and beyond which they were not permitted to venture. If a mufti were queried about a case, he had first to look for its solution in the works of *ẓāhir al-riwāya*. Were he to find it there and discover that all three masters were in agreement upon it, he had to answer the query in accordance with it; he would not give his own solution, even though he might be a highly qualified *mujtahid*. If there was disagreement, Abū Ḥanīfa and one of his two disciples having one opinion, then that was the opinion to be adopted. If Abū Ḥanīfa stood alone, however, then the opinion of his two students could be adopted if it were more agreeable and appropriate to the situation in which the case arose.[13] In certain branches of the law, such as commercial transactions and agricultural leases, the opinions of Abū Yūsuf and Shaybānī were, by the consensus of later jurists, often deemed preferable to those of Abū Ḥanīfa.[14] In all instances where resort had to be made to the second and third ranks of the hierarchy, the jurist was to follow the authoritative doctrine of the *muta'akhkhirūn* (later jurists), subject to general agreement; otherwise he was to opt, through his own *ijtihād*,[15] for what he deemed appropriate.

Now, between the limitations imposed by the school tradition and the meager allowances of legal theory, there remained little latitude for customary practices to penetrate the walls of established or otherwise authoritative legal doctrine, especially that enshrined in *ẓāhir al-riwāya*. The consequences of this virtually systematic narrowing of latitude were, at least theoretically, grave. The theoretical formulation of the law, partly on its own, but also partly in reaction to the realities of legal practice, never succeeded in recognizing custom as an independent and formal legal source. Indeed, even when compared with the so-called supplementary sources, custom never managed to occupy a place equal to that which the latter had attained in the hierarchy of legal sources. As a formal entity, it remained marginal to the legal arsenal of the four schools, although the Ḥanafites and Mālikites seem to have given it, at least outwardly, more recognition than did the other two schools, however informal this recognition might have been.

Some remarks on the history of custom in the Ḥanafite school should therefore suffice to show its relatively marginal place in the law, at least on the formal level of legal theorization. Despite the fact that this school insisted, like all the others, that for a jurist to qualify as a *qāḍī* he had to be fully aware of the social customs prevailing within his jurisdiction, the intention behind this requirement was by no means to make custom a normative or formal source of the law. This requirement must not, therefore, be equated with its counterpart, namely, that the *qāḍī* ought to possess proficient knowledge of the four formal sources.[16] Knowledge of the four sources was required so that law might be derived therefrom. But knowledge of custom was expected in order that this law might be applied in light of whatever customary values were in force in the specific locale where the *qāḍī* had jurisdiction. Damages pertaining to livestock, for instance, could differ in monetary or barter value from one region or even village to the next. To properly assess such damages in terms of barter equivalence, the *qāḍī* had to have adequate knowledge of local customs.

The *qāḍī*'s knowledge of custom also constituted a prerequisite in those relatively few cases where Islasmic law was by default inapplicable, for standard legal logic dictated conclusions that might lead to unreasonable or unbearable hardship. The Ḥanafite jurist Ibn Māza (d. 536/1141),[17] for instance, argues that the *qāḍī* should possess such knowledge "because *qiyās* may be abandoned in favour of custom. It is to be recognized that we have permitted *istiṣnā'* due to its being customary,[18] although *qiyās* dictates that it should not be admitted."[19]

It is not without significance that despite its presence in various areas of the law, custom ultimately failed to gain a place among the formal sources. This failure becomes all the more striking because Abū Yūsuf, a foremost Ḥanafite authority and second only to Abū Ḥanīfa himself, seems to have recognized it as a source.[20] But for reasons that still await further research to discern them, Abū Yūsuf's position failed to gain majority support and was in effect abandoned.[21] Instead, throughout the five or six centuries subsequent to Abū Yūsuf, the Ḥanafite school upheld the fundamental proposition that textual sources unquestionably override custom.

The discourse of Ḥanafite texts during this period reflects their strong commitment to this proposition, since its vindication on the grounds that the textual sources are superior to custom was universally accepted.[22] While occasional references to custom remained part of the same discourse, it is nonetheless significant that such references appear fleetingly as contingent entities intermittently relevant to the law. In Ibn Sahl Sarakhsī's highly acclaimed *Mabsūṭ*, for instance, both explicit reference and allusion to custom appear a number of times in connection with a variety of topics.[23] In the context of rent, for instance, he states the maxim, "What is known through custom is equivalent to that which is stipulated by the clear texts of revelation."[24] It is clear, however, that the maxim is not cited with the purpose of establishing a universal legal principle but rather as a justification for a highly specific doctrine concerning the rent of residential property. If a house is rented and the contract includes no stipulation as to the purpose for which it was rented, then the operative assumption—which the said maxim legitimizes—would be that it was leased for residential and not commercial or other purposes. The tendency to confine custom to very specific cases, which is evident in Sarakhsī's work, is only matched by its acceptance under the guise of other formal principles, such as *istiḥsān* and consensus.

It is no doubt true that the application of custom under a variety of methodological disguises such, as *istiḥsān* and consensus, amounts to little more than a denial of the form of nonreligious elements in the law. The form of such elements had to conform to the parameters of legal methodology before their qualified assimilation into law became possible, that is, if they were allowed a place in the law at all. Why qualified? Because there appear to have been serious difficulties in assimilating all customary elements by means of such formalizing devices. Custom was often treated in the law and law books qua custom, pure and simple, this being an unambiguous indication of the inability of jurists to introduce it into the law under the guise of established methodological tools.[25] While the cumulative increase in the instances of custom was evident, there was still no formal place for it in the methodological and theoretical scheme, no doubt because legal theory and methodology had become too well established to allow for a structural and fundamental change.

An Attempted Solution

Evidence suggests that by the tenth/sixteenth century, the jurists found it necessary to account for custom in a manner that adequately acknowledged its role in the law but that did not disturb the postulates and basic assumptions of legal theory. In the Ḥanafite school, Ibn Nujaym (d. 970/1563) seems to have been one of the more prominent jurists to undertake the articulation of the relationship between law, legal theory, and custom.[26] In his important work *al-Ashbāh wal-Naẓā'ir*, he dedicates a chapter to custom, significantly titled "al-'Āda Muḥakkima" ("Custom Determines Legal Norms").[27] The first issue traditionally discussed in the exposition of legal sources is *ḥujjiyya* (authoritativeness), namely, a conclusive demonstration through *dalīl qaṭ'ī* (definitive textual support) that the source in question is valid, admissible, and constitutes an authoritative basis for further legal construction. But all Ibn Nujaym can adduce in terms of textual support is the allegedly prophetic report "Whatever Muslims find good, God finds it likewise,"[28] which is universally considered to be deficient. Ibn Nujaym acknowledges that the report lacks the final link with the Prophet, insinuating that it originated with Ibn Mas'ūd.[29] Al-Ḥaṣkafī al-'Alā'ī also observes that after an extensive search he could find it in none of the hadith collections except for Ibn Ḥanbal's *Musnad*.[30] Curiously, despite his obvious failure to demonstrate any authoritative basis for custom—a failure shared by the entire community of Muslim jurists—Ibn Nujaym proceeds to discuss those areas in the law in which custom has traditionally been taken into account.[31] After listing a number of legal cases acknowledged by the community of jurists as having been dictated by customary conventions, he argues that in matters of usury not stipulated by the revealed texts, custom must be recognized. Those commodities that are measured by volume and/or by weight and that have been regulated by the revealed texts as lying outside the compass of usurious transactions are in no way affected by customary usage, of course. This, he maintains, is the opinion of both Abū Ḥanīfa and Shaybānī but not that of Abū Yūsuf, who, as we have seen, permitted the intervention of custom. Abū Ḥanīfa and Shaybānī's opinions, he further asserts, are strengthened by a number of later jurists who argued that a clear *naṣṣ* (text) cannot be superseded by considerations of custom.[32]

Ibn Nujaym distinguishes between two types of custom, namely *'urf 'āmm* (universal) and *'urf khāṣṣ* (local). The former prevails throughout Muslim lands, whereas the latter is in effect in a restricted area or in a town or village.[33] When the former does not contravene a *naṣṣ*, the authoritative doctrine of the Ḥanafite *madhhab* (school) is that it ought to be taken into consideration in legal construction. The contract of *istiṣnā'* is but one example in point.[34] The Ḥanafites, however, differed over whether local custom has any legal force. Najm al-Dīn al-Zāhidī (d. 658/1259), for instance, refused to acknowledge that local custom had any such force, since the weight of local considerations is negligible.[35] Others, such as the Bukhāran jurists, disagreed. Indeed, as quoted by Ibn Nujaym, Zāhidī gives us to understand that these jurists were the first in the history of the Ḥanafite school to advocate such an opinion.[36] But Zāhidī emphatically states that the *al-ṣaḥīḥ* (correct opinion) is that local practices are effectively insufficient to establish themselves as legally admissible customs.

Ultimately, however, the question is not whether local custom can or cannot generate legal norms, for it was clear to the jurists that such customs cannot yield universal and normative legal rules, but only, if at all, particular ones: "Al-ḥukm al-'āmm lā yathbut bil-'urf al-khāṣṣ [A universal rule simply cannot emanate from a local custom]."[37] This, Ibn Nujaym asserts, is the authoritative doctrine of the *al-madhhab*, although a good number of Ḥanafite jurists have issued fatwas on the basis of local custom and in contravention of this doctrine. It is interesting that Ibn Nujaym finally takes the side of these jurists, in a conscious and bold decision to go against the *madhhab* doctrine.[38]

Ibn Nujaym's recognition of custom as an extraneous legal source represents only a later stage in a checkered historical process that began with the three founders of the Ḥanafite school. Sarakhsī's recognition of custom on a case-by-case basis is but one illustration of the success of the thesis of divine origins of the law, a thesis that ensured the near decimation of Abū Yūsuf's doctrine advocating a certain formal role for custom among the legal sources. But the serious demands imposed by custom persisted. The practices and writings of the Bukhāran jurists, among others, were conducive to a process in which the informal role of custom as a source of law was expanded and given more weight. Ibn Nujaym's writings, in which he selectively but skillfully draws on earlier authorities, including the Bukhārans, typify the near culmination of this process.

Ibn ʿĀbidīn: The Background

The process reached its zenith with the writings of the last major Ḥanafite jurist, the Damascene al-Sayyid Amīn Ibn ʿĀbidīn (1198/1783–1252/1836), whose career spanned the crucial period that immediately preceded the introduction of Ottoman *tanẓīmāt* (reform period, 1839–1876). There is no indication that Ibn ʿĀbidīn held an official post in the state, and he seems to have been distant from the circles of political power. His training and later career were strictly traditional: He read the Quran and studied language and Shāfiʿite law with Shaikh Saʿīd al-Ḥamāwī. Later, he continued his legal studies with Shaikh Shākir al-ʿAqqād, who apparently persuaded him to convert to Ḥanafism. With him he studied arithmetic, law of inheritance, legal theory, hadith, quranic exegesis, Sufism, and the rational sciences. Among the texts he read with his shaikh were those of Ibn Nujaym, Ṣadr al-Sharīʿa, Ibn al-Humām, and of other significant Ḥanafite authors.[39] His successful career brought him distinction in several spheres, not the least of which was his rise to prominence as a highly celebrated author and mufti. As a professor, he seems to have had an equally successful career involving, among other things, the privilege of bestowing *ijāza*s (certificates) on important men such as the Ottoman Shaikh al-Islam ʿĀrif Ḥikmat Bey.[40]

True, Ibn ʿĀbidīn flourished before the *tanẓīmāt* started, but he was already witness to the changes that began to sweep the empire long before. When his legal education began, the Niẓām-i Cedid of Selim III was well under way, and when his writing career reached its apex, Maḥmūd II and his men centralized, in an unprecedented but immeasurably crucial move, the major charitable trusts of the empire under the Ministry of Imperial Pious Endowments, which was established in 1826.[41] These significant developments, coupled with the changes that Damascene society experienced due to Western penetration and intervention, already effected a new outlook that culminated not only in the *tanẓīmāt* reforms but also in a rudimentary rupture with traditional forms.[42] Ibn ʿĀbidīn's writings do not mirror any clear sense of crises, either in epistemological or in cultural terms, but they do reflect a certain measure of subtle and latent impatience with some constricting aspects of tradition.

Sometime in 1243/1827, Ibn ʿĀbidīn wrote a short gloss on his *ʿUqūd*

Rasm al-Muftī, a composition in verse that sums up the rules that govern the office of *iftā'* (act of issuing fatwas by the mufti), its functions, and the limits of the mufti's field of hermeneutics.[43] In the same year, he authored a *risāla* (treatise) in which he amplifies his commentary on one line in the verse, a line that specifically addresses the role of *'urf* (custom).[44] Having been written at the same time, cross-references between the two *risāla*s are many.[45] The disintegration of textual boundaries between the two treatises is further enhanced by constant reference to, and juxtaposition with, his super-gloss *Ḥāshiyat Radd al-Muḥtār*. In the latter, he also refers,[46] in the past tense, to his two *risāla*s, and in the two *risāla*s, in the same tense, to his *Ḥāshiya*.[47] This synchronous multiple cross-referencing suggests that Ibn 'Ābidīn authored his two *risāla*s during the lengthy process of writing the *Ḥāshiya*.

Establishing for these treatises a chronological order, or the absence thereof, is particularly important here because a correct analysis of Ibn 'Ābidīn's concept of custom depends on the relationship of his epistemological and authority-based assumptions in *Nashr al-'Urf* to the hierarchy of authority that he sets forth in and that governs the discourse of his *Ḥāshiya*.[48] That *Nashr al-'Urf* and *Ḥāshiya* were authored simultaneously and that the former in fact represents a discursive extension of the latter suggests that Ibn 'Ābidīn continued to uphold the structure of authority and epistemology as he laid it down in his *Ḥāshiya*, and as it was articulated in the Ḥanafite school for at least a few centuries before him. It is precisely the resolution of the tension between this structure of authority and the role he assigned to custom in the law that presented Ibn 'Ābidīn with one of the greatest challenges.

A New Solution

The declared raison d'être of *Nashr al-'Urf* is that custom presents the jurist with several complexities that Ibn 'Ābidīn's predecessors had not adequately addressed.[49] (In treating this presumably neglected area, Ibn 'Ābidīn seems to promise a certain measure of originality.) A careful reading of the *risāla* reveals that these complexities revolve around custom as a legal source, as well as around its relationship to both the unambiguous revealed sources and the authoritative opinions embodied in *ẓāhir al-riwāya*.[50] But before proceeding to unravel these complexities, Ibn 'Ābidīn attempts a definition of *'āda* (custom). Here, as elsewhere in the *risāla*, the mode of discourse is selective citation and juxtaposition of earlier authorities, a mode that has for centuries been a common practice of the author-jurist. However conventional or novel they may be, arguments are presented as falling within the boundaries of authoritative tradition, for they are generally adduced as the total sum of quotations from earlier authorities, cemented together by the author's own interpolations, interventions, counterarguments, and qualifications. Through this process, new arguments acquire the backing of tradition, represented in an array of voices that range from the highly authoritative to the not-so-authoritative. This salient feature of textual elaboration makes for a discursive strategy that we must keep in mind at all times, whether reading Ibn 'Ābidīn or others.

Having defined custom, Ibn 'Ābidīn attempts to demonstrate that its authoritativeness—as for any legal source in order to qualify as such—must be anchored in the revealed texts. Here Ibn 'Ābidīn falls back on Ibn Nujaym's by now familiar argument that is itself exclusively based on Ibn Mas'ūd's weak tradition. Realizing the weakness of the tradition and thus the invalidity of this argument, he remarks that custom was so frequently resorted to in the law that it was made as an *aṣl* (principle), as evidenced in Sarakhsī's statement: "What is known through custom is equivalent to that which is stipulated by the clear texts of revelation."[51] But Ibn 'Ābidīn's compensatory argument does nothing to conceal the fact that custom could never find any textually authoritative vindication. Nor does justification in terms of frequent use in the law lead to anything but a petitio principii, namely, that custom should be used in the law because it is used in the law. Be that as it may, Ibn 'Ābidīn states his piece and moves on, being little, if at all, perturbed by his own, and tradition's, failure to persuade on this matter.

The real issue for Ibn 'Ābidīn was one of more immediate and practical concern. It was one that is made problematic through the introduction of two competing opinions on the relationship between custom and the doctrines of *ẓāhir al-riwāya*. In his *Qunya*, Zāhidī is reported to have maintained that neither the mufti nor the *qāḍī* should adopt the opinions of *ẓāhir al-riwāya* to the utter exclusion of custom. Both Hindī[52] and Bīrī[53] cited Zāhidī's argument, apparently approving its conclusion. Ibn 'Ābidīn argues that these assertions raise a problem, since the common doctrine of the school is that the opinions of *ẓāhir al-riwāya* remain binding unless the *al-mashāyikh* (leading legal scholars) decide to replace them by other opinions that have been subjected to *taṣḥīḥ*.[54] The problem is accentuated in those areas of the law where the opinions of *ẓāhir al-riwāya* were constructed on the basis of revealed texts of an unambiguous nature and/or sanctioned by the conclusive authority of consensus. In these areas, custom does not, nor should it, constitute a source, for unlike the texts, it may simply be wrong. In what seems to be an attempt to accentuate this problem, Ibn 'Ābidīn invokes Ibn Nujaym's statement to the effect that custom must be set aside in the presence of a text and, conversely, that it may be taken into consideration only when no text governing the case in question is to be found.

Before Ibn 'Ābidīn begins his treatment of this problem he introduces, in the footsteps of Ibn Nujaym, the distinction between universal and particular custom. Each of these two types is said to stand in a particular relationship with both the unambiguous revealed texts and *ẓāhir al-riwāya*, thereby creating a fourfold classification. A typical fifth/eleventh- or sixth/twelfth-century jurist would normally treat this fourfold classification under four separate headings, but Ibn ʿĀbidīn, in a markedly less organized and structured discourse, reduces them to a two-part discussion, one treating custom's relationship with the unambiguous revealed texts and the other its relationship with *ẓāhir al-riwāya*.

In line with traditional juristic epistemology, it remains Ibn ʿĀbidīn's tenet that whatever contravenes, *min kulli wajh* (in every respect), the explicit and unequivocal dictates of the revealed texts are void, carrying neither legal effect nor authority. The case of intoxicants affords an eloquent example of this sort of contravention. The key element in the formulation of this tenet is the clause "in every respect," a clause that quite effectively limits the boundaries of those texts that engender exclusive authority by removing from their purview all cases that posit no straightforward or direct contravention of these texts. A partial correspondence between the text and custom does not therefore render the latter inadmissible, for what is being considered in such cases is the corresponding part, not the differential. That part, therefore, particularizes the text but does in no way abrogate it. However, custom must be universal for it to have this particularizing effect. If universal custom can particularize a text, then it can, a fortiori, override a *qiyās,* which is no more than a probabilistic inference. *Istiṣnāʿ*, as we have seen, is a case in point.[55]

Turning to particular custom, Ibn ʿĀbidīn makes the categorical statement that, according to the school's authoritative doctrine, it is not taken into consideration. But this rather forward statement of doctrine is undermined by the introduction of a succession of qualifying and opposing opinions by other jurists. Before doing so, however, he states, on the authority of earlier jurists, the school's traditional doctrine, thereby engaging in what amounts to polemical maneuvering. As might be expected, Ibn Nujaym's weighty attestation is given first, the intention being to introduce not so much an affirmation of the school's doctrine but mainly Ibn Nujaym's partial qualification and exception that many jurists have issued fatwas in accordance with a particular custom.[56] This is immediately followed by another, more drastic statement made by Ibn Māza, who reported that the Balkh jurists, including Naṣīr b. Yaḥyā[57] and Muḥammad b. Salama,[58] permitted, among other things, a certain type of rent, which is otherwise deemed prohibited. The permissibility of this type was justified on the grounds that the practice was not explicitly regulated by the texts and that it had become customary among the people of Balkh. The license of this exception in no way meant that the principles of rent were set aside. If this type of rent was permitted, it was deemed to be an exception, in the same manner *istiṣnāʿ* represents an exception to the principle that the object being sold must at the time of sale be in existence.

But Ibn Māza does not, in the final analysis, agree with the Balkh jurists. Having fully stated their case, he cautions that exceptions, made through *takhṣīṣ* (particularization) on the basis of a particular custom, are not deemed valid because the weight of such a custom is negligible and that this engenders *shakk* (doubt), which does not exist in the case of *istiṣnāʿ*, a pervasive practice that has been shown to exist *fī al-bilād kullihā* (in all regions). In support of Ibn Māza, Ibn ʿĀbidīn interjects Ibn Nujaym's discussion of a particular custom, which is in turn based on a series of citations from other jurists. Here, he concludes that *qiyās* cannot be abandoned in favor of a particular custom, although, as we have seen, some of Ibn Nujaym's authorities do recognize it. The commentators, Ibn ʿĀbidīn argues, have asserted that wheat, barley, dates, and salt are to be sold, without exception, by volume, while gold and silver are to be sold by weight. This rule is dictated by a well-known and explicit prophetic tradition. Thus, the sale of wheat by weight and of gold by volume is unanimously considered null and void, whether or not it is sanctioned by custom. The explicit texts must always stand supreme. However, other commodities that carry no stipulations in the texts may be sold in accordance with the custom prevalent in a certain society.[59]

An apparently hypothetical interlocutor is made to state, on Aḥmad b. Muḥammad b. Jaʿfar al-Qudūrī's authority, that Abū Yūsuf allowed custom to prevail over the prophetic tradition concerning usury in the sale of certain commodities. Accordingly, gold might be sold in volume if custom dictated that it should be so.[60] This departure from the imperatives of the revealed texts therefore justifies the practice of usury and other unlawful matters as long as custom requires it.

Taking this to be a distortion of Abū Yūsuf's position, Ibn ʿĀbidīn argues that what the master meant to do was to use custom as the *ratio legis* of the textual prohibition. If the prophetic tradition dictated measurement by weight for certain commodities and by volume for others, it was merely because it was the custom to do so at the time of the Prophet. Had custom been different, it is entirely conceivable that the prophetic tradition might have permitted the sale of gold by volume and that of barley by weight. Therefore, Ibn ʿĀbidīn concludes, "If custom undergoes change, then the legal norm (*ḥukm*) must change too. In taking changing and unprecedented custom into consideration, there is no violation of the texts; in fact, if anything, such consideration constitutes adherence to [the imperatives of] the texts."[61] At this point, Ibn ʿĀbidīn hastens to add that certain pecuniary practices prevalent in his time—such as "buying *darāhim* for *darāhim*" or borrowing money on the basis of face value (or by count, *ʿadad*)—do not, in fact, constitute violations of the texts, thanks to Abū Yūsuf's doctrine. "May God abundantly reward Abū Yūsuf for what he did for the people of these times of ours. He saved them from the serious affliction that is usury."[62]

The liberties granted with regard to borrowing money at face value, and not by weight or volume, were reached by means of a *takhrīj* (legal interference) representing a direct extension of Abū Yūsuf's doctrine.[63] This was originally Sa'dī Afandī's *takhrīj*, confirmed later by Sirāj al-Dīn Ibn Nujaym (d. 1005/1596) and others.[64] Ismā'īl b. 'Abd al-Majīd al-Nābulusī, however, thought the entire juristic construction needless, since the coins struck by the state had a specific weight, and borrowing or exchange by denomination was effectively the same as representation of weight.[65] Yet Ibn 'Ābidīn introduces Nābulusī's argument only to disagree with it. It may have been the case, he maintains, that in Nābulusī's time, coins were equal in terms of weight and value; nevertheless, *fi zamāninā* (in our own day), each sultan struck currency of lower quality than that struck by his predecessor. The practice in those days involved the use of all sorts of currency, some containing a high ratio of gold and silver as well as those of a lower quality. When people borrow, for instance, they do not specify the type of currency, rather only the number, for when repayment becomes due, they may use any type of currency as long as the value of the amount paid equals that which had been borrowed.[66] Had it not been for Abū Yūsuf's doctrine, these types of transactions could have been said to involve usury, because the weight of the coins borrowed was never identical to that with which repayment was made. If, on the other hand, such transactions were to be regulated by Abū Ḥanīfa's and Shaybānī's doctrines—which require the stipulation in the contract of the type of currency and the year of minting—the outcome would surely be objectionable, for all pecuniary contracts and transactions would be deemed null and void. Their doctrines would thus lead to *ḥaraj 'aẓīm* (great difficulties), because they would also necessarily entail the conclusion that the people of our age are unbelievers. The only way out of this quandary, Ibn 'Ābidīn asserts, is to go by Abū Yūsuf's doctrine, which is left as the only basis of practice.[67]

In Abū Yūsuf's weaker doctrine over and against the other one—also held by Abū Ḥanīfa and Shaybānī—there is an undeniable difficulty. Bypassing three authoritative doctrines by the most influential figures of the school in favor of a weak opinion certainly called for an explanation. Ibn 'Ābidīn alludes to two possible solutions, one by upholding custom qua custom as a sufficient justification, the other by resorting to the notion of *ḍarūra* (necessity).[68] But Ibn 'Ābidīn does not articulate the distinction between these two means of justification, for he immediately abandons custom in favor of necessity. This is to be expected. Rationalizing the relevance of Abū Yūsuf's doctrine and the need for it by means of custom amounts to rationalizing custom by custom, an argument involving the fallacy of a petitio principii. Falling back on necessity is thus left as the only logical choice.

Although the notion of necessity has been used to justify a number of departures from the stringent demands of the law, it is, like custom, restricted to those areas upon which the explicit texts of revelation are silent. Abū Yūsuf, for instance, was criticized when he held the opinion—which ran against the dictates of prophetic Sunna—that cutting grass in the sacred precinct was permissible due to necessity. In this case, Ibn ʿĀbidīn does not seem to agree with Abū Yūsuf, his reasoning being that since the Prophet excluded from the prohibition the *idhkhir* plant,[69] we must conclude that the prohibition remains in effect, and that removal of the prohibition due to necessity is applicable only to that particular plant. More important, the hardship that may result from the prohibition against cutting the grass pales into insignificance when compared with the consequences of forcing a society to change its habits and customs. Ibn ʿĀbidīn lists a number of cases in which hardship was mitigated due to necessity but then concludes that these cases are in no way comparable to the enormity of the hardship resulting from the imposition of a legal norm that contradicts prevailing social customs.

Having thus established necessity a fortiori, Ibn ʿĀbidīn seeks to locate it in the hierarchy of school doctrine. Probably drawing on Ibn Nujaym, who argued that a good number of Ḥanafite jurists issued fatwas on the basis of local custom, Ibn ʿĀbidīn asserts that the acceptance of local custom as a basis for a particular legal norm has become one of the opinions of the school,[70] albeit a *qawl ḍaʿīf* (weak opinion). Now, necessity renders the adoption of such an opinion permissible.[71] But this constitutes a serious departure from the mainstream doctrine of the school according to which the application of weak opinions is deemed strictly forbidden, for it violates, inter alia, the principles of consensus.[72] Furthermore, hermeneutically, weak opinions are considered void for they belong to the category of the *mansūkh* (abrogated), it being understood that they have been repealed by a *rājiḥ* (sound or preponderant) opinion. The later Shāfiʿites, however, adopt a less rigorous position on this matter than the Ḥanafites, and hence it is to them that Ibn ʿĀbidīn turns for a way out of his quandary. In one of his fatwas, the influential Taqī al-Dīn al-Subkī (d. 756/1355)[73] states—concerning a case of *waqf* (charitable trust)—that a weak opinion may be adopted if it is limited to the person and matter at hand and if it is not made transferable to other cases, be it in the courts of law or in *iftāʾ*.[74] But Ibn ʿĀbidīn apparently finds that having recourse to a Shāfiʿite authority insufficient. To enhance Subkī's view, he refers the reader, among other things, to Marghīnānī's *Mukhtārāt al-Nawāzil*,[75] a well-known work that commentators on the same author's *Hidāya* often use in the writing of their glosses.

There, Marghīnānī held the opinion that the blood seeping from a wound does not nullify ablution, an opinion that Ibn 'Ābidīn admits to be not only unprecedented but also one that failed to gain any support among the Ḥanafites during or after Marghīnānī's time. Although he fully acknowledges that the opinion is *shādhdh* (irregular), he nonetheless argues that Marghīnānī stands as an illustrious Ḥanafite, one of the greatest in the school and considered among the highly distinguished *aṣḥāb al-takhrīj*.[76] Therefore, he continues, his opinion ought to be considered sound and the application of a weak opinion must thus be allowed on a restricted basis when it is deemed necessary to do so.[77] Why only in a restricted sense? Because given its weak nature, it is not considered universal in the sense that a local custom gives rise to a legal norm that is applicable only to the city, town, or village where that custom is predominant.

Ibn 'Ābidīn's reasoning here entails a fundamental leap that he does not address, much less justify. The restricted practice, which has been deemed permitted by the four schools, usually termed *fī ḥaqqi nafsihi*, is a principle traditionally limited to the person exercising legal reasoning, the *mujtahid*. For example, a heretical *mujtahid* is allowed to apply his own legal formulations to himself (*fī ḥaqqi nafsihi*), but he is barred from issuing fatwas for Muslims.[78] Subkī himself appears to have made just such a leap in allowing the principle to apply to a *waqf* beneficiary, and Ibn 'Ābidīn went even further in imposing its application upon the inhabitants of a village, town, and even a city. It is important to observe that in the final analysis, it is immaterial whether Ibn 'Ābidīn vindicates each and every step he takes in the construction of his arguments. Just as the anomalous opinions of Subkī and Marghīnānī were readily brought into Ibn 'Ābidīn's discursive strategies to serve an end, so will Ibn 'Ābidīn's own conclusion be utilized to score further points by future generations of jurists.[79] The question that seems to matter most at this point—namely, whether local custom can lawfully give rise to a particular ruling—has been solved, at least for those who share Ibn 'Ābidīn's assumptions and viewpoint.

Custom and Society

Thus far, local custom has been shown to be capable of yielding a particular rule in the locale in which it is predominant, even when contradicted by the dictates of a clear text.[80] What remains to be clarified is the relationship between custom and those opinions derived from the texts in *ẓāhir al-riwāya* by means of inferential reasoning. This is perhaps the most central theme of *Nashr al-'Urf*, and an important one in *Sharḥ 'Uqūd al-Muftī*.[81] Ibn 'Ābidīn avers in these two works that such opinions are arrived at by *mujtahids* on the basis of a number of considerations, not the least of which are the customary practices prevalent at the time when these opinions were formed. The need for taking customary practices into consideration explains the theoretical requirement that the *mujtahid* must possess precise knowledge of the habits and customs prevalent in the society that he serves.[82] The *mujtahid*'s reasoning and the results it yields, therefore, reflect a particular combination of law and fact, the latter being, in part, if not entirely, determined by custom. If these practices differ from time to time, or from one place to another, they would lead the *mujtahids* to different legal conclusions, depending on the time and place. This, Ibn ʿĀbidīn argues, explains why the later *mujtahids* (*mashāyikh al-madhhab*) diverged in a number of areas from the rules that had been established by the school founders, the prevailing assumption being that had these founders faced the same customs that the later *mujtahids* encountered, the founders would have formed the same opinions as their later counterparts came to hold.

Here, Ibn ʿĀbidīn cites at least a few dozen cases in which *mashāyikh al-madhhab* differed with the founding masters.[83] One example in point is the later permission to hire Quran teachers, a type of hire contract prohibited by the early Ḥanafites. During the early era of Islam, Quran teachers are said to have received state stipends, which in time came to a halt. It was argued that if the prohibition of this type of hire contract were to continue, then the teachers would starve together with their families, or the Quran would cease to be taught. Another example is the regional and chronological variation in the law of *waqf*. In Anatolia, for instance, it is customary to dedicate cash or coins as *waqf*, when it is the authoritative doctrine of the school that moveable property cannot be used as charitable trusts.[84] In "our region," Ibn ʿĀbidīn notes, such has never been the practice. An example of diachronic change is the practice of dedicating the farmer's axe as *waqf*, which used to be customary in Syria during earlier periods "but unheard of in our times."[85] The change in the habits of a society must therefore lead to a correlative change in the law. But it is important to note, as Ibn ʿĀbidīn does, that such a legal change is not precipitated by a change in the law as a system of evidence or as a methodology of legal reasoning. Instead, it is one that is stimulated by changing times.[86] (This rather plain remark bears much significance, for it amounts to a stern proposition, which we have proven elsewhere, that the mechanisms of legal change are embedded in the very structure of Islamic law.)[87]

The impressive list of cases compiled by Ibn ʿĀbidīn is intended to demonstrate that the jurisconsult "must not stubbornly adhere to the opinions transmitted of *ẓāhir al-riwāya* without giving due attention to society and the [demands of the] age it lives in. If he does, he will cause many rights to be lost, and will thus be more harmful than beneficial."[88] "The jurisconsult must follow custom even though it might contradict the authoritative opinions of *ẓāhir al-riwāya*."[89] Both universal and local customs are included under these generalizations. "If local custom opposes the school doctrines (*al-naṣṣ al-madhhabī*) that have been transmitted on the authority of the school founder (*ṣāḥib al-madhhab*), it is to be taken into consideration."[90]

Having reached this conclusion by what he takes to be an inductive survey of the law, Ibn 'Ābidīn goes on to say that the jurisconsult must treat both local and universal customs as equal insofar as they override the corpus of *ẓāhir al-riwāya*. The only difference between them is that universal custom produces a universal legal norm, whereas local custom effects a particular norm. Put differently, the legal norm resulting from a universal custom is binding on Muslims throughout Muslim lands, while local custom is binding in the village or town in which it prevails.[91] These conclusions Ibn 'Ābidīn seeks to defend and justify at any expense. Here, he introduces a statement reportedly made by Aḥmad al-Ḥamawī in his *Ḥāshiya 'alā al-Ashbāh*, a commentary on Ibn Nujaym's work. In this work, Ḥamawī remarked that from Ibn Nujaym's statement that "a local custom can never yield a universal legal norm," one can infer that "a local custom can result in a particular legal norm."[92] Obviously, there is nothing in the logic of entailment that justifies this inference. But Ibn 'Ābidīn accepts Ḥamawī's conclusion readily and unquestioningly.

The principles that justify the dominance of local custom over the school's authoritative doctrine also justify, with equal force, the continuous displacement of one local custom by another. If a local custom could repeal those doctrines that had been established by the school founders, then a later local custom, superseding in dominance its forerunner, can override both the forerunner and the *ẓāhir al-riwāya*. This much is clear from Ibn 'Ābidīn's statement that the local custom that overrides the school's authoritative doctrine includes both old and new local customs.[93] The legitimization of this continuous modification lies in Ibn 'Ābidīn's deep conviction that the founding fathers would have held the same legal opinions had they encountered the same customs that the later jurists had to face.[94] This is one of Ibn 'Ābidīn's cardinal tenets that he nearly developed into a legal maxim.

Conclusion

There is no doubt that custom has always presented the Muslim jurist and legal practitioner with one of his most serious challenges. It was at the juncture of law and custom that questions of friction, contradiction, compromise, and synthesis were posed. Ibn 'Ābidīn's discursive elaborations on custom are particularly significant because the presence of these challenges in his writings is evidently meaningful and intense and, for us, instructive since he wrote at a time in which fundamental social, cultural, and epistemological transformations were beginning to take place.

Ibn ʿĀbidīn's discourse is instructive from a number of perspectives, not the least of which is the presence in it of a complex and multilayered hermeneutical texture. Functioning within the context of a school authority, Ibn ʿĀbidīn's discourse was dominated by the ever-present perception of a legal tradition within which he had to function and beyond which he could not tread. But the tradition was by no means so constraining. Rather, it offered multiple levels of discourse originating, chronologically, in centuries of legal evolution and, geographically, in far-flung regions dominated by Ḥanafite as well as other schools. This rich multiplicity afforded Ibn ʿĀbidīn, as it did others, a large measure of freedom to include or exclude opinions at will. Opinions from distant and immediate predecessors were selectively cited and juxtaposed. They represented at the same time the dominant weight of the tradition and the means by which the tradition itself could effectively be manipulated. The author—the manipulator—cements the selective citations that make up the building blocks of his discourse through the medium of interpolations, interventions, counterarguments, and qualifications. Although the manipulator's presence in the text that he produces more often than not seems minimal, it is he who decides how the tradition and its authority are to be used, shaped, and reproduced. It is a remarkable feature of Islamic legal discourse that it was able to reproduce this varied and multilayered tradition in a nearly infinite number of ways. The interpretative possibilities seem astounding.

Ibn ʿĀbidīn's discourse on custom is also particularly instructive in the way it invokes the weak and minority positions in the tradition. These positions are made, by necessity, to juxtapose with the authoritative doctrine of the school, that which represents the dominant mainstream of legal doctrine and practice. The initial impulse that propelled the minority position was Abū Yūsuf's opinion, which had largely been abandoned by Ibn Nujaym's time. Abū Yūsuf's opinion was revived through the device of necessity, a device that must have seemed handy when all other hermeneutical ventures appeared to be without prospect of success. Ibn ʿĀbidīn's hermeneutics also entailed the manipulation of other minor opinions, such as those of Subkī and Marghīnānī. In this hermeneutical exercise, which turned the ladder of doctrinal authority right on its head, Ibn ʿĀbidīn's skills as a polemicist, author, and textual strategist are not to be underestimated. Admittedly, however, they involved certain flaws in logical argumentation, flaws that were certainly more a result of the strains inherent in Ibn ʿĀbidīn's hermeneutically exacting venture than they were a reflection of his competence as a reasoner.

The difficulties Ibn ʻĀbidīn encountered were the result of the conflict between his loyalty to the authoritative hierarchy of Ḥanafite doctrine and the demands that custom imposed, not only as a set of individual legal cases but, more important, as a source of law. For as a body of individual legal cases, custom was fairly successfully incorporated into law, a fact abundantly attested to in the works of early jurists and exemplified, as we have seen, in Sarakhsī's *Mabsūṭ*. But in attempting, as Ibn ʻĀbidīn did, to raise the status of custom to that of a legal source, there arose a distinct difficulty in squaring this source not only with *ẓāhir al-riwāya* but also with the legal methodology that sustained both the doctrinal hierarchy and the theological backing of the law. That Ibn ʻĀbidīn was entirely loyal to the hermeneutical imperatives of the Ḥanafite school and at the same time a vehement promoter of custom *as a legal source* makes him a jurist sui generis. It is almost certain that none of his precursors attempted to raise custom to such a methodologically formal status, and it is definitely true that none after him insisted upon an exclusive loyalty to the authoritative hierarchy of the school's doctrine.

Ultimately, however, Ibn ʻĀbidīn succeeded in constructing an argument that elevates custom to the status of a legal source capable of overriding the effects of other sources, not excluding much of the Quran and the Sunna. It is not far-fetched, then, to view his contribution as a first step, paving the way to modern legal reform, albeit a step that, expectedly, suffered from what might be called epistemological schizophrenia. The strained and coerced arguments that were based on such authorities as Marghīnānī and Aḥmad al-Ḥamawī exemplify the fundamental hermeneutical difficulties brought about by split loyalty to two contradictory imperatives, namely, the divine decree as construed and constructed in the school's doctrine and the humanistic considerations of the law.

Ibn ʻĀbidīn's success was not achieved without a heavy price, however. The implications of his doctrine are grave, especially in light of historical developments in the century or so after his death. True, he did take into serious account the school's doctrine and the methodology that sustained it, for after all, this was the source of his conceptual difficulties. In the final analysis, though, he, in effect, sacrificed the entire structure of law and legal methodology in favor of custom. His subtle qualifications, exceptions, and discursive maneuvering do give the distinct but misleading impression that he ploughed traditional terrains using traditional tools. But the fact is that he used the concept of necessity, which had always been a relatively minor element in the law, to raise custom in both of its types to the status of a supreme source. This is perhaps the most important fact about Ibn ʻĀbidīn's discourse on custom. And it is here that Ibn ʻĀbidīn is strikingly modern, in the sense that he not only anticipated such doctrines as those of Muḥammad Rashīd Riḍā but, in fact, excelled over them in producing more sophisticated arguments while still remaining, at least formally, operative within and loyal to the boundaries of traditional authority. In the discourse of Ibn ʻĀbidīn and that of the majority of modern reformers, necessity is made to justify any end, including the repeal of traditional legal methodology.[95]

If traditional legal doctrine and methodology were sacrificed in the interest of custom, the authority of Ḥanafism as a personal school was not. Here lies a major difference between Ibn ʻĀbidīn and the modern reformers. The latter not only abandoned the old school structures but also argued against them, which explains why they made recourse directly to revelation and passed in silence over school authority. A major argument of theirs is that the Quran and the Sunna meant to speak to the first Muslims, the Arabs, in a language to which they could relate. Likewise, the new laws that came down through revelation took into account the customs and habits of the Arabs and would have been different had these customs and habits been otherwise. This direct confrontation with the revealed texts was not part of Ibn ʻĀbidīn's legal scholarship. Being a Ḥanafite, his frame of reference was his school, and Abū Ḥanīfa and his two chief disciples the ultimate authorities. It was their interpretation of the texts that counted, not the texts as such. But even so, his assertion that Abū Ḥanīfa would have reached different legal conclusions had he lived in a different age is again strikingly modern, and in this *articulated* form is not, insofar as I can tell, to be found in works authored prior to Ibn ʻĀbidīn.

That Ibn ʻĀbidīn saw both universal and local customs as being capable of yielding legal norms does not, substantively, set him apart from the modernists who stated their preference for a humanistic law in more modern and utilitarian terms. His notion of custom and the connotations he attached to it are the traditional equivalent to humanistic considerations of social exigency. In other words, what the modernists of the twentieth century did was to take a short-cut whereby custom and the epistemology that sustained the system that produced it were a priori excluded. Ibn ʻĀbidīn operated within the traditional structures and had, therefore, to face custom head on. That he was not part of the Ottoman state apparatus, and that he preceded the massive waves of legal reform, is an eloquent testimony to the ability of Islamic law to transform itself and adapt to significant change. Ibn ʻĀbidīn, the product of his own times, was therefore not only the last great Ḥanafite but also the first jurist par excellence to offer a program of legal reform in the Ottoman Empire.[96]

Notes

I should like to thank Amy Singer, Selim Deringil, Zachary Lockman, Iris Agmon, and other workshop participants for their perceptive remarks and questions on this chapter.

1. This is usually expressed by the Arabic dictum "*inna-mā shurri'at al-aḥkām li-maṣāliḥ al-'ibād.*" See, for example, Sayf al-Dīn al-Āmidī, *al-Iḥkām fī Uṣūl al-Aḥkām*, 3 vols. (Cairo: Maṭba'at 'Alī Ṣubayḥ wa-Awlādihi, 1387/1968), Vol. III, p. 81; Abū Isḥāq Ibrāhīm al-Shāṭibī, *al-Muwāfaqāt fī Uṣūl al-Aḥkām*, 4 vols. (Cairo: Maṭba'at al-Madanī, 1969), Vol. II, pp. 3, 27, and passim.

2. Āmidī, *Iḥkām*, Vol. I, p. 148; Jamāl al-Dīn Ibn al-Ḥājib, *Muntahā al-Wuṣūl wal-Amal fī 'Ilmayy al-Uṣūl wal-Jadal*, ed. M. Badr al-Dīn al-Na'sānī (Cairo: Maṭba'at al-Sa'āda, 1326/1908), p. 37; Muwaffaq al-Dīn Ibn Qudāma, *Rawḍat al-Nāẓir wa-Junnat al-Munāẓir*, ed. Sayf al-Dīn al-Kātib (Beirut: Dār al-Kitāb al-'Arabī, 1401/1981), p. 116.

3. See n. 7 below.

4. On the supplementary sources, see Wael B. Hallaq, *A History of Islamic Legal Theories* (Cambridge, UK: Cambridge University Press, 1997), pp. 107–117; Rudi Paret, "Istiḥsān and Istiṣlāḥ," *Shorter Encyclopaedia of Islam* (Leiden: E.J. Brill, 1974), pp. 184–186.

5. Gideon Libson, "On the Development of Custom as a Source of Law in Islamic Law," *Islamic Law and Society* 4 (1997): 131–155.

6. On the process of this transformation, see Hallaq, *History*, pp. 19, 23, 107 ff., 112 ff., 131 ff.

7. Āmidī, *Iḥkām*, Vol. III, pp. 62, 72, 74–75, and passim; Ibn al-Ḥājib, *Muntahā al-Wuṣūl*, pp. 124 ff.; Fakhr al-Dīn al-Rāzī, *al-Maḥṣūl fī 'Ilm Uṣūl al-Fiqh*, 2 vols. (Beirut: Dār al-Kutub al-'Ilmiyya, 1408/1988), Vol. II, pp. 319–344. On the rationalistic nature of *munāsaba* and its relationship with *maṣāliḥ mursala*, see Hallaq, *History*, pp. 88, 112–113, 132.

8. See Wael B. Hallaq, *Authority, Continuity, and Change in Islamic Law* (Cambridge, UK: Cambridge University Press, 2001), Chapter 4.

9. Fakhr al-Dīn Ḥasan b. Manṣūr al-Ūzajandī Qāḍīkhān, *Fatāwā Qāḍīkhān*, printed on the margins of *Fatāwā al-Hindiyya*, Vols. I–III (repr.: Beirut: Dār Iḥyā' al-Turāth al-'Arabī, 1400/1980), Vol. I, p. 3; Wael B. Hallaq, "From *Fatwās* to *Furū'*: Growth and Change in Islamic Substantive Law," *Islamic Law and Society* 1 (1994): 39.

10. On ranking the five Ḥanafite masters in terms of hierarchical doctrinal authority, see 'Alā' al-Dīn Muḥammad 'Alī al-Ḥaṣkafī (al-'Alā'ī), *al-Durr al-Mukhtār*, printed with Ibn 'Ābidīn's *Ḥāshiyat Radd al-Muḥtār*, 8 vols. (repr.: Beirut: Dār al-Fikr, 1399/1979), Vol. I, pp. 70–71.

11. Ḥājjī Khalīfa, *Kashf al-Ẓunūn 'an Asāmū al-Kutub wal-Funūn*, 2 vols. (Istanbul: Maṭba'at Wakālat al-Ma'ārif al-Jalīla, 1941–1943), Vol. II, p. 1281; Ibn 'Ābidīn, *Ḥāshiya*, Vol. I, p. 69.

12. Ḥājjī Khalīfa, *Kashf al-Ẓunūn*, Vol. II, p. 1281.

13. Ibn 'Ābidīn, *Ḥāshiya*, Vol. I, p. 71.

14. Qāḍīkhān, *Fatāwa*, Vol. I, p. 3; "*wa-fī al-muzāra'a wal-mu'āmala wa-naḥwihimā yukhtāru qawluhumā li-ijtimā'i al-muta'akhirīn 'alā dhālika.*"

15. Ibid. It is to be noted that *ijtihād* here does not necessarily carry the connotation of fresh legal reasoning of the type that involved a direct confrontation with the revealed texts. Although the possibility of direct encounter is never entirely excluded, it is the weighing of various existing opinions and what this juristic activity entailed that is here termed *ijtihād*.

16. See 'Umar Ibn 'Abd al-'Azīz al-Ḥusām al-Shahīd Ibn Māza, *Sharḥ Adab al-Qāḍī*, ed. Abū al-Wafā' al-Afghānī and M. al-Hāshimī (Beirut: Dār al-Kutub al-'Ilmiyya, 1414/1994), p. 19; Qāḍīkhān, *Fatāwa*, Vol. I, p. 3. For other sources, see 'Umar Jīdī, *al-'Urf wal-'Amal fī al-Madhhab al-Mālikī* (Rabat: Maṭba'at Faḍāla,

1982), pp. 85 ff. This requirement was to undergo some change during the later period, when knowledge of the *madhhab*, as the authoritative doctrine of the school, replaced expertise in the four sources. See Hallaq, *Authority*, Chapter 3.

17. For a biographical account, see Zayn al-Dīn Ibn Quṭlūbughā, *Tāj al-Tarājim fī Ṭabaqāt al-Ḥanafiyya* (Baghdad: Maṭba'at al-Muthannā, 1962), pp. 46–47; Abū al-Wafā' Muḥammad al-Qurashī, *al-Jawāhir al-Muḍī'a*, 2 vols. (Haydarabad: Maṭba'at Majlis Dā'irat al-Ma'ārif al-Niẓāmiyya, 1332/1913), Vol. II, pp. 560–561.

18. *Istiṣnā'* is a manufacturing contract whereby a sale is concluded with the condition of future delivery. The contract may also be one of hire, such as when a person gives a blacksmith a certain amount of metal so that the latter manufactures therefrom a certain pot or container, for a stipulated payment. Being of the same type as the *salam* contract (involving the ordering of goods to be delivered in the future for a price paid in the present), *istiṣnā'* goes against the principles of *qiyās*, which require the avoidance of risk by stipulating that the object of sale be in existence at the time the contract is concluded. Both labor and the option of examination are conditions for validity. See Shams al-A'imma al-Sarakhsī, *al-Mabsūṭ*, 30 vols. (Cairo: Maṭba'at al-Sa'āda, 1906–1912), Vol. XV, pp. 84 ff.

19. Ibn Māza, *Sharḥ Adab al-Qāḍī*, p. 19.

20. Muḥammad Ibn 'Ābidīn, *Nashr al-'Urf fī Binā' Ba'ḍ al-Aḥkām 'alā al-'Urf* in *Majmū'at Rasā'il Ibn 'Ābidīn* (N.p., 1970), Vol. II, p. 118 (henceforth cited as *Nashr*).

21. Until, that is, Ibn 'Ābidīn not only rejuvenated interest in his position but essentially revived it, as we shall see later.

22. Zayn al-Dīn Ibn Nujaym, *al-Ashbāh wal-Naẓā'ir* (Calcutta: al-Maṭba'a al-Ta'līmiyya, 1260/1844), p. 131 (on the authority of Ẓahīr al-Dīn b. Aḥmad); Jalāl al-Dīn al-Suyūṭī, *al-Ashbāh wal-Naẓā'ir fī Qawā'id wa-Furū' Fiqh al-Shāfi'iyya* (Beirut: Dār al-Kutub al-'Ilmiyya, 1399/1979), p. 93. For Marghīnānī's statement that "an explicit textual ruling is stronger than a custom and one does not abandon something stronger in favour of something weaker," see Libson, "Development of Custom," p. 145.

23. See n. 24. For a biographical account of Sarakhsī, see Ibn Quṭlūbughā, *Tāj al-Tarājim*, pp. 52–53.

24. Sarakhsī, *Mabsūṭ*, Vol. XV, p. 130; "*al-ma'lūm bil-'urf kal-mashrūṭ bil-naṣṣ*." See also Vol. XV, pp. 85–86, 132, 142, 171; Vol. XII, p. 142, and passim. Also see 'Abd Allāh b. Mawdūd al-Mūṣilī, *al-Ikhtiyār li-Ta'līl al-Mukhtār*, ed. Maḥmūd Abū Daqīqa, 5 vols. (Beirut: Dār al-Kutub al-'Ilmiyya, n.d.), Vol. II, p. 18.

25. It would, in this context, be instructive to explore the possible reasons that lie behind the incorporation of customary practices into law through these two distinctly different channels, namely, direct incorporation (= custom qua custom) and incorporation via formal and supplementary sources. Granting, as I do, the valid explanation in terms of chronological developments (whereby custom came into law as part of the evolutionary processes that gave rise to both positive law and legal theory), there remains the question as to why the supplementary and formal sources of law could not permit, under their own name, the total absorption of customary practices in the later period.

26. Carl Brockelmann, *Geschichte der arabischen Literatur*, 2 vols. (Leiden: E.J. Brill, 1943–1949); 3 supplements (Leiden: E.J. Brill, 1937–1942), Vol. II, pp. 401–403.

27. Ibn Nujaym, *Ashbāh*, p. 129.

28. "*Mā ra'āhu al-Muslimūna ḥasan fa-hwa 'inda Allāhi ḥasan*."

29. Ibn Nujaym, *Ashbāh,* pp. 129–130.

30. Ibn 'Ābidīn, *Nashr*, p. 115; Suyūṭī, *Ashbāh*, p. 89. This *ḥadīth* is also used by Muḥammad b. al-Ḥasan al-Shaybānī in justification of consensus. See Wael B. Hallaq, "On the Authoritativeness of Sunni Consensus," *International Journal of Middle East Studies* 18 (1986): 431.

31. An inductive survey of the instances of custom that have been incorporated into law appears to have been often offered as a substitute for a proof of *ḥujjiyya*, although such a substitute clearly involved begging the question. It is perhaps the jurists' acute awareness of the pernicious effects of circularity that prevented them from claiming the inductive survey to constitute a solution to the problem of *ḥujjiyya*.

32. Ibn Nujaym, *Ashbāh*, p. 131.

33. Ibid., p. 137; Ibn 'Ābidīn, *Nashr*, p. 132. On universal and local customs, see Baber Johansen, "Coutumes locales et coutumes universelles," *Annales Islamologiques* 27 (1993): 29–35.

34. See n. 18 above.

35. For a biographical notice, see Ibn Quṭlūbughā, *Tāj al-Tarājim*, p. 73; Brockelmann, *Geschichte*, Vol. I, p. 382 (475).

36. Ibn Nujaym states that these Bukhārans formulated this opinion (*aḥdathahu ba'ḍ ahl Bukhārā*), it being almost certain that their opinion is a reflection of their juridical practices. See his *Ashbāh*, p. 138.

37. Ibid., p. 137.

38. Ibid., p. 138; "*lākin aftā kathīr min al-mashāyikh bi-i'tibārihi, fa-aqūlu 'alā i'tibārihi*."

39. For Ibn 'Ābidīn's biographical notices, see Khalīl Mardam Bey, *A'yān al-Qarn al-Thālith 'Ashar fī al-Fikr wal-Siyāsa wal-Ijtimā'* (Beirut: Mu'assasat al-Risāla, 1977), pp. 36–39; 'Abd al-Razzāq al-Bīṭār, *Ḥulyat al-Bashr fī Tārīkh al-Qarn al-Thālith 'Ashar*, ed. M. B. Bīṭār, 3 vols. (Damascus: Maṭbū'āt al-Majma' al-'Ilmī al-'Arabī, 1963), Vol. III, pp. 1230–1239; Khayr al-Dīn al-Ziriklī, *al-A'lām*, 8 vols. (Beirut: Dār al-'Ilm lil-Malāyīn, 1980), Vol. VI, p. 42.

40. Mardam, *A'yān*, p. 37.

41. See Madeline C. Zilfi, "The *Ilmiye* Registers and the Ottoman *Medrese* System Prior to the Tanzimat," in *Contributions à l'histoire économique et sociale de l'Empire ottoman* (Leuven: Éditions Peeters, 1983), pp. 309–327, at pp. 312–313.

42. For a general history of Damascus during this period, see George Koury, "The Province of Damascus" (Ph.D. dissertation, University of Michigan, 1970); Yūsuf Na'īsa, *Mujtama' Madīnat Dimashq*, 2 vols. (Damascus: Ṭlās, 1986). It is to be noted that the Westernized bent of Ottoman reforms since 1839 was already obvious, despite the perceptive argument made by Butrus Abu-Manneh that the 1839 Gülhane rescript was inspired by Islamic principles. (Abu-Manneh's argument, however, does not account for the treatment in this rescript of religious minorities, a treatment that can hardly be sustained by traditional Islamic principles.) See his article, "The Islamic Roots of the Gülhane Rescript," *Die Welt des Islams* 34 (1994): 173–203.

43. *Sharḥ al-Risāla al-Musammā bi-'Uqūd Rasm al-Muftī*, in *Majmū'at Rasā'il Ibn 'Ābidīn,* 2 vols. (N.p., n.d.), Vol. I, pp. 1–53 (henceforth cited as *Sharḥ 'Uqūd*).

44. *Nashr*, p. 114; the line runs as follows: "*wal-'urf fī al-shar' la-hu i'tibār / li-dhā 'alayhi al-ḥukm qad yudār*."

45. *Nashr*, pp. 114, 125, and passim; *Sharḥ 'Uqūd*, p. 48 and passim.

46. Ibn 'Ābidīn, *Ḥāshiya,* Vol. IV, pp. 364, 434, 519, and passim.
47. *Nashr*, p. 139 and passim; *Sharḥ 'Uqūd*, p. 15.
48. Ibn 'Ābidīn, *Ḥāshiya,* I, pp. 70 ff. See also *Sharḥ 'Uqūd*, pp. 16–18.
49. *Nashr*, p. 114.
50. That is, the *naṣṣ*, as distinguished from ambiguous texts that are by definition capable of more than one interpretation. See Abū al-Walīd al-Bājī, *Kitāb al-Ḥudūd fī al-Uṣūl* (Beirut and Homs: Mu'assasat al-Zu'bī, 1392/1973), pp. 42 ff. The ambiguous, equivocal texts did not present a challenge to custom because their hermeneutical effects were indeterminate.
51. *Mabsūṭ*, XV, p. 130; "*al-ma'lūm bil-'urf kal-mashrūṭ bil-naṣṣ.*"
52. In *Khizānat al-Riwāyāt*. Brockelmann, *Geschichte*, Vol. II, p. 221 (286).
53. Whom I could not identify.
54. On *taṣḥīḥ*, see Hallaq, *Authority*, Chapter 5.
55. *Nashr*, p. 116.
56. See n. 38 above.
57. Muḥammad al-Mudarrisī, *Mashāyikh Balkh min al-Ḥanafiyya*, 2 vols. (Baghdad: Wizārat al-Awqāf. Silsilat al-Kutub al-Ḥadītha, 1979), Vol. I, pp. 53, 76, and see index at Vol. II, p. 942.
58. Ibid., Vol. I, pp. 53, 89, and see index at Vol. II, p. 938.
59. *Nashr,* p. 118.
60. Cf. Aḥmad b. Muḥammad b. Ja'far al-Qudūrī, *Mukhtaṣar* (Beirut: Dār al-Kutub al-'Ilmiyya, 1997), p. 87.
61. *Nashr*, p. 118.
62. Ibid.
63. On *takhrīj* and its relationship with the doctrines of the schools' founders, see Hallaq, *Authority*, Chapter 2.
64. In his *al-Nahr al-Fā'iq*. See Brockelmann, *Geschichte*, S II, p. 266.
65. Probably, Ismā'īl b. 'Abd al-Majīd al-Nābulusī (d. 1043/1633). See Brockelmann, *Geschichte*, S II, p. 476.
66. For a detailed discussion of fiscal issues in law, see Ibn 'Ābidīn, *Tanbīh al-Ruqūd 'alā Masā'il al-Nuqūd*, in his *Majmū'at Rasā'il Ibn 'Ābidīn,* Vol. II, pp. 58–67.
67. *Nashr*, p. 119. Also see ibid., pp. 119–124, where similar arguments are made.
68. Ibid., p. 120.
69. An aromatic plant that grew around Mecca and was used, when cut, in decorating houses and in funerals. See Jamāl al-Dīn Ibn Manẓūr, *Lisān al-'Arab*, 15 vols. (repr.: Beirut: Dār Ṣādir, 1972), Vol. IV, pp. 302–303.
70. It is worth noting that Ibn 'Ābidīn stresses the point that for a local custom to be considered a valid legal source, it must thoroughly permeate the society in which it is found. See *Nashr*, p. 134.
71. Ibid., p. 125; "*al-qawl al-ḍa'īf yajūzu al-'amal bi-hi 'inda al-ḍarūra.*"
72. *Sharḥ 'Uqūd*, pp. 10–11, 48.
73. For a biographical notice, see Tāj al-Dīn al-Subkī, *Ṭabaqāt al-Shāfi'iyya al-Kubrā*, 6 vols. (Beirut: Dār al-Ma'rifa, 1906), Vol. VI, pp. 146–227.
74. *Sharḥ 'Uqūd*, p. 49; "*yajūz taqlīd al-wajh al-ḍa'īf fī nafs al-amr bil-nisba lil-'amal fī ḥaqqi nafsihi, lā fī al-fatwā wal-ḥukm.*"
75. Brockelmann, *Geschichte*, Vol. I, p. 378 (469); Burhān al-Dīn al-Marghīnānī, *al-Hidāya: Sharḥ Bidāyat al-Mubtadī*, 4 vols. (Cairo: Muṣṭafā Bābī al-Ḥalabī, 1400/1980), Vol. I, pp. 3–9.

76. *Sharḥ 'Uqūd*, pp. 49–50. On *takhrīj* and those who practiced it, see Hallaq, *Authority*, Chapter 2.

77. *Sharḥ 'Uqūd*, p. 50.

78. 'Uthmān b. 'Abd al-Raḥmān Ibn al-Ṣalāḥ, *Adab al-Muftī wal-Mustaftī*, ed. Muwaffaq 'Abd al-Qādir (Beirut: 'Ālam al-Kutub, 1986), p. 107.

79. That is, assuming that the traditional structures of the law were allowed to survive.

80. Although the contradiction is seen in terms of *takhṣīṣ,* or particularization. See the paragraph ending with n. 55 above.

81. *Nashr*, p. 128 (1. 17); *Sharḥ 'Uqūd*, pp. 46 ff.

82. *Nashr*, pp. 128–130.

83. Ibid., pp. 126–128.

84. For a detailed study of this practice, see J. E. Mandaville, "Usurious Piety: The Cash Waqf Controversy in the Ottoman Empire," *International Journal of Middle East Studies* 10 (1979): 295–304.

85. Ibn 'Ābidīn, *Ḥāshiya,* Vol. IV, p. 364.

86. *Nashr*, p. 126.

87. See Hallaq, *Authority*, Chapters 5–6.

88. *Nashr,* p. 131; *Sharḥ 'Uqūd*, p. 47.

89. *Nashr,* pp. 131–132, restated at p. 133.

90. Ibid., p. 133.

91. Ibid., p. 132.

92. Aḥmad al-Ḥamawī, *Sharḥ al-Ashbāh,* printed with Ibn Nujaym's *Ashbāh,* p. 137; *Nashr*, p. 132.

93. *Sharḥ 'Uqūd*, p. 45; *Nashr*, p. 133.

94. *Nashr*, pp. 128, 130; "*law kāna Abū Ḥanīfa ra'ā mā ra'aw, la-aftā bi-hi*" (at p. 130, 1. 15); *Sharḥ 'Uqūd*, p. 14.

95. On Muḥammad Rashīd Riḍā and other modern reformers, see M. Kerr, *Islamic Reform: The Political and Legal Theories of Muḥammad 'Abduh and Rashīd Riḍā* (Berkeley: University of California Press, 1966); Hallaq, *History*, pp. 214–220.

96. Nearly all the essential features of Ibn 'Ābidīn's theory that we have discussed here appear in the *Majalla*: (1) Need is equivalent to necessity *(al-ḥāja tanzil manzilat al-ḍarūra*); (2) necessity renders lawful what is otherwise illicit (*al-ḍarūrāt tubīḥ al-maḥẓūrāt*); (3) hardship constitutes grounds for mitigating the law *(al-mashaqqa tajlib al-taysīr*); (4) custom, be it universal or local, determines legal norms (*al-'āda muḥakkima*); (5) what is known by custom has the force of a contractual stipulation (*al-ma'rūf 'urfan kal-mashrūṭ sharṭan*); (6) what is dictated by custom has the force of an unambiguous divine text (*al-ta'yīn bil-'urf kal-ta'yīn bil-naṣṣ*); legal norms change with changing times *(taghayyur al-aḥkām bi-taghayyur al-azmān*). See *Sharḥ al-Majalla*, 2 vols. (repr.: Beirut: Dār al-Kutub al-'Ilmiyya, 1923), articles 17, 21, 32, 36, 39, 43, 45. See also the prologue at Vol. I, pp. 9–14.

4

The Damascus Affair and the Beginnings of France's Empire in the Middle East

Mary C. Wilson

Micro-history, "an approach to the past through one exemplary event or person," has not really caught on in the writing of Middle Eastern history.[1] And the genre within micro-history that uses a judicial proceeding to explore connections and cleavages between lives lived and the outlines of known history is entirely absent. One can think of trials that might be so used: the trial that led to the hanging of four Egyptian peasants after the Dinshaway incident in 1906, for example, or the trial of Layla Ba'albaki on obscenity charges in Beirut in 1964. But perhaps there is not enough documentation, or enough accessible documentation, to make these cases exploitable in such a manner. There is, however, at least one trial that took place in the Middle East that has produced a mountain of accessible documentation: the 1840 ritual murder trial in Damascus. Although the Damascus trial is not precisely an exemplary event, as it is the only time in the Arabic-speaking Middle East that an accusation of ritual murder resulted in a trial and a death sentence,[2] its very strangeness demands investigation. The Damascus trial found sixteen Jews of Damascus guilty of killing a Capuchin missionary, Père Thomas, and his servant, Ibrahim Amara, in order to use their blood in the baking of matzoh for Passover. This story roughly follows the classic outlines of ritual murder accusations as they emerged in Europe in the twelfth century, though here Père Thomas and Ibrahim Amara were not children and their bodies did not exhibit miraculous powers.[3]

The Damascus affair, as it was called at the time and since, is not a new subject to historians. Most recently, Jonathan Frankel has explored the discussions of the affair in the European press of the time in order to illuminate midcentury European attitudes toward the place of Jews in the modern state.[4] No one who has written about the affair, however, has paid close attention to the official report of the investigation and trial.

Writing about the affair may be divided into two schools. The first school believes that Jews do practice ritual murder and that Jews killed Père Thomas and Ibrahim Amara to use their blood for ritual purposes.[5] Writers in this school reproduce or summarize the text of the official record of the accusation and trial, but they do not analyze it. For them, it speaks for itself and confirms their prior belief in the demonic nature of Judaism and of Jews. The second school rejects the accusation of ritual murder and finds the evidence presented in the Damascus case to be unsound.[6] Although the writers of this school are certainly correct in their analysis of the evidence, they have not closely read the official record beyond that needed to reject the evidence presented in it.[7]

Neither school convincingly answers the question, What happened to Père Thomas? The conclusions of school one, as of the trial that took place in Damascus, are belied by the torture used to produce them and inconclusive physical evidence.[8] School two suggests alternatives based on hearsay, but these, too, lack evidence.[9]

As satisfying as it would be to know what happened to Père Thomas, this seems not only impossible after the passage of 160 years but perhaps not even the most interesting question that could be posed of the documentary record. For historians, the most significant question is not what happened to Père Thomas and Ibrahim Amara but why that question was answered with a story of ritual murder.[10] This focus takes us back to the realm of micro-history and a close reading of the manner of telling a story. The way the story of ritual murder is told in the judicial proceedings may reveal who wanted the story told. Once we know who wanted it told, we may be able to ask why. Thus, we may unfold from the small events of lived lives new understandings of time and place.[11]

The official report of the investigation and trial exists in manuscript versions in both French and Arabic in the archives of the Quai d'Orsay in Paris and in Arabic in the Dar al-Watha'iq in Cairo; it was first published in 1846 in French.[12] It is written in two voices, third-person narrative and first-person recorded speech. It begins in the third person with a narrative describing how Père Thomas came to be missed and how the French consul in Damascus began the investigation into his disappearance. Why the French consul began the investigation did not need to be explained in the official record; everyone knew that since Père Thomas was under French protection in Damascus, it was the consul's duty to find out what happened to him.

The opening narrative relates that several European missionaries and doctors noticed Père Thomas's absence and told the French consul. The consul went to the monastery where Père Thomas lived to see for himself.

There, "he found the street full of inhabitants of various creeds, and who said in a unanimous voice: 'Yesterday Père Thomas was in the Jewish quarter, and there is no doubt that he disappeared there along with his servant.'"[13] Thus, the investigation was set off in the direction of the Jewish quarter in a manner that masks any individual accuser and that gives the credence of unanimous judgment to the statement.[14]

This carefully shaped third-person narrative continues until a suspect is brought before the governor of Damascus. Then recorded speech takes over in the form of questions and answers. Recorded speech later gives way to narrative and narrative to recorded speech as more suspects are rounded up and questioned and as material evidence is gathered and its relevance written into the trial record. It is in the recorded speech sections of the investigation that the story of ritual murder is first told. The secretary who recorded the questions and answers also recorded the conditions under which the suspects were questioned: "Friday the 11th of the lunar month. The barber Suleiman, questioned in a pressing manner, was asked to tell the real circumstances relating to this affair; but as nothing was got out of him, the order was given to beat him, and after several lashes of the kourbadj, he avowed. . . ."[15]

The story of ritual murder is repeated over and over throughout the trial narrative, first by suspects beaten and offered clemency, then by the men they accused. The story comes out fitfully, in response to the use of force and the promise of clemency or at least of release from immediate pain. In all four people died: two witnesses whose stories did not accord with the story of ritual murder and two of the accused.[16]

Most of the time the official record does not name who took part in interrogations, other than the accused. The passive voice dominates: "He was asked. . . ." The questioners were many, but the governor of Damascus was, finally, the official in charge. He was a civil official appointed by and responsible to Mehmed Ali who had ruled geographical Syria from Cairo since 1831. The interrogations took place in his *diwan* (court of the provincial governor) in front of whomever happened to be there to do some bit of government business.[17]

On 28 February, three weeks after Père Thomas had disappeared, the presumed murder was first described in all its gory detail. For that key session, there is a list of those present: Hathiq Bey, an officer of Mehmed Ali's mounted artillery; M. Massari, the governor's physician; the Comte de Ratti-Menton, the French consul; and M. Beaudin, the chancellor of the French consulate.[18] Since the narrative given voice that day solved the case, the listing of those present was perhaps a way to underline its importance and its veracity; these things really were said because they were heard by important people. Or perhaps it was a way to underline the cooperation between the French and Mehmed Ali's officials. When the governor of

Damascus wrote his overlord in Cairo about the day's testimony, he mentioned only the most important hearers: an officer representing Cairo's military authority in the region and the French consul.[19]

On this day, two suspects, both Jewish, were questioned: Sulayman the barber and Murad, the servant of one of the accused. Both had been flogged on previous occasions, and both had been promised immunity in exchange for "the truth." The barber described the murder, the careful collection of blood in a copper basin, and the dismemberment and disposal of the body. The servant corroborated the story of dismemberment and disposal. Then the French consul asked the servant: "What do they do with the blood?" And the servant replied: "It is for the [feast of the] unleavened bread." The French consul asked: "How do you know?" And the servant replied: "I heard them say that the blood was for the [feast of the] unleavened bread." The officer followed: "Since you did not see the blood, how did you know that it was for the [feast of the] unleavened bread?" And the servant replied: "I asked for what reason did you make blood flow, they told me that it was for the [feast of the] unleavened bread."[20]

At two defining moments of the investigation, the French consul, through his actions, shaped or is represented as shaping a narrative of ritual murder. First, he began the investigation and directed it, or as it was told, followed the crowd's lead, to the Jewish quarter. Second, he was present at the *diwan* on the day the complete story of the murder was told for the first time, and he asked the question that revealed the motive of ritual murder. The French consul was satisfied with the answer his question received. The next day he wrote to Paris for the first time to report Père Thomas's disappearance. He also reported, and embraced, what the investigation had found—that Père Thomas had been killed by Jews to use his blood for ritual purposes.[21]

The official record of the trial thus shows the importance of the French consul to the telling of the tale of ritual murder. His role is amplified in documentation outside of the official trial report. Here the evidence shows that whenever the investigation flagged, the French consul and those under him kept it moving. When guards searched the Jewish quarter on the governor's orders and found nothing, the French consul intervened to find something. He got a man out of debtors' prison to do the job, and through him turned up the first suspect, Sulayman the barber.[22] The consul kept Sulayman at the French consulate for a week before sending him on to the governor of Damascus for questioning. Once he was sent on, he named names and told the story of ritual murder. Similarly, when the investigation turned to the disappearance of Père Thomas's servant, Ibrahim Amara, the chief "witness" was arrested by the consul and kept at the consulate for six or seven days before he was turned over to the governor for the official interrogation. Like Sulayman, this man named names and told a story of ritual murder.[23]

There are numerous records of the consul telling the governor whom to question, whom to hold, and whom to release. When the local guards did not move fast enough, the consul himself arrested suspects.[24] What does all this reveal? It reveals the French consul's active participation in moving the story of ritual murder along at crucial moments. He not only wanted to protect or vindicate a French protégé, he wanted this particular story told. He was not alone; the governor of Damascus and the chancellor of the French consulate were two other key figures in its telling. The governor of Damascus was responsible for torture; the chancellor rounded up suspects. But the consul was the link between these two. It was on his authority that suspects rounded up by the chancellor were detained and delivered to the governor.[25] Therefore, in what follows, I will concentrate on the French consul to consider in what ways a story of ritual murder might have served his interests.

The Comte de Ratti-Menton arrived in Damascus in November 1839. Three months later, Père Thomas and his servant disappeared. As the ritual murder trial in Damascus became known in Europe, so attention turned to the consul and his role in it. Many applauded his vigorous pursuit of Père Thomas's supposed murderers, especially in France.[26] Those who criticized him sought an explanation in his political identity.

> That the representative of France in the year 1840 should be imbued with prejudice, and the rancor of religious hatred and persecution, appeared so extraordinary, that I inquired into who and what he was, and learned in reply that he is a Legitimist of the oldest and worst school—an adherent of the imbecile and fanatical party who by their folly brought about the revolution.[27]

The consul, Benoit Ulysse Laurent François de Paule, the Comte de Ratti-Menton, came from an aristocratic and military family that had served the crown before the revolution. I do not know the whereabouts of his mother or father during the French Revolution, but it is possible that they were émigrés because the consul was born in Puerto Rico in 1799. By the early 1820s, he had succeeded his father as the Comte de Ratti-Menton and had returned to France along with the rest of the amnestied nobility. Thereafter, his career followed a pattern common to the prerevolutionary aristocracy: He joined the diplomatic corps. French governments of all stripes throughout the nineteenth century preferred diplomats who were aristocrats, trained by their families in the niceties of etiquette and so very reassuring to the monarchies of Europe who were France's partners in diplomacy. He was a royalist, even perhaps an ultra, as the correspondent to

The Times suggested, but he did not have the resources to abjure government service altogether and so he adapted to the changes of government in France and served in the consular corps until his retirement in 1862.[28]

That the count was a royalist could suggest that he brought the church into his politics. But in the eastern Mediterranean one did not need to be a royalist, a clericalist, or even a Catholic to patronize the local Catholic community and to see it as an avenue for French influence. France had Catholic missionaries under its umbrella. Beyond the Catholic orders, France was beginning to extend its patronage to the regional Catholic and Maronite populations.

The competition for local allies became intense in 1839–1840 given the growing tensions for control of the eastern Mediterranean between the Ottomans and their European allies on the one hand and Mehmed Ali and France on the other. It was especially so in Mount Lebanon, which was populated by two compact minorities, the Maronites and the Druze, and which was seen as the geographical key in the coming struggle.[29] Mount Lebanon was a formidable barrier protecting inland areas from the coast. Inland, the forces of Mehmed Ali could be expected to defeat Ottoman forces as they had before. The coast, which Britain's navy had blockaded in the summer of 1839, was where British troops would land. If the mountain held firm, Mehmed Ali might have had a chance of retaining control of inland Syria and even of defeating British troops on inhospitable terrain.

The problem for Mehmed Ali was that there was opposition in Mount Lebanon to his policies of taxation, conscription, and disarmament. The British patronized the Druze and encouraged their rebellion; there was no contradiction here between wooing potential clients who were chafing under Mehmed Ali's rule and British policy to weaken Mehmed Ali in favor of a restoration of Ottoman power. The French were in a far more difficult situation. There was a contradiction in French policy between France's support for Mehmed Ali on the one hand and its desire to extend French patronage to the Maronites, numbers of whom were on the verge of rebellion, on the other.

For some, French policy and personal attachment to the church worked in opposite directions. Those in official positions seem to have hewed to the official French line of supporting Mehmed Ali, or at least they did not encourage rebellion against him. Others, mainly missionaries and adventurers, encouraged Maronites to rebel, hoping thereby to create for France a Catholic protectorate in the eastern Mediterranean.

The French consul in Beirut, M. Bourée, experienced this contradiction acutely. In his analysis, three related developments made his position difficult in 1840. The idea of rebellion against Mehmed Ali had spread among the Maronites from the Druze who were being encouraged by Britain. The French were being accused of not supporting the Maronites because they were protecting Mehmed Ali from the other European powers. And the Maronites were therefore being enticed into Britain's embrace. He urged strongly that if France decided to "place the Vice Roi [Mehmed Ali] among the number of independent powers, we absolutely must not give up by that, either in rights or in language, the position of protector [of the Maronites]."[30] In the end, though, Consul Bourée left Beirut; he could not maintain his balance between France's official policy of verbal and diplomatic support for Mehmed Ali on the one hand and rebellion on the part of some Maronites on the other.[31]

Bourée's life was made difficult by French adventurers like Vicomte Onffroy. In April 1840 the vicomte established himself in Zuq Mikha'il, in the foothills next to the coast and close to the Jesuit college at Antourah, ostensibly to learn Arabic.[32] Within a month he had created a sensation in Beirut by publicly proclaiming his support for the Maronite rebels. The rebels called him the French prince, and some appear to have thought he was the king's nephew sent to show the king's support and that French boats were sure to follow.[33] For M. Bourée, the vicomte's "presence in the thick of them [the rebels] would have hurt his countrymen without any benefit for the cause that he wished to serve."[34] By July, Onffroy was in serious trouble in the midst of competing powers; he demanded that Bourée get him on the first boat out or he would invoke British protection by virtue of his birth in Jamaica.[35] This would have fed the notion among Maronites that Bourée most feared—that Britain offered better protection than France.

The Comte de Ratti-Menton did not face this dilemma as acutely as did M. Bourée. There was not, in Damascus, a large Catholic community on the verge of rebellion. He was, though, very sensitive to European competition for Catholic and Christian clientele. And like Onffroy, Ratti-Menton thought the Christians wished to separate themselves completely from Muslim rule and come under the protection of France.[36] The disappearance of Père Thomas gave him an opportunity, and the imperative, to demonstrate France's protective powers to the local Catholic community and by extension to the whole of the Catholic, and Christian, population in the region. By getting Mehmed Ali's governor to vigorously pursue a ritual murder accusation, he could demonstrate that France and Mehmed Ali together served Catholic interests. Beyond demonstrating the simple protection of one protégé, the ritual murder story conjured up a threat to the whole Christian/Catholic community that the French could deal with: the Jews. When Mehmed Ali exonerated the accused Jews in September 1840, Ratti-Menton was beside himself. He felt that the reputation of France had thereby suffered irreparable damage.[37]

For Ratti-Menton, as for his defender at the head of government in Paris, Adolphe Thiers, perhaps the accusation of ritual murder was nothing more than a handy prejudice married to a simple political calculation. "If the Jews are to be held innocent of the refined slaughter of Father Thomas, it will be necessary to accuse the Mohammedans and Christians. This is a sad alternative."[38] And an apparently unacceptable one for France in the competition for local support as Istanbul and the other European powers lined up against Mehmed Ali and France in the struggle for Syria. It is striking that in explaining what happened to Père Thomas, the French consul told a story that implicated not just individuals but a whole group.[39]

In the summer of 1840 the Comte de Ratti-Menton reported to Paris that the Christians of the eastern Mediterranean had sincere affection for France and wished to be free of Muslim rule. Had he intended, by telling a story of ritual murder in Damascus, to create notions of Catholic solidarity in Syria and France alike? Perhaps, but there is only circumstantial evidence. Five years later, such notions had gained currency in France and were beginning to take hold in the Middle East.

In 1845 Druze-Maronite clashes in Mount Lebanon sparked an outpouring of sympathy in France for the Maronites on the basis of a shared Catholicism. This sympathy, already in the making in 1840, had been augmented by the appearance in 1844 of a book by the Maronite archbishop and representative to the Vatican, Nicolas Murad.[40] Written in French and dedicated to Louis Philippe, the fifty-page book articulated a history of the Maronites in two politically significant ways: as the most faithful of all Christian communities in the Orient to Catholic beliefs and as the community with the longest and closest ties to France. In 1846 a two-volume work about the 1840 events in Mount Lebanon and Damascus, *Relation historique des affaires de Syrie depuis 1840 jusqu'en 1842*, was published in Paris.[41] Here we can finally see clearly the ritual murder trial in Damascus being used to excite French support for Christians in the region.

At first glance, the two volumes of *Relation historique* seem oddly coupled. The first volume is about Mount Lebanon and the coast in the period of the defeat of Mehmed Ali and the Ottoman restoration. In it, the Maronite community is depicted as a victim first of Mehmed Ali's government and then of Ottoman rule after the restoration. The second volume is about the ritual murder trial in Damascus; it published for the first time the official report of the investigation and supporting documents and correspondence. The pairing of these two apparently dissimilar narratives could be explained by simple chronology. The investigation into Père Thomas's disappearance in Damascus happened to occur at the time of the British and Ottoman conquest of Mount Lebanon and the restoration of Ottoman control there. In the context of 1845–1846, however, the two stories come together in an arresting way. *Relation historique* shows in both volumes a beleaguered Catholic population threatened by Jews in Damascus and by Druze and bad government in Mount Lebanon. The two volumes, written by Achille Laurent and published by the ultramontane-leaning press,

Gaume Frères, can further be read as an argument for French intervention on the basis of Catholic solidarity. This solidarity failed to materialize in Mount Lebanon in 1840 but could yet be acted upon in 1846 to save the Maronites of Lebanon and to further French interests there.

Achille Laurent not only brings together the events in Mount Lebanon and Damascus in his book, he also brings together the Vicomte Onffroy and the Comte de Ratti-Menton. Onffroy's exploits in Lebanon in 1840 are regaled with a note of bravado in volume I; Ratti-Menton, as the chief exposer of ritual murder, is the hero of volume II. All three men—Laurent, Onffroy, and Ratti-Menton—were members of the Société Orientale, founded in Paris in 1841. Nicolas Murad, author of the 1844 tract on the Maronites, was an honorary member. The aim of the society was to defend French interests and the Christian population in "the Orient," which it defined as east of the longitude running from pole to pole through Paris. "This aim," the founders insisted, "is truly national. . . . Catholic interest and French interest are one in the Orient."[42]

The Société Orientale did not succeed in getting France to intervene in Mount Lebanon in 1845 and 1846, but its aim of promoting Catholic interests as French interests was successful in strange quarters. Adolphe Cremieux, the prominent French Jew who had gone to Egypt with Sir Moses Montefiore in 1840 to save the Jews of Damascus and who must have regarded the Comte de Ratti-Menton with the utmost repugnance, upbraided the Chamber of Deputies in 1846 in terms straight from the count's lexicon.

> The Christians of Lebanon! They have, in fact, been your brothers for centuries, not only in religion, but brothers in war, brothers on the fields of battle. They have been there in all circumstances. Saint Louis found them. Napoleon found them. . . . Very well then, destroy the work of Saint Louis and your kings, annihilate with one blow the Christian population which has the same faith, the same God, the same religion as you.[43]

As in Natalie Zemon Davis's *The Return of Martin Guerre*, micro-history creates strange bedfellows. By looking at a judicial proceeding in Damascus, we can see royalists and republicans, clericalists and anti-clericalists, anti-Semites and Jews coming together to manipulate ties of Catholicism in order to extend French influence in the Middle East. We can also see the deployment of European anti-Semitism to create such ties.

Notes

1. Edward Berenson, *The Trial of Madame Caillaux* (Berkeley: University of California Press, 1992), p. 8.

2. See, for example, Jacob Landau, "Ritual Murder Accusations and Persecutions of Jews in 19th-Century Egypt," *Sefunot*, Annual for Research on the Jewish Communities in the East (Publications of the Ben Zvi Institute, The Hebrew University, Jerusalem), vol. 5 (1961): 415–460. He finds Greeks to have been the prime instigators.

3. Regarding the genesis of ritual murder accusations, see Gavin Langmuir, "Thomas of Monmouth: Detector of Ritual Murder," in his collection of articles, *Toward a Definition of Antisemitism* (Berkeley: University of California Press, 1990). Regarding standard shapes of the accusation, see Ronnie Po-Chia Hsia, *The Myth of Ritual Murder: Jews and Magic in Reformation Germany* (New Haven, Conn.: Yale University Press, 1988); and Alan Dundes (ed.), *The Blood Libel Legend: A Case Book in Anti-Semitic Folklore* (Madison: University of Wisconsin Press, 1991). The story of ritual murder had rarely appeared in the Middle East before 1840. Uriel Heyd found traces of two accusations in fifteenth- and sixteenth-century Anatolia in Ottoman records. The alleged victims were grown Muslim men. Uriel Heyd, "Ritual Murder Accusations in 15th- and 16th-Century Turkey," *Sefunot,* vol. 5 (1961): 135–150.

4. Jonathan Frankel, *The Damascus Affair* (Cambridge, UK: Cambridge University Press, 1997).

5. Exemplars of the first school include: Achille Laurent, *Relation historique des affaires de Syrie depuis 1840 jusqu'en 1842*, Vol. II (Paris: Gaume Frères, 1846); Giambattista da Mondovi, *Relazione del Padre Tomaso da Calangiano di Sardegna missionario apostolico cappuccino. Il processo verbale diretto contro gli Ebrei di Damasco nel'anno 1840* (Marseille, 1850); no author, *Aceldama* (Cagliari: Stab. Tip. G. Dessi, 1896); Jean Driault, *L'assassinat du Père Thomas et le Talmud* (Paris: Edition da la Vieille France, 1922). The first prejudicial use of the 1840 accusation in Arabic publications is Habib Effendi Faris, *Sarakh al-Bari* (Cairo: H. Faris, 1891). Recently, Mustafa Tlas, *Fatir Sahyun* (Damascus: Tlasdar, 1987), has reproduced and summarized the official record as what really happened to Père Thomas.

6. Exemplars of the second school include: L. H. Loewenstein, *Damascia* (Rodelheim: J. Lehrberger, 1841); A. M. Hyamson, "The Damascus Affair—1840," *Transactions of the Jewish Historical Society of England* 16 (1952): 47–71; Ursula Henriques, "Who Killed Father Thomas?" in V. D. Lipman (ed.), *Sir Moses Montefiore—A Symposium* (Oxford: Oxford Centre for Postgraduate Hebrew Studies and Jewish Historical Society of England, 1982); Tudor Parfitt, "'The Year of the Pride of Israel': Montefiore and the Damascus Blood Libel of 1840," in Sonia and V. D. Lipman (eds.), *The Century of Moses Montefiore* (Oxford: Oxford University Press, 1985); Frankel, *The Damascus Affair.*

7. This sentiment is perhaps akin to historians' reluctance to use inquisitorial records noted by Carlo Ginzburg in "The Inquisitor as Anthropologist," in his *Clues, Myths, and the Historical Method* (Baltimore: Johns Hopkins University Press, 1989).

8. The doctors who declared bits of flesh and bone discovered in a Damascene sewer to be Père Thomas's had only their eyes as instruments of identification.

9. The alternatives are based on a report by G. W. Pieritz, *Persecution of the Jews at Damascus* (London: London Society for Promoting Christianity Amongst the Jews, 1840). Pieritz, a missionary in Jerusalem with the London Society for Promoting Christianity Amongst the Jews, and himself a convert, was sent to Damascus to refute the accusation of ritual murder. His report presents two alterna-

tive endings for Père Thomas: that he was last seen leaving town or that he quarreled with a muleteer and a merchant and was later murdered by one of them.

10. Here I am paraphrasing the question Gavin Langmuir put to "The Life and Passion of Saint William the Martyr of Norwich" in order to discover the origins of the medieval accusation of ritual murder. See Langmuir, *Toward a Definition*, p. 209.

11. Besides Berenson, the best-known micro-histories based in judicial proceedings are Natalie Zemon Davis, *The Return of Martin Guerre* (Cambridge: Harvard University Press, 1983), and Carlo Ginzburg, *The Cheese and the Worms: The Cosmos of a Sixteenth-Century Miller* (London: Routledge and Kegan Paul, 1980).

12. Cairo, Dar al-watha'iq, Mahafiz al-sham, 52/3/87/29; Paris, Ministère des Affaires Étrangères [hereafter MAE], Affaires Diverses Politiques [hereafter ADP], Turquie, vol. 4; London, Public Record Office, FO 78/410; Achille Laurent, *Relation historique des affaires de Syrie depuis 1840 jusqu'en 1842*, Vol. II (Paris: Gaume Frères, 1846). The archival versions and the printed version confirm each other although they are not exact copies.

13. Laurent, *Relation historique*, Vol. II, p. 8. Asad Rustum, *Materials for a Corpus of Arabic Documents Relating to the History of Syria Under Mehemet Ali Pasha*, Vol. V (Beirut: American Press, 1933), p. 2. I have chosen to cite Laurent and Rustum as more accessible sources than the archival versions. They are also paginated, which makes citation easier. I would also like to note that Rustum, unlike Laurent, is not an adherent of school one. He reproduces the trial report as a historical document without any comment as to the veracity of the verdict.

14. A crowd voicing the accusation is a standard part of European narratives of ritual murder.

15. Laurent, *Relation historique*, Vol. II, pp. 12–13; Rustum, *Materials*, Vol. V, p. 4.

16. Paris, MAE, ADP, Turquie, vol. 4, pp. 511–514, "Notice relative aux tourmente et mauvais traitement soufferte par les condamnés étant les meurtriers du P. Thomas."

17. Several sources mention in passing the presence of people doing business with the governor but not involved in the investigation and trial. Laurent, *Relation historique*, Vol. II, p. 23; Rustum, *Materials*, Vol. V, p. 8; Mikhayil Mishaqa, *Murder, Mayhem, Pillage, and Plunder: The History of Lebanon in the 18th and 19th Centuries*, trans. Wheeler Thackston (Albany: State University of New York Press, 1988), p. 197.

18. Cairo, Dar al-watha'iq, Mahafiz al-sham 52/3/87/29, testimony on 25 dhu'l-hijja, not paginated. Rustum, *Materials*, Vol. V, p. 8. Paris, MAE, ADP, Turquie, vol. 4, "Traduction du journal (ensemble de procès verbaux) relatif à la disparition du Père Thomas et de son domestique," p. 18. This is one of the few places where Laurent (*Relation historique*, Vol. II, p. 24) does not completely reproduce the archival record. The archival record gives the day and lists those present before relating the questions asked and answered. Laurent lists the day but does not name those present, and it is only through the text of questions and answers that we can see that the French consul and Hathiq Bey were present. This difference, though small, suggests that Laurent's version was reproduced from a preliminary version sent to the French government and later replaced by a cleaned-up text. The preliminary version begins on p. 44 of MAE, ADP, Turquie, vol. 4.

19. Cairo, Dar al-watha'iq, Mahafiz al-sham, 52/3/51/29, 26 Dhu'l-hijja 1255 [29 February 1840], no. 444.

20. Laurent, *Relation historique*, Vol. II, pp. 34–35; Rustum, *Materials*, Vol. V, p. 12.

21. Paris, MAE, ADP, Turquie, vol. 4, Ratti-Menton to MAE, 29 February 1840.

22. Paris, MAE, ADP, Turquie vol. 4, pp. 571–584.

23. Cairo, Dar al-watha'iq, Mahafiz al-sham 52/3/51/29, copy of a report, 21 muharrem 1256, no 22.

24. Nantes, MAE, Damas 72, Ratti-Menton to Sharif Pasha, 22 February 1840, 10 March 1840, and 17 April 1840.

25. "L'affaire relative à l'assassinat . . . a été poursuivie par M. le Cte de Ratti-Menton, qui a été parfaitement secondé par le gouverneur générale de la Syrie." Paris, MAE, Correspondance Politique Consulaire [hereafter CPC], Turquie, Alexandrie, vol. 10, p. 9, Cochelet to Thiers, 2 April 1840. Of course, the French were disposed to view the local government as less active than themselves, and the styles of correspondence of the governor and the consul are completely different. The consul tends to highlight his activity on behalf of French interests. The governor presents himself only as a recorder and reporter. See, for example, Cairo, Dar al-watha'iq, 52/2/87/29, Mehmed Sharif to Mehmed Ali.

26. See Frankel, *The Damascus Affair*, on European attitudes.

27. *The Times* (London), 18 May 1840, p. 5, "The Jews in Damascus, Private correspondence, Paris, May 12." The author is not indicated.

28. All personal information was gleaned from his personnel file at the Ministère des Affaires Etrangères. Paris, MAE, Personnel Série 1, Ratti-Menton.

29. Mishaqa, *Murder, Mayhem*, p. 208. Paris, MAE, CPC, Turquie, vol. 12, Ratti-Menton to Thiers, Damascus, 16 September 1840.

30. Paris, MAE, CPC, Turquie, Beyrouth, vol. 1, Bourée to MAE, Beirut, 27 June and 10 July 1840.

31. Nantes, MAE, Beyrouth, Série A, 25, MAE to Bourée, 29 July 1840. Bourée returned to Beirut as consul after the Ottoman restoration.

32. The French ambassador in Istanbul instructed the consul in Beirut to help Onffroy all he could as a traveler who belonged to a very good family. Nantes, MAE, Beyrouth, Série A, 24, Pontois to Bourée, 22 March 1840.

33. Laurent, *Relation historique*, Vol. I, pp. 21–22; Paris, MAE, CPC, Turquie, vol. 11, Ratti-Menton to Thiers, 27 July 1840.

34. Nantes, MAE, Beyrouth, Série A, 25, Cochelet to Bourée, 18 June 1840.

35. Nantes, MAE, Beyrouth, Série A, 24, Onffroy to Bourée, 12 July 1840.

36. Paris, MAE, CPC, Turquie, vol. 11, Ratti-Menton to Thiers, Damascus, 17 July 1840.

37. Nantes, MAE, Beyrouth, Série A, 25, Ratti-Menton to Desmeloizes, 6 and 12 September 1840.

38. S. Posener, *Adolphe Crémieux: A Biography* (Philadelphia: Jewish Publication Society of America, 1940), p. 97.

39. See Ussama Makdisi, *The Culture of Sectarianism* (Berkeley: University of California Press, 2000), for an analysis of Europe's and especially France's role in the creation of sectarianism in Lebanon.

40. Nicolas Murad, *Notice historique sur l'origine de la nation maronite et sur ses rapports avec la France, sur la nation druze et sur les diverses population du mont liban* (Paris: Librairie d'Adrien le Clere et Cie., 1844). The book was published by an ultramontane press.

41. Laurent, *Relation historique,* Vols. I and II.

42. Ibid., Vol. I, unnumbered page before p. 1.

43. Posener, *Adolphe Crémieux*, pp. 130–131.

5

The Gender of Modernity: Reflections from Iranian Historiography

Afsaneh Najmabadi

Since the early 1980s, feminist theory and scholarship have radically transformed "doing history." Broadly speaking, this transformation has taken two forms: writing women's history (sometimes referred to as retrieval history, as telling herstory) and introducing "gender as a useful category of analysis" into history writing.[1] Within Middle Eastern studies, the first project—retrieval history—has already produced a number of thorough historical works.[2]

"Established" Middle Eastern history, however, has been more resistant to the introduction of gender. For instance, present histories of Iranian modernity, with precious few exceptions, are gendered through the exclusion of women and the neglect of gender.[3] Not only are women largely absent, the existing historical narratives are not structured analytically by notions of gender. Sometimes separate chapters about Iranian women in the modern period are included. Yet this kind of inclusion, by keeping women virtually insulated from the overall historical narrative, signals the absence of women in the larger story and reinforces the irrelevance of gender to the analytical frame of the work. One author has called Iranian women's history "a kind of 'patch-work,'" necessitated by a lack of sources for writing fuller histories.[4] The problem of sources can, of course, be a real one. For instance, compared to Ottoman history, comparable periods of Safavid, and even more so Zand and Afsharid Iran, may be said to lack sources of the same scope as the rich Ottoman court records and state archives. But this has never led any historians of Iran to conclude that one cannot do Iranian history. A variety of existing sources have been used to "do history." So the claim of a lack of sources becomes a claim about a lack of information about women in the same existing historical sources. But then, perhaps, we are not facing so much a void of information in the sources as gender-oblivious readings of these sources. If gender is used analytically, sources about men can also become sources about women, or perhaps more accurately, they become sources about how "man" and "woman" are constituted.

The complaint about the lack of sources indicates a set of assumptions about doing history, and in particular about doing women's history. For instance, it assumes the stability and the already-given meaning of the category "woman." It assumes that bits of information about women can be culled from sources across time and genre and pulled together to produce a history of women. It aspires to compensate for the absence of women from current histories by simple retrieval and addition. Yet if we do not assume atemporal meanings for concepts, we can no more do so with the concept "woman." One task of reading historical sources through a gender lens is to figure out the very construction of woman in these sources. Writing women's history in this sense then becomes a radically different kind of history writing, with an inherent "troubling ambiguity." For it is "at once an innocuous supplement to and a radical replacement for established history."[5] Disjointed narratives of women's history as patchwork on existing history, by continued compartmentalization of women, leave the gender-obliviousness of histories of modernity unchallenged. Gender, however, is not only a "useful category of historical analysis" but a centrally structuring category for the study of modernity—for modernity is a thoroughly gendered construct. As noted by Rita Felski:

> If our sense of the past is inevitably shaped by the explanatory logic of narrative, then the stories that we create in turn reveal the inescapable presence and power of gender symbolism. This saturation of cultural texts with metaphors of masculinity and femininity is nowhere more obvious than in the case of the modern. . . . Whether these [individual or collective human] subjects are presumed to be male or female has important consequences for the kind of narrative that unfolds. Gender affects not just the factual content of historical knowledge—what is included and what gets left out—but also the philosophical assumptions underlying our interpretations of the nature and meaning of social processes.[6]

Concepts central to imagining and constructing a modern Iran, for instance, were envisaged in terms related to concepts of femininity and masculinity. From the late eighteenth century through the first decades of the twentieth century, Iranian modernity was shaped through rearticulation of such pivotally important concepts as *millat* (nation), *sīāsat* (politics), *vaṭan* (homeland), and *'ilm* (knowledge).[7] The genderedness of this crafting has received little, if any, attention. Nation was largely scripted and visualized as a brotherhood—at least until the last decade of the nineteenth century when women began to claim their space as sisters in the nation. The modern notion of *vaṭan,* on the other hand, was envisaged as female—as a beloved and/or as a mother.[8] Closely linked to the maleness of *millat* and femaleness of *vaṭan* was the concept of *nāmūs* (honor). As *millat* changed from a religious to a national community, *nāmūs* was also delinked from *nāmūs-i Islām,* its religious affiliation, and reclaimed as *nāmūs-i Irān,* a national concern.[9] Slipping between the idea of *'iṣmat* (purity of woman) and integrity of the nation, in both cases *nāmūs* was constituted as subject to male possession and protection; sexual and national honor intimately constructed each other.[10] Symbolically, the Iranian national logo, first formally adopted in 1836, was a male lion with a female sun. Over the following century, the lion became more manly, the sun less evidently feminine, eventually losing all facial features, and making the national logo thoroughly masculinized.

The gendered construction of these central notions of modernity has had significant political consequences for how the changes in notions of gender and sexuality and, in particular, womanhood were articulated in the emergence of Iranian modernity. The rearticulation of the language of honor into the language of political mobilization, and the production of homeland as woman, crafted woman of modernity as a category of manly possession and protection. The universal citizen turned out to be a manly citizen. At the same time, the modernist discourse, by striving toward a general notion of equality before the law and articulation of general rights of citizens, provided women with a discourse to claim a new space for themselves in public, to script themselves as occupants of that politically powerful notion of the Iranian nation. The category "modern woman" was crafted within the tensions posed by these conflictive tendencies inside the same discursive space of nationhood.

To write a gendered history of modernity has important repercussions for writing women's history. Transformations of concepts of woman and man did not occur only on the level of reimagining how men and women of modernity would be different from their predecessors. The gendered rhetoric and symbolism of modernity in turn became productive of new notions of man and woman, while setting the limits of possibility for the lives and experiences of men and women.[11]

This chapter will suggest some additional sources, but more strongly, ways of reading these sources that I hope will be productive for gendering a history of Iranian modernity. I will use largely visual material. The use of visual texts as primary material for history writing immediately faces the challenge of priority historians usually accord to textual evidence over visual material. When historians do use visual material, it is largely used illustratively rather than analytically. That is, at a certain point in the text, the historian includes an illustration as a pleasing final touch for a textually supported narrative, as its visual mirror. However, when presenting an argument articulated through visual documentation, one is often asked if one could produce supporting texts. If such textual support can be provided, then the argument acquires a solidity that it seemed to lack otherwise. Although in an important sense visuality has precedence over textuality—after all, we see before we talk and surely before we read and write—we seem to need a distance from, and express distrust and disavowal of, visual material. One is rarely asked to produce visual material in support of a textually developed argument. Written texts have a self-sufficiency that visual texts are assumed to lack. I am not suggesting to reverse this common priority of textual over visual. The challenge, rather, resides in learning how to "read" visual texts historically and to use methods of visual interpretation to craft a historical argument.[12]

For the purpose of doing a gendered history of modernity, the use of visual sources opens up whole new domains to a historian. In the case of nineteenth-century Iran, for instance, we have an abundance of representations of women. But, as I have argued elsewhere, the referential point of these paintings cannot be assumed to be actual women.[13] This can be a source of disappointment and frustration, for Qajar art seems to be largely devoid of any social information.[14] However, using gender analytically can turn these visual texts into rich sources for study of gender and sexuality.

This proposition requires another shift, taking us away from the assumption of "art as mere reflection of reality" to considering art as constitutive of meaning. As elaborated by Griselda Pollock:

> As representation the term stresses that images and texts are no mirrors of the world, merely reflecting their sources. Representation stresses something refashioned, coded in rhetorical, textual or pictorial terms, quite distinct from its social existence. Representation can also be understood as "articulating" in a visible or socially palpable form social processes which determine the representation but then are actually affected and altered by the forms, practices and effects of representation. . . . Finally, representation involves a third inflection, for it signifies something represented to, addressed to a reader/viewer/consumer.[15]

Looking at Qajar art with an eye for representations of gender and sexuality offers us important reading possibilities. In the rest of this chapter, I will attempt to tease out a possible meaning for one feature of Qajar representation of women: the baring of the breast. A figure that appears repeatedly in Qajar art is the bare-breasted woman.[16] Although nude females as well as females whose breasts are visible through transparent clothing do appear in Safavid and Zand art, the bare-breasted woman, or women with breasts emphatically displayed through style of dress or association with fetishistic objects, seems to be a heavily accented theme in Qajar painting. In Safavid art, for instance, the figure of exaggeratedly décolleté woman is occupied by representations of European women.[17] In addition to representations of European women and the many bare-breasted women of pleasure (dancers and acrobats, wine and food servers, musicians—see Figure 5.1), other bare-breasted women of Qajar art include angels, and woman and child figures reminiscent of Mary and Child paintings.

The figure of a bare-breasted woman, in other words, constitutes a "figure of repetition" in Qajar art. Previously, I had argued that the Qajari bare-breasted woman emerged at the culmination of a process of eroticization of the breast linked with Iranian men's perceptions of women in Europe.[18] European woman as the site of paradisaic eroticism was focalized on the breast, which in turn contributed to the eroticization of the breast in Persian male imagination. I now want to propose that eroticization of the woman's breast and representation of the bare-breasted woman as a figure of repetition are linked with another important Qajar development: the disappearance of *ghilmān* as a figure of desire. *Ghilmān,* along with *ḥūr,* comes from quranic verses that describe paradisaic pleasures.[19] The terms are commonly understood to refer to male and female eternally young beauties, respectively. Sexual meanings were constituted for *ghilmān* as much as for *ḥūr* in many genres of Persian and Arabic literature. In Arabic language, this constitution is now reflected in the root location for *ghulām* (pl. *ghilmān*) itself, coming under *gh/l/ṃ*, to be excited by lust, be seized by sexual desire.[20] Similarly, in Persian, connections are well established in the word *ghulām* and even more so in its plural *ghilmān*.[21] This was definitely the case in nineteenth-century writings, which is the relevant discursive domain for my argument here. As I have documented elsewhere, when Iranians wrote about European beauties, more often than not the phrases of praise went in couples: *ḥūrī*s and *ghilmān*s, beautiful young women and men.[22]

A striking feature of Qajar art is the virtual absence of male homoerotic couples. From earlier periods, namely Safavid Iran, we have both male-male and male-female embraces that are often catalogued as "amorous couple." By the late Zand/early Qajar period, we are left with only male-female couples, and as Layla Diba has noted, from early Qajar on, there is a noticeable absence of amorous couples altogether.[23] This absence is accompanied by a veritable abundance of female objects of desire, most notably as entertainers of various types, ladies of male pleasure. What can we make of this transformation?

If we read visual sources as a simple reflection of reality, we may be tempted to conclude that whereas in earlier times male homoeroticism was an openly celebrated theme (in literature even more so than in paintings),[24] Qajar Iran marks a radical change in sexual mores and erotic sensibilities that are, in turn, reflected in the disappearance of male-male erotic representations. There is good historical ground, in fact, to argue for the heterosexualization of love in nineteenth-century Iran.[25] Yet I want to suggest that

Figure 5.1
"A Girl Playing a Guitar," by Abdū 'l-Qāsim, 1816. Former Amery Collection.
Reprinted in Falk, *Qajar Paintings*, Plate 20.

the situation is more complex than the mere presence or absence of male homoeroticism. For one thing, how would we then explain the disappearance of the female-male amorous couple? Surely, if read as simply a representation of heterosexual pleasure, the female-male amorous couples should have multiplied.

To get around this paradoxical situation, I suggest that previous readings of female-male couples as amorous couples may have been a misreading, or at least a missed reading. If we expand the field of visuality beyond the visual text itself by bringing in the eye of the viewer (and the eye of the painter), we no longer have a dyad but triangles of desire. What erotic desires can we speculate are circulated and generated through these triangles? If we assume a male viewer (and/or painter), a female-male loving couple (see Figure 5.2) no longer need be viewed as a representation of heteroeroticism but becomes implicated in a complex set of desires: First, the desire for the male in the painting (as expressed by the female in the painting) constructs the male figure as an object of desire that the male viewer could also desire.[26]

In other words, the heteroerotic desire in the visual text can be conducive of homoerotic pleasure and desire outside the text. A similar point could be made about the male painter. In other words, the representation of heteroeroticism within the visual text cannot be assumed necessarily to mirror heterosexual inclinations of the painter, nor simply be presumed generative of heteroeroticism in the viewer. There is as strong a circulation/generation of desire on the other side of the triangle between male painter or viewer and the male figure in the text. Not only can both male and female figures in the visual field be imagined as objects of desire for the (presumably male) viewer/painter, the viewer/painter could be imagined to desire identification as the object of desire with either of them. He could desire to be the male object of desire for a female or, alternatively, be in the place of the female, desired by another male.[27] This kind of masqueraded identification may not have been necessary or dominant when male-male amorous couples were openly represented and celebrated. Yet it may have become an important development for Qajar transformations, as we will see.

The suggestion of reading the female-male couple not as simply an amorous couple but as a multiple scene of desire is grounded in iconic points, which I analyze at greater length elsewhere.[28] These include the fact that the male figure in the male-female amorous couple is always a very young man, never with a mustache, at most with a hint of a newly emerging mustache, that icon of young man's beauty: He may be a *nawkhat*, but never an adult man.[29] In other words, male-male scenes of desire are not representations of an older man and a young man, as one would expect of a realistic representation. Book illustrations related to the latter theme are of

Figure 5.2
"Embracing Lovers." Attributed to Muhammad Sadiq, Shiraz, c. 1770–1780. Oil on canvas, 59 x 38 inches. Collection of Eskandar Aryeh. Reprinted in Diba and Ekhtiar, *Royal Persian Paintings*, Plate 27, p. 156.

quite a different character. Frequently, the older man is an abject figure, in desperate love with a cruel young beauty, as in "The Dervish Picks Up His Beloved's Hair," and "The Fickle Old Lover Is Knocked Off the Rooftop."[30] Moreover, both male and female beauties in these paintings have identical features (see Figure 5.2). In contrast, when love scenes between a particular man and woman are depicted, the male figure bears the marks of an adult man: He has a pronounced mustache (rather than being represented as a *nawkhatt*), heavy sideburns, or a beard.[31]

What allows this interpretive move to be made even more forcefully for the Zand and Qajar male-female scene of desire in the text is *the strong outward gaze*, a late Safavid/early Zand development. The direct gaze, like direct address in a text, is an invitation; in scenes of desire, it invites the viewer to become an accomplice in the pleasures of the visual text, to become actively engaged in the production and circulation of desire in and out of the visual text. This invitational gaze strongly tilts the triangle of desire between the couple in the text and the viewer with an induction of the latter into the scene of desire. A possibility thus suggests itself for the disappearance of the male-male scene of desire: that the determined outward gaze disrupted the internal homoeroticism of the text so strongly in favor of that between the text and the viewer/painter that it made simultaneous presence of two male points of reference in the visual text redundantly disruptive of engendering desire between a male viewer/painter and the text. The presence of a female figure in the text along with a male one, however, assuming a difference between female-male versus male-male desire, would not pose similar viewing challenges. In this particular scene (Figure 5.2), what is remarkable is that the female beauty is looking outward, but the male is not. Nor is he looking at her—a pose typically expected of a realist rendering of an amorous couple. He is looking away, not only away from her but more intriguingly away from the viewer; it is an averted gaze, as if playing coy with the viewer. The averted gaze speaks to the ambivalence of youthful masculinity, a transitional age for a young man, being the most desired by the world of adult men he is about to join. His averted gaze and coy smile, as well as other facial features, resemble strongly "A Girl Playing Mandolin" by the same artist.[32] In other words, his features and poses put him in the same iconic position as that of a female figure of pleasure, an object of desire, rather than that of a desiring male subject. The cup of wine completes the paradisaic scene of desire, the promise of *ghilmān*, *ḥūr*, and wine to the good male believer in the afterlife—pleasures, two of which are forbidden to him on earth. In other words, what has often been read as representation of the real, that is, the male-female amorous couple as a spectacle of heterosexuality, I suggest we can read as a spectacle of hetero- and homoerotic desire if we bring the viewing eye into the dynamic of viewing and ask, What kinds of desire could the painting produce in a (male or female, hetero- or homoerotically inclined) viewer? The amour in the young amorous female and male couple could then be read as amour circulating between the viewer and the painting as a spectacle of *ḥūr* and *ghilmān*.

This possibility may have become consolidated through a process specific to this period of Iranian cultural transformation. Iranians became acutely aware that Europeans considered older man/younger man love and sexual practices very prevalent in Iran and that they considered it a vice. This is a theme that goes back to at least Chardin.[33] Chardin's travelogue remained immensely influential for Europeans who subsequently visited Iran.[34] Later travelers seem to have followed Chardin looking for things as reported by him and perhaps saw what they had anticipated to see. Could this have been part of the repeated seeing and reporting of the prevalence of male homosexuality, always linked with maltreatment of women, in Iran? M. Tancoigne, for instance, in a journal entry written in Tehran on 10 February 1808, echoed Chardin closely:

> I judge of them, therefore, as I see them. . . . I have, besides, still other vices to reproach them with; the most serious is their injustice and indifference to a sex which elsewhere forms all the charm and happiness of our existence. Women are merely, in the estimation of these men, beings created solely for their pleasure. Preserved by their education and habits from the pains and vicissitudes of love; incapable, on the other hand, by their religious prejudices, of appreciating its delights and enjoyments, they have degraded that sentiment to the excess of reserving it at times for their minions, and of turning it into a crime against nature. Many of their poems turn entirely on this inconceivable degeneracy; and their moral depravity is such that far from making a mystery of this new species of amorous intrigue, they appear, on the contrary, to take pride in it; speak publicly of their minions, as if they were speaking of their mistresses.[35]

Could one of the effects of this repetition have been the pressure on Iranian men in contact with Europeans to dissimulate and disavow male homosexuality? Could this pressure have contributed to the process of heteronormalization of male sexuality in Qajar Iran? Some of the Iranian men traveling to and writing about Europe used similarly strong language to disavow European perceptions. Mīrzā Fattāḥ Khān Garmrūdī, traveling through Europe in 1838, wrote:

> With all this corruption and the unseemly state [in Farang (Europe) that he had been so far describing and documenting], they write books condemning and moralizing people of Iran. In particular, Fraser has insinuated and exaggerated a great deal. For instance: that Iranian people [men] are greatly inclined toward young beautiful boys and some commit evil acts with them. Yes, in all nations of the world, some deeply ignorant people, over-

> come by spirit of lasciviousness and satanic temptations, commit some unacceptable practices. But the people of Farang who are known for all kinds of ill reputes, and especially for this evil act, who have houses of young men [male brothels—*amradkhānah*], similar to houses of prostitution [*qaḥbah'khānah*], who go to these places all the time, pay money and commit this evil act—it is totally unfair that they, who are known to engage in this evil practice, would tell off people of Iran and attribute this practice to us and write about it in books.[36]

In retaliation, he continued by telling homophobic tales about English men.[37]

This anxiety over Europeans' judgment of Iranian sexual concepts and practices remained a preoccupation throughout the nineteenth century. Ibrāhīm Saḥḥāfbāshī, sightseeing in London in 1897, reported—with no indication of moral outrage or disapprobation, however—two occasions in which he had been propositioned by English men. Rejecting their advances, he commented that it was a pity that Iranians had been defamed while the English seemed to practice sodomy widely, despite harsh laws against it.[38]

Open disavowal and homophobic retaliation may have been only one response to this scrutiny. Dissimulation and "cross-representation" could have been another: The disappearance of the male beloved from visual representation, similar to what we witness as his disappearance from love poetry in this period, could have been an alternative resolution. I am suggesting that as "another gaze" came onto the scene of desire, for those Iranian men interacting with Europeans who came to Iran, or those traveling to Europe, as if an intruder had walked into one's private chamber, the scene of homoerotic desire had to be covered, to be masqueraded. The female-male loving couple in this context can be read as a masquerade of desire: The European viewer could read the male-female couple as a scene of heteroeroticism, while for the Iranian male viewer, the young male beauty, looking directly at him, or averting his gaze, could continue to stand for his *shāhid*, his beautiful male testimony to divine perfection.[39] I want to suggest tentatively that *one marker of modernity became the transformation of male homoeroticism into masqueraded hetero-eros*. This masquerade could not but affect homoeroticism itself. The disappearance of *ghilmān* in their own right from visual representation left the field in sole occupation of *ḥūrīs*.[40] Read in this way, the disappearance of the amorous male-female couple now acquires a different meaning: It becomes the disappearance of *ghilmān* from the scene of desire, leaving us with abundant scenes of beautiful females only—thus the proliferation of female figures in nineteenth-century Qajar art.

It is in connection to the emergence of this female figure of desire in Qajar art that I suggest we could also read the baring of the breast. Another common scene of European travelogues' description of Iran was that of dances in weddings and other festivities.[41] What many of these travelers seem to have found most disturbing was the spectacle of young boys being dressed and made up as female dancers to perform on these occasions. Both Tancoigne and George Keppel report on young men transdressed as female entertainers in men's festivities and express their deep "disgust."[42] In his journal entry at Khoi, on 8 November 1807, Tancoigne wrote:

> A magnificent feast was prepared for us at the Khan's. . . . The banquet was long, and animated by music: Persian dancers were also engaged to enliven the scene. Lascivious postures, varied to infinity, composed all the art of those dancers, who are generally boys—their profession, despised as it is by the Persians, is however very lucrative. Cloyed in very early life with all kinds of enjoyments, the nobility know no better means of amusing their satiety, and they never have a festival at home without this brutal accompaniment.
>
> Those dancers are dressed in female habits, and hold metal castanets in each hand: they generally begin their exercises by various feats of strength and agility; then, changing their gestures and movements, they exhibit all that debauchery and luxury ever invented by the most refined profligacy.[43]

The description of these dancing scenes was intimately linked with expressed disgust about male-male homosexual practices. If, as I have suggested, disavowal of these practices became an important concern for Iranian men in the nineteenth century, then the bare-breasted female entertainers of Qajar art acquire yet another layer of meaning: The baring of the breast becomes another way of emphasizing that these dancers were women and not young men; it became another way of disambiguating the gender-undifferentiated figure of desire into a pronouncedly feminine one. It is as if the bare-breasted female entertainers emphatically and repeatedly say, "Look! We are young women, not young adolescent men."

Display of breast and its emphatic visual construction through arrangements with objects, flowers, or fruits (Figure 5.3) became a distinct mark of womanhood. This process, at once, intensified eroticization of the breast and heterosexualization of eros. In "Reading for Gender Through Qajar Art," I had focused on the former process by largely looking at the bare breast as a signifier of cultural difference, marking Europe from Iran, with European women marked as figures of male pleasure and Qajari bare-breasted women as a replicated substitute figure of desire from "elsewhere." My reading in this chapter, by placing the figure of the female object of desire, the *ḥūrī*, in the context of her disappeared male counterpart, the *ghilmān*, suggests a local scene as well for transformation of desire in Qajar Iran.

The disappearance of *ghilmān* and the repeated appearance of bare-breasted female figures both performed the same cultural labor: that of het-

Figure 5.3
"A Girl in Outdoor Costume Holding an Apple." Period of Fath 'Ali Shah.
Former Amery Collection. Reprinted in Falk, *Qajar Paintings*, Plate 17.

eronormalization of desire, at least in its public visual presentation and appearance. A similar phenomenon happened in Persian literature, as the cup bearer and *shāhid* of classical poetry became transformed into female figures (something linguistically possible in Persian, unlike Arabic or Urdu, since the language has no gender markings). Today's illustrated copies of Hafiz poetry, for instance, depict these figures as women, and modernist interpreters of that poetry insist on the metaphorical nature of homoerotic love when the text does not allow them to insist on reading the beloved as female. The modernist imagination insists on reading the heteroerotic masquerade of homoeroticism as real.

Notes

An earlier version of this chapter benefited enormously from critical comments by Houman Sarshar, Natalie B. Kampen, and Layla Diba. I thank them all.

1. See Joan Wallach Scott, "Women's History," in Peter Burke (ed.), *New Perspectives on Historical Writing* (Cambridge, UK: Polity Press, 1991), pp. 42–66; and Joan Wallach Scott, *Gender and the Politics of History* (New York: Columbia University Press, 1988).

2. Among them: Judith Tucker, *Women in Nineteenth-Century Egypt* (Cambridge, UK: Cambridge University Press, 1985); Parvin Paidar, *Women and the Political Process in Twentieth-Century Iran* (Cambridge, UK: Cambridge University Press, 1995); Beth Baron, *The Women's Awakening in Egypt* (New Haven, Conn.: Yale University Press, 1994); Margot Badron, *Feminists, Islam, and Nation* (Princeton, N.J.: Princeton University Press, 1995); Leslie Pierce, *The Imperial Harem* (Oxford: Oxford University Press, 1993); Marnia Lazreg, *The Eloquence of Silence* (New York: Routledge, 1994); Zehra Arat, *Deconstructing Images of the Turkish Woman* (Basingstoke: Macmillan, 1998).

3. For a more detailed critical assessment of this issue, see Paidar, *Women and the Political Process*, "Introduction: Marginalisation of Gender and Approaches to Women in Middle Eastern Studies."

4. Hammed Shahidian, "Dushvārīhā-yi nigārish-i tārīkh-i zanān dar Irān," *Iran Nameh* 12, no. 1 (Winter 1994): 81–128; quote from p. 83.

5. Scott, "Women's History," p. 49.

6. Rita Felski, *The Gender of Modernity* (Cambridge: Harvard University Press, 1995), p. 1.

7. See Mohammad Tavakoli-Targhi, "Refashioning Iran: Language and Culture During the Constitutional Revolution," *Iranian Studies* 23 (1990): 77–101; and M. Tavakoli-Targhi, "The Formation of Two Revolutionary Discourses in Modern Iran: The Constitutional Revolution of 1905–1906 and the Islamic Revolution of 1978–1979" (Ph.D. dissertation, University of Chicago, 1988).

8. See Afsaneh Najmabadi, "The Erotic *Vaṭan* [homeland] as Beloved and Mother: To Love, to Possess, and to Protect," *Comparative Studies in Society and History* 39 (1997): 442–467.

9. See Tavakoli-Targhi, "Refashioning Iran."

10. See Beth Baron, "The Construction of National Honour in Egypt," *Gender and History* 5 (1993): 244–255; Afsaneh Najmabadi, "*Zanhā-yi millat:* Women or Wives of the Nation," *Iranian Studies* 26 (1993): 51–71.

11. For a fine paper on the labor of rhetoric in production of gender, see Susan E. Shapiro, "A Matter of Discipline: Reading for Gender in Jewish Philosophy," in Miriam Peskowitz and Laura Levitt (eds.), *Judaism Since Gender* (New York: Routledge, 1997), pp. 158–173.

12. On the possibilities, problems, and challenges of using visual texts as an indispensable source for historians of women, see Margaret R. Miles, *Image as Insight: Visual Understanding in Western Christianity and Secular Culture* (Boston: Beacon Press, 1985). For important observations and critical suggestions about the interaction between written and visual texts, see Mieke Bal, *Reading "Rembrandt": Beyond the Word-Image Opposition* (Cambridge, UK: Cambridge University Press, 1991).

13. Afsaneh Najmabadi, "Reading for Gender Through Qajar Art," in Layla S. Diba and Maryam Ekhtiar (eds.), *Royal Persian Paintings: The Qajar Epoch 1785–1925* (London: Brooklyn Museum of Arts in association with I. B. Tauris, 1998), pp. 76–89.

14. See Layla S. Diba's observation with regards to the Amory collection, in "Persian Painting in the Eighteenth Century: Tradition and Transmission," in *Muqarnas*, Vol. VI, ed. Oleg Grabar (Leiden: E. J. Brill, 1989), pp. 147–160.

15. Griselda Pollock, *Vision and Difference: Femininity, Feminism, and Histories of Art* (London: Routledge, 1988), p. 6. See also Linda Nochlin, *Women, Art, and Power, and Other Essays* (New York: Harper and Row, 1988).

16. See, for instance, Diba and Ekhtiar, *Royal Persian Paintings*, Plates 56, 57, 58, 65. For other representations, see Figure 9 in Diba, "Persian Painting in the Eighteenth Century"; Figure 5 in Maryam Ekhtiar, "The Qajar Visual Aesthetic: Highlights from The Brooklyn Museum Collection," *Orientations* (July 1989): 46–53; Figure 2 (p. 225) and Figure 10 (p. 230) in R. W. Ferrier, *The Arts of Persia* (New Haven, Conn.: Yale University Press, 1989); and many of the reproductions of the paintings formerly in the Amery Collection in S. J. Falk, *Qajar Paintings: Persian Oil Paintings of the 18th and 19th Centuries* (London: Faber and Faber Ltd., in association with Sotheby Parke-Bernet, 1972).

17. See, for instance, Plate 48/Folio 93, "Two Ladies with a Page," 'Alī Qulī Jabbādār, 1674 A.D., in *The St. Petersburg Muraqqa* (Milano: Leonardo arte, 1996), described on p. 65.

18. See Najmabadi, "Reading for Gender Through Qajar Art."

19. For instance, Sura 44, verses 51–54; 52: 20–24; 56: 17–24; 55: 46–58, 70–74; and 76: 19–20.

20. See, for instance, Hans Wehr, *A Dictionary of Modern Written Arabic*, ed. J. Milton Cowan (Ithaca: Cornell University Press: 1966).

21. In Muhammad Mu'īn, *Farhang-i Fārsī* (Tehran: Amīr Kabīr, 1985), some of the meanings under *ghulām* are: (1) boy (from birth until beginning of youth), (2) boy who has developed sexual passion, and (3) boy who is made love to, *amrad.*

22. Afsaneh Najmabadi, *Women with Moustaches and Men without Beards: Gender and Sexual Anxieties of Iranian Modernity*, forthcoming, chapter 2, "Shaykh Ṣan'ān and Heteronormalization of Love." At the conference, *The Qajar Epoch: Culture, Art, and Architecture*, 1–4 September 1999, at the School of Oriental and African Studies, London University (co-sponsored by the Iran Heritage Foundation), where I presented a paper, "Gendered Transformations: Beauty, Love, and Sexuality in Qajar Iran" (to be published by the *Journal of Iranian Studies*), the question of whether *ghilmān* has the sexual meaning I am attributing to it was raised. The denial of a sexual meaning for *ghilmān* strikes me as a disavowal of homoeroticism, to put it mildly! It is intriguing that many current sources, such as

the *Encyclopaedia of Islam*, that have an entry for *ḥūr* do not have an entry for *ghilmān* (A. J. Wensinck [Ch. Pellat], "*Ḥūr*," in *Encyclopaedia of Islam,* Vol. III (Leiden: E. J. Brill, 1971), pp. 581–582.) *Encyclopaedia of Islam* has an entry under *ghulām* and even though the author notes the meaning of the word in Arabic as "a young man or boy . . . *ghulām amrad* 'beardless,'" it does not pay any attention to this layer of meaning (D. Sourdel, Vol. II, 1965, pp. 1079–1091, quote from p. 1079). Only C. E. Bosworth's subsection on *ghulām* in Persia includes a paragraph on "the sexual aspect" of the relationship between master and slave (p. 1082).

23. Layla S. Diba, "Early Qajar Period: 1785–1834," in Diba and Ekhtiar, *Royal Persian Paintings*, pp. 169–171.

24. J. W. Wright, Jr., and Everett K. Rowson (eds.), *Homoeroticism in Classical Arabic Literature* (New York: Columbia University Press, 1997). See also C. M. Naim, "The Theme of Homosexual (Pederastic) Love in Pre-Modern Urdu Poetry," in Muhammad Umar Memon (ed.), *Studies in the Urdu Gazal and Prose Fiction*, South Asian Studies Publication Series No. 5 (Madison: University of Wisconsin, 1979), pp. 120–142.

25. See Najmabadi, *Women with Moustaches and Men without Beards.*

26. This point was first brought to my attention by Dick Davis in the context of discussing Jami's *Yūsuf and Zulaykhā.* Correspondence with author, 9 November 1997.

27. I am grateful to Houman Sarshar, whose insightful suggestions opened up this reading possibility.

28. Afsaneh Najmabadi, "Gendered Transformations: Beauty, Love, and Sexuality in Qajar Iran," forthcoming in *Journal of Iranian Studies.*

29. *Nawkhatt*, adolescent young man with the first thin growth of a mustache, celebrated as the most beautiful and desired youth. Yet at the same time, that sign of beauty heralded the beginning of the end of his status as the object of desire for adult men and his own movement into adult malehood. It signaled the beginning of his loss to the lover.

30. Marianna Shreve Simpson, with contributions by Massumeh Farhad, *Sultan Ibrahim Mirza's Haft Awrang: A Princely Manuscript from Sixteenth-Century Iran* (Washington, D.C., and New Haven, Conn.: Freer Gallery of Art and Yale University Press, 1997), Folio 59a and Folio 162a, respectively. See Paul Sprachman, "*Le beau garçon sans merci:* The Homoerotic Tale in Arabic and Persian," in Wright and Rowson, *Homoeroticism in Classical Arabic Literature*, pp. 192–209.

31. See, for instance, Figure I: "Shirin Presents a Jug of Milk to Farhad," artist unknown, Iran, late fifteenth to early sixteenth century, p. 105 in Diba and Ekhtiar, *Royal Persian Paintings;* or Figure 34(a) "Zal Wooing Rudaba," by Lutf 'Ali Khan, dated between 1854 and 1864, in *The Cambridge History of Iran*, Vol. VII, eds. Peter Avery, Gavin Hambly, and Charles Melville (Cambridge, UK: Cambridge University Press, 1991).

32. "A Girl Playing Mandolin," Muhammad Sadiq, Shiraz, dated circa 1770–1780, Figure VIII, in Diba and Ekhtiar, *Royal Persian Paintings*, p. 157. The male-female couple on p. 156 (Figure 5.2 in this chapter) is attributed to the same artist.

33. See Ronald W. Ferrier (trans. and ed.), *A Journey to Persia: Jean Chardin's Portrait of a Seventeenth-Century Empire* (London: I. B. Tauris, 1996), pp. 22, 118, and 176, on Chardin's observations and judgment on the prevalence of male homosexuality and unfavorable conditions of women in Safavid Iran.

34. "I have occasionally named Chardin, the most accurate of all the French

travelers who have written on this country, for a European visitor might even at this day go all over Persia with his book as guide, except as it regards the costume, which has undergone a total change," wrote the editor to the English translation of M. Tancoigne who had traveled to Iran attached to the Embassy of General Gardane. See *A Narrative of a Journal into Persia and Residence at Teheran* (London: printed for William Wright, by W. Shackell, 1820); quote from p. vii. Tancoigne, himself, throughout his narrative, refers to Chardin as an authority. Among more well-known English travelers, both James Morier and Sir Robert Ker Porter repeatedly refer to Chardin's descriptions as a point of reference for their own report, though Ker Porter also refers to Morier and Sir Hartford Jones. See James Morier, *A Journey Through Persia, Armenia, and Asia Minor, to Constantinople, in the Years 1808 and 1809* (London: Longman et al., 1812); and Sir Robert Ker Porter, "At the Court of Fath Ali Shah," in B. W. Robinson and Gianni Guadalupi (eds.), *Qajar: Court Paintings in Persia* (Milan: Franco Maria Ricci, 1990), pp. 53–207.

35. Tancoigne, *A Narrative of a Journal*, p. 174.

36. Mīrzā Fattāḥ Khān Garmrūdī, *Safarnāmah*, ed. Fatḥ al-Dīn Fattāḥī (n.p., 1969), p. 962.

37. Ibid., pp. 962–964.

38. *Safarnāmah-'i Ibrāhīm Saḥḥāfbāshī Ṭiḥrānī,* ed. Muḥammad Mushīrī (Tehran: Shirkat-i mu'allifān va mutarjimān-i Irān, 1978), pp. 50–52, 57–58.

39. This masquerading move may have some similarities to one in eighteenth-century Urdu literature: "Avoiding the ambiguous *gazal-e muzakkar* of Persian, i.e., the lyric in which a male lover seemingly addressed another male, the Urdu poets of South India . . . adopted the Indian tradition of having a female address a male." Naim, "The Theme of Homosexual (Pederastic) Love," p. 121. Carla Petievich is currently working on a manuscript and translation of this genre of poetry from Urdu to English.

40. Though *ghilmān* disappear from explicit scenes of desire, they continue throughout the nineteenth century to make the stage in other guises; among them as young men next to young women in narrative paintings of the Shaikh Ṣan'ān story, where the scene of his receiving wine from the Christian maiden is depicted; the figure of Yūsuf in the many scenes of the Yūsuf and Zulaykhā story, and figures of male Sufis. See, for instance, Figure 29b ("Shaykh San'an and the Christian Girl," c. 1830, p. 84), and Plate 85 ("Nur 'Ali Shah," Ismail Jalayir, c. 1865, p. 259), both in Diba and Ekhtiar, *Royal Persian Paintings*. Depictions of Yūsuf are numerous, especially the scene where Zulaykhā invites women of the town to come and admire Yūsuf's beauty.

41. See, for instance, Sir Henry Layard (who traveled to the region in 1840–1842), *Early Adventures in Persia, Susiana, and Babylonia* (London: John Murray, 1887), Vol. I, pp. 332–333.

42. Tancoigne, *A Narrative of a Journal*, p. 67; George Keppel, *Personal Narrative of a Journey from India to England . . . in the Year 1824* (London: Henry Colburn, 1827), Vol. II, p. 47.

43. Tancoigne, *A Narrative of a Journal*, pp. 67–68.

Part 2

Globalization Then and Now

6

From Liberalism to Liberal Imperialism: Lord Cromer and the First Wave of Globalization in Egypt

Roger Owen

The recent emphasis on globalization has encouraged an interest in comparisons with what might be called the first wave of modern globalism in the decades before World War I.[1] Then, too, there was a similar process of an intensified global interconnectedness, manifest most obviously in the economic sphere but also characterized, as now, by the impact of a growing political and cultural interaction, promoted by some groups and interests and found intensely threatening by others. It was also characterized, then as now, by the problem of international debt and the strong belief that economic good heath was to be found in free trade, low taxes, and limited government.

There are significant differences between the two periods of intensified globalization as well. Certainly the most important is that the first wave was accompanied by the rise of the new imperialism, which brought much of the non-European world under direct European control. This, in turn, encouraged a growing intra-imperialist rivalry based in large measure on an awareness of unequal power and the need to catch up with, and if possible overtake, the front-runners, Britain and France. One result was the appearance of more intense forms of nationalism, protectionism, and particularism, as well as of a strong emphasis on the notion of a racial hierarchy in which a country's place in the world was largely determined by the color and, to a lesser extent, by the ethnicity and religion of its people. In the British context, with which I am most familiar, this late-nineteenth-century worldview is usually contrasted unfavorably with the much more universalist, free trading, anticolonial orthodoxies promoted among the middle classes at midcentury by the likes of Richard Cobden, John Bright, and, later, William Ewart Gladstone.[2]

What I would like to attempt in this chapter is to investigate the marriage of globalization with imperialism in terms of the life of one of those men, Evelyn Baring (later Lord Cromer), who lived through many of the essential stages of this process as a result of his service in Egypt. In the early part of his life, first as a young officer in the British garrison on Corfu, then as private secretary to the viceroy of India (1872–1876) and finance member of the viceroy's council (1880–1883), as well as during his first period in Egypt (1876–1880), he was a firm believer in free trade, in the right of self-determination, and in the kind of human universalism to be found in thinkers from Voltaire to John Stuart Mill. He approved, for example, of the transfer of the Ionian Islands to Greek control; he actively promoted local fiscal self-government in India; and he came back to Egypt in 1883 a firm believer that that country, too, should be returned to the government of its own ruling class.[3]

But then began a process of rapid personal change in which a growing belief in the importance of continuing the occupation, combined with an almost visceral distrust of Gladstone's handling of matters of the empire, caused him to follow the path pursued by so many of the old Whigs from liberalism to liberal imperialism. This, in turn, led to an increasing emphasis on the racial inferiority of the Egyptians as part of his justification for a continued British presence, as well as to policies designed to reduce the amount of international control in Egypt in such a way as to leave it, in form if not in name, a British protectorate.[4] Even his continuing belief in the central importance of free trade now had an imperial component. It allowed him to believe that there was no basic conflict of economic interest between Britain and its colonies and protectorates. And it could be used to demonstrate his concern for the welfare of the peasant majority in India and Egypt who, under his aegis, were able to benefit from duty-free imports of food and clothing, whether they understood the economic principles involved or not.[5]

Historical Biography: Comments on the State of the Field

The use of biography to illustrate some of the prominent features of a particular age has long been part of the Anglo-American historical tradition. In its modern form, it can be said to have begun with the one- or two-volume "lives" of Victorian Age public figures, which—though generally designed to place their subjects in the best possible light—often contained enough material from the individuals' personal letters and diaries to provide unguarded insights into their feelings, their ideas, and their position within the governing elite. What was generally missing, however, was any real concern for the political and social context within which such lives had been led, no doubt on the valid assumption that this would already be perfectly familiar to most members of the then much smaller reading public.

Attitudes began to change around World War I, marked by the introduction of a new note of openness and honesty in the writing of the lives of public figures and a willingness to subject their actions to a greater degree of analysis and criticism. This trend is generally associated with the publication of Lytton Strachey's *Eminent Victorians* (1918) in which the lives of four exemplary and much revered British figures—Cardinal Manning, Florence Nightingale, Dr. Thomas Arnold, and General Gordon—were presented in an unusually bad light. But it is probably better seen in the larger context provided by the growing interest in psychological analysis based on the work of Sigmund Freud, as well as by a greater willingness to view knowledge of the personalities and, to some extent, the private lives of public men and women as essential to the understanding of their political behavior. This did not necessarily have to involve an exploration of dark secrets, like Strachey's emphasis on Gordon's drinking, Florence Nightingale's later senility, or Manning's self-righteous manipulation of the truth. The task could be accomplished more gracefully by a writer like Harold Nicolson whose *Curzon: The Last Phase 1919–1925* (1934) demonstrates how much there is to learn from a close analysis of the personal strengths and weaknesses of an important British statesman when it comes to understanding the successes and failures of Britain's post–World War I diplomacy, especially in the Middle East.

However, it was really only with the emergence of the French Annales school of historians after World War II that biography emerged as an important tool for an understanding, not just of the political but also the sociocultural history of an age. One good example is Lucien Febvre's *Philippe II et Franche-Comté* (1911) in which a study of the king's life is used to highlight large questions concerning the social dynamics of his day. Enthusiasm for this new initiative quickly found its way to the United States, leading to such seminal works as Felix Gilbert's *Machiavelli and Gucciardini: Politics and History in Sixteenth-Century Florence* (1965). A few years earlier, David Landes's *Bankers and Pashas* (1958) had amply demonstrated how the lives of two Frenchmen could be used to illustrate important aspects of Egypt's slide into bankruptcy in the 1860s as well as to understand the force of the unequal power relationships that drove most of these developments along.

Later, when both French and U.S. historians seemed to lose interest in this biographical approach, it continued to thrive in Britain where, for example, a central feature of the heated discussion concerning the economic, political, and ideological causes of the seventeenth-century civil war was the research into the lives of some of its key participants conducted by someone like Christopher Hill in his *Intellectual Origins of the English*

Revolution (1965) and *Levellers and the English Revolution* (1983). Others to write with a similar focus on the intersection between biography and a rapidly changing sociopolitical context were E. P. Thompson, for example, in his *Romantics: England in the Revolutionary Age* (1997), and Lawrence Stone in *Crisis of the Aristocracy 1558–1641* (1965).

More recently there has been a marriage of the older, more popular type of biography with these newer forms of more highly contextualized works in order to demonstrate how particular individuals or families negotiated their way through the difficult waters of nineteenth- and twentieth-century public life, both influencing, and being influenced by, the major currents of their time. One particular subset takes its cue from late-nineteenth-century global issues that have assumed new contemporary importance, such as banking and international finance or the management of international debt. As far as international finance is concerned, one could cite Niall Ferguson's *The World's Banker: The History of the House of Rothschild* (1998) and Jean Strouse's *Morgan: American Financier* (1999), with the latter's arresting account of how, in the absence of an interventionist central bank, Morgan himself used his own vast resources and personal contacts to contain the 1907 world financial crisis. As for the use of biography to explore both the development of notions of managing economic relations between countries and those moments, like 1919 and 1944–1945, when wholesale changes can be effected, one could point to Robert Skidelsky's three-volume life of the influential British economist John Maynard Keynes.[6]

In the case of Evelyn Baring—whose own official biography was published in 1932 by the Marquess of Zetland—I propose to focus on one particular period of his life as a means of highlighting some of the global themes outlined above and the way they shaped one man's response to the rapidly changing world around him. After a brief introduction to his worldview just before and then just after his return to Egypt in 1883, I will then go on to look in somewhat greater detail at some of the central issues that emerged during the particularly tense decade, 1895–1904, in which he worked to remove much of the old system of international control over the Egyptian economy as a prelude to what he hoped would be its replacement with a much more direct type of British rule.

Cromer's Worldview in the Early 1880s

Cromer spent two periods in Egypt between 1877 and 1880, first as one of the four commissioners of the Caisse de la Dette Publique, then in the latter part of 1879 and the first months of 1880 as one of the two controllers who directed the Anglo-French management of Egyptian finance. As he himself described the system in a report written in April 1880, the controllers had no "executive authority" but acted as advisers to the government with "full powers to investigate all financial affairs." They worked closely with the chief minister, Riaz Pasha—Cromer notes they occupied adjoining offices in the Ministry of Finance—directing the process of reform from behind the cover provided by the ruler and his cabinet. This, for him, was obviously the ideal arrangement and one that he believed might allow the Egyptian government to preserve itself from direct foreign control.[7] It was this arrangement, too, that he recommended should be revived after the strong challenge to foreign control mounted by forces under the leadership of Colonel Ahmad 'Urabi had been overcome by British troops in the late summer of 1882.[8]

Nevertheless, Cromer had only been back in Egypt for a few months in the autumn of 1883 when he convinced himself that the ruler's authority had been undermined to such an extent that the old system could not be successfully revived. A less charitable view might be that he had quickly come to the conclusion that he himself could not manage things in the same old, behind-the-scenes way. In his mind there now seemed no midpoint between indirect control and the establishment of a British protectorate. And it was the latter that he now began to maneuver toward through his persistent advocacy of a permanent military occupation.

Coming as he did from colonial India, and relying as he did on the service of many advisers recruited from the Indian service, it was not surprising that his many local critics believed that India was now to be his one and only model.[9] But this does seem to have been quite the case. Whatever he may have wished in his heart of hearts, he was now a member of the British diplomatic service, constantly in touch with the British Foreign Office, and so made increasingly aware of the international complexity of the British position in Egypt. The French, bitter at having had to surrender their position as joint managers of the country's finance, used their seat on the Caisse de la Dette to exercise a regular veto over proposals of which they disapproved. Meanwhile, the German chancellor, Otto von Bismarck, proved particularly adept at using diplomatic support over matters Egyptian to extract British concessions elsewhere.

In these circumstance, there was nothing for Cromer to do but to acknowledge what he already knew—that the world was connected by a web of international interests—even while he might rail against many of its Egyptian manifestations.[10] As he described the situation in the chapter in *Modern Egypt* devoted to "The International Administrations":

> Trade, with its handmaids, the railway and the telegraph, does not appear to have bound nations together in any closer bonds of amity than existed in the days of slow locomotion and communication. On the other hand,

> the European body politic has become more sensitive than heretofore. National interests tend towards cosmopolitanism, however much national sentiments and aspirations may tend towards exclusive patriotism. The whole world is quickly informed of any incident which may occur in any part of the globe. Not only in the cabinet of every Minister, but in the office of every newspaper editor the questions to which its occurrence instantly give rise are, how does this circumstance affect the affairs of my country? What course should be taken to safeguard ours interests? It is more difficult than heretofore to segregate a quarrel between any two states. In a certain sense Europeans, in spite of themselves, have become members of a single family, though not always a happy family. They are all oppressed by one common dread, and that is that some accident may precipitate a general war. . . . A certain power of acting together has thus been developed among the nations and Governments of Europe, and it cannot be doubted that the world has benefitted by the change. In all the larger affairs of state, internationalism constitutes a guarantee of peace.[11]

But what about the situation outside Europe? As he is quick to point out, "internationalism" was also present in many non-European territories as well. In his words:

> [C]ases sometimes arise which involve prolonged supervision and control in the interests of the European powers, but which do not justify exclusive action on the part of any one of them, or which, if they are to justify it, are of a nature not to allow exclusive action without a risk of discord in respect of the particular nation by whom it is to be exercised.[12]

Then comes the special pleading. In Egypt, he asserts:

> [T]he results cannot be said to be encouraging to those who believe in the efficacy of international action in administrative matters. What has been proved is that international administrations possess admirable negative qualities. They are formidable checks to all action and the reason why they are so is that, when any action is proposed, objections of one kind or another generally occur to some members of the international body. . . . Hence, for all purposes of action, administrative internationalism may be said to tend towards the creation of administrative impotence.[13]

As we now know, these words were actually written at a time (probably in the mid-1890s) when Cromer himself was actively planning a campaign against the various forms of internationalism—the Caisse de la Dette, the Mixed Tribunals and the remains of the Anglo-French dual control as they affected the railways, the State Domains and the Daira Saniyya—that he believed stood in the way of his exclusive management of Egypt's finances in the interest of policies that would so benefit Egyptians of all classes that they would have little interest in supporting either the khedive or the country's nationalist politicians.[14] In what follows, I would like to look more closely at some aspects of this campaign in order to learn more about the way in which Cromer juggled, and was himself influenced by, a variety of powerful forces, both international and (in his terminology) "exclusive," as they interacted in one particular locale, Cairo, and during one particularly intense period, 1896–1907. I will begin by saying something about the situation in Cairo itself before going on to analyze the major events of those years.

Cairo in the Late 1890s

By the mid-1890s, what is best described as the Anglo-Egyptian government was firmly in the hands of Lord Cromer and a small group of Britons of whom, from an economic point of view, the most important was the financial adviser, Sir Elwin Palmer, up to 1898, and then Sir Eldon Gorst, 1898–1904. Although Cromer himself tended to emphasize that his was very much a one-man band, other senior officials had a fair degree of latitude to make policy (as we shall see), particularly at times of crisis (for example, the events leading up to the reconquest of the Sudan) or when (as happened in 1898) Cromer was preoccupied by his own personal concerns, notably his first wife's fatal illness. Other important actors and interests included the various local representatives of the European powers, notably the six council members of the Caisse de la Dette, the bondholders (the vast majority of whom were French), and the European and locally based bankers, financiers, and investors of whom the most prominent were Sir Ernest Cassel, Ernest Cronier, and their Egyptian associates among the largely Jewish families such as those of Suarès, Rolo, Cattaui, and de Menasce.

All were united by various alliances and understandings at various levels—international, national, and personal—in which three sets of perceptions were of particular importance. First, all accepted that the British presence was a necessary safeguard for the proper payment of the interest on the debt and, therefore, of the value of the shares in the debt itself. This understanding extended to the French government and its local representatives who tended to use their position on the Caisse, not—as Cromer saw it—to block every one of his initiatives but as a mechanism for maintaining what remained of French interest in an Egypt managed by Britain.[15] Second, the economic progress of Egypt, combined with Cromer's increasing willingness to award public works contracts to private entrepreneurs, made a personal association with the senior British officials in the government ever more attractive. To say the very least, it seems to have released an explosion of entrepreneurial imagination. Third, it had become a well-known fact that Cromer was anxious to increase the flow of British capital to Egypt.[16]

What also gave the financial scene in Cairo its special flavor was the seasonal nature of international contact there. By in large, Europeans came to Egypt for the winter, while Cromer and his colleagues spent long summers in Europe when they had plenty of opportunity to maintain contacts and to make new deals. Even a momentary glance at Gorst's diary reveals something of the intensity of this interaction. For example, in 1901, he records that he met Cassel in London and then went to stay with him at his house near Newmarket in July, and then met him again in Aswan in November and several times in Cairo in January 1902, with the same pattern repeated the following summer and winter including their joint presence at the opening of the Aswan Dam in December 1902.[17] Of course, such opportunities also existed for the same kinds of people in many other places as well—London combined with Cowes, Ascot, and the shooting seasons; or Washington, D.C., and Newport, Rhode Island, for example—but there seems to have been something extra intense and extra cosmopolitan about the Cairo scene, especially when it was combined with the almost obligatory voyage up the Nile in December or January.

The Economic Impact of the Sudan Campaign, 1896–1904

As most histories assert, Cromer himself was most upset by the British government's decision to send a military expedition up the Nile to assist in the restoration of Italian prestige after news of the battle of Adowa in March 1896.[18] He had already determined to go ahead with plans to build the first Aswan Dam and was unhappy at the prospect of having to spend Egyptian funds on the military expedition as well. However, he soon came to see that there were certain advantages to be gained from the situation, particularly after his request to be given £E500,000 from the reserve fund had been challenged by the French (and Russian) members of the Caisse. From then on, events began to turn his way with a vengeance, even if it remains unclear (to me) just how much he, himself, was actually responsible for creating the opportunities then presented. It seems, for example, that Horatio Herbert Kitchener was just as effective as Cromer—perhaps even more so—in persuading the British chancellor of the Exchequer to offer the loan, later turned into a grant, which played the key role in getting round the French veto and so inaugurating the process of putting an end to the blocking power of the Caisse.[19]

However, Cromer himself is probably to be praised (if praise is the right word) for three other vital ingredients. One was his ability to persuade the British foreign secretary, Lord Salisbury, that preparations for the construction of the Aswan Dam should proceed, pari passu, with the reconquest of the Sudan, on the grounds that the increase in agricultural taxation it would promote would help Egypt greatly to pay its share of the costs of the campaign.[20] A second was his long cultivation of Sir Ernest Cassel, who was to play a vital role in the complicated deal with Messrs. Ayrd and Company, the firm of contractors that actually built the dam.[21] This had the additional advantage of ending the virtual monopoly that the Rothschilds had exercised over loans to Egypt and introducing a player who, if not totally committed to British interests, was much more malleable than the Rothschilds had ever allowed themselves to be.[22] Although Pat Thane asserts that the reasons why Cassel took over the management of the Sudan loan are "uncertain," it would seem from Cromer's correspondence with Lord Salisbury and his nephew, Lord Revelstoke, that he (Cassel) was more willing than they to run the slight risk involved in raising funds that went beyond Egypt's internationally agreed borrowing powers.[23] Third, Cromer's obvious commitment to the introduction of British capital not only gave the green light to Cassel and those British officials like Palmer who joined (and were encouraged to join) his camp but also provided the incentive for influential local financiers like Raphael Suarès to hedge their bets with France by involving themselves much more closely with British-sponsored interests.[24] This had the further advantage, from Cromer's point of view, of increasing the discomfiture of the French government, which soon came to the conclusion that it could do little to reverse the adverse tide of events without losing the support of both bondholders and local capitalists, all of whom had a vested interest in the further progress of the Egyptian economy.

The years 1897–1898 saw three related developments that testify both to the possibilities presented by the new situation and, from Cromer's own point of view, to some of its major disadvantages as well. These were the Aswan Dam contract, the establishment of the National Bank of Egypt, and the agreement to liquidate the Daira Saniyya loan. All three involved Sir Ernest Cassel, and all three were actively promoted by Sir Elwin Palmer, safe in the knowledge that he was following the Cromer line. Cromer was known to be particularly anxious to find a way of financing the Aswan Dam not subject to international veto.[25] He was equally anxious that the new bank should be an Anglo-Egyptian institution.[26] And he was certainly ready to see the end of any one of the Anglo-French administrations as a result of debt liquidation, even if, as Samir Saul asserts (basing himself on French sources), Cromer himself was not properly informed of the exact details of the Saniyya agreement signed in July 1898.[27] Later, however, he was privately very critical of various aspects of the deal, notably what he terms the "scandalous profits" that its promoters made from the sale of the Daira Saniyya lands.[28]

It is difficult not to assume, though probably impossible to prove, that the latter two initiatives were in some sense a reward for Cassel's help with the first. That they were also an obvious reward for Palmer himself, who held shares in the Daira Saniyya Company and who also resigned from the government to become the first director of the bank, was something that Cromer was forced to recognize in due course.[29] So, too, did Gorst, Palmer's successor as financial adviser, who quickly realized that his own future was best served by becoming a better interpreter and executor of Cromer's own wishes than his predecessor.[30] And it was the two of them together who formed the vital partnership that, building on the momentum created by the French defeats in 1898, went on to solidify the British position still further by means of a series of successful negotiations with the Caisse over the release of reserve funds, followed by the Franco-Egyptian commercial convention of 1902 and then the Anglo-French Treaty of 1904, which gave Britain carte blanche as far as control over Egypt's finances was concerned. While their initial plan had been to try to marginalize what was left of the power of the Caisse by another huge conversion, which would have gotten rid of much of the remainder of the Egyptian debt, Cromer himself was quick to see that the high-level Anglo-French maneuvering over Morocco—a process with which he himself was closely involved—provided an even better opportunity to persuade the French government to abandon what was left of its veto rights over the way Egypt spent its taxes.

The lessons drawn by Cromer and Gorst from the deals made in 1897–1898 were also of great importance. In 1899 Gorst was instrumental in preventing Cassel from pushing though the same kind of scheme for the domains land as he had for the Daira Saniyya, preferring, instead, to sell the land over time to the profit of the government itself.[31] Subsequently, both he and Cromer also turned down a variety of schemes to privatize the Egyptian railways on the grounds that, where there was a natural monopoly, private enterprise, deprived of the stimulus of competition, had no obvious advantages over state management.[32] In both cases, this had the additional advantage of providing a sop to the French by way of a continuation of the existing Anglo-French management, a strategy of conciliation now possible once the major instruments of French intervention had been removed.

It was, perhaps, inevitable that the new situation should also encourage a more clearly defined notion of state interest, albeit one in which it was Cromer himself who continued to decide what was best for the Egyptian economy. One aspect was a growing distrust of both the excesses of private capital and its ability to get in the way of his own schemes, as manifest by his great irritation at Cassel's loan of £E500,000 to the khedive in 1904 in exchange for certain "concessions."[33] More important was his sense of possession and control once the British could manage things on their own as they thought best. This provided an incentive to amend some of the economic principles that Cromer himself held dear, notably by way of the government assistance offered to the failing sugar company in 1905. It also encouraged thoughts of a more national approach to Egypt's financial problems, as with Cromer's (private) suggestion to Lord Revelstoke of Baring Brothers that what Egypt needed was not the badly managed National Bank—still under Palmer's direction and criticized even by Cassel for offering its board members nonperforming loans—but something that he styled a "banks of banks," a lender of last resort ready to impose some proper discipline on all the rest.[34]

This, in turn, contributed to Cromer's developing notion of where an Anglo-Egyptian government's legitimacy might lie, one based on acting in the true interests of what he called all the "dwellers" of the Nile. Such views may have been first expressed in the early draft of *Modern Egypt.* They were certainly present in his farewell speech to Gorst when he left Egyptian service for the Foreign Office in 1904. There he praised his departing colleague as someone who had carried out the policy of "Egypt for the Egyptians" in the only sense that that policy was practicable and beneficial to all concerned. Such a policy, he argued, was not one that implied that Egypt was to be governed solely by native Egyptians. Rather, "It is a policy that does imply that the touchstone to be applied to every Egyptian question is to inquire how far this or that proposal is in the true interests of the dwellers of Egypt, of whatsoever nationality and creed they may be."[35]

Further gloss can be found in a private letter to St. Loe Strachey, the editor of *The Spectator*, in 1906 in which Cromer compares his vision of Egypt and its people to that of Wilfred Blunt. When Blunt spoke of the Egyptians, he meant the Muslims: "But when I speak of Egypt I mean all the dwellers in Egypt. . . . My aim is to fuse them all together and to move in the direction of making a nation of them, including the Europeans who have become more or less Egyptianised."[36]

The aim, as Cromer saw it, was twofold: to reduce the role of what he called "internationalism" by moving, not toward nationalism but to his version of a "cosmopolitanism" in which representatives of the different groups resident in Egypt were to be elected to a second, non-Egyptian legislative council on the basis of interest rather than national origin. Hence, in a memorandum, several versions of which were drafted between March and June 1905, he suggested that there be fourteen such elected representatives (two Mixed Court judges and eight persons representing commercial and four representing landed interests) plus eleven government nominees.[37]

Once in place, the various powers with capitulatory rights would be expected to delegate their collective veto to this new body, although Britain would still retain its own as a guarantee that the rights of foreign residents would continue to be respected. The council would then discuss legislative proposals put to it by the Egyptian government, which, if agreeable and not subject to a British veto, would become the law of the land and, equally important, acceptable to the Mixed Courts.

The logic is clear: An Egypt no longer under internationalist control was to be governed exclusively by Britain, but in the interests of what Cromer had come to see as a polyglot population from all the corners of the globe. Egyptian nationalism was to be sidelined, giving time for the operation of one of Cromer's pet views that the Egyptians would only develop the skills needed to administer themselves if they learned from the Europeans and Europeanized natives who lived among them. It also followed from his own understanding of the complexities of Egypt's special situation. For one thing, he believed that the European powers would never agree to the abolition of the Mixed Tribunals unless their own resident nationals felt quite comfortable in Egypt. For another, what he took to be Egyptian interest could only be properly protected by maintaining the complicated balancing act in which the country needed to present itself as a national entity in some contexts (for example, in order to protect the Suez Canal from the designs of French or Russian admirals) and as under a species of international control in others (for example, the use of the notion of a condominium to avoid the extension of the capitulations to the Sudan.[38]

The Years of Anticlimax and Failure, 1905–1907

There is no doubt that the Anglo-French agreement of 1904 was a particular personal triumph for Lord Cromer, representing not only the culmination of his long campaign to reduce French official influence over Egypt's finances but also a platform for the further consolidation of British control.[39] However, in the event, the latter proved extremely difficult to realize. On the one hand, successive British governments refused to take the basic step that, in Cromer's opinion, was necessary to clear away the last vestiges of international control, that is, to come out directly with a statement that the occupation was going to be permanent. On the other hand, there was an embarrassing list of difficulties and disasters, including mounting criticism of Cromerian policies from both Egyptian nationalists and British radicals, the Taba border dispute with Ottoman Turkey, the mishandling of the Dinshawai affair, and finally the economic crisis beginning just before Cromer's own resignation in March 1907. Indeed, such was the growth of popular opposition to Cromer himself that the authorities were worried enough to take special precautions to prevent anti-Cromerian outbursts on the streets of Cairo during his last few days there.[40]

Part of this was the result of events quite beyond Cromer's own control—for example, the impact of the sweeping Liberal electoral victory of 1906. His failing health was another factor, as was his sense of not being properly supported by his British colleagues. Indeed, as he was to assert in an addition to his *Biographical Notes* (1905), he made a great mistake in staying on in Egypt after his health had begun to break down during his last years.[41] Nevertheless, it is also important to note that there was something deeply flawed about his attempt to use the post-1904 freedom to match economic progress with a new political structure in Egypt. As can be seen from his last two annual reports, he was (in Peter Mellini's words) "groping for some sort of new direction."[42] However, this was not one of allowing the Egyptians a larger share in their own administration but involved, instead, the rather paradoxical combination of greater participation by both the British and the local Europeans in Egyptian rule.

How is this to be explained? Clearly it had much to do with the fact that Cromer had been in Egypt too long, that he had grown more and more autocratic over time, that the primacy he attached to economics over politics produced a number of significant blind spots in his grasp of political affairs, and, finally, that he had allowed his prejudices about Egyptians and their administrative incompetence to harden into dogma. Nevertheless, there were what might be called structural factors involved as well. One was the way in which he had managed to detach Egypt almost completely from governmental oversight from London. As he boasted to his nephew, Lord Revelstoke, in 1903: "The main reason why Egypt has been a success is that practically the system has been one of Egyptian 'home rule.' I very rarely refer anything to London, and whenever I do, I always tell them what they have to do. They are most pleased to know."[43]

There is much here that is also reminiscent of the dispute Cromer himself had been involved in, as a loyal adjutant of Lord Northbrook, in his unsuccessful attempt to prevent Lord Salisbury, the new secretary of state for India in 1874, from dictating policy from London, on the grounds that it was only the men on the spot who could understand Indian interests properly.[44] Government for such men was a matter of expertise and local knowledge, not easily shared either with the democratically elected governments in London or with the (in their eyes) even less expert local politicians. But this, of course, was to cut them off from the free play of criticism and from the stimulus provided by receiving contradictory flows of advice.

A second structural factor was the continued existence of an international dimension that, via the capitulations and the presence of the foreign communities, remained beyond Cromer's power to control. He could circumvent it in Sudan by the simple instrument of the condominium. But not in Egypt where any basic change in status required pan-European assent. Hence, it made a kind of sense to try to disarm the foreign communities, not only by offering them a generous share of investment opportunities but also by trying to devise a mechanism in which they would feel politically and legally safe enough to abandon the protection of their special status. My own conclusion is that thirty years of wrestling with the international conundrum in Egypt had encouraged him to miss the nationalist wood for the small clumps of foreign trees.

A final point concerns Cromer's understanding of the central role played by the management of the press and of the manipulation of public opinion in imperial government. He first learned some of the basic techniques in India from 1872 onward and, later, perfected more of them in Egypt with a system of subsidies, leaks, and planted articles, all in the interests of making the best possible presentation of the Anglo-Egyptian government's case. But two can play the same game. And he seems to have become more than usually discomforted by the way in which the Egyptian nationalists fed special items of news to their radical supporters in England like the member of Parliament John Robertson, or the journalist Theodore Rothstein. One ill-considered response was to try to obtain the support of Christian groups in Britain, notably the Church Missionary Society, to counter liberal opposition to his policies on the basis of their shared commitment to the protection and improved well-being of the Copts.[45] It would seem that for Cromer, as for others like Samuel Huntington nearly a century later, an essential component of globalization was the manipulation of transglobal religious identities.

Conclusion

I have taken as my starting point Cromer's own understanding of the nature of the period of global internationalism through which he was living. License for this comes from my own observation that references to present-day globalization are generally more in the nature of an exhortation or an ideological intervention than a serious attempt to define a concrete historical process. Nevertheless, this understanding did not come out of the air, as it were, but was the result of his own experience of government in one particular part of the globe where the contending forces of late-nineteenth-century internationalism and imperial exclusivity were particularly apparent. Partly because of this, partly because of his habitual attempt to reduce the practice of government to a set of hard and fast principles, Cromer made a serious effort to use such experience in the service of what he took to be British national interest, but within the constraints (as well as opportunities) provided by various types of transnational forces he encountered, whether those stemming from international commitments and the European balance of power or from the various combinations of national and international capital as they presented themselves in an Egyptian context.

Like all such inevitably partial understandings, it enabled him to recognize certain trends and not others. Like Lord Salisbury of the 1890s for whose diplomatic skills he came to have the greatest respect, he tried to see Britain's worldwide interests as interconnected and in many ways dependent upon one another.[46] His comments on the decline of Egypt's traditional crafts and services show him to be a keen observer of the process that would later be called "modernization." Nevertheless, for a whole variety of reasons, he was unable to recognize either a growing Egyptian nationalism or any kind of native ability at self-administration. This was an essential ingredient in his basic—and endlessly repeated—justification for the maintenance of the British occupation. Power and permanence were what mattered in situations where local consent was never likely to be obtained. Just as important, his blindness also stemmed from what he took to be the failure of the local governing class combined with his aristocratic distaste for democracy and his marked distrust of the administrative abilities of the representatives of the native groups within Egyptian society, which he dissected in *Modern Egypt* with such pseudosociological zeal.

If we step back from these immediate concerns, we can also see that Cromer was engaged in the not unfamiliar (to us) task of trying to define what was state interest in the context of an open economy dependent on foreign capital for its further development. No doubt, a native Egyptian government, had one been allowed, would have looked at the situation in a somewhat different light. But Cromer, being a foreigner, as well as a representative of the British national interest, was driven, logically I would argue, toward an early version of the notion of an international "trusteeship" in which his right to manage Egypt was based on his ability to convince the European powers that he was doing it in everyone's best interests, including that of the Egyptians themselves. This has always been a difficult claim to sustain for long. Perhaps the best we can say is that it must have looked somewhat more convincing than the one made contemporaneously by King Leopold of the Belgians over the Congo.

The same long-distance lens may also allow us better to determine the longer-term trajectory involved. In Egypt's "developmental phase" under Ismail Pasha, the state—as well as the ruler as state—made sure to accumulate large resources of land, agricultural and manufacturing capacity, and public utilities (for example, the railways), which it was then forced to surrender to international control as a result of its international bankruptcy. Then, when the value of these same assets began to rise as a result of Cromer's successful management of the export economy, they provided a magnet for local and foreign financiers culminating in what could have been simply a free-for-all sell-off from the late 1890s onward. However, this in turn prompted Cromer and Gorst to attempt to formulate a new version of state interest in which the remaining resources were guarded and managed in such a way that the state itself was able to maintain control over policy subject to the usual constraints to be found in any open, capitalist, early-twentieth-century economy.

In final conclusion, what I have tried to do in this chapter is, first, to illustrate the importance of the global or international component in the study of the pre-1914 Middle East and, second, to demonstrate one of the ways that this might be done by concentrating on the experience of one central figure as he encounters, and then tries to manage, the interplay of powerful global forces in one central, contested space. It is my belief that this opens up a new perspective, encouraging us to go beyond old narratives and to pose new questions. It can also allow us to draw strength from both contrasts and comparisons with the second wave of globalization that we are experiencing all around us just now.

Notes

1. For example, Paul Hirst and Graeme Thompson, *Globalisation in Question* (Cambridge, UK: Polity Press, 1996); Paul Bairoch, "Globalisation, Myths, and Realities," in R. Boyer and D. Drache (eds.), *States Against Markers: The Limits of Globalisation* (London: Routledge 1996), pp. 173–192.

2. Thomas R. Metcalf refers to this "crisis of liberalism" in his "Ideologies of the Raj," in *The New Cambridge History of India*, Vol. III, No. 4 (Cambridge, UK: Cambridge University Press, 1994), pp. 47, 52–55. See, also, Bernard Semmel, *The Liberal Ideal and the Demon of Empire: Theories of Imperialism from Adam Smith to Lenin* (Baltimore: Johns Hopkins University Press, 1993).

3. See the views he expressed in his "Very Confidential Memorandum on the Present Situation in Egypt," Simla, 18 September 1882, Public Records Office [hereafter PRO], Foreign Office [hereafter FO] 633/99, which include the statement that, whatever the faults of 'Urabi himself: "I do not see that the Egyptians, considered as a nation, have done to forfeit their right to self-government."

4. These views are most succinctly expressed in Evelyn Baring, *Modern Egypt*, Vol. II (New York: The Macmillan Company, 1908), Chapters 34–37. But they can be found expressed in more or less the same terms in a dispatch written on the subject of "Who are the Egyptians?" in the late 1880s: Sir E. Baring to the Marquis of Salisbury, Cairo, 14 December 1887. Egypt. Confidential 1168, a copy of which can be found in PRO, FO 633/98.

5. For example, Evelyn Baring, "Recent Events in India," *The Nineteenth Century* 14 (October 1883): 587–588.

6. Robert Skidelsky, Vol. I, *John Maynard Keynes: Hopes Betrayed, 1883–1920* (London: Macmillan, 1983), Vol. II, *John Maynard Keynes: The Economist as Saviour, 1920–1937* (London: Macmillan, 1992), and Vol. III, forthcoming.

7. Evelyn Baring, "Memorandum on the Present Situation of Affairs in Egypt," PRO, FO 78/3142, 387b–390a.

8. Evelyn Baring, "Very Confidential Memorandum on the Present Situation in Egypt," 18 September 1882, Cromer Papers, PRO, FO 633/99.

9. Amira Sonbol (ed.), *The Last Khedive of Egypt: Memoirs of Abbas Hilmi II* (Reading, UK: Ithaca, 1998), pp. 248–249; Nubar Pasha, *Mémoires de Nubar Pasha* (with Introduction and Notes by Mirrit Butros Ghali) (Beirut: Librairie du Liban, 1983), p. 507.

10. For his views on free trade versus protectionism, see Cromer to St. Loe Strachey (editor of *The Spectator*), 10 July 1903 (?), PRO, FO 633/7.

11. Baring, *Modern Egypt,* pp. 301–304.

12. Ibid.

13. Ibid.

14. Cromer sent a draft of *Modern Egypt* to Milner for comment in 1896.

15. See, in particular, the compelling argument in Samir Saul, *La France et l'Egypte de 1882 à 1914: Intérêts économiques et implications politiques* (Paris: Ministère de l'Economie, des Finances et de l'Industrie, 1997), chapter 14. Saul's argument is well supported by the views of the French ambassador to London as reported by Lord Salisbury in his dispatch to Lord Cromer, London, 20 February 1896, PRO, FO 633/7.

16. For example, Cromer's letter to Carver outlining the importance he attached to establishing a British chamber of commerce in Egypt, Cairo, 18 December 1895, PRO, FO 633/8.

17. Notes relating to Gorst's diary kindly lent to me by Dr. Peter Mellini.

18. For example, John Marlowe, *Cromer in Egypt* (London: Elek Books, 1970), pp. 195–196.

19. Ibid., p. 207.

20. Ibid., pp. 226–227.

21. For information about Cassel's financial activities, see Pat Thane, "Financiers and the British State: The Case of Sir Ernest Cassel," *Business History* 28, no. 1 (January 1986): 80–99. According to Thane (p. 83), his first involvement with Egypt seems to have been in connection with the 1888/89 loan. Some time thereafter he took to spending the winter months in Cairo, often in the company of the family of his American business partner, Jacob Schiff. See Kurt Grunwald, "'Windsor-Cassel'—the Last Court Jew," *Leo Baeck Institute Year Book* 14 (1969): 137.

22. Until 1898, Cromer often complained about how difficult it was to deal with the Rothschilds but, nevertheless, recognized that (1) they were the most acceptable to the powers represented on Caisse, and (2) they had sufficient power to block any other deal. For example, Baring to Goschen, Cairo, 11 February 1888, PRO, FO 633/9. Also Cromer to Salisbury, Cairo, 4 December 1897, PRO, FO 633/6.

23. Thane, "Financiers and the British State," p. 86. Salisbury to Cromer, London, 19 February 1897, and Cromer to Revelstoke, Cairo, 2 February 1898, PRO, FO 633/7.

24. Saul, *La France et l'Egypte*, pp. 640, 647–651.

25. Ibid., p. 640. See also Cromer to Lord John Revelstoke, Cairo, 2 February 1898, PRO, FO 633/8.

26. Cromer to Lord Hillingdon, Cairo, 21 May 1898, PRO, FO 633/8.

27. Saul, *La France et l'Egypte*, p. 651. Saul does not give an exact source, but

a reading of this particular section of his account would suggest that the information must have come from Gay-Lussac, the French controller of the Daira Saniyya.

28. Cromer to Revelstoke, Cairo, 6 December 1903, *Baring Archive* (London), 203076, "Partners" File, Supplementary Set. Cromer was also critical of Dr. Crookshank, the British controller of the Daira Saniyya for purchasing Daira lands for his own private gain. See Cromer to Crookshank, Cairo, 28 June 1900, PRO, FO 633/8.

29. Saul, *La France et l'Egypte*, p. 648. Jeffrey G. Collins also asserts that promoters fraudulently maintained that Daira Saniyya was not making a profit, *The Egyptian Elite Under Cromer, 1882–1907* (Berlin: Klaus Schwarz Verlag, 1984), p. 351. But he offers no evidence. It is more likely that the promoters simply stated that profits could have been higher. However, the main point is that it suited a Cromer-led government at this time to liquidate Egypt's debts in whatever way possible.

30. Peter Mellini, *Sir Eldon Gorst: The Overshadowed Proconsul* (Stanford, Calif.: Hoover Institute Press, 1977), pp. 70–71.

31. Saul, *La France et l'Egypte*, p. 659.

32. Ibid., p. 661.

33. Thane, "Financiers and the British State," p. 92. Thane gives no source, however, and is certainly wrong to state that the loan was encouraged by Gorst and led Cromer to dismiss him from Egyptian government service.

34. Cromer to Revelstoke, 22 February 1906, *Baring Archive*, 203076, "Partners" File, Supplementary Set.

35. Cromer, *Speeches and Miscellaneous Writings*, Vol. I (1912).

36. Cairo, 18 May 1906, PRO, FO 633/8.

37. For example, Cromer: "Rough notes to serve as a basis for further discussions on the question of revising the system of legislation at present in force in Egypt," 14 March 1905, PRO, FO 881/8616. This initiative is well discussed in Barbara Allen Roberson, "Judicial Reform and the Expansion of International Society: The Case of Egypt," Ph.D. dissertation, London School of Economics and Political Science (1998), pp. 243–247.

38. See, for example, Cromer to Admiral J. Fisher, Cairo, 19 March 1903, and Cromer to Sir Reginald Wingate, Cairo, 25 January 1904, PRO, FO 633/8.

39. According to Lord Sanderson, the permanent undersecretary at the Foreign Office: "The actual determining cause of the Entente was Lord Cromer's anxiety for an arrangement with France which would let him place Egyptian finances on a more satisfactory footing and pave the way for the abolition of the Capitulations"; quote in Marlowe, *Cromer in Egypt*, p. 253,

40. Mellini, *Sir Eldon Gorst*, p. 138.

41. *Biographical Notes* (in the possession of Last Esme Cromer), addition dated 2 August 1910, p. 1.

42. *Sir Eldon Gorst*, p. 133.

43. Cairo, 7 May 1903, *Baring Archive*, 203076, "Partners" File, Supplementary Set.

44. This bitter affair, which led to Northbrook's premature resignation, is well described by Edward L. Moulton in his *Lord Northrook's Indian Administration 1872–1876* (London: Asia Publishing House 1968), pp. 261–276.

45. Mellini, *Sir Eldon Gorst*, pp. 124–128.

46. See his comments to his nephew, Maurice Baring, in the latter's *The Puppet Show of Memory* (London: Cassel, 1987), p. 178.

7

Late Capitalism and the Reformation of the Working Classes in the Middle East

Joel Beinin

From Economic Nationalism to Neoliberalism

Since the early 1970s the working classes of the Middle East have been socially reorganized while their political salience has been discursively reconfigured. These processes have been accompanied by a transition from economic nationalism, industrially biased statist development, and populist politics toward integration into the world economy, encouragement of private enterprise, and upward redistribution of the national income. State-led development and import-substitution industrialization were key components of the social policies advanced by Gamal Abdul Nasser in Egypt, the Ba'th in Syria and Iraq, and the Algerian National Liberation Front (FLN) from the 1950s to the 1970s. The political and economic programs of these authoritarian-populist regimes were designated "Arab nationalism" and "Arab socialism." Turkey pursued comparable policies after the 1960 military coup: The 1961 constitution and 1963 labor code sought to include workers in political life and protect their living standards, while maintaining corporatist-style control over their trade unions. Even pro-Western Tunisia pursued a brief experiment with socialism in the 1960s.

Egypt began to retreat from Arab socialism in 1968, even before Nasser's death, although full elaboration of a new orientation was delayed until 1974.[1] Tunisia abandoned its socialist experiment in 1969. The 1980 military coup in Turkey installed a regime committed to neoliberal economic policies. Monocausal or globalist explanations for the demise of statist development policies in the Middle East—Guillermo O'Donnell's theorization of the transition from populist to bureaucratic authoritarianism,[2] interpretations stressing pressures from the United States and Great Britain during the ascendancy of Reagan-Thatcher efforts to roll back economic nationalism,[3] or the all-pervasive power of the International Monetary Fund (IMF) and the World Bank[4]—must be modified by the particularities of each case. Rivalries within ruling parties, the social balance of forces, and collective actions of workers and others have influenced the timing and character of these transitions.

The global context for the demise of state-led development in the Middle East was the end of the long wave of post–World War II capitalist expansion regulated by the institutions established at the 1944 Bretton Woods conference: the IMF, the International Bank for Reconstruction and Development (now the World Bank), and the General Agreement on Tariffs and Trade (GATT, precursor to the World Trade Organization). The Bretton Woods system was an international expression of Fordism-Keynesianism: a regime of mass production, mass consumption, mass democratic politics, and a New Deal/social-democratic, social safety net in the metropolitan capitalist (Organization for Economic Cooperation and Development, OECD) countries. Its success was based on the preeminence of the U.S. economy, the U.S. dollar, and U.S. military power.

The Bretton Woods system began to break down in the late 1960s. The resurgent economies of Japan and Europe threatened the preeminence of the U.S. economy, which was burdened with funding "Great Society" social programs and the Vietnam War and an upsurge of trade union struggles.[5] Delinking the dollar from gold in 1971 symbolized the relative decline of the U.S. economy. The rise of the Organization of Petroleum Exporting Countries (OPEC) in the 1960s also weakened U.S. capital by undermining the hegemonic position of the "Seven Sisters" (Mobil, Exxon, Chevron, Texaco, Gulf, Shell, and British Petroleum) in the international petroleum industry and shifting the balance of power and revenue flows from multinational oil corporations to oil-exporting states until the price collapse of 1985–1986 facilitated a corporate recovery.

Oil price spikes following the 1973 Arab oil embargo and the Iranian revolution of 1979 are commonly associated with the global recessions of 1974–1975 and 1980–1982 and a decade of stagflation (stagnation and inflation). This recessionary period, the longest and deepest since the end of World War II, marked the demise of Fordism-Keynesianism. But while the twelvefold increase in the international price of oil—from $2.70/barrel in 1973 to $32.50/barrel in 1981—contributed to the inflationary element of the stagflation syndrome, the recessions were not caused primarily by increased oil prices. Domestic factors in the OECD countries were more significant: insufficient capital investment exacerbated by Reagan-Thatcher monetarist policies designed to eliminate inflation and break the bargaining power of organized labor.

During the oil boom of the 1970s, a deluge of petro-dollars washed over the Middle East, lubricating the transition to a new economic order. Oil-exporting states came to control enormous concentrations of petroleum revenues. International lending to Middle Eastern countries increased sharply. For non-oil-exporting states, high oil prices contributed to a debt crisis, signaled regionally by foreign-exchange shortages in Egypt in 1976 and Turkey in 1977–1979, and globally by the 1982 Mexican default. Hard-currency shortages, a common problem in late stages of import-substitution industrialization, and foreign debt made Middle Eastern states more vulnerable to pressure from previously repressed bourgeois elements and from the Bretton Woods institutions, with differences in timing due to local circumstances.

The Washington Consensus

The IMF and the World Bank began promoting the transition from public enterprises and import-substitution industrialization to export-led development, private enterprise, and integration into the world capitalist market following a "successful" intervention in Chile after the 1973 coup that deposed the democratically elected socialist government. The debt crisis of the 1980s allowed the Bretton Woods institutions and the U.S. government to promote this program—the neoliberal Washington consensus—even more forcefully by attaching conditions to the loans offered to ease the debt crisis (stabilization) and restructuring economies of debt-stricken countries so as to enable them to continue repaying their debts in the future (structural adjustment). The typical IMF/World Bank stabilization and structural adjustment program raised the cost of food and other basic consumer goods, cut government spending on social services, and reduced investments in the public sector. Workers, government bureaucrats, and others on fixed incomes bore a disproportionate share of the pain of these austerity measures.

Advocates of the Washington consensus believe that all things being equal, individuals are rational actors and markets distribute goods most efficiently. Designating it as "science" enhances the social power of this belief. Few advocates of the Washington consensus argue that an economy should privilege the interests of local and multinational capital and international financial institutions. It just happens to work out that way when neoliberal policies are dogmatically applied.

The neoliberal belief system can never be proven because all things are never equal, and unpredictable political events often intervene to affect how economies operate. For example, the 1980 military coup cleared the way for aggressive implementation of the IMF structural adjustment plan in Turkey. Cancellation of nearly half of Egypt's $55 billion foreign debt in return for participating in the U.S.-led coalition against Iraq in the Gulf War opened the way to concluding a successful agreement with the IMF and gave the regime sufficient political capital to begin the long-delayed privatization of public-sector enterprises.

Lest they appear to be "unscientific," even moderate critics adopt the rhetoric of the Washington consensus.[6] Who can be opposed to economic "stabilization," or "structural adjustment"? These benign terms and others like "reform," "liberalization," "efficiency," and "rationalization" are nearly universally employed to describe the economic transformations envisioned by neoliberals. "Cutting public investments in housing, health, and education," "upward redistribution of income," "increasing inequality," "diminishing the influence of trade unions," "increasing the power of private capital," and "upward redistribution of access to agricultural land" are more difficult to defend. Yet these are the common effects of the neoliberal program, at least in the short and medium run.

Proponents of the Washington consensus often argue that despite the immediate pain, these policies will promote economic growth and thereby increase the incomes of the poor in the long run. Bent Hansen carefully examined the Turkish case, widely considered a successful example of neoliberal reform based primarily on the rapid growth in exports of manufactured goods in the 1980s. Hansen demonstrates that economic growth from 1962 to 1977 under a regime of state planning and import-substitution industrialization was as good as that of the 1980s. He concludes: "[T]he verdict would seem to be that expected benefits of reform and liberalization programs have at best materialized unevenly and rather slowly."[7] Hansen speculates that the long-term effects of the new policy may not yet be evident, and it may not have been possible to sustain high levels of growth with an import-substitution strategy past the mid-1970s. But Turkey's recurrent economic crises suggest that Washington consensus policies are not about to succeed. After a decade of structural adjustment programs, the World Bank admitted that there was no straightforward way to assess their success and no conclusive evidence on growth.[8]

Social and Discursive Disorganization of the Working Classes

Large numbers of Turkish workers began migrating to Europe, especially Germany, in the 1960s. As many as 135,000 migrants a year found jobs abroad during 1968–1973. When Germany and Europe closed their doors to new migrants during the 1974–1975 recession, many Turks and Kurds had established permanent communities. In the late 1980s, Turkish labor migration resumed, reaching a level of about 50,000 a year. Saudi Arabia and Libya were now the principal destinations.[9]

While the 1974–1975 recession curtailed opportunities for work in Europe, oil-exporting states began to embark on massive construction and development schemes financed by petroleum revenues. Millions of skilled and unskilled workers and peasants from Arab countries with little or no oil—Egypt, Sudan, Jordan, Palestine, Syria, Lebanon, and Yemen—migrated to Saudi Arabia, Kuwait, and Libya and earned many times what they could at home. Egypt was the largest Arab labor exporter. One well-informed observer estimated that 3.5 million Egyptians, about one-third of the entire labor force, migrated at some time during 1973–1985, primarily to Saudi Arabia, Libya, and Iraq.[10] At the peak of oil-boom-induced labor migration, more than 5 million Arabs worked in the Gulf countries; half as many North Africans were working in Europe.[11] The Tunisian Ministry of Social Affairs estimated that migrants made up 11.6 percent of the total labor force.[12]

Remittances of migrant workers partially recirculated petro-dollars and became an important factor in several national economies. Turkish workers sent home enough hard currency to cover the national trade deficit in 1972 and 1974; declining remittances contributed to the 1977–1979 foreign exchange crisis.[13] In Egypt, transfers of migrant workers constituted the single-largest source of foreign exchange amounting to 12 percent of the gross domestic product in the mid-1980s. By 1988, at least 20 percent of the labor force worked abroad, and annual official transfers of migrant workers reached about $3.2 billion; unofficial transfers were estimated at $2 billion to $4 billion.[14]

Rapid urbanization, high levels of unemployment and underemployment, and the possibilities of labor migration weakened the position of working people in the coalitions that supported authoritarian-populist regimes pursuing state-led import-substitution industrialization. The new circumstances made it difficult to organize workers as a social and political force in any framework. The continuity and effectiveness of communities, institutions, and traditions of organization and collective action that might have facilitated such organization were undermined.

As part of their critique of colonialism, authoritarian populists advocating state-led import-substitution industrialization popularized the idea that an economy should serve "the people." They were neither entirely successful nor entirely sincere in implementing this vision, but it was fundamental to their political legitimacy. Despite pro forma rhetoric about raising incomes of the poor, neoliberal policies were promoted by the Bretton Woods institutions and the U.S. government as an end in themselves. Joan Nelson observes that "it is roughly accurate to argue that in the early 1980s the international financial and development agencies pressed debtor governments to subordinate virtually all other goals to stabilization and adjustment."[15] This single-mindedness is a symptom of a discursive shift in conceptualizing what an economy is and for whose benefit it should function. Delegitimizing questions about whose interests economies serve made neoliberalism an appropriate discursive accompaniment to the social disorganization of the working classes and the fitful integration of the Middle East into the new international capitalist order of post-Fordist, post-Keynesian flexible accumulation.

The Washington consensus tends to eliminate altogether the working class as a social category, since its presence recalls the social compact of the era of authoritarian populism that the new economic order cannot fulfill. A salient expression of this inclination is the widely used textbook by Alan Richards and John Waterbury, *A Political Economy of the Middle East.*[16] The first edition includes the subtitle *State, Class, and Economic Development.* This was removed from the second edition, and the conceptual framework of the study was redesigned, replacing "class" with "social actors." This might be understood as eliminating a residue of Marxist dogmatism, although the first edition of the text was hardly sympathetic to the interests of workers or peasants and focused primarily on the role of the state in economic development. "Social actors" is an amorphous term not necessarily incompatible with the concept of class. Its main task in this context is to avoid asking: Are there structural contradictions in capitalist economies, and in whose interests are such economies most likely to operate?

Because most trade union federations in the Middle East were subordinated to ruling parties or states that adopted a corporatist approach to labor relations after independence, state-centered approaches to politics often considered them to be insignificant in determining economic and social policy. Typical of this orientation is Waterbury's study of Egypt under Nasser and Anwar al-Sadat,[17] which devotes minimal attention to workers or peasants. Others have argued that labor is a significant social and political force but focus their attention on the bargain between the elites of national trade union federations and the state.[18] This orientation can easily lead to ignoring the significance of collective actions of local union leaders or ordinary workers. Ellis Goldberg and Marsha Pripstein Posusney are exceptional among political scientists in insisting on the significance of the actions of rank-and-file workers.[19]

The following three case studies have been selected because Tunisia, Turkey, and even Egypt to a certain extent were considered IMF success stories, while Egypt is the emblematic case for the entire Middle East and the site of long-term, remedial Washington consensus policies.[20] The cases demonstrate the importance of local circumstances in the social contest over implementing Washington consensus policies. National trade union federations, local union officials, rank-and-file workers, and heterogeneous urban crowds protested the limits of import-substitution industrialization and corporatism and resisted the imposition of neoliberal policies and the political order that accompanied them. Their resistance altered the timing and extent to which neoliberal programs were implemented and mitigated their social costs. But against a triumphalist global structure of power and discourse proclaiming "there is no alternative," it was unable to reverse the trend or articulate a comprehensive new policy.

Tunisia

The Union Générale Tunisienne de Travail (UGTT) was historically the strongest trade union federation in the Middle East. It was intimately tied to the Neo-Destour Party, which led the independence struggle, and its successor, the Socialist Destour Party (PSD). Rivalries within the UGTT culminating in the ouster of the minister of national economy and former UGTT secretary general Ahmad Ben Salah in 1969 were among the causes for Tunisia's abandonment of its brief socialist experiment.

Ben Salah advocated austerity measures to build socialism. His base in the UGTT, primarily unions of white-collar civil servants, was more willing and able to make sacrifices to build a socialist future than blue-collar workers who followed Habib Achour and were more loyal to President Habib Bourguiba. Their patronage connection to the minister of national economy enabled teachers and other civil servants to win salary increases in 1968, while the more militant blue-collar workers did not receive raises. In the summer and fall of 1969, phosphate miners, railway workers, and dockers loyal to Achour launched wildcat strikes protesting the regime's austerity program.[21] Lower-paid, blue-collar workers no longer willing to tolerate the erosion of their wages and working conditions became functional allies of capitalists, especially large landowners of the Sahel, in ousting Ben Salah and his policies.

President Bourguiba engineered the installation of his ally, Achour, as secretary general of the UGTT in January 1970. The UGTT and the PSD were purged of opposition elements. A corporatist agreement between the UGTT and the employers' association (Union Tunisienne de l'Industrie, Commerce et l'Artisanat)—including a minimum wage, a small salary increase, and collective contracts—was imposed in 1972. To complement these undemocratic measures, in 1974 Bourguiba had himself declared "president for life."[22]

Unions of teachers, bank employees, university professors, engineers, and other educated, higher-paid, white-collar workers—Ben Salah's base of support within the UGTT—began a sustained campaign of resistance to the new economic policies. Some white-collar union activists had been radical students in the 1960s; others had ties to the Communist Party. Achour tried to purge these elements from the national leadership of the UGTT by eliminating the representatives of the teachers' and the Post, Telegraph, and Telephone workers' unions.[23]

The central issue for labor in the 1970s was the rising cost of living. Using government figures, the UGTT estimated that consumer prices increased 36 percent from 1970 to 1977 while average real wages increased only 18 percent from 1971 to 1975. White-collar workers led the way in launching wildcat strikes unauthorized by the UGTT central leadership throughout the 1970s.[24] Continuing wildcat strikes undermined the social pact negotiated between the UGTT and the government in 1977. Achour, under pressure from rank-and-file unionists who urged the UGTT to declare a general strike against the cost-of-living increases, defended the wildcat strikers and ultimately announced his open opposition to the regime by resigning from the leadership bodies of the PSD. The UGTT held a highly successful general strike on 26 January 1978, accompanied by rioting of the urban poor. At least 100 people died in clashes with security forces that day. In response, the government jailed Achour and other UGTT leaders and imposed a new executive committee on the union.[25]

The government of Muhammad Mzali (1980–1986) sought to avoid further conflict with the UGTT. In the fall of 1983 an IMF mission visited Tunisia and convinced Mzali to lower the budget deficit by cutting subsidies on consumer products. Mzali announced the cuts on 29 December, raising the price of bread, pasta, and semolina by 70 percent. In response, rioting began in Gafsa and other southern cities and then spread to Tunis in early January. More than 100 people died in clashes with security forces before the government rescinded the price increases.

In late 1985 the government began a new campaign of repression against the UGTT. Achour was again placed under house arrest. PSD militias occupied the union offices. During 1986 most of the UGTT leadership was imprisoned, as the government faced a foreign exchange crisis. The government resolved the crisis by accepting an IMF standby credit of $180 million in exchange for adopting the standard Washington consensus stabilization policy package: devaluation of the dinar, government budget cuts, liberalization of the trade regime, and a commitment to privatize public sector enterprises.

The first priority of the new regime established by the coup d'état of Zayn al- 'Abidin Ben 'Ali on 7 November 1987 was to implement the IMF stabilization plan. In response, there were 2,586 strikes during the next six years, far more than the 1,761 in the seven years preceding the general strike of 26 January 1978. Most were conducted without approval of the

UGTT central committee. Despite the repression of 1985–1986 and the intervention of the Ben 'Ali regime in its affairs, UGTT members continued to engage in collective acts of resistance. The regime faced the choice of breaking the union or enticing it into a new alliance.

The rise of the Islamic Tendency Movement and its successor al-Nahda as the strongest opponents of the regime in the mid-1980s tilted the balance toward the option of a renewed corporatist bargain between the regime and the union. Ben 'Ali intervened heavily in the renewal of the UGTT to strengthen its secularist elements. The fight against political Islam created pressures for a new state-union alliance in which strikes over wages and working conditions became rare, and there was no longer a contest over fundamental economic policy. The UGTT embarked on a new era of collaborative relations with the government and the Union Tunisienne de l'industic, du Commerce et de l'Artisanat. In 1992, Secretary General Isma'il Sahbani, who was installed at the 1989 national congress consecrating the government-supervised "rehabilitation" of the UGTT declared: "Our union . . . is trying to adapt to changes in the international economic system, the structural adjustment program, the new world order, and the market economy."[26]

Egypt

After the devastating defeat by Israel in the 1967 war, unionized workers supported the government's austerity measures. The first expressions of resistance to wage reductions were in response to exposures of corruption and mismanagement in the public sector in 1968.[27] The death of Nasser in September 1970 and al-Sadat's consolidation of power through the arrest of leading Nasserists on 15 May 1971 created an opening for the expression of demands that first emerged during the 1965–1966 crisis of import-substitution industrialization but were postponed by the 1967 war.

During 1971 and 1972 strikes in several large public enterprises, as well as demonstrations of thousands of private-sector textile workers in Shubra al-Khayma, a historic bastion of the left, challenged the regime with the largest collective actions of workers since the early 1950s. The government responded with the classic combination of conciliation and repression. The General Federation of Egyptian Trade Unions (GFETU) denounced the August 1971 strike of the Iron and Steel Company workers in Helwan.[28] Strike leaders were fired or transferred to other workplaces. The mill's unit of the state's single party, the Arab Socialist Union, was dissolved, and the local union leaders were isolated. Prime Minister 'Aziz Sidqi visited Shubra al-Khayma after the demonstrations and promised to raise the minimum wage and improve sick-leave policy for private-sector workers.[29]

The strikes and demonstrations of the early 1970s were accompanied by a resurgence of former communists who dissolved their parties and joined the Arab Socialist Union after spending four years in jail during the Nasser regime. They won leadership positions in several local unions and national union federations in the July 1971 elections. One of them, Ahmad al-Rifa'i, was positioned to become the GFETU president. He and other like-minded leftists decided instead to support the regime's candidate, Salah Gharib, hoping that avoiding a clash with the regime would encourage President al-Sadat to expand trade unions' freedoms and their room for political action.

After briefly collaborating with the leftists who supported his election, in March 1973 Gharib purged the left from the GFETU executive committee and canceled both the annual convention and the executive committee elections.[30] Political miscalculation of some leftist labor leaders, perhaps due to years of isolation from rank-and-file union members, strengthened Gharib's hand and deprived the rank-and-file upsurge of potential organizational and political support. The GFETU became a reliable element of al-Sadat's ruling coalition.

President al-Sadat's announcement of a new *infitah* (open door) economic policy in April 1974 heralded the end of state-led development. Its good showing in the 1973 war gave the regime sufficient public credit to introduce the new policy without significant organized opposition. GFETU leaders did not openly oppose *infitah* policies and limited themselves to resisting the liquidation of the public sector and other measures they feared would reduce the standard of living and job security of their constituents. Even this limited opposition contributed substantially to obstructing structural changes in the Egyptian economy during the oil boom. Service and rent activities—U.S. aid, oil exports, tolls from the reopened Suez Canal, renewed international tourism, and remittances from migrant workers—generated sufficient hard currency to avert a crisis. This allowed the government to avoid policy choices that would endanger its support from the legions of managers as well as clerical and blue-collar workers employed in public enterprises and the state apparatus.

The first post-*infitah* urban protest erupted dramatically and unexpectedly with no organizational support from the GFETU or leftist political leaders. On 1 January 1975, workers commuting to the southern Cairo industrial suburb of Helwan occupied the Bab al-Luq railway station; others sat in at the plant. Textile workers in Shubra al-Khayma proclaimed a solidarity strike and occupied several mills. In addition to economic demands, workers raised political slogans, including a demand for the resignation of the prime minister. Strikes and collective actions over economic issues took place during 1975–1976 in Cairo, al-Mahalla al-Kubra, Helwan, Alexandria, Tanta, Nag' Hammadi, and Port Said.[31] The movement was concentrated among workers in large public-sector enterprises: the major beneficiaries of Nasserist development policies.

In 1976 an IMF mission visited Egypt and recommended that the government cut its budget by reducing subsidies on basic consumer goods, raising their prices by 25 to 50 percent. Immediately after the price increases were announced, demonstrations and riots erupted on 18–19 January 1977. The protests—the largest popular collective action in twenty-five years—were concentrated in Cairo and Alexandria, spread throughout the country, and threatened to topple the regime. Factory workers initiated and played a prominent role in these actions, joined by students, the unemployed, and others in the urban crowd.

Al-Sadat portrayed himself as a great democrat opposed to Nasser's authoritarianism. But a chilly, repressive climate descended upon Egypt from the 1977 riots until al-Sadat's assassination by radical Islamists in 1981. The government blamed the left for inciting the riots and brought many suspected communists to trial. In fact, the legal and illegal left were surprised by the extent of popular anger and its insurrectionary character.[32] The intellectual Marxist monthly *al-Tali'a*, which dared to explain that though it did not endorse the violence, the anger of the masses was justified, was closed. *Al-Ahali*, the weekly of the legal leftist Tagammu' Party, was intermittently proscribed. The regime's unsubstantiated suspicion that communist organizations incited the riots guaranteed that communist parties would remain illegal. Law 3 of 1977 was enacted to allow the government to punish striking workers with hard labor.

Many workers in large public enterprises did have a Nasserist or Marxist-inspired understanding of their situation. Other elements of the urban crowds in January 1977 were moved by Islamic sentiment expressed by the trashing of the casinos on Pyramids Road, long identified by the Muslim Brothers as symbols of foreign-influenced moral dissolution.[33] Although public-sector workers were sometimes quite militant in the 1970s and 1980s, many skilled and experienced workers as well as unskilled workers and peasants who migrated to the oil-exporting countries absented themselves from the struggle over the open-door policy. Those in the vast "informal sector" were largely quiescent and difficult or impossible to organize. Years of Nasserist repression of the left, subsequent efforts of the left intelligentsia to collaborate with the regime, and mistaken assessments of the early al-Sadat regime by those same intellectuals meant there was no oppositional discourse articulating a role for workers and their potential allies.

Hosni Mubarak began his rule in 1981 by alleviating the repressive measures of his predecessor. He ordered the 1,300 political prisoners arrested without charges on the eve of al-Sadat's assassination released. The press and opposition political parties were given more leeway. An electoral alliance of the Muslim Brothers and the Wafd Party was permitted to participate in the 1984 parliamentary elections. A more ideologically compatible Muslim Brothers–Socialist Labor Party (SLP) electoral alliance was formed in 1987.

Mubarak risked angering the IMF by resisting its demands for further reduction of subsidies, exchange-rate unification, and privatization of the public sector. The more open atmosphere of the early Mubarak era permitted a significant increase in strikes and other workers' collective action. Some fifty to seventy-five actions a year were reported in the press from 1984 to 1989, surely not a comprehensive enumeration.[34] The left actively participated in struggles involving confrontations with the state: the massive strike and uprising of textile workers in Kafr al-Dawwar in September–October 1984; the strike at the Misr Spinning and Weaving Company in February 1985; the railway workers strike of July 1986; and two sit-in strikes at the Egyptian Iron and Steel Company in Helwan in July and August 1989. Workers' shop-floor resistance and enterprise-level militancy and the bureaucratic maneuvers of the GFETU continued to be major factors delaying full implementation of the Washington consensus economic program until after the 1991 Gulf War.[35] Opposition forces made some headway in enterprise-level trade union committees in the elections of 1991 and 1996, but the state's candidates continued to dominate the GFETU and the national federations.

Cancellation of nearly half of Egypt's foreign debt as a reward for participation in the Gulf War prepared the way for a new agreement with the IMF in May 1991. As foreign currency reserves and other macroeconomic indicators improved, the Mubarak government began to privatize state-owned enterprises in earnest. To encourage privatization, the regime proposed a new unified labor law, which was not enacted by the end of the decade. The legal reorganization of the trade union movement was resisted by the GFETU, the left, and the Islamic current in the labor movement because of fears that it would diminish workers' rights and enhance the state's repressive capacity. The national GFETU leadership embraced the proposed law, hoping that it would legalize strikes and reinforce control over rank-and-file union members alienated by what they perceived as the leadership's weakness in defending their interests.

Turkey

The populist atmosphere of the post-1960 coup years encouraged an upsurge of labor and left activism. The Turkish Labor Party (TLP) was formed in 1961, although the Communist Party remained illegal. In 1967 the Confederation of Revolutionary Trade Unions (DISK) was established as an alternative to the state-sponsored Türk-Iş trade union federation. By the late 1970s the TLP and other left forces mobilized some 400,000 workers to affiliate with DISK. In an attempt to block the labor upsurge, the conservative Justice Party government amended the electoral law to reduce the parliamentary representation of the TLP and enacted labor legislation favoring the Türk-Iş federation and hindering DISK's ability to organize. More than 100,000 workers responded to these measures by blocking the Istanbul-Ankara highway on 15–16 June 1970, immobilizing the entire Istanbul-Marmara region. They battled the police and army with clubs in what the regime described as "the dress rehearsal for revolution."[36]

Student-based, new left groups, imagining that the country was in a revolutionary situation, began to rob banks, attack U.S. institutions, and kidnap U.S. soldiers. These actions undermined and discredited the workers' social movement, which nonetheless continued to grow. From 1 January to 12 March 1971, more days were lost to strikes than in any full year since 1963, except 1966.[37] The military coup of 12 March 1971 sought to control the social conflict and political violence by declaring martial law and banning the TLP.

The coup broke the new student left but was less successful with the workers' movement. Strike action declined somewhat during the mid-1970s but began to increase in 1978 and reached unprecedented proportions in 1980. DISK sponsored May Day demonstrations in Istanbul in 1976, 1977, and 1978, with as many as 500,000 participants. The 1979 demonstration was banned by martial law.[38]

The increased cost of oil imports, declining remittances from workers in Europe, reduced foreign aid due to the 1974 invasion of Cyprus, and heavy borrowing from commercial banks at high interest rates created a foreign exchange crisis in 1977–1979. Despite its social-democratic commitments, Bulent Ecevit's Republican People's Party (RPP) government negotiated debt-rescheduling arrangements with creditors under IMF supervision. The IMF austerity measures caused enough of the RPP's urban supporters to defect in the October 1979 Senate elections to return Süleyman Demirel and the Justice Party to power. Demirel's economic adviser, Turgut Özal, designed an IMF-approved austerity plan, announced on 24 January 1980, that devalued the Turkish lira by more than 30 percent (on top of the 43 percent devaluation previously imposed by Ecevit) and raised consumer prices by about 70 percent. Özal feared that political pressures would not allow him to implement his program fully. Political violence and strikes throughout 1980 provided the pretext for the military coup of 12 September 1980.

The junta banned DISK and arrested hundreds of trade union leaders. The Türk-Iş federation was permitted to continue functioning, but strikes were outlawed, and an arbitration board was established to settle wage disputes. The 1983 labor code institutionalized labor's subordination to capital. With all organized opposition broken, Özal convinced the junta to allow him to implement his economic program without political interference.[39] This program succeeded in increasing industrial exports significantly in the 1980s, though workers paid a heavy price for this success. As the regime eased its repression, they moved to recover their losses. From 1987 to 1991, the average annual number of strikes was greater than the previous peak year of 1980.[40] Collective bargaining agreements of 1989–1991 included significant wage increases but still failed to compensate for the wage erosion of the previous period.[41]

The 1980 military coup that consolidated Özal's ascendancy and his electoral victory as leader of the Motherland Party in 1983 were a reaction against the intense political violence and social conflict of the 1970s. While the mobilization of Turkish workers from the 1960s to the 1980s more closely resembles Marxian class politics than any other Middle Eastern case, the social conflict cannot be reduced to an expression of class struggle. It also involved a student-based new left, an Islamist challenge to Kemalist secularism, an upsurge of Kurdish ethnic sentiment and a right-wing effort to repress it, a sectarian contention between Sunnis and Alevis, and other social cleavages. All these were exacerbated by personal rivalry between Demirel and Ecevit. Moreover, the working class was not unified. Unionized workers were divided among DISK, based mainly in the private sector; Türk-Iş, based primarily in the public sector; and the much smaller National Action Party–led Confederation of Nationalist Trade Unions and the Islamist Hak-Iş. Only 1.5 million of the 6 million workers covered by social security were unionized in 1980. Other cleavages within the working class included the social adjustment difficulties of migrants returning from Europe in the mid-1970s.[42] The labor movement was socially isolated and made little effort to form a political alliance with peasants.

Nonetheless, the politicization of the labor movement and the transformation of the RPP into a social-democratic party threatened the Turkish business class much more so than the new left urban guerrilla activity of the early 1970s. Both workers and industrialists benefited from import-substitution industrialization, but the populist guarantees of the 1961 constitution allowed organized workers to fight fiercely to maintain and extend their gains during the post-1973 recessionary period. Özal's neoliberal economic policies and the repression of the labor movement were a victory for the Turkish business class. Yet they were unwilling to fight for it on their own because they had benefited from statist development and because of their historic political timidity. Thus, an unanticipated consequence of the collective action of unionized workers and their political allies among the intelligentsia was the consolidation of a bourgeois pole in Turkish politics during the 1980s.

Results and Prospects

The cases examined here support some limited generalizations about politics, economics, and the fate of workers after the demise of Middle Eastern Fordism-Keynesianism. In the era of authoritarian populism, the autonomy of trade union movements, particularly their radical elements, was sharply limited. Washington consensus policies heralded further repression and declines in political freedom. In Turkey and Tunisia, implementation of these policies was preceded by military coups. In Egypt, although a limited democratic opening accompanied the new policies, the regime cracked down hard on the opposition when the going got rough. Strikes and other forms of collective action challenged the corporatist integration of the organized trade union movement as the regimes of state-led import-substitution industrialization entered crises and escalated as local elites implemented Washington consensus solutions to the crises. Opposition trade unionists and political leaders were repressed. The limited democratic openings did not include the legalization of communist or Islamic parties (with the limited exception of the Welfare/Virtue Party in Turkey), and the right to strike was limited.

Egypt, Turkey, and Tunisia recovered from the balance-of-payments crises that provided the opening for imposing Washington consensus policies. In Tunisia and Turkey, the combination of state repression, renewed social spending, and the threat of political Islam led to a new corporatist bargain between the trade unions and the state. Efforts to negotiate such a bargain in Egypt did not come to fruition by the end of the 1990s, in part due to the relative weakness of the workers' collective action against *infitah* policies. The Egyptian strikes and demonstrations of 1975–1977 and 1984–1989 were less substantial than the Tunisian strike waves of the mid-1970s and mid-1980s or the Turkish labor actions of the early and late 1970s and late 1980s–early 1990s. Unlike Turkey, the most radical actions were concentrated in the declining public sector, not the private sector encouraged by the open-door policy.[43]

The riots of January 1977 in Egypt and January 1984 in Tunisia exemplify a new form of urban social protest that became common in response to imposition of Washington consensus policies: "IMF food riots." Other Middle Eastern examples include Morocco (1981), Sudan (1985), and Jordan (1989 and 1996). The Tunisian general strike of 26 January 1978 and the September–October 1984 strike and riot at the textile mills in Kafr al-Dawwar in Egypt are mixed cases: traditional labor actions commingled with violence of urban crowds directed broadly against the state and its symbols of authority.

The diffuse and sporadic character of these protests—spontaneous rioting or localized labor strikes rather than a sustained campaign of political and economic action—is due to the structural heterogeneity of urban workers in the post-1973 era and the delegitimization of all forms of class-based and leftist politics. Collective action of unionized workers, even if well organized, radical, and militant, was only one component of popular protest against the Washington consensus. Workers were unable to organize a counterhegemonic bloc of forces around themselves. Therefore, their collective actions could do no more than delay or modify the implementation of Washington consensus policies.

Islamist forces attempted to capitalize on the decline of the left, forming a rival trade union federation in Turkey and contesting elections in the state-authorized trade union federations of Egypt and Tunisia. They were not successful in replacing the left as the principal advocates of workers in large-scale modern enterprises.[44] Unionized urban workers seem to be one of the social groups least attracted to the forms of political Islam that have inspired resistance to capitalist globalization in the Middle East and beyond.

Democracy did not do well in the era of neoliberal ascendancy. Over and above the coup that brought Ben 'Ali to power in 1987, Tunisia became more authoritarian after a wave of rural economic reorganization began in 1990.[45] The Islamist al-Nahda remains illegal; there have been repeated reports of the regime's detention and torture of political opponents; and no real opposition parties participated in the 1994 elections. After July 1992, Egypt underwent a broad political deliberalization in response to the challenge of armed Islamist groups and opposition to the new economic policies.[46] A revised penal code replaced prison terms with forced labor. Security cases were routinely transferred to military courts with less independence than civil courts. At least 10,000 political detainees were held under the state's emergency powers; many were reportedly tortured. The parliamentary elections of 1990 and 1995 were significantly less free than those of the 1980s and resulted in greater majorities for the ruling National Democratic Party.

Following the 1980 coup in Turkey, both the political left and right were smashed, as the junta strove to depoliticize society. In January 1981, a European Economic Community committee estimated that there were 30,000 political detainees. Many of them were tortured. One consequence of Washington consensus policies has been redistribution of national income away from working people toward self-employed individuals and corporations. Statistics on such matters are more than usually unreliable, but the overall trend is clear. According to the World Bank, in the early 1990s real wages in manufacturing in Algeria, Egypt, Syria, Jordan, Morocco, and Tunisia were at or below their 1970 levels.[47]

In Tunisia, the incomes of self-employed individuals increased 68 percent during 1970–1977, after Arab socialist policies were abandoned, while profits increased over 115 percent.[48] Income distribution grew more unequal from 1975 to 1986, as the richest 20 percent of the population increased its share of total consumption from 22 percent to 50 percent while the share of the poorest 20 percent stagnated at 5 to 6 percent.[49]

In Egypt, real wages stagnated from 1973 to 1987 as the government gradually implemented *infitah* policies. Public-sector wages rose somewhat during the late 1970s and early 1980s but by 1987 retreated to just below the 1973 level. Private-sector wages increased more during the boom years but fell back to only 15 percent greater than the 1973 level by 1987.[50] Real wages in manufacturing rose nearly 50 percent from 1975 to 1982 but fell 40 percent from 1985 to 1995.[51] Income distribution worsened. From 1981 to 1991, the Gini coefficient rose from 0.32 to 0.38 in the urban sector and 0.29 to 0.32 in rural areas. The biggest losers in this period were the middle 40 percent of households, followed by the lowest 30 percent.[52]

The Turkish statistics seem the most complete and reliable. In the decade after the implementation of Washington consensus policies in 1980, real wages in the public sector declined by 39 percent, and civil service wages declined 13.5 percent. Real wages in the private sector increased by 16.6 percent. This last figure suggests a success for the new economic policies. However, it must be judged in the context of increasingly unequal income distribution. An expression of this tendency is the decline of the "popular" factor shares in the national income. From 1980 to 1988, the share of agriculture in the national income declined from 26.66 percent to 13.20 percent. Wages and salaries, which rose steadily as a percentage of national income from 1963 to 1978, declined from 23.87 percent to 15.80 percent. Rents, profits, and interest increased from 49.47 percent to 71 percent.[53] The decline in real wages in manufacturing was the main factor increasing the competitiveness of Turkey's manufactured exports in the 1980s, the main claim to success of the Washington consensus policies.[54]

Washington consensus policies have so far failed to create sufficient jobs to employ those excluded from the shrinking public sector or those displaced from agriculture. In the mid-1990s unemployment rates in the Middle East were higher than anywhere else in the world: about 10 percent in Turkey (down considerably from 25 percent in 1986); 15 percent in Egypt, Morocco, and Tunisia; 20 to 25 percent in Algeria, Jordan, and Yemen; and about 20 percent in the West Bank and Gaza Strip, frequently exacerbated by the closure of the Israeli economy to Palestinian workers.[55]

Although poverty levels were low by international standards, Washington consensus policies did not significantly alleviate poverty. According to the World Bank, the segment of the Egyptian population under the poverty line ($30 a month) rose 30 percent from 1985 to 1990. Using Egyptian household income data, Karema Korayem calculated that in 1990–1991 urban poverty was one-and-a-half times the level of

1980–1981, while rural poverty more than doubled. Calculations based on household expenditure data yielded an increase of 20 percent in rural poverty and 84 percent in urban poverty over the same period.[56]

The World Bank believes that in Morocco and Tunisia poverty levels declined by nearly half.[57] However, Samir Radwan disputes the Bank's method for defining the poverty line and argues that in Tunisia, between 1975 and 1985, poverty decreased by only one-fifth, and 23 percent of all wage earners lived in poverty. Moreover, there was no trickle down in rural areas where families own few productive resources. The alleviation of poverty in the face of worsening income distribution in Tunisia was largely due to remittances of migrant workers, not the internal capacity of the economy to generate good-paying jobs. Thus, the structural transformation of the economy was not self-sustaining.[58]

Washington consensus policies were certainly not the only cause of declining wages, high unemployment, and persistent poverty. Import-substitution industrialization regimes may have reached the limits of their possibilities in the late 1960s and early 1970s. International economic factors—oil price fluctuations, the possibilities for migrant workers, and the reduced rate of growth in the OECD countries in the post-1973 recessionary period—all played a role. But by the criteria of job creation, alleviation of poverty, and equity, Washington consensus policies cannot be considered a success.

By 1995 the World Bank had become so concerned about this state of affairs that it issued a special report, *Will Arab Workers Prosper or Be Left Out in the Twenty-First Century?* The report made obeisance to the primacy of markets obligatory but also argued for the first time that laissez-faire policies were inadequate to set minimum standards for wages, working conditions, collective bargaining, and to reduce income insecurity. The Bank called for a "broad vision of a new social contract that is realistic and capable of benefiting most workers."[59] It is too soon to tell if this change of tone will influence the more antipopular orientation of the IMF and the U.S. government. But the Bank's defection from neoliberal orthodoxy and the vigorous protests against the World Trade Organization in Seattle in 1999 suggest that history has not quite ended.

Notes

1. Mark N. Cooper, *The Transformation of Egypt* (Baltimore: Johns Hopkins University Press, 1982).

2. Guillermo O'Donnell, "Reflections on the Patterns of Change in the Bureaucratic-Authoritarian State," *Latin American Research Review* 12 (1978): 3–38.

3. Walden Bello with Shea Cunningham and Bill Rau, *Dark Victory: The*

United States, Structural Adjustment, and Global Poverty (London: Pluto Press, 1994).

4. Gouda Abdel-Khalek, "Looking Outside or Turning NW? On the Meaning and External Dimension of Egypt's Infitah, 1971–1980," *Social Problems* 28 (1981): 394–409; Galal A. Amin, *Egypt's Economic Predicament: A Study in the Interaction of External Pressure, Political Folly, and Social Tension in Egypt, 1960–1990* (Leiden: E. J. Brill, 1995); Tim Niblock, "International and Domestic Factors in the Economic Liberalization Process in Arab Countries," in Tim Niblock and Emma Murphy (eds.), *Economic and Political Liberalization in the Middle East* (London: British Academic Press, 1993), pp. 55–87.

5. Robert Brenner, *Turbulence in the World Economy* (London: Verso, 1999).

6. Joan Nelson, "Overview: The Politics of Long-Haul Reform," in Joan Nelson (ed.), *Fragile Coalitions: The Politics of Economic Adjustment* (Washington, D.C.: Overseas Development Corporation, 1989), pp. 3–26.

7. Bent Hansen, *The Political Economy of Poverty, Equity, and Growth: Egypt and Turkey* (Oxford: Oxford University Press, 1991), pp. 391–395.

8. World Bank, *World Development Report 1991: The Challenge of Development* (Washington, D.C.: The World Bank, 1991), p. 114.

9. Turkey, State Institute of Statistics, *Türkiye Istatistik Yıllığı* (Istanbul: Prime Minister's Office, 1973–1995).

10. Alan Richards and John Waterbury, *A Political Economy of the Middle East,* 2nd ed. (Boulder, Colo.: Westview Press, 1996), p. 371.

11. World Bank, *Will Arab Workers Prosper or Be Left Out in the Twenty-First Century? Regional Perspectives on World Development Report 1995* (Washington, D.C.: The World Bank, 1995), p. 6.

12. Samir Radwan, Vali Jamal, and Ajit Ghose, *Tunisia: Rural Labour and Structural Transformation* (London: Routledge, 1991), pp. 23–24.

13. Feroz Ahmad, *The Making of Modern Turkey* (London: Routledge, 1993), p. 177.

14. Delwin A. Roy, "Egyptian Emigrant Labor: Domestic Consequences," *Middle Eastern Studies* 22 (1991): 552, 579.

15. Nelson, "The Politics of Long-Haul Reform," p. 14.

16. Alan Richards and John Waterbury, *A Political Economy of the Middle East: State, Class, and Economic Development,* 1st ed. (Boulder, Colo.: Westview Press, 1990); Richards and Waterbury, *A Political Economy of the Middle East,* 2nd ed.

17. John Waterbury, *The Egypt of Nasser and Sadat: The Political Economy of Two Regimes* (Princeton, N.J.: Princeton University Press, 1983).

18. Robert Bianchi, "The Corporatization of the Egyptian Labor Movement," *Middle East Journal* 40, no. 3 (Summer 1986): 429–444; Robert Bianchi, *Unruly Corporatism: Associational Life in Twentieth-Century Egypt* (New York: Oxford University Press, 1989); Michael Christopher Alexander, "Between Accommodation and Confrontation: State, Labor, and Development in Algeria and Tunisia" (Ph.D. dissertation, Duke University, 1996).

19. Ellis J. Goldberg, *Tinker, Tailor, and Textile Worker: Class and Politics in Egypt, 1930–1954* (Berkeley: University of California Press, 1986); Marsha Pripstein Posusney, *Labor and the State in Egypt: Workers, Unions, and Economic Restructuring, 1952–1996* (New York: Columbia University Press, 1997).

20. Karen Pfeifer, "How Tunisia, Morocco, Jordan, and Even Egypt Became IMF 'Success Stories' in the 1990s," *Middle East Report,* no. 210 (Spring 1999): 23–27.

21. Alexander, "Between Accommodation and Confrontation," pp. 109–124.

22. Ibid., pp. 151–158.

23. Ibid., p. 179.

24. Ibid., pp. 158–162.

25. Dirk Vandewalle, "From the New State to the New Era: Toward a Second Republic in Tunisia," *Middle East Journal* 42, no. 4 (Autumn 1988): 607–608.

26. Michael Christopher Alexander, "State, Labor, and the New Global Economy in Tunisia," in Dirk Vandewalle (ed.), *North Africa: Development and Reform in a Changing Global Economy* (New York: St. Martin's Press, 1996), pp. 177–202.

27. Posusney, *Labor and the State in Egypt*, p. 142.

28. Ibid.

29. Huwayda 'Adli, *al-'Ummal wa'l-siyyasa: al-dawr al-siyyasi li'l-haraka al-'ummaliyya fi misr min 1952–1981* (Cairo: al-Ahali, 1993), p. 268; A. Baklanoff, *al-Tabaqa al-'amila fi misr al-mu'asira* (Damascus: Markaz al-Abhath wa'l-Dirasat al-Ishtirakiyya fi al-'Alam al-'Arabi, 1988), pp. 216–224.

30. Posusney, *Labor and the State in Egypt*, pp. 95–100.

31. 'Adli, *al-'Ummal wa'l-siyyasa*, p. 268; Baklanoff, *al-Tabaqa al-'amila*, p. 225; Joel Beinin, "Will the Real Egyptian Working Class Please Stand Up?" in Zachary Lockman (ed.), *Workers and Working Classes in the Middle East* (Albany: State University of New York Press, 1994), pp. 247–270.

32. Beinin, "Will the Real Egyptian Working Class Please Stand Up?" pp. 248–258.

33. Ibid., pp. 260–261.

34. Omar El Shafei, "Workers, Trade Unions, and the State in Egypt: 1984–1989," *Cairo Papers in Social Science* 18, no. 2 (Summer 1995): 36.

35. Posusney, *Labor and the State in Egypt*, pp. 208–243.

36. Ahmad, *The Making of Modern Turkey*, pp. 145–147. See also Robert Bianchi, *Interest Groups and Political Development in Turkey* (Princeton, N.J.: Princeton University Press, 1984), p. 202; Ronnie Margulies and Ergin Yıldızoğlu, "Trade Unions and Turkey's Working Class," *Merip Reports,* no. 121 (February 1984): 15–20, 31.

37. Ahmad, *The Making of Modern Turkey*, p. 235.

38. Margulies and Yıldızoğlu, "Trade Unions and Turkey's Working Class," p. 18.

39. Ahmad, *The Making of Modern Turkey*, pp. 177–183.

40. *Türkiye Istatistik Yıllığı* (1995), p. 285.

41. A. Erinç Yeldan, "The Economic Structure of Power Under Turkish Structural Adjustment: Prices, Growth and Accumulation," in Fikret Şenses (ed.), *Recent Industrialization Experience of Turkey in a Global Context* (Westport, Conn.: Greenwood Press, 1994), pp. 77, 80–81; Ahmad, *The Making of Modern Turkey*, p. 211.

42. Metin Kara, "The Workers as a Class Were Defeated," *Merip Reports,* no. 121 (February 1984): 21–27.

43. El Shafei, "Workers, Trade Unions, and the State in Egypt," p. 36.

44. Alexander, "Between Accommodation and Confrontation," pp. 344, 374–378; Michael Willis, *The Islamist Challenge in Algeria: A Political History* (New York: New York University Press, 1996), p. 178; Alexander, "State, Labor, and the New Global Economy in Tunisia"; Joel Beinin, "Political Islam and the Trade Union Movement in Egypt," paper presented to the conference on Globalization, Political Islam, and Urban Social Movements (University of California, Berkeley, 6–8 March 1998).

45. Stephen J. King, "The Politics of Market Reform in Rural Tunisia" (Ph.D. dissertation, Princeton University, Princeton, N.J., 1997).

46. Eberhard Kienle, "More Than a Response to Islamism: The Political Deliberalization of Egypt in the 1990s," *Middle East Journal* 52 (1998): 219–235.

47. World Bank, *Will Arab Workers Prosper?* p. 4.

48. Alexander, "Between Accommodation and Confrontation," p. 162.

49. Karen Pfeifer, "Between Rocks and Hard Choices: International Finance and Economic Adjustment in North Africa," in Vandewalle, *North Africa,* p. 46; Radwan, Jamal, and Ghose, *Tunisia*, pp. 49–52, 61–62.

50. Posusney, *Labor and the State in Egypt*, p. 137.

51. Hansen, *The Political Economy of Poverty*, p. 473; Kienle, "More Than a Response to Islamism," p. 233.

52. Karima Korayem, "Structural Adjustment, Stabilization Policies, and the Poor in Egypt," *Cairo Papers in Social Science* 18, no. 4 (Winter 1995–1996): 25–26.

53. Birol A. Yeşılada and Mahır Fısunoğlu, "Assessing the January 24, 1980 Economic Stabilization Program in Turkey," in Henri J. Barkey (ed.), *The Politics of Economic Reform in the Middle East* (New York: St. Martin's Press, 1992), pp. 199–200; John Waterbury, "Export-Led Growth and the Center-Right Coalition in Turkey," in Tevfik F. Nas and Mehmed Odekon (eds.), *Economics and Politics of Turkish Liberalization* (Bethlehem, Penn.: Lehigh University Press, 1992), p. 66.

54. Hansen, *The Political Economy of Poverty*, pp. 415–418.

55. World Bank, *Will Arab Workers Prosper?* p. 2; Richards and Waterbury, *A Political Economy of the Middle East,* 2d ed., p. 134.

56. Korayem, "Structural Adjustment," p. 22.

57. World Bank, *Will Arab Workers Prosper?* pp. 3–5.

58. Radwan, Jamal, and Ghose, *Tunisia*, pp. 52–61, 89.

59. World Bank, *Will Arab Workers Prosper?* p. v.

Part 3

Recovering Lost Voices in the Age of Colonialism

8

Exploring the Field: Lost Voices and Emerging Practices in Egypt, 1882–1914

Zachary Lockman

This chapter was originally written for a workshop whose organizers asked participants to address a common set of themes and questions. In an effort to comply, I gave my contribution a rather programmatic cast, which has largely been preserved in this version. I will begin by laying out some of the theoretical and historiographical issues with which I have been grappling in my ongoing research project on aspects of Egyptian society and culture in the late nineteenth and early twentieth centuries. Then I will offer some material that illustrates what I am trying to get at.

The literature on Egypt of the 1882–1919 period has been dominated by diplomatic and political history—in which Anglo-Egyptian relations occupy center stage—and by a mode of intellectual history that is rather traditional by contemporary standards. The question that most crucially informs that intellectual history is how members of the Egyptian elite grappled with, and eventually adopted in whole or in part, concepts and ideas that originated in Western Europe. This process is presumed to be the key catalyst of social change: Members of the educated elite encountered certain initially alien ideas, tried to make sense of them in terms of their own cultural preconceptions, and ultimately deployed them in their own society through their writings or embodied them in new or "reformed" institutions by which means these ideas ultimately affected the lower classes.

As a result, the history of this period has usually been written not only "from above," from the perspective of elites linked to or seeking to influence the state, but also as a narrative of modernization whose central drama is the struggle of the enlightened (i.e., Europeanized) middle and upper classes to assimilate and transplant Western-inspired ideas and institutions.

This chapter depicts the outmoded and socially pernicious traditionalism of the retrograde and unruly rural and urban masses as a key obstacle to progress, which requires that those masses be remolded into a body of self-disciplined and self-motivated Western-style individuals fit to be citizens of a newly reawakened Egyptian nation ready to assume its rightful place in the modern world.

That most late-nineteenth- and early-twentieth-century Egyptian intellectuals (and not a few since) saw themselves and their society in this way is certainly true. And the best analyses of those intellectuals' concerns and debates, most notably Albert Hourani's classic *Arabic Thought in the Liberal Age*, remain indispensable.[1] Nonetheless, this literature is insufficient in several respects. For one, it has tended to focus on the same handful of individuals (especially Jamal al-Din al-Afghani, Muhammad 'Abduh, Rashid Rida, Qasim Amin, Ahmad Lutfi al-Sayyid, Muhammad Husayn Haykal, and a few others) and on the sources and evolution of their ideas as manifested in their published writings. In contrast, the work of a host of less well-known but prolific and, at the time, significant writers, journalists, and other intellectuals have received very little attention, despite the fact that these second- and third-tier writers grappled with more or less the same issues as 'Abduh or Rida or Lutfi al-Sayyid, though often in a more popular and accessible style, and enjoyed a substantial readership.

One does not have to claim that the work of these writers was as intellectually original or powerful as that of the "usual suspects" on whom the literature has focused in order to argue that any effort to reconstruct the dynamics and currents of intellectual and cultural life in turn-of-the-century Egypt requires that they be given due attention. In just the same way, one could not develop a reasonably comprehensive and in-depth analysis of U.S. public culture in the 1980s and 1990s by focusing exclusively on the work of Clifford Geertz, Stanley Fish, and Harold Bloom while ignoring people like Robert Bly, Deborah Tannen, Robert Bennett, and even, heaven help us, George Gilder—not to mention media personalities like Oprah Winfrey, Dr. Ruth Westheimer, and many others—though future generations of scholars may ultimately not deem the latter to have been among the great thinkers of our age.

At the same time, studies of even that small number of luminaries whose work has been most closely analyzed have tended to treat each of them in relative isolation, even though, whether for the late-twentieth-century United States or for turn-of-the-century Egypt, grasping what these intellectuals were about and gauging the impact of their work would seem to require locating them and their work in their interrelated contemporary intellectual, political, social, and cultural contexts. Here a concept deployed by Sami Zubaida provides a useful starting point. In an essay entitled "The Nation State in the Middle East," Zubaida discusses the emergence in the later nineteenth century of a "whole complex of political models, vocabularies, organisations and techniques" that constituted and animated a "political field of organisation, mobilisation, agitation and struggle."

> The vocabularies of this field are those of nation, nationality and nationalism, of popular sovereignty, democracy, liberty, legality and representation, of political parties and parliamentary institutions, as well as various ideological pursuits of nationalism, Islam and socialism. These ideas are underpinned by structural and institutional transformations: urbanisation and the dissolution or weakening of many primary communities, urban and rural, the emergence and widening of an individualised (but not always universalised or impersonal) labor market in which the state is a major if not the major employer, and crucially the spread of education and literacy, aided by the technical means of printed communication, of what Benedict Anderson called "print capitalism."[2]

Admirable as Zubaida's formulation is, it should, I think, be expanded to include the domain of cultural production more broadly, encompassing all forms of prose and poetry, written and oral, as well as music, song, theater, and so on, since that domain often overlapped with, influenced, and was influenced by what Zubaida defines as the political field. (Just as, to turn once again to the contemporary United States, the writings of Bly and Tannen but also the fiction of Tom Clancy, E. L. Doctorow, Norman Mailer, Toni Morrison, Stephen King, and even Louis L'Amour—and of course, the movies—are inextricably cultural and political at one and the same time, while the right's hatred for Bill Clinton seems to have been animated not so much by his policies as by what he was deemed to represent culturally.) I, therefore, use the term *cultural-political field* to denote the emerging arena of cultural politics in Egypt, that new social space in which, in the second half of the nineteenth century and on into the twentieth century, many of the issues that are still central to the cultural politics of the Arab world—modernity, tradition, cultural authenticity, liberty, democracy, nationalism, Islam, and the role, rights, and status of women—were first extensively debated in a myriad of books, periodicals, and pamphlets, but also in plays, poems, songs, and other forms of cultural expression.[3]

The task of elucidating the contours and dynamics of this field in its complexity and dynamism is still at an early stage. At this point we have some broad surveys of various domains (theater, the press, literature), some studies of individual intellectuals and literary figures, some work on social history, a few thematic studies, and various odds and ends. Nonetheless, there has already been substantial progress. For example, until quite recently the story of the emergence of women's status and rights as a hotly debated issue in Egyptian society focused almost exclusively on one elite writer, Qasim Amin, and the responses his books elicited from a few other members of the elite. However, thanks to the pioneering work of a number of scholars (among them Leila Ahmed, Margot Badran, Beth Baron, Marilyn Booth, Juan Cole, and Judith Tucker), we have begun to acquire a much better understanding of the historical antecedents and conditions of the possibility of the emergence of this issue as a key focus of cultural-political contention and the complex ways in which it was bound up with a range of other sociopolitical transformations and conflicts. Among other things, it is now clear that Qasim Amin's interventions were preceded by the appearance of periodicals targeting an emerging literate middle- and upper-class female audience and addressing some of the same issues he would later raise. A substantial number of writers, publishers, editors, investors, and readers, female as well as male, were thus involved in the processes associated with the emergence in Egypt of the issue of women's rights and status, enlarging the circle of people (and the networks of personal and institutional relationships) that scholars need to make sense of.

But it is not enough simply to do for a wider range of less well-known participants in turn-of-the-century Egyptian cultural-political life what Albert Hourani and others like Israel Gershoni and James Jankowski in their *Egypt, Islam, and the Arabs* have already done so well for a number of prominent elite intellectuals, namely, to trace the origin and evolution of the ideas about liberty, the nation, modernity and tradition, science, reason, and faith, which they espoused and the responses they elicited from other intellectuals.[4] To understand this cultural-political field more adequately, we will need to bring to bear on Egypt the kinds of approaches already well developed by cultural and social historians working on many other times and places. This entails shifting our focus from *ideas* to *practices* (including discursive practices), which I prefer to Zubaida's "complex of models, vocabularies, organisations and techniques."[5] That is, instead of merely trying to trace how members of literate and educated strata assimilated and sought to disseminate a limited set of abstract ideas, we would do well to try to broaden our perspective by addressing a much wider range of social practices, including those ideas but also the modes in which they were produced, engaged with, and received, and a great many other things besides.

To return to my earlier example, the emergence of women's rights and status as an issue in Egypt was not simply the product of Qasim Amin's exposure to contemporary European ideas about women or of the rise of print capitalism; it was also bound up with the emergence of new social strata as a consequence of the creation of a new kind of state in Egypt, as well as with a range of social and economic transformations, the development of new forms of Arabic and of Arabic-language literary culture, and the spread of new practices of reading that were, in turn, connected with changing conceptions of individuality and sociability, in ways that scholars of modern Egypt have only recently begun to explore.[6]

At the same time, focusing on social practices rather than on abstract ideas should allow us to move beyond the elite and more adequately explore changing modes of life, work, identity, and sociability among the peasant and poor urban (and overwhelmingly nonliterate) majority of Egyptian society. The kind of intellectual history that focuses only on the ideas that members of the elite were grappling with will almost inevitably exclude the nonliterate, or at best implicitly regard them (as the elite itself regarded them) as passive objects of a state-sponsored project of reform and moral uplift. By contrast, a form of sociocultural history that focuses on practices and representations offers at least the theoretical possibility of bringing even nonliterate Egyptian peasants, urban crafts workers, peddlers, domestic servants, and others into the historical narrative as people who were actively engaged with social transformation, rather than being relegated to the residual (and passive) category of tradition until redeemed by their social superiors' efforts at reform and/or by nationalism's appropriation of them as citizens of the nation.

This is not to deny or downplay the difficulties involved in doing research on the social and cultural history of nonliterate, lower-class people; those difficulties are painfully obvious and all too real. It simply suggests that by broadening our focus and asking different kinds of questions—by delving into how people worked, lived, associated with one another, socialized, spent leisure time, dressed, decorated their homes, told stories, and related to the expanding power of the state, as well as the ways in which these practices were represented, how people defined themselves and others along various axes of identity—we may improve our prospects for understanding this particular society at a specific historical moment and the ways in which it was changing.[7]

Lost Voices

By way of illustrating my argument about widening the scope of historical inquiry to include intellectuals who are today not well known or altogether forgotten, but who at the time were widely read and figures of some political and/or cultural significance, I would like to offer two examples. The first, 'Abd al-'Aziz Jawish, is, in fact, not entirely obscure. Hourani discusses him briefly in *Arabic Thought in the Liberal Age* (though he renders his name as 'Abd al-'Aziz Shawish), calling him a "violent orator" who "developed the ideas of Mustafa Kamil in the direction of Islamism and pan-Ottomanism." "His one achievement," Hourani writes, "was to bring the latent suspicion of Muslims and Copts to the surface, for almost the only time in the modern history of Egypt."[8] Jacques Berque mentions Jawish only in passing, calling him a "corrosive journalist" while characteristically suggesting that it would be desirable to know more about him and other personalities of contemporary significance and the relationships among them.[9] Gershoni and Jankowski refer to Jawish as the publicist of the Nationalist Party (al-Hizb al-Watani) and as an advocate of Muslim solidarity.[10] In his *Colonising Egypt*, Timothy Mitchell highlights a different dimension of Jawish's life, his work as an educator.[11] A number of other scholars, Egyptian and foreign, have also discussed Jawish, usually very briefly and in passing.[12]

Here, I can only offer limited evidence in support of my argument that 'Abd al-'Aziz Jawish and people like him merit more serious and more nuanced scholarly attention. Jawish was a complex and interesting figure, and a better understanding of who he was, how he saw the world, and why what he had to say appealed to a fair number of his contemporaries would help us understand his times more fully.

Shaikh Jawish, as he would become known, was born into Alexandria's Maghribi community in 1876 and as a youth went to Cairo to study at al-Azhar. He remained there only briefly, though, before transferring to Dar al-'Ulum, founded in 1872 to produce teachers of Arabic for the state school system; he graduated in 1897. He spent some eight years in Britain, studying pedagogy and then teaching Arabic at Oxford University. He returned to Egypt to serve as an inspector at the Ministry of Education and in 1903 published what quickly became the country's standard textbook on pedagogy, *Ghunyat al-mu'addibin*. In 1908, after the death of the Nationalist Party's founder, Mustafa Kamil, Jawish quit his government post to become editor of the party's organ, *al-Liwa'* (and, in 1910, of its successor, *al-'Alam*).

In that capacity Jawish soon earned the enmity of the British authorities for the often vitriolic (but nonetheless politically effective) character of his journalism. Some Egyptians shared British officials' animosity toward Jawish, especially when Jawish (largely for tactical political reasons) played a key role in stirring up anti-Copt sentiment. But many others saw him as an effective and courageous champion of the national cause and of an Islam under attack by "crusading colonialism." Yet while certainly an advocate of Islamic solidarity and of Egypt's connection with the Ottoman Empire, Jawish's stances on contemporary cultural-political issues make it difficult to pigeonhole him. For example, he became deeply involved in the controversies over government plans to restructure al-Azhar in 1908–1911. Though he generally defended al-Azhar against what he saw as the British-controlled government's attempts to destroy the autonomy of this bastion of Egyptian-Muslim identity and give near-absolute power to its government-appointed shaikh, and though he opened his newspaper's pages to protesting Azharis, he was no reactionary. Jawish supported the broadening of the institution's curriculum to include modern subjects, and in 1911, despite the bitter opposition of most of its *'ulamā'*, he organized a study mission to France for a number of Azhari students. The clothing he had those students wear while abroad reflected his vision of how a proper modern Azhari should dress: European-style suits and the traditional Azhari turban. Jawish went so far as to advocate admitting female students to al-Azhar. Taha Husayn has left a moving account (written from the perspective of 1955) of the influence Shaikh Jawish had on him and other young educated Egyptians before official harassment forced Jawish (along with the Nationalist Party's leader, Muhammad Farid) into exile in 1912.[13]

Unlike Jawish, who retains at least a small niche in the historical literature, Salih Hamdi Hammad is today completely unknown. Yet in the decade and a half before World War I, he was a prolific writer whose articles and books constituted significant and interesting interventions in contemporary debates and who seems to have had a substantial readership, though its size and range are difficult to gauge. I have not yet been able to find out a great deal about his life. He was born in 1865, the son of Hammad 'Abd al-'Ati Pasha, indicating an upper-class social background; suggestively, however, though Salih Hamdi Hammad himself held the title of bey, he does not seem to have used it, at least in his published work. He published a number of books and articles (notably in Shaikh 'Ali Yusuf's conservative-nationalist *al-Mu'ayyad*) as well as several translations into Arabic. He died in Cairo in 1913 at the age of forty-eight.[14]

I have not yet been able to locate all his published works, but what I have so far found suggests that second-tier writers like Hammad should not be as neglected as they have been. Perhaps his most interesting work is *Nahnu w'al-ruqiy* (We and progress), published in 1906. In this book Hammad details what he sees as the defects of Egyptian society, which like many of his middle- and upper-class contemporaries he understands not as social-structural but as essentially moral and cultural. Remedying those defects and making Egypt (and other "Eastern countries"— *al-bilad al-sharqiyya*) properly civilized and modern is therefore predicated, first and foremost, on the inculcation of individual endeavor and striving—in effect, of a reformed and properly modern personality, freed of the ignorance, indolence, and bad habits that he believes characterizes most Egyptians, especially those of the lower classes. Hammad goes on to discuss what should be done to correct the defects of Egyptian society in various domains, including health, trade and industry, and culture. He devotes a chapter to the Sudan, using the term *isti'mar* (colonialism) quite positively to denote Egypt's relation to it; indeed, it would seem that being a colonizing power is for Hammad a sign of modernity and civilization. Hammad regards the Sudan primarily as a source of wealth for Egypt and as an underpopulated but fertile land in which Egypt's surplus population could be resettled; he has no great interest in the Sudanese as such, who hardly figure in his analysis.[15]

If Hammad is clear about the many ways in which Egypt should emulate European civilization in order to become properly modern, he is also clear about what Egypt should reject: socialism and anarchism toward which he expresses great horror and loathing and which he fears may undermine and destroy the bases of European civilization. Egypt and other Eastern countries can and should follow the path of civilizational progress that the West has blazed, a course that, Hammad insists, is entirely compatible with Islam, properly understood as a faith that fosters science and rationality.

In another book, *Hayatuna al-adabiyya* (Our cultural life), first published in 1907, Hammad lays out, rather abstractly and formalistically, his prescription for proper modes of social, political, and cultural life, showing the clear influence of contemporary European social thought, but with hardly a mention of Islam. A second edition published in 1913 included translated passages from Cicero and Volney. By contrast, Hammad's 1913 book *Adab al-Islam* (The culture of Islam) is something of a popularization and extension of Muhammad 'Abduh's reformulated version of Islam, almost a sort of manual for correct modern Muslim belief and living.

Taken as a whole, the body of Hammad's published work may well seem eclectic and inconsistent. But it is precisely the evolution and inner logic of his thinking, as he and his contemporary readers perceived it, that needs to be recovered, and it is in any case high time we ceased measuring Egyptian (and other non-Western) intellectuals against some illusory Western standard of pristine intellectual consistency and modernity, instead of trying to grasp them in their own (sometimes contradictory) terms and properly contextualizing them—a job that obviously remains to be done, for Hammad and for many others. Books like these, written for a broad audience, were received at the time as contributions to lively ongoing debates and may ultimately help elucidate aspects of social and cultural change in Egypt that are not immediately apparent in works of greater originality, erudition, and lasting fame.

Youth, Manhood, and the Nation

I would now like to turn from neglected intellectuals to some of the new practices and representations that were associated with the constitution of a new cultural-political field in late-nineteenth-century Egypt. In his admirable study of the social, cultural, and political roots of the nationalist movement that emerged in Egypt in the later 1870s, Juan Cole discusses an oppositional political grouping that called itself Young Egypt.[16] The adherents of this grouping obviously modeled themselves on recent or contemporary European nationalist movements, perhaps especially Young Italy. Underpinning this term was a narrative central to nationalisms everywhere: The ancient nation that had for centuries been silenced by alien domination was now reawakening to national life and striving for independence, so as to take its rightful place among the civilized and modern nations of the world. In this image, the nation was simultaneously very ancient, with roots in the prehistoric or quasi-historic past, and utterly new, reborn into the full vigor of youth. Despite the brief existence of this small group in Egypt, however, this conception of Egypt as "young" does not seem to have played any very great role in the nationalist upsurge of the pre-1882 period, nor was it associated with any vanguard role being assigned to young people.

By contrast, from the 1890s young people—mainly young men—begin to constitute a publicly recognized social category in Egypt, and youthfulness begins to appear as a politically and culturally significant element in public discourse. This development was obviously connected with the emergence of students in the higher schools as a newly distinctive, highly politicized, and increasingly self-conscious group in Egyptian society, indeed as the vanguard of the new nationalist movement that would achieve Egypt's freedom and put her on the path to modernity. Students came to see themselves as members (or, at least, future members) of a new social elite, an elite based on knowledge, individual merit, and commitment to the national cause, rather than on wealth or inherited social rank, and thus as the social element from which the nation's future leaders would be drawn. In the process, youthfulness itself acquired a positive value, associated with physical and mental vigor and a capacity for self-sacrifice on behalf of the nation.

Obviously, youthfulness in this context had a strong class dimension: It was educated, middle-class youth (members of the *effendiyya*) rather than lower-class youth, who came to see themselves, and to be seen by their social peers, as the nation's vanguard. The new discourse in which this vision was manifested constituted a new form of social capital in Egyptian society and thus an implicit challenge to an older regime of social knowledge and social power based on deference to age, to other forms of knowledge, and to the established social hierarchy. Youthfulness was a thoroughly gendered category as well. Given that virtually all of these young students were male, it is not surprising that the image they had of themselves as the saviors and future leaders of the nation was inextricably bound up with new notions of masculinity, including a new interest in physical prowess and strength as evidence of manhood and as a means by which the honor of the nation (often represented as female) was to be redeemed.[17]

It was, of course, Muhammad 'Ali who first established schools of a new type to train military, technical, and administrative cadres for his state. Sa'id and Ismail had, to varying degrees, continued this policy, but Lord Cromer, who was Egypt's de facto ruler from 1883 to 1907, was opposed to higher education for Egyptians, for fear of producing an oversupply of unemployed and discontented intellectuals; in fact, he scaled back state spending on education at every level, reducing it to about 1 percent of the budget. In 1881, some 70 percent of students received government assistance; by 1892 the proportion had fallen to 27 percent. Nonetheless, the number of schools and of students in Egypt increased dramatically after 1882, as foreign residents and Egyptians stepped in to fill the gap left by the state's withdrawal or inactivity. By 1914, the country had 68 state schools, 328 private foreign schools, and 739 private Egyptian schools.[18]

The number of Egyptians enrolled in these institutions was certainly miniscule when compared with the explosion of post-elementary and post-secondary education in the Egypt of the 1950s and 1960s. Before World War I, the total number of secondary and post-secondary students throughout the country was probably still below10,000. Nonetheless, by the first decade of the twentieth century there were already enough students in the new higher and professional schools, especially but not only in Cairo, to begin to allow them to be seen (and to see themselves) as a unique and significant social group, distinguished from the vast majority of the country's population (the poor masses but also the idle rich) by their education, the kinds of career trajectories for which it prepared them, and the social status it brought, along with certain modes of attire and sociability—but also by their high degree of political involvement. That significant numbers of such students were concentrated in institutions located in the heart of Cairo, Egypt's capital and largest city, further enhanced their social weight.

Mustafa Kamil, who in the mid-1890s emerged as a central figure in the reviving Egyptian nationalist movement, owed a good part of his success to his precocious recognition of the emerging group identity and potential political significance of students. He grasped early on that the struggle for independence could not be won by force of arms—the debacle of 1882 had demonstrated the futility of that route—but only through the mobilization of public opinion in Egypt and in Europe (especially France). In 1893, still only nineteen years old and a student at the Khedival Law School, he founded *al-Madrasa*, apparently Egypt's first periodical published by and targeted at students enrolled in the higher schools. In the years that followed, he and his fellow nationalists worked hard to develop their base among students and graduates of the higher schools—that is, among young (and relatively young) men like themselves.

In 1905, their efforts led to the creation of a new organization, the Higher Schools Club, through which they sought to organize students and graduates of the capital's advanced educational institutions. This was the first of what might be called nationalist "front organizations" created to mobilize members of specific social groups. Predating the formal establishment of the Nationalist Party itself by almost two years, it claimed 773 members by the end of 1909. Established in rented rooms in Qasr al-Nil Street, the club provided members with lectures, trips, social services, a library (Nationalist Party leader Muhammad Farid would donate his personal library to the club), and a place to spend leisure time in like-minded company.[19] Students organized in the Higher Schools Club constituted a good portion of the Nationalist Party's activist cadre before World War I.

Egypt's first student strike followed the formation of the Higher Schools Club by only a few months. In January 1906 the Ministry of Education, dominated by its British adviser, Douglas Dunlop, promulgated new rules for the law school, which required that all students who failed any year of study be dismissed. The law students protested these regulations by boycotting classes. Mustafa Kamil's *al-Liwa'* strongly supported the students and sought to link their grievances to the national cause. After a week or so the students returned to classes, in return for a government promise to look into their complaints.[20] A modest beginning, perhaps, but from that time on, students in Cairo (and especially those at the law school) were to be in the forefront of nationalist agitation. Two years later, when Khedive 'Abbas Hilmi signaled his acquiescence in British rule by attending the parade of British troops held in front of 'Abdin Palace to celebrate the birthday of King Edward VII, nationalist law students gathered at the gate of their school (conveniently located adjacent to the palace) and chanted "Long live the khedive! Long live independence!"[21]

The law students' use of the strike as a means of protest was soon emulated by other Cairo students. These included engineering students, who in November 1908 boycotted classes to protest conditions at their school, and thousands of the *talaba* (students) of al-Azhar who in 1909 boycotted their studies to protest government proposals to reorganize their curriculum and institution—a struggle in which, as we have already seen, Shaikh Jawish was deeply involved. The nationalist press was quick to support the students and link their grievances with the broader national question; student activism thus inevitably became politicized. By the end of the century's first decade, political activism had come to be seen as a key feature of student life, launching a tradition that would persist down through the decades, indeed down to the present.

The students were moreover now frequently depicted as the front-line soldiers of Egyptian nationalism, the youthful vanguard of an ancient nation now awakening and asserting its vitality and its right to freedom after long centuries in the darkness of foreign (Ottoman and then British) misrule. It was a striking sign of the times that Mustafa Kamil's youthfulness—he was still in his twenties when he became a major public figure—could be cast as a political asset rather than as a liability. The positive valuation of youth, which he both took advantage of and greatly stimulated, enabled him to present himself as Egypt's tribune, representative of an ancient land now reborn into national youth and vigor. His untimely death in 1908 at the age of thirty-four enabled his supporters to cast him as a youthful martyr to the cause of Egypt's independence, further enhancing the image of educated young people as the social element that, by virtue of its command of modern knowledge and essential skills and its willingness to sacrifice for the nation, would play a crucial role in the struggle for freedom and progress. It is true that Mustafa Kamil's successor Muhammad Farid was somewhat older, and in 1919 the leadership of the nationalist struggle would be in the hands of considerably older men. But the image of youth and of students as the shock troops of the nation and its future leaders persisted, manifesting itself also in the emergence of Misr al-Fatat (influenced by Italian fascism and similar movements) in the 1930s and in the image of themselves as selfless young reformers that the Free Officers sought to project when they seized power in July 1952.

There exists a nice account, written in the 1930s, of how one young Egyptian student became an ardent nationalist, around 1904, an account that also provides some insight into the practices and discourse in which this new form of identity was manifested. Quite appropriately, his "conversion" took place in a coffeehouse, a social institution that was rapidly proliferating and in which members of the new *effendiyya* were increasingly spending much of their leisure time. The student is ʻAbd al-Rahman al-Rafiʻi, who would become a Nationalist Party activist and leader and go on to write chronicles of the Egyptian nationalist movement and biographies of his idols, Mustafa Kamil and Muhammad Farid.

> When *al-Liwa'* appeared in 1900 I was still a pupil in the preparatory division of the Ras al-Tin School in Alexandria, where my father had assumed the post of mufti at the Shariʻa Court. I had not yet become discerning enough to read the newspapers, and I went through most of the secondary division oblivious to them as well. During 1904 I began going every week or so to a charming *baladi* coffeehouse on Ras al-Tin Street, toward the palace of Muhsin Pasha. Its owner, al-Hajj Ahmad, would serve us lemonade, which was so delicious that his coffeehouse became famous for it. He would tell us about the newspapers, including *al-Liwa'*, but I did not understand its program, nor the programs of the other newspapers, nor did I have in my mind any image of Mustafa Kamil, for I had not yet seen or heard him. I was then fifteen years old. When I went to Cairo and entered the Law School (1 October 1904), a coffeehouse near the School, named Qahwa al-Huquq and owned by *al-hawaja* André, caught my eye. The other law students and I liked this name and spent our free time and our evenings there. It was there that I began to read *al-Liwa'* with understand-

> ing and comprehension and came to like its spirit and its articles; it became the school at which I learned the principles of nationalism, as it was the school of nationalism for an entire generation.[22]

Successive classes of students at the law school would maintain and pass on their institution's reputation as a nationalist bastion, right down to the spring of 1919, even though martial law made open protest virtually impossible during the war years. So when the law students helped touch off the countrywide anticolonial uprising that erupted in March 1919 by leaving their classrooms and taking to the streets to protest the arrest and deportation of the leaders of the Wafd, they were following a trail blazed by an earlier generation of students. It was thus the height of verisimilitude for Najib Mahfuz, in his *Bayn al-Qasrayn*, to have made young Fahmi 'Abd al-Jawad of al-Gamaliyya, struck down by British bullets during a demonstration in 1919, a law student.

A number of new practices emerged in the two decades before World War I that, in association with the new discourses of nationalism, of individual and collective identity and sociability, of how a proper modern person should live, work, dress, and comport oneself, were both constituted by and constitutive of a new cultural political field.[23] These practices included a reconceptualization of youthfulness and of masculinity that was bound up in complex ways with the spread of nationalism; middle-class young men going to new kinds of higher schools (especially law); new media like the nationalist press and new ways of reading them, often in specific social spaces (for example, the coffeehouse located near the school); and new forms of collective action (student organizations, the student strike, the protest demonstration in the streets). Exploring these practices does not, of course, obviate analysis of the abstract ideas about the nation, liberty, and so on that appeared in the speeches and writings of Mustafa Kamil, Ahmad Lutfi al-Sayyid, and others; rather it helps situate those ideas within the broader (and highly contested) cultural-political field within which they originated, circulated, and acquired social power.[24]

Nationalizing Islam (Islamizing Nationalism?)

I would like to offer one last illustration of the kind of thing I am trying to get at. Albert Hourani and others have provided excellent analyses of the thought of Muhammad 'Abduh and the divergent directions in which those who regarded themselves as his disciples—including Rashid Rida and Ahmad Lutfi al-Sayyid—developed his way of thinking about Islam. We have already seen how people like Shaikh Jawish espoused a form of Egyptian nationalism in which Muslim solidarity played an important part and very deliberately set out to bring Azharis into the nationalist camp. At the same time, other Nationalist Party leaders and activists were seeking to appeal to popular Egyptian Muslim sentiment by "nationalizing" Islamic practices and texts, again demonstrating the importance of cultural politics as an arena of struggle.

In January 1908, nationalist secondary-school students in Cairo and other cities organized social occasions to celebrate the beginning of the new *hijri* (Muslim calendar) year, very self-consciously emulating and countering the celebrations held by resident Europeans to mark the beginning of the new year as reckoned by the Gregorian calendar. They were in effect inventing a tradition as a way of asserting cultural-political equality, for the beginning of the new *hijri* year had up to that point been neither a day of great religious significance nor a day on which government offices were closed. Similar celebrations were held the following year as well, and the noted nationalist poet Hafiz Ibrahim even composed and recited a *qasida* (a poem that follows an ancient Arabic structure) to mark the occasion. This attempt by the nationalists to invent a potentially powerful new Islamic-nationalist tradition apparently worried the Egyptian government, and in January 1909 the cabinet of Prime Minister Butrus Ghali announced that henceforth all government offices would be closed on the *hijri* new year's day,[25] which gave the day a cultural and political significance it had not previously had.

A few months later, during the festivities marking *mawlid al-nabi* (the Prophet's birthday), nationalist students and Azhari *talaba* in Cairo again took the initiative. They set up their own large tent, at whose entrance they hung two large lamps covered with cloth on which the following quranic verses and hadiths (sayings ascribed to the Prophet) were inscribed:

- Consult with them in the conduct of affairs
- [God favors] those who consult among themselves
- The best struggle is that of he who speaks truth to an unjust ruler
- If God wishes good for a ruler, he gives him a sincere minister; if the ruler forgets, the minister reminds him, and if he remembers, the minister assists him. But if God wishes a ruler ill, he gives him an evil minister; if the ruler forgets, the minister does not remind him, and if the ruler remembers, the minister does not assist him.[26]

The message was directed not so much at the British as at the khedive, 'Abbas Hilmi, who seemed to have made his peace with the occupation and from whom the nationalists were demanding a constitution. These nationalist activists obviously felt that the rich tradition of Islam offered them tools they could make good use of in their struggle to mobilize popular support. We do not really know how people participating in the *mawlid* festivities perceived or responded to this intervention. That it took place at all, however, reminds us yet again how correct Sami Zubaida was to insist that Islam has been an important part of the modern cultural-political field all along, with a variety of sociopolitical forces selectively appropriating (and, of course, thereby transforming) Islamic discourses, symbols, and institutions and deploying them to achieve various ends. And it reinforces the argument that the writings of elite intellectuals may not tell us all we need to know about the political, ideological, and cultural struggles of that crucial era.

The material I have presented here has, I hope, helped clarify the arguments I advanced at the outset. Fruitful avenues for further research may be opened up, yielding significant new insights by (1) getting away from the premises of modernization so deeply embedded in our conception of history and of the world; (2) expanding the range of social phenomena we seek to understand in order to grasp more fully the transformations that Egypt underwent in this period; and (3) trying to explore nonelite as well as elite perceptions, identities, and behavior and the various and complex ways in which all Egyptians made sense of, and engaged with, the changing world in which they lived.

Notes

1. Albert Hourani, *Arabic Thought in the Liberal Age* (Oxford: Oxford University Press, 1962; Cambridge, UK: Cambridge University Press, 1983).

2. Sami Zubaida, "The Nation State in the Middle East," in *Islam, the People, and the State: Political Ideas and Movements in the Middle East* (London: I. B. Tauris, 1993), pp. 145–146.

3. In this connection, Jacques Berque's monumental but underutilized *Egypt: Imperialism and Revolution* (London: Faber and Faber), first published in French in 1967, and in English in 1972, merits mention as well as renewed and careful attention. Berque's profound knowledge of (and empathy for) Egypt and his essentially phenomenological approach to history led him to pay attention to many individuals and cultural-intellectual conjunctures and currents largely ignored by other historians. As a result, this very important work continues to offer important insights and point to promising avenues for further research.

4. Israel Gershoni and James P. Jankowski, *Egypt, Islam, and the Arabs: The Search for Egyptian Nationhood, 1900–1930* (Oxford: Oxford University Press, 1986).

5. For a somewhat outdated but nonetheless still useful discussion of the concept of "practice," see Sherry B. Ortner, "Theory in Anthropology Since the Sixties," *Comparative Studies in Society and History* 26 (1984): 126–166.

6. For an interesting discussion of publishing and reading, and more broadly of how to study popular culture, see Roger Chartier, *The Cultural Uses of Print in Early Modern France* (Princeton, N.J.: Princeton University Press, 1987). For a more general discussion of approaches to cultural history, see Roger Chartier, *Cultural History: Between Practices and Representations* (Cambridge, UK: Polity Press, 1988).

7. Khalid Fahmy's current research on the emergence of forensic medicine in Egypt and popular appropriations of it in the period before 1882 offers an outstanding example of a promising avenue of inquiry. I also cannot resist mentioning a very exciting dissertation in progress on Egyptian craftsmen and small traders and their "guilds" in the 1864–1914 period, by John Chalcraft of New York University's Department of History.

8. Hourani, *Arabic Thought*, pp. 208–209.

9. Berque, *Egypt,* p. 256.

10. Gershoni and Jankowski, *Egypt*, pp. 7, 17, 27.

11. Timothy Mitchell, *Colonising Egypt* (Cambridge, UK: Cambridge University Press, 1988), pp. 89, 101.

12. For a not very adequate biography, see Anwar al-Jundi, *'Abd al-'Aziz Jawish: min ruwwad al-tarbiyya w'al-sahafa w'al-ijtima'* (Cairo: al-Dar al-Misriyya lil-Ta'lif wal-Tarjama, 1965).

13. In al-Jundi, *Jawish*, pp. 179ff.

14. Khayr al-Dīn al-Ziriklī, *al-A'lām,* 8 vols. (Beirut: Dār al-'Ilm lil-Malāyān, 1980), Vol. III, pp. 275–276.

15. Eve Troutt Powell, *A Different Shade of Colonialism: Egypt, Great Britain, and the Mastery of the Sudan* (Berkeley: University of California Press, forthcoming).

16. Juan R. I. Cole, *Colonialism and Revolution in the Middle East: Social and Cultural Origins of Egypt's 'Urabi Movement* (Princeton, N.J.: Princeton University Press, 1993), pp. 153–155, passim.

17. On representations of Egypt as female, see Beth Baron, "Nationalist Iconography: Egypt as a Woman," in James Jankowski and Israel Gershoni (eds.), *Rethinking Nationalism in the Arab Middle East* (New York: Columbia University Press, 1987), Chapter 6. Wilson Jacob of New York University's Joint Ph.D. Program in History and Middle Eastern Studies is currently pursuing a very promising dissertation research project on changing conceptions and practices of masculinity in late-nineteenth- and early-twentieth-century Egypt.

18. These numbers do not include primary schools. For an overview of education in Egypt in this period, see Robert Tignor, *Modernization and British Colonial Rule in Modern Egypt, 1882–1914* (Princeton, N.J.: Princeton University Press, 1966).

19. 'Abd al-Rahman al-Rafi'i, *Mustafa Kamil: ba'ith al-haraka al-wataniyya* (Cairo: Maktab al-Nahda al-Misriyya, 1939), p. 195.

20. Ibid., pp. 195–197.

21. 'Abd al-Rahman al-Rafi'i, *Muhammad Farid: ramz al-ikhlas w'al-tadhiyya* (Cairo: Maktab al-Nahda al-Misriyya, 1948), pp. 77–79.

22. al-Rafi'i, *Mustafa Kamil*, pp. 145–146.

23. I am thinking, for example, of Mustafa Kamil's exhortations on the "free life" (*al-hayya al-hurra*)—namely, an independent profession that he and others argued was morally preferable to the dependency and subservience that a government job entailed. In 1898 he told a gathering of students at the Ezbekiyya gardens that "[t]here is no doubt that you will not be able to engage in enlightening the nation and guiding it properly unless you are in the free life, striving for yourselves in the path of life, not employed in some department or office and receiving your fixed salary at the end of every month, which will kill in you the sentiment of independence and suppress in your souls personal freedom and your propensity for great deeds." In al-Rafi'i, *Mustafa Kamil*, p. 113. In part, Mustafa Kamil and others may have taken this stance because government service meant subordination to British

superiors, unlike during the preoccupation period when Egyptian officials and army officers—including the fathers of both Mustafa Kamil and Muhammad Farid—could plausibly see themselves as the builders of a new Egyptian state, albeit one that was subject to the often arbitrary authority of the khedive. Though later nationalists would advocate a more vigorous state role in promoting social reform, and a government job would be widely coveted, the cohorts that came of age in the 1890s and early 1900s were strongly imbued with the tenets of late-nineteenth-century European liberal individualist thought.

24. Almost everywhere, participatory and spectator sports have, since the late nineteenth century, become a crucial mode of sociability and a key arena in which local, regional, national, and often ethnic or racial identities—not to mention conceptions and practices of gender!—are forged and reproduced. There has unfortunately been little research on the introduction and spread of organized sports, especially football/soccer, in Egypt, though it would probably shed some very interesting light on a range of questions.

25. See al-Rafi'i, *Muhammad Farid*, pp. 91–92.

26. Ibid., p. 104. The original in Arabic:

- washawirhum fi'l-amr
- wa'amruhum shura baynahum
- afdal al-jihad man qala kalimat haqq 'inda sultan ja'ir
- idha arada Allah bi'amir khayran ja'ala lahu wazir sidq—in nasa dhakkarahu wa'in dhakara a'anahu; wa'idha arada bihi ghayr dhalika ja'ala lahu wazir su'—in nasa lam yudhakkirhu wa'idha dhakara lam yu'inhu.

9

Slaves or Siblings? Abdallah al-Nadim's Dialogues About the Family

Eve M. Troutt Powell

In the 1890s, when the British occupation of Egypt was well entrenched, the make-up of the family and the structure of households had become explosive issues in the political struggle between British officials, Egyptian nationalists, and other intellectuals. The image of the family had evolved into being a symbol of timeless stability, yet also a target of cultural reform. The ideal of the family had become paradoxically synonymous with religious tradition, cultural morality, modernity, and a teleological sense of progress.[1] For nationalists, reformers, and educators alike in Egypt, the ideals of family values also bore a defensive significance. The traditions of the Egyptian family were seen as a cultural buffer against the British occupation. If reforms were needed to strengthen the intellectual and economic independence of women in Egyptian homes, it was often felt that such sensitive issues were best left to Islamic teachers, not to external, foreign supervision.

British officials, in their turn, often castigated this idealization of the Muslim Egyptian family as a prison for women, who were chained by gender seclusion, veiling, and a lack of education. One can read in the documents of Lord Cromer and his associates in the Foreign Office how Egyptian Muslim women were often likened to slaves, and this metaphor raised yet another controversy—the much diminished but still contentious presence of slaves within Egyptian households that many in Europe found reprehensible. In defense, Egyptian clerics and lawyers pointed out that these slaves, the vast majority of whom were from sub-Saharan East Africa, were not at all the victims of violence that their counterparts in the Caribbean or in the U.S. South were, but instead were quickly and fully embraced by the households that purchased them as family members. One finds this argument again and again, as this chapter will demonstrate. But one man took a different stance—the nationalist thinker and orator Abdallah al-Nadim. His approach to the issue of family and slavery differed a great deal from many of his colleagues, in his attempts to seriously argue from the perspective of Sudanese slaves themselves. As such, his work is very valuable in re-evaluations of the nineteenth-century discourse on African slavery in the Islamic Middle East. His perspective offers a dimension that complicates the binary of "good masters/bad masters," which dominated the arguments of his Egyptian and British contemporaries, and enables us to explore the issue of abolition in the Middle East in a new light.

This chapter will focus on two articles written by al-Nadim and published in his last journal, *Al-Ustaadh*, in 1892. These pieces present a unique and complicated investigation of the institution of the family in Egypt, an institution that al-Nadim recognized as undergoing great and volatile upheaval, with grave consequences for the country. The first dialogue, "*Sa'id wa Bakhita*," represents a conversation between two manumitted Sudanese slaves in Cairo trying to decide what their next step should be, now that they were free. The second, a group of articles organized as "Question" then "The Answer" in a series, explores how different classes of women in Egypt labor within their own households and situates domestic slaves as the instruments by which Egyptian mothers evaded their moral obligations to the raising of children. Both place slaves firmly in the middle of the controversy about family, which was so politically charged at the time, while drawing sometimes surprising conclusions about the relationship between domestic slavery and the position of working-class women.

Debating the African Slave Trade

After several years of resistance, Khedive Ismail, ruler of Egypt, submitted to the increasing volume of petitions, appeals, and outright pressure from the British government and signed the Anglo-Egyptian Convention for the Suppression of the Slave Trade, in 1877. The convention prohibited trade in African slaves, a trade that was at that time concentrated in the Egyptian-dominated Sudan and along the Red Sea coast. Ismail had been able to extend Egyptian control of this particular coast only with the cooperation of the British government, which had itself become involved in supporting the policies of the Anti-Slavery Society in Zanzibar, Oman, and Tanganyika. As the politics of anti-slavery grew more powerful in England, they affected and then shaped the negotiations between the Egyptian ruler and the British government.[2] They also proved powerful enough to persuade many in the British government that the Muslim rulers and potentates of East Africa could not be trusted to remain in power, precisely because of the existence of slavery in this region.

The anti-slavery movement gained momentum in England from the stories about the trade published by explorers like Dr. David Livingstone, Richard Burton, John Hanning Speke and James Grant, and Sir Samuel Baker. Their narratives about the havoc against innocents that slavery wrought were reprinted in newspapers and served as the evidence for what became a massive, evocative human-rights campaign against the African slave trade. Interestingly, many of these writers noticed how much more gentle slavery was within Islamic regions, after the trauma of enslavement was accepted. As Speke wrote in 1863,

> [T]he slave in this new position finds himself much better off than he ever was in his life before, with this exception, that as a slave he feels himself much degraded in the social scale of society, and his family ties are all cut off from him—probably his relations have all been killed in the war in which he was captured. Still, after the first qualms have worn off, we find him much attached to his master, who feeds him and finds him clothes in return for the menial services which he performs.[3]

But even such mildness cannot, for Speke, obviate the ultimate horror of the slave trade. "Slavery begets slavery," he wrote. "To catch slaves is the first thought of every chief in the interior; hence fights and slavery impoverish the land, and that is the reason why Africa does not improve."[4]

Egypt's long domination of the Sudan, Ismail's ambitions to further extend Egypt's control of the Nile Valley, and the numbers of Egyptians involved in the trade in slaves all made the khedive and Egypt clear targets for the concerned attention of the abolition movement. Ismail tried to counter these suspicions by employing European military officials to help his government fight the trade and to gain greater international standing. Sir Samuel Baker was one of these individuals hired to fight the slave trade in the Sudan, in 1869. Ten years after his expedition, he described his mission in the following terms:

> It was thus that the Khedive determined at the risk of his popularity among his own subjects to strike a direct blow at the slave trade in its distant nest. To insure the fulfillment of this difficult enterprise, he selected an Englishman, armed with a despotic power such as had never been entrusted by a Mohammedan to a Christian.
>
> The slave trade was to be suppressed; legitimate commerce was to be introduced, and protection was to be afforded to the natives by the establishment of a government.
>
> The suppression of the slave trade was a compliment to the European Powers which would denote the superiority of Egypt, and would lay the first stone in the foundation of a new civilization; and a population that was rapidly disappearing would be saved to Africa.[5]

However, Baker's fateful phrase "the establishment of a government" caused many abolitionists to wonder what kind of authority would be institutionalized, and it increased British suspicions that Ismail himself was trying to colonize vulnerable African lands. The convention of 1877 only increased anti-slavery watchfulness. In a few short years, many Egyptians would, in turn, begin to question British motivations, noticing how much more control of African territories was falling into British hands and wondering if abolitionism was simply imperialism spelled differently. Even more worrying, the khedive had signed the convention while his treasury had been bankrupted due to excessive borrowing from European banks, and a great deal of the government's finances were being supervised by European financiers. By 1884, the date by which the decree was to be put into full effect, Ismail had been deposed, the 'Urabi rebellion put down, the Mahdiyya had gained control of most of the Sudan, and the British were in full occupation of Egypt. Those who had foreseen the loss of Egyptian independence in the increased attention of Europeans into the slave trade now felt, unfortunately, vindicated.

This moment of crisis further exposed the embarrassments of slavery. The British now possessed the authority to more fully explore the presence of African slaves in Egypt. Lord Cromer, the British consul general, created manumission bureaus throughout the country, with a solid supply of primarily European investigative agents. He also created the Cairo Home for Freed Slave Women to train former slaves for paid domestic labor.[6] This proximity to Egyptian society exacerbated tensions between the British and Egyptians, and the tension increased as castigation of Egyptian Muslim culture became international. In 1888, for example, a Parisian cleric, Cardinal Lavigerie, gave a sermon condemning Islamic attitudes about slavery. An Egyptian law student named Ahmed Shafik heard this sermon and responded to it in a long presentation that he gave in 1890 at the Khedivial Geographic Society in Cairo, which was quickly printed. In his response, Shafik pointed out that European abolitionists often equated slavery in Islam with the physically much harsher institutions of slavery in the West. This was a mistake, Shafik stated, not only in its refusal to recognize the complicity of the Christian religious institutions with slavery but also in its blindness to the mildness with which slaves in the Islamic world were treated. Shafik asserted that, unlike in the Americas where slaves were stigmatized socially by their race, slaves were intimately integrated into Egyptian homes.[7] And the historical record usually bears out Shafik's assertions. However, as both Ehud Toledano and Jay Spaulding have pointed out, this has projected an oversimplified view of domestic African slavery. Slavery in rural areas of Egypt and the Ottoman Empire was often much harsher than the domestic slavery practiced in Cairo and other big cities. In what

Toledano cites as "core" areas, though, slaves were generally well treated. Still, the reiteration of the much-heralded "mildness" of the institution often disabled contemporaries and historians from recognizing "the vulnerability and the powerlessness of Ottoman slaves, especially bondwomen, vis-à-vis their owners."[8]

Domesticity, Slavery, and the Labors of Love

Many British officials were extremely curious about the defenselessness of female slaves and based their conclusions on evidence gathered by officers employed in the manumission bureaus around Egypt. Unlike Ahmed Shafik, however, these men took the ease with which black slaves entered Egyptian households as a token of Egyptian backwardness. "It must not be forgotten," wrote one official to Lord Cromer, "that in this country the selling of slaves from a Musulman [Muslim] point of view is considered legal, that amongst natives the custom of employing paid female servants, is far from general: so that the possession of slaves or even the selling of them, does not offend public morality as it would in a civilized country."[9] It was also widely believed that the inaccessibility of the women's quarters created conditions in which slavery flourished. As another officer summed up in 1886, "[T]he inmates of a harem, moreover, are so secluded that it would often be difficult to find whether a Negro girl was treated, within harem walls, as a free servant or a slave."[10]

Through the testimony of slaves freed at British-run manumission bureaus, British agents and officials gained access to the private domestic environment of many Egyptian families. With no other means of investigating the lives of women, many British government officials synecdochally equated "the harem" with the slaves; all Egyptian women were considered virtual slaves in their own homes. These judgments, glimpses, and speculations created an erotic, exotic discourse about the lives of Egyptian women and ignored the small but growing numbers of Egyptian women journalists and writers publishing their own ideas about the future of the Egyptian family.[11] How were Egyptians to respond to these equations of family with slavery?

One of the most sensitive and interesting responses to this uncomfortable situation was written by Abdallah al-Nadim, who had returned from a decade-long exile to Egypt after the defeat of the 'Urabi rebellion, and who had started, almost immediately, a new newspaper called *Al-Ustaadh* (The teacher). Actually, the British authorities had given al-Nadim's brother permission to launch the paper and had warned that current politics were not to be directly addressed. Al-Nadim thus had to approach the issue of slavery from a carefully articulated framework. He created a dialogue, in Egyptian colloquial Arabic, between two recently freed slaves, Sa'id and Bakhita, in which the two try to figure out what to do with the rest of their lives.

The dialogue begins when Sa'id meets Bakhita and asks her where she is now working. She answers that she has no work and that she wishes they were still slaves, still being cared for and fed by their masters. Sa'id reminds her that they were also regularly beaten by these same masters, and Bakhita concedes that she finds pleasure in freedom, but she still laments: "We came from our country like beasts [*zay al-bahayim*] and it was our masters who taught us about Islam [*al-kalaam wal-hadith*] and taught us about cleanliness, food, drink, how to dress and how to speak properly since we spoke in a way that no one could understand." Continuing to praise the kindness of her masters, Bakhita recounts how she was like a daughter to her mistress—"if my master tried to beat me, she would argue and yell at him. We always held hands, even when we were eating our meals."[12]

Sa'id, however, remembers physical torments and the terrible journey with the slave dealers more vividly than he does any kindness from his former masters. But Bakhita makes one point on which they both agree: that it is confusing and difficult to parcel themselves out to different households, to work for one household one month and another the next. Slavery is not better than freedom, she admits, but the uncertainty of independent living is too hard to tolerate. Sa'id agrees that the precarious employment situation of former slaves is very dire, and he tells Bakhita that he thinks the government should take responsibility for them and give to every manumitted slave a plot of land from royal estates and the necessary machinery and tools. After all, he says, they used us to cultivate a lot of land, year after year, in addition to the government having conscripted so many soldiers out of the Sudan. Sa'id says he's even heard that the Ottoman sultan offered such a gesture to the Sudanese, from whose agricultural bounty the empire is profiting.[13]

This was a daring and singular suggestion on al-Nadim's part, asking the Egyptian government to take responsibility for the futures of the men and women formerly enslaved by Egyptians. He also recognized, in this dialogue, how difficult it was for freed slaves to find an independent place for themselves in society, particularly for women. Much to Sa'id's annoyance, Bakhita cannot stop referring to her previous "masters," even as her friend tries to get her to see them as simply the *al-jama'a al-'aghniyya* (wealthy class) who could help create a new entrepreneurial collective of their former slaves.[14] Sa'id envisions the freed slaves as storekeepers and as contractors with their own teams of workers. Sa'id imagines Sudanese working in a wide range of fields, not only as the servants that many had been for so long. Bakhita balks at the impossibility of Sa'id's dreams, but he ends the dialogue with a challenge and a hope. "We'll publish this conversation in *Al-Ustaadh* and we'll see what progressive people will do with us."[15]

Language and the Family

Al-Nadim knew that many of his pieces were read out loud, which would thus force his readers to articulate this challenge to themselves as well as to illiterate listeners. The reader would therefore become both subject and object for a brief moment, before he and his listeners began to discuss the merits of al-Nadim's points.[16] Unlike the earlier, comic dialogues of the playwright and journalist Ya'qub Sanu'a, in which Sudanese characters regularly mispronounce Egyptian dialect, al-Nadim offered no indication of accent in this discussion. One wonders if the dialogue would have provoked a greater sense of inclusion of slaves among Egyptians or whether it was just an exercise in cultural ventriloquism. Would people have read this dialogue out loud, mimicking Sudanese or Nubian accents? Would the last sentence—"we'll see what progressive people do with us"—have felt like a rebuke of such mimicry or have been an effective means of driving the point of Sa'id's humanity even further home?

It is also interesting how the dialogue treated gender roles. Sa'id wishes several times that the government would provide them with the plots of land they deserve, then the Sudanese could marry each other and create the sort of family life that he feels they deserve.[17] The idea of marriage accompanies the suggestion of the Sudanese getting the chance to create their own community. While it would be dependent on the investments of previous employers, it would be an independent community, liberated from the homes of wealthy Egyptians. Several sentences later, Sa'id repeats the wish for respectability and for the rights of the Sudanese to marry and create homes with their women, "our sisters."[18] But Bakhita has more trouble envisioning this kind of family setting, so rooted does her loyalty remain to her former mistress, to whom she was like a daughter.[19] Bakhita's heart is intimately connected to her Egyptian "family." She is not ready to become the matriarch of her own family. She is paralyzed in a kind of perpetual childhood, not able to take up her position as a mature Muslim woman. Al-Nadim thus held up proper marriage within Islam as an ideal, and with Bakhita's incapacity to even imagine herself as an active part of this ideal, he demonstrates one sad consequence of long years of servitude. Thus, he also contradicted the traditional assertion that slavery had taught the Sudanese how to be civilized by revealing a woman stunted by her "education." Bakhita's social stagnation thus presents an important disjuncture in the dialogue. While Bakhita did not mature under the institution of slavery,

Sa'id clearly did grow into a thinking, articulate man ready and able for independence, self-supporting labor, and his own family. Such a disjuncture leaves important questions about where al-Nadim thought women fit within the construct of the family.

Labor, Women, and the Family

Ahmed Shafik's earlier insistence that slaves formed part of the Egyptian family involved another equally controversial discourse between British officials and Egyptians, and between Egyptians themselves, that the Egyptian family was an institution of "civilization" for any slaves within. Abdallah al-Nadim's dialogue between Sa'id and Bakhita also problematizes this ideal within an Islamic context, by showing its lack of success. Bakhita is bereft without slavery and unable to mature, leaving questions about the situation of free women within the household. These were provocative questions that encompassed fears about the future of the Egyptian nation itself. Lord Cromer launched a significant salvo when he stated that the situation of women in Egypt, which he viewed as tragically backward, would prevent Egyptians from the political sovereignty so many desired, because Islam was the intractable fiber of Egyptian society. This immutable foundation meant that Egyptian women would forever be slaves in despotic households ruled by unthinking men.[20] Cromer prescribed as an antidote the transformation of the Egyptian household into an accessible site where educated women could rear children unhandicapped by gender segregation and veiling.[21]

In his published views on the Egyptian family, Lord Cromer translated post-Darwinian British conceptions of the proper Victorian family and the idea that the nation represented such an archetype. As Anne McClintock has written, in this idealization of a particular kind of nuclear family, "a women's *political* relation to the nation was thus submerged as a *social* relation to a man through marriage. For women, citizenship in the nation was mediated by the marriage relation within the family."[22] Interestingly, Abdallah al-Nadim inferred that women's political relationship to the nation was mediated by the amount of work they performed for their families, and that this labor was different among the various social classes of Egyptian society.

Al-Nadim structured one article, "*Su'al*" (Question), around the idea of the equality between men and women, asking his readers to discuss whether there was such equality among themselves, and send him their answers. He urged his readers to consider the different circumstances of Egyptian women, which he outlined clearly in the subsequent article "*Jawab*" (Answer): the fellah in her rural poverty and her poor counterpart in the cities, as well as middle-class and wealthy women, both of whom he located only in urban areas.

With great detail, in long lists of chores and household details, al-Nadim describes the labors of the peasant woman. Awake before dawn, she feeds the livestock, bakes bread for her family, gives her husband and children breakfast, milks the cows, cleans the house, washes the family's clothes, and brings the livestock out to pasture. If she is a fellah from a certain area of the delta, she also must pack patties of manure for fuel. Her family responsibilities are to her husband and her children; no other member, such as a mother-in-law or cousins, is mentioned. But the truly remarkable labor performed by the fellah is her ease in giving birth, without interrupting her other duties: "I saw a hugely pregnant woman go from her village to get clover for the water buffaloes one day. After several hours labor pains overtook her while she was alone. She gave birth, wrapped the baby next to the clover, and carried this on her head, returning with two bundles. She passed by us, laughing, and told us of her happy accomplishment."[23] Labor, in all its meanings, cannot stop the sturdy peasant woman. Her labors make the family and keep it together.

In a second article published two weeks later, al-Nadim investigates the working lives of the city woman. The poor woman in the city wakes up before her husband, prepares breakfast for him and for the children, cleans the house, washes the clothes, perhaps does some piecework as well, like embroidery or making handkerchiefs, or teaches her daughters to do the same. Her work is difficult but not described in nearly the same amount of detail that al-Nadim used to portray the fellah woman. The *mutawasita* (middle-class woman) has a slave or a servant who does the necessary cleaning and cooking. Sometimes the *mutawasita* helps the domestics, but if it's a beautiful day outside, she has the time to put on a clean dress and go out to enjoy it.[24] As for the wealthy urban woman, she has so many slaves and servants that she does not work at all, except when absolutely necessary. Life requires her only to make sure that the household work gets done.[25]

All women bear the work of pregnancy, birth, and rearing children, work that al-Nadim says all women love. Among the fellahin, birth is invariably easy, as it is for the urban poor, too. But middle-class and wealthy women have a more difficult time with labor and giving birth and are more susceptible to commonplace "women's sicknesses," which are quickly cured. All of these classes of women love their children and the pleasure of raising them, but wealth deprives upper-class women from knowing this pleasure, since servants and slaves provide the child care. From all this, al-Nadim concludes that the fellah works much harder than her husband, that the poor city woman works as hard as her husband, that the middle-class woman works less than her husband, and that the wealthy woman has no work at all, except being beautiful. Thus, only the poor women equal men in their labors. And using an image of the wealthy harem that Lord Cromer himself would have found familiar, "*fa innahuna 'ala firash al-raha fi-l-layl wa al-nahar*" (rich women rest on their comfortable beds night and day).[26]

In this short series, and the dialogue "*Sa'id wa Bakhita,*" al-Nadim connects the issues of slavery and the ideal of the Egyptian family to the phenomenon of labor. The hardest worker in the family is the most honorable, the most equal to men because of the generosity of her work. It is interesting that the archetypal Egyptian woman who earns this honor is the peasant woman whose toil differs the most from the domestic servant or slave (both of whom exist only in the city, in al-Nadim's construction). Domestic slaves in Egypt, for the most part, did not perform agricultural work. In al-Nadim's portrayal, the least equal to men is the wealthy woman, who loses all dignity and status. Furthermore, slaves disrupt the balance of the family in two important ways. Their very presence in the household enables the middle-class or wealthy woman to evade her own domestic and maternal responsibilities. Second, their living in the households of others prevents them from forming their own true families, where their hard work will be shared by their husbands, and where such hard work forms the basis of a real cooperative, a family unit. And so, this contemporary observer of late-nineteenth-century Egyptian life debases the wealthiest women of his society, making their lives less meaningful than that of slaves, and inversely elevates the poor fellah as the ultimate care-giver, and the slave woman gains her dignity through what she has wrongly been denied—her own family and home.

Notes

1. Anne McClintock, *Imperial Leather: Race, Gender, and Sexuality in the Colonial Contest* (New York: Routledge, 1995), p. 357.

2. Ehud Toledano, *The Ottoman Slave Trade and Its Suppression: 1840–1890* (Princeton, N.J.: Princeton University Press, 1982), pp. 224–225. See also British and Foreign Anti-Slavery Society Papers, British Empire, Box G-26, Rhodes House, St. Antony's College, Oxford University, for the petitions brought directly before the khedive from delegations of the society's members.

3. John Hanning Speke, *Journal of the Discovery of the Source of the Nile* (Mineola, N.Y.: Dover Publications, 1996), p. xxvii.

4. Ibid., p. xxvii.

5. Sir Samuel W. Baker, *Ismailia: A Narrative of the Expedition to Central Africa for the Suppression of the Slave Trade* (London: Macmillan and Company, 1879), p. 4.

6. Judith Tucker, *Women in Nineteenth-Century Egypt* (Cambridge, UK: Cambridge University Press, 1985), p. 190.

7. Ahmed Shafik, "L'Esclavage au point de vue musulmane," *Bulletin de la Société de Géographie de l'Egypte* 5 (1892): 465.

8. Ehud Toledano, *Slavery and Abolition in the Ottoman Middle East* (Seattle: University of Washington Press, 1998), p. 19.

9. Public Records Office [hereafter PRO], Foreign Office [hereafter FO] 84/1770, Colonel Schaefer to Lord Cromer, 18 April 1886.

10. PRO, FO 84/1770, Report of C. G. Scott Moncrieff, "Cairo Home for Freed Women Slaves, May 1886."

11. Beth Baron, "Mothers, Morality, and Nationalism in Pre-1919 Egypt," in Rashid Khalidi et al. (eds.), *The Origins of Arab Nationalism* (New York: Columbia University Press, 1991), p. 272.

12. "Sa'id wa Bakhita," *Al-Ustaadh* 13 September 1892, reprinted in Abdallah al-Nadim, *Al-A'daad al-Kamila li majallat al-Ustaadh*, Vol. I (Cairo: Al-Hi'yyat al-'amma lil-kitaab, 1994), p. 91.

13. Ibid., p. 93.

14. Ibid., p. 92.

15. Ibid., p. 93.

16. Sabry Hafez, *The Genesis of Arabic Narrative Discourse* (London: Saqi Press, 1993), p. 84.

17. "Sa'id wa Bakhita," p. 92.

18. Ibid., p. 93.

19. Madiha Daws, "Al-'Amiyya al-misriyya 'inda 'Abdallah al-Nadim," *Buhuth nadwah al-ihtifal bi-dhikry maruur ma'itah 'am 'ala wafaa' 'Abdallah al-Nadim* (Cairo: Al-Majlis al-'Ala lil-Thaqafah, 1997), p. 295. Dr. Daws makes an interesting point about the different styles of dialect used by men and women in al-Nadim's work.

20. Evelyn Baring (Lord Cromer), *Modern Egypt* (New York: The Macmillan Company, 1908), Vol. II, p. 138.

21. Timothy Mitchell, *Colonising Egypt* (Cambridge, UK: Cambridge University Press, 1988), p. 112.

22. McClintock, *Imperial Leather*, p. 358.

23. Abdallah al-Nadim, *Al-a'daad al-kamilah li majallah al-ustaadh*, vol. 1, "Jawab," 20 September 1892, p. 118.

24. Abdallah al-Nadim, *Al-a'dad al-kamilah*, vol. 1, "Tabi' al-jawab 'an al-rajil w'al-mar'a," 4 October 1892, p. 160.

25. Ibid., p. 160.

26. Ibid., p. 161.

10

Shaikh al-Ra'is and Sultan Abdülhamid II: The Iranian Dimension of Pan-Islam

Juan R. I. Cole

The question of whether individual identity is singular or plural has serious implications for how we write Middle Eastern history, particularly cultural and intellectual history. Even canny studies of Middle Eastern thinkers often assume that the individual demonstrates a certain consistency in his or her views about basic issues in reform, modernity, and tradition. Social scientists have long recognized, however, that everyone's identity is situational and is influenced by one's particular social environment at any one time.[1] The Pan-Islamic project of Sultan Abdülhamid II, which involved, in part, attempting to cobble together an alliance of Ottomans and Iranians from various forms of Islam to stand against Western imperialism, is a promising venue for considerations of multiple identity. This project openly assumes that it is possible to be a Shiite and yet a supporter of the Sunni sultan, to be Turcophone Sunni and yet an ally of Persian-speaking Twelvers (the main group of Shiites). Moreover, Shiism itself was in a state of flux in the nineteenth century, throwing up schools like the esoteric Shaikhis and even new religions like Babism and the Baha'i faith, and many of the intellectuals involved in the movement had such heterodox origins. The layered and somewhat fluid character of their identities is exemplified by Abu al-Hasan Mirza "Shaikh al-Ra'is" Qajar (1848–1921), a prince, a poet, a Shiite clergyman, a political activist, and a secret member of the heterodox Baha'i religion.

The idea of an Ottoman-Iranian political and cultural alliance against European encroachments, which was intensively explored by Istanbul around 1886–1894, on the surface had much to recommend it. The Ottomans lost Tunisia to the French in 1881 and Egypt to the British in 1882, on top of major losses to the Russians in 1878. The Qajars watched with apprehension from the mid-1860s as the Russians advanced determinedly into Central Asia, conquering the Turkmen just to Iran's east, and eyed uneasily the vast British empire to their southeast. The idea of such an alliance was wrought up with Abdülhamid II's project of Pan-Islam, which had several virtues as a platform on which to pursue the diplomatic alliance. Pan-Islam as an anti-imperial ideology posited that the office of the caliph in Istanbul was key to rallying Muslims worldwide against European encroachments on Muslim territory. It could therefore form a framework in which both reactionary and progressive intellectuals could unite around the caliphate in a way they could not be expected to unite around an absolute monarchy like the Ottoman sultanate. Bringing the shah of Iran into the equation, however, made it far more intricate, since it was much harder to convince Iranian progressive intellectuals to support Nasir al-Din Shah for the sake of Pan-Islam. Moreover, the caliph was in competition with the shah for influence among, for instance, the Shiite Muslims of Iraq, which complicated any *political* alliance between the sultan and the shah.

Anti-imperialism drove a great deal of the politics of the Ottoman and Qajar states in the late nineteenth century. All three of the major political trends of the time—absolutism, elite reformism, and parliamentarianism—were elaborated with regard to their utility in maintaining the autonomy of the remaining Middle Eastern governments from European colonialism. Abdülhamid II (r. 1876–1909), who favored absolutism and Pan-Islam, pointed to the success of Russia in becoming a great power under the tsars. The Ottoman experience also exercised a lively influence on Iran, in part brokered by the some 17,000 Iranian merchants and intellectuals settled in Istanbul.[2] Ottoman absolutism gave way to reformist oligarchy under the Tanzimat in the 1830s through the 1860s, as well as to an increasing secularization of law and some political institutions. In 1865–1876 the Young Ottomans and their allies made an effective argument for a parliamentary solution to the imperial threat and to local problems, showing themselves sympathetic to a populist Islam. From 1878 through 1908, Sultan Abdülhamid veered back toward absolutism and even toward theocracy, as he proclaimed himself caliph. Absolutist opponents of the parliamentarists as well as moderate reformers who hoped for a far-future democracy pointed out that that movement's moments of greatest success, such as the 1876 constitutional revolution in Istanbul and the 1881–1882 'Urabist revolution in Egypt, were followed by humiliating defeats at the hands of colonial powers (Russia and Britain, respectively) who took advantage of the turmoil of revolution and the divisions among the deputies.[3] In Iran, which was more rural and isolated from Europe than the Ottoman Empire, the struggle in the nineteenth century was between the absolutists around Nasir al-Din Shah and the elite reformers such as Mirza Husayn Khan Mushir al-

Dawlih, who sought Tanzimat-type change from the top down in the 1870s. The absolutists won in Tehran, and not until 1905 was there a significant movement for parliamentarism in Iran.

These swings in political strategy and public mood affected the political career of Shaikh al-Ra'is. He played an important role in the Istanbul-based Pan-Islamic movement of the 1880s and 1890s, siding to some extent with the absolutist rule of Abdülhamid II for the sake of making a united front against Western colonial incursions. Shaikh al-Ra'is was born in Tabriz into the household of a prince who had made an unsuccessful bid for the throne and so lived his early life out under house arrest. After a fling as a cadet in the early 1860s, he accompanied his widowed mother to Mashhad and entered the seminary, ultimately becoming an accomplished Shiite *mujtahid* (jurisprudent). Shaikh al-Ra'is eventually became a secret believer in the globalist Baha'i religion, a moderate and reformist successor to the Babis that resembled in some respects the Saint-Simonians in France.[4] Dissimulating his heterodoxy, he nevertheless completed his studies in Ottoman Iraq with the great Shiite professors of the day and then returned to Mashhad. He was forced to leave again, however, after coming into conflict with the new Qajar governor of Khurasan. Shaikh al-Ra'is's gradual journey toward being a revolutionary began with this experience of suffering at the hands of a tyrannical Qajar official against whom no effective political reply could be made, but he still had not completely lost faith in his ability to acquire the cooperation of absolute monarchs for his reformist ends.

He relocated in the mid-1880s to Istanbul. Mirza Muhammad Husayn Farahani heard him preach there late in 1885 when he broke his journey home after the same pilgrimage. In a passage concerning the Iranian ambassador to Istanbul, Muhsin Khan Mu'in al-Mulk, he wrote disapprovingly of Shaikh al-Ra'is preaching in the Shiite mosque there and being honored by Muhsin Khan. Farahani no doubt disapproved of Shaikh al-Ra'is because of the rumors that swirled around him that the latter had heretical inclinations toward the Baha'i faith and toward the ideals of liberty and progress.

Shaikh al-Ra'is did more than preach in mosques while in Istanbul. He began explorations of a possible Pan-Islamic alliance between Iran and the Ottoman Empire. The ground for a Pan-Islamic enterprise had been laid by activists such as the Young Ottoman Namik Kemal and the Iranian political theorist Sayyid Jamal al-Din al-Afghani from the late 1870s, as well as by other thinkers and journalists. According to Iranian diplomat Mirza Malkum Khan, a group of "fanatics" around Sultan Abdülhamid had convinced him that the Europeans intended to force the Ottomans out of Europe altogether and that the only way to riposte was for the sultan to gather to himself the kind of support from the Islamic world as a whole that only recognition as caliph could generate. The sultan determined to send out a proclamation of his station as caliph to Egypt, India, Iran, and Central Asia.[5]

The new project was promoted in the Ottoman press. As Jacob Landau has shown, the Istanbul newspaper *Osmanli*, published from 1880 to 1885, took a strong Pan-Islamist line, with authors arguing for the unity of Muslims under the banner of the sultan-caliph.[6] The turn to a Pan-Islamic diplomacy coincided with increasingly better relations between Iran and the Ottoman Empire.[7] Beyond the question of Iranians in Iran, the plan to foster more friendly relations did have a certain appeal within the empire to the thousands of Iranian Shiites in Istanbul and Ottoman Iraq, despite the antipathy between Sunnis and Shiites.[8] The background of the idea of an Ottoman-Iranian alliance among Iranian expatriates would have to be traced in the expatriate Persian newspapers of the time.[9] Shaikh al-Ra'is was only one of a large number of reformers thinking along these lines.

At a meeting with Cevdet Pasha, minister of justice, and Riza Pasha, immigration commissioner, on 26 August 1886, Shaikh al-Ra'is began by putting forth the general proposition that the power and influence of every *millat* (nation) is dependent on its leaders being united and in accord.[10] The unity of the Muslim peoples, he maintained, could only be achieved by turning to the sultan and convening a council to exert efforts for the unity of the Ottoman Empire and Iran. He insisted that Muslim society at that point had no greater enemy than conflict between those two states.

Cevdet Pasha replied that in general he agreed with these sentiments but added that it seemed to him unlikely that competition between the two states could be eliminated.

Shaikh al-Ra'is agreed that monarchs tend to want quick influence. If the two sultans of Islam were, he says, to consider themselves equals and brothers and were to safeguard the religion, then it would become a simple matter to reform the condition and the thinking of the people. He added, "As someone who could be called a spiritual leader of the Twelver Shi'ites, I am ready to write a book and publish it, calling the people to a unity of the body of Islam (*ittihad-i hay'at-i Islamiyyat*), saying: 'O Shi'ites: Do you really wish to see the body of Islam weak and divided before powerful enemies?'"[11] He goes on to ask them if this was really what 'Ali (d. 661), the first Shiite imam, would have wanted, at a time when the enemies of the Muslim holy law were themselves fully united and were attacking the Muslims with all their power.

Cevdet Pasha and Riza Pasha then pressed Shaikh al-Ra'is on what practical steps could be taken toward Pan-Islam.

The prince-*mujtahid* replied that first, Ottoman newspapers must change the way they speak of Iran, avoiding the asperity then common in their columns. Second, special newspapers must be founded to promote Pan-Islam and make clear to the sultan's subjects that he favored unity with Iran. Third, the sultan might make some gifts to the Twelver Shiite shrine cities in Arab Iraq and issue permits for upkeep and remodeling to be carried out on the shrines, so as to attract the hearts of the Shiites. Fourth, special favor should be shown by the sultan to the Shiite clergymen resident in Iraq, who dwelled under Ottoman sovereignty. Bigoted movements that contributed to disunity should be curbed, and no differences between the two parties (Sunnis and Shiites) should be countenanced. Fifth, the ban on intermarriage between Ottomans and Iranians should be lifted. Sixth, the Ministry of Publications must be instructed not to allow attacks on Shiism to be published.

Cevdet Pasha and Riza Pasha both agreed that these were reasonable measures, as long as the Iranian state also changed its style and undertook similar reforms. Shaikh al-Ra'is wrote up his account of the meeting three days later, on 29 August 1886, and submitted it to the Iranian embassy in Istanbul, which passed it on to the Ottoman court. It is alleged that in the aftermath of this meeting, Shaikh al-Ra'is briefly edited an Istanbul newspaper *Itthad-i Islam* (Pan-Islam). It is not clear whether the Ottoman state ultimately adopted any significant number of Shaikh al-Ra'is's suggestions, but it does seem that his and many others' complaints about the state of the shrine cities were listened to. Abdülhamid gilded the shrine of 'Ali in Najaf and dug canals to bring water to the perennially arid city in 1888 and 1893.[12]

Nasir al-Din Shah would certainly have been made aware of Shaikh al-Ra'is's high-level Ottoman contacts and of his promotion of Pan-Islamic ideals in Istanbul. He no doubt worried that the dissident prince would become a political pawn in Ottoman hands if he were allowed to stay there. In early 1887, he therefore ordered the ambassador, Mu'in al-Mulk, to induce Shaikh al-Ra'is to return to Iran, with pledges of his safety. Shaikh al-Ra'is later observed that he had had his eyes open and knew that the shah's pledge that he would receive a different sort of treatment in Iran than before was untrustworthy but that he nevertheless complied.[13]

In early winter, 1887, Sultan Abdülhamid II responded to the prince's overtures of the previous summer by summoning Shaikh al-Ra'is for a royal audience, with both the Iranian ambassador to Istanbul, Mu'in al-Mulk, and his attaché, Mirza Asadu'llah Khan Nazim al-Dawlih, present.[14] Mu'in al-Mulk was celebrated for his excellent relations with the Sublime Porte.[15] They gathered at the Hamidiye Mosque and after prayers went to the sultan's palace. Permission was given to Shaikh al-Ra'is, Mu'in al-Mulk, and Nazim al-Dawlih to sit on chairs.

Shaikh al-Ra'is explained that Nasir al-Din Shah had repeatedly and insistently given an order that he return to Iran. "Since it is obligatory to obey the Padishah of Islam, if royal permission is given I will be leaving in a few days."[16]

The sultan asked Shaikh al-Ra'is to give his greetings to the shah and to convey his feelings of oneness with him. He noted that Nazim al-Dawlih had brought a formal letter from the shah and a reply had been written but not yet sent.

Abdülhamid II then remarked, "The enemies of Islam are united. It is good that these two Islamic governments be as one."

Shaikh al-Ra'is concurred, recalling the saying of the Prophet that "Unbelief is a single community (*al-kufr millah wahidah*)," and remarking that it was therefore fitting that Islam be united. He hoped that the harmony of the two states would be uninterrupted.

The sultan expressed a desire that Shaikh al-Ra'is would keep him apprised of his news through the ambassador.

The Qajar prince replied, "My sincerity requires it." The sultan said he hoped that they would meet again, and Shaikh al-Ra'is suggested it might be during his forthcoming planned pilgrimage. Mu'in al-Mulk noted, "Moreover, his son is here." This was a reference to one of Shaikh al-Ra'is's two sons by his first wife, known as Shaikh-i Baha'i, who was being educated in a special Ottoman military academy for sons of Iranian notables.[17] In the course of his discussions with the Ottoman leaders, Shaikh al-Ra'is had promised to write a book on Pan-Islam, a promise that he eventually followed through on.

In fall of 1890, Shaikh al-Ra'is was imprisoned. I have been unable to determine if his political activities at that point had to do with discontent over the tobacco monopoly granted by Nasir al-Din Shah to a Colonel G. E. Talbot, a British entrepreneur, or for how long he languished in the fortress. In January of 1892 Nasir al-Din Shah finally bowed to public pressure and canceled the tobacco monopoly, after which the political turmoil in the country gradually subsided. Iranian merchants and intellectuals in Istanbul, such as Aqa Khan Kirmani, as well as Shiite ulema in the Ottoman shrine cities, had played a prime role in agitating against it, which had changed the terms of the Ottoman-Iranian relationship.[18] Istanbul was now harboring Iranian thinkers who had publicly opposed the shah. In response, Aqa Khan Kirmani wrote to Malkum Khan around 1892. Nasir al-Din Shah put pressure on Istanbul to keep the Shiite ulema of Ottoman Iraq from continuing to intrigue against him in the wake of the tobacco revolt, though he noted that relatively few such clergymen felt comfortable continuing to intervene in politics, in part for fear of undermining the Iranian state.[19]

Shaikh al-Ra'is was allowed to depart from Mashhad with his entire family on 10 April 1892, heading for Ashkhabad in Russian territory. Shaikh al-Ra'is then proceeded with his family to Istanbul, from which he made another pilgrimage, though he returned to reside in the Ottoman capital upon his return. There he was again welcomed by the large Iranian community of expatriates, especially, he says, by the Azerbaijanis (Shaikh al-Ra'is had spent his childhood in Tabriz and spoke the Azeri as well as the Qajar Turkic dialects). He also had initially friendly meetings with Asadu'llah Khan Tabataba'i Nazim al-Dawlih, the former chargé who had become the Iranian ambassador to the Sublime Porte in the spring of 1891.[20] He stayed in Istanbul for one year upon his return from pilgrimage, until the end of 1893.

Shaikh al-Ra'is's return to Istanbul coincided with the arrival there of Sayyid Jamal al-Din al-Afghani from London to join the sultan's circle.[21] Abdülhamid II was still interested in promoting the notion of Pan-Islam or the unity of all Muslims, Sunni and Shiite, under his religious leadership, writing in his memoirs:

> The caliphate and the Shi'ites. Islam must work toward the end of reinforcing its bonds. It would discover great profit were the Muslims found in China, India, Central Africa, and in the entire world to draw near one another. It is regrettable that we have not managed to reach entire agreement with Iran on this point. Moreover, we have every interest in drawing nearer so as to put an end to the games of the Russians and the British. In my palace at Yildiz, a celebrated man of science, Sayyid Jamal al-Din, gave me hope when he said, "it is possible for the Sunnis to unite with the Shi'ites to the extent that the former stand ready to prove their good will." If what he told me can prove true, this would be of exceptional interest for Islam. The ambassador of Iran at Istanbul, Haji Mirza Khan, promised me his help in guiding this vast enterprise to a good conclusion. Jamal al-Din rallied certain ulama in Iran, in the same manner that he attracted to himself a number of high functionaries. Thus, if it is possible to arrive at a total accord with regard to the envisioned goal, a great step will have been taken and the two states will be much closer.[22]

Iran and Shiism posed geostrategic problems for any hope of uniting Ottomans with Central Asian and Indian Muslims. As a former consul to some Azeri cities, Ali Riza Bey, wrote, "Shiism intervened like a vast uncrossable sea," and he blamed this sectarian divide created by Shiite Iranians for separating the Central Asian Sunnis from any realistic hope of succor from their Middle Eastern co-religionists as the Russian imperialists moved into the region.[23]

The issue of Iran and Shiism was also, as Selim Deringil has shown, the subject of a stream of memoranda to the Sublime Porte from Sunni officials in Ottoman Baghdad, who worried mightily about the Iranian and Shiite influence there. Late in 1891 the sultan had brought eight poor Shiite children and two Sunnis from Iraq to study in Istanbul.[24] On 31 January 1892 a Baghdad official complained of the widespread authority in Iraq of Iranian-influenced Shiite clergy, even in the Ottoman army and police, and urged that Sunni teachers should be sent and the stipends of Sunni seminarians increased to offset it.[25] In spring of 1892 Sulayman Hüsnü Pasha wrote from Baghdad that a book of correct Muslim doctrine should be compiled and should be promulgated in Ottoman Iraq by trained Sunni clergymen to offset the enormous influence of the Shiite clergy there. He compared Mirza Hasan Shirazi, the supreme exemplar of the Shiites resident in Samarra' to the pope, detailed his alleged role in the tobacco revolt, and said he "has more influence and power than the shah of Iran." He urged education to instill allegiance to "our Master and the Caliph of all Muslims."[26] In another, undated memorandum, an official urged that the Ottoman state "turn" the influence exerted by the Shiite clergy, which was possible because most of them were Arabs and Ottoman subjects.[27] (This was also the hope held out by Sayyid Jamal al-Din and Shaikh al-Ra'is.) Most writers on the subject, such as Ottoman ambassador in Iran Ali Galip Bey, proposed a contradictory set of measures that included steps to attract the allegiance of the Shiites to the caliph in Istanbul while at the same time urging the same caliph to take aggressive measures to support Sunni missionary work among Ottoman Shiites, which surely would have alienated the latter from him.[28]

Nikki Keddie found and translated the account of what happened next, presumably in fall or early winter 1892, given by Afdal al-Mulk Kirmani, the brother of the Azali figure Aqa Khan Kirmani:

> The Ottoman Sultan came to believe in the unity of the different Islamic groups and asked Sayyed Jamal ed Din to write to the Shi'ite ulama in Iran and Iraq and call them to unity. The late Sayyed Jamal ed Din . . . said if he had the power of the sultanate and the necessary money . . . he could accomplish this great work with the help of a circle of patriotic intellectuals (*mellat parast*). The Ottoman Sultan gave guarantees and obligations for this. The Sayyed formed a society of Iranian and other Shi'ite men of letters who were in Istanbul. This Society was made up of twelve men: Novvab Vala Hajj Sheikh ol Ra'is, Feizi Efendi Mo'allem Irani, Reza Pasha Shi'i, Sayyed Borhan ed Din Balkhi, Novvab Hossein Hindi, Ahmad Mirza (who had just come from Iran to Istanbul), Hasan Khan (the Iranian Consul General), Mirza Aqa Khan Kermani, Sheikh Ahmad Ruhi, myself (Ruhi's brother), Abdol Karim Bey and Hamid Bey Javaherizadeh Esfahani.[29]

In 1892–1893 members of the group, including Shaikh al-Ra'is, carried on a series of discussions with Ottoman officials aimed at laying the groundwork for a thoroughgoing ideology of Pan-Islam. Ironically, of course, this group of twelve contained a number of highly heterodox figures, and several of them had extremely bad relations with Nasir al-Din Shah. Sayyid Jamal al-Din, who secretly inclined to the cabalistic Shaikhi school of Shiism, was in Iran from 1889 to 1892, when he was expelled for involvement in oppositional politics and his role in protesting the grant of a tobacco monopoly to a Briton. Immediately as the sayyid arrived in Istanbul in 1892, Nasir al-Din Shah had Nazim al-Dawlih demand Sayyid Jamal al-Din's imprisonment, but the sultan begged off on the grounds that he could hardly imprison a guest he had called to his capital. He did force Sayyid Jamal al-Din to forswear further public attacks on Nasir al-Din Shah, whom the sayyid said he had "forgiven."[30] Aqa Khan Kirmani and Ahmad Ruhi had been Azali Babis and married the daughters of Babi leader Mirza Yahya "Subh-i Azal" Nuri (an exile in Cyprus) but had then moved toward atheism and nationalist chauvinism; both hated Nasir al-Din Shah and had agitated against the tobacco monopoly. Shaikh al-Ra'is was a secret Baha'i and had been expelled from Iran twice for insubordination against the governor of Khurasan, and was in the shah's bad books. That Abdülhamid chose to work through this motley crew (though admittedly as a group they were among the more eloquent and important Iranian reformist thinkers of the time) raised severe questions about whether he could gain the trust and cooperation of the shah.

In an autobiographical note written after the constitutional revolution many years later, Shaikh al-Ra'is described the events in Istanbul after his third pilgrimage: "I intended to settle in Istanbul, and I associated with the late, peerless philosopher, Sayyid Jamal al-Din Afghani. Still, this was contrary to the desires of the Iranian ambassador. Because of his interference and intervention, nothing could happen. Mirza Aqa Khan Kirmani, the martyr to liberty, was a conduit for correspondence."[31] His continued affection for Afghani and his circle was thus still evident a decade and a half later.

While in Istanbul, through his renewed contact with Aqa Khan Kirmani, Shaikh al-Ra'is began taking an interest in the work of Mirza Malkum Khan. Malkum had been a long-time reformist thinker and had served in the foreign ministry but more than once suffered the shah's wrath, as in 1862 when he was exiled for having founded an Iranian form of freemasonry. Perhaps as a way of redeeming himself, he then broke decisively with Nasir al-Din Shah and began a dissident newspaper, *Qanun* (The law), which argued for a rule of law, supported Abdülhamid II and Pan-Islam, supported the tobacco revolt, and from 1892 began calling for parliamentary governance in Iran.[32] Malkum had been influenced by Saint-Simonian and Masonic ideas about human unity and also began a "League of Humanity" (Majma'-i Adamiyyat). Hamid Algar tells us that Malkum's *Qanun* reported the prince-*mujtahid's* presence in Istanbul: "Now Shaikh al-Ra'is has joined him [Sayyid Jamal al-Din], and it is said that he is attempting with the support of the Sultan, to become the supreme manifestation (*mazhar-i a'zam*)." As Algar notes, the meaning of the latter phrase is unclear but probably has some reference to a Babi or Baha'i idea of spiritual progress (Baha'u'llah, e.g., spoke of the spiritually perfected human being as the supreme talisman (*tilism-i a'zam*) and considered human beings manifestations [*mazhar*s] of the attributes of God. While in Istanbul, Shaikh al-Ra'is not only deepened his knowledge of Malkum's League of Humanity, but he also joined a Masonic lodge. Algar understandably finds it odd that an anticolonial Pan-Islamist would affiliate himself to a European-dominated organization.[33] But, in fact, Shaikh al-Ra'is was not a reactionary who disliked the progressive aspects of European civilization.

Shaikh al-Ra'is clearly fell out with the Iranian ambassador, Nazim al-Dawlih. It has been alleged by some historians that the Iranian state began to suspect Shaikh al-Ra'is of intriguing with the Ottoman government against it.[34] Given that he had joined a circle of known opponents of Nasir al-Din Shah, this assertion seems perfectly reasonable and may in part explain the deteriorating relations with the ambassador. Nazim al-Dawlih wrote Nasir al-Din Shah, complaining about Shaikh al-Ra'is. The shah wrote back entirely agreeing with the sentiments expressed by his ambassador and insisting that Shaikh al-Ra'is must by any means be brought back to Tehran. It has also been alleged by some historians that Shaikh al-Ra'is came into conflict with Sayyid Jamal al-Din over the latter's intrigues against Nasir al-Din Shah.[35] This assertion is untrue. First of all, as we have seen, the Ottomans pressured Sayyid Jamal al-Din to cease publicly attacking Nasir al-Din Shah. Second, in a letter written 3 June 1894 from Bombay to a friend in Istanbul, Shaikh al-Ra'is asks him to convey his "'*ishq*" (passionate love) for the "Great Sayyid" (that is, Sayyid Jamal al-Din).[36]

Aqa Khan Kirmani alleged that the Ottomans, seeking better relations with Iran in part because they wanted to ward off any Iranian support for the Armenians who were showing restlessness in eastern Anatolia at that time, declined to grant asylum to Shaikh al-Ra'is.[37] Under enormous pressure from the Iranian court, he left Istanbul in December 1893 or early January 1894 after having spent only about a year and a half there. There is a sense in which he was forced out of Istanbul in the interests of Pan-Islam.

Shaikh al-Ra'is did follow through on his pledge to write a book on Pan-Islam, but only after he had left Istanbul, visited the Baha'i leader 'Abd al-Baha in 'Akka, and gone on to India in March 1894. There he was put up in Bombay by a relative, the young Aqa Khan III. The latter was only a teenager (he had been born in 1877 and succeeded his father in 1885) and was unlikely to have been Shaikh al-Ra'is's real patron. Rather, his mother, Shams al-Muluk, was a Qajar princess (a granddaughter of Fath-'Ali Shah through one of his daughters and so a first cousin of Shaikh al-Ra'is). It seems most likely that she was his real host, though norms of gender segregation prohibited biographers from putting it that way.

Although the Aqa Khan was young, according to his later memoirs he already resented the bigotry of his largely Twelver clerical tutors and expresses disapproval of their casting aspersions on any of the companions of the Prophet, so that issues of Pan-Islam may already have been being broached in his household. (It is not impossible that his discussions with Shaikh al-Ra'is, who had come from Istanbul, were among the factors that led the Aqa Khan to seek and obtain an audience with Sultan Abdülhamid II only a few years later). Shaikh al-Ra'is's stay in India proved even briefer than his sojourn in Istanbul had been. He was amused at the religious diversity of Bombay, saying that one could see in the streets every day the embodiments of the medieval Muslim works on comparative religions such as Shahristanis' *Milal* (Communities) and the *Dabistan-i Madhahib* (School of religions).[38]

In his short book begun in India, *Pan-Islam* (*Ittihad al-Islam*), Shaikh al-Ra'is begins by saying his object in writing it is to revive Islam.[39] His first aim is to differentiate Islam from Christianity and other religions and to exalt it above the others. He asserts that Islam is the best of the religions, as demonstrated by the Quran verse, "Today I have completed for you your religion." He insists that no religion is more beneficial than Islam or better able to bestow prosperity on humankind. He denies any desire to detract from previous religions, but insists that these were temporary, with appointed lengths assigned to their dispensations. He interprets the ordaining of a further religion, Islam, that supplants previous faiths as in accordance with the Shiite doctrine of *bada'*, which holds that God changes his mind, but urges that this abrogation be seen as a sign of divine grace rather than as a matter for regret.

This argument is drawn from Babi-Baha'i thought on "progressive revelation," and obviously has the drawback within an Islamic framework that it strongly implies that Islam, too, could conceivably be abrogated and a new "prescription" written by a God who changes his mind. Moreover, the mainstream Muslim view of the religions is that all were restatements of the same basic faith, rather than being "progressive" over time, and that the problem was not that they became outmoded but that they became corrupted over time from their static pristine purity, which a new revelation restored. Shaikh al-Ra'is appeals to progressive revelation in this context, however, as a useful way to deflect the claims of the Christian missionaries that their religion was the most advanced. Perhaps aware of how he might be accused of veering into heterodoxy, he is careful to invoke the doctrine that Muhammad is the seal of the prophets and Islam is everlasting (though both "seal" and "Islam" are sufficiently ambiguous words—the latter can mean mere submission to God—that he need not have been lying so much as dissimulating here). Indeed, he boasts, the civilized nations of the non-

Muslims had recently found themselves constrained to adopt some of the provisions of the holy Law, such as the prohibition on alcohol, or allowing divorce (*Ittihad al-Islam*, pp. 12–15).[39]

After a general defense of Islam, Shaikh al-Ra'is turns to the vexed issue of the differing Sunni and Shiite conceptions of religious leadership. Early Sunnis vested authority in a caliph, whether oligarchically chosen or hereditary, drawn from the noble Quraysh clan. Shiites felt that the successorship to the Prophet should have gone to his cousin and son-in-law 'Ali in the first instance, and then have been passed to the lineal descendants of 'Ali and the Prophet's wife, Fatima. Twelver Shiites refer to 'Ali and his eleven descendants as imams, and they hold that the twelfth imam disappeared into a supernatural occultation from which he would one day return, rather as Christians hope for the return of Christ. Shiites have in history tended to view the first three caliphs now venerated by Sunnis as loathsome usurpers of the rights of the House of the Prophet, and in folk practice pronounced curses on them during Shiite mourning sessions and processions commemorating the martyrdom of the imams. Obviously, Shiite antipathy toward the early caliphate (and the general idea of a non-'Alid caliphate) stood firmly in the way of the Pan-Islamic enterprise, and Shaikh al-Ra'is attempts to combat it.

He argues that the Prophet's influence ensured high ethical standards among all his companions in Mecca and helpers in Medina (the former mostly supported Abu Bakr and the latter had tended to support 'Ali and so could be counted as primitive proto-Shiites). Shaikh al-Ra'is does throw a sop to the Shiites by saying that later generations turned the caliphate into a monarchy and that these kings were seduced by the baubles of this world, contributing to a decline in Muslim religious zeal. He condemns the Umayyads. He focuses on 'Ali as a sympathetic figure (note that he is both the fourth Sunni caliph and the first Shiite imam, and so a natural icon for Pan-Islamists) and points to his willingness to compromise and seek arbitration in his conflict with Mu'awiyah (pp. 30–37).

What, then, can be done to address Islam's plight, which he compares to that of "a fevered person on his death bed"? He replies that the only way to throw off this illness in the body of Islam is for "the two mighty states and the two august communities of Islam to renew their fraternal sentiments under the shadow of the Muslim creed" (i.e., "There is no God but God and Muhammad is his Prophet," something all Muslims agreed upon). He dismisses that idea he says was put forward by some, that the doctrines of the various Muslim sects could be unified, noting that it is difficult almost to the point of impossibility to change established beliefs. "My purpose," he avows, "is not that Sunnis become Shi'ites or Shi'ites Sunnis." Rather, he says, the question is whether the two branches of Islam have more in common with one another in regard to monotheism and the basic principles of Islam than they do with other Abrahamic faiths (the "people of the Book"). After all, he points out, the Prophet Muhammad called for unity with Christians and Jews, and the Quran rejoiced when Christian Byzantium defeated "pagan" Persia. But today, he says, were one of the two branches of Islam to vanish, the members of the other would rejoice!

Shaikh al-Ra'is now makes some concrete suggestions for Sunni-Shiite conciliation and unity, similar to those he had earlier broached to Cevdet Pasha and Riza Pasha. First, he says, a treaty of friendship must be enacted between the Ottoman and the Iranian states renewing their friendship, and both must make a spiritual commitment to exalt the word of Islam. Moreover, all Muslim states not in a vassal relationship to either of these, whether emirates or limited constitutional regimes, should also join them in this new effort. The impetus for such unity and avoidance of intra-Muslim conflict, he stresses, comes from the unique situation facing the Middle East in the 1890s, when for the first time excellent communications allow Westerners to acquire good intelligence on the domestic affairs of the states of the region, and to spread their influence throughout the East. Thus, every step taken that weakens *saltanat-i Islam* (Muslim monarchy) is destructive of religion and state.

In short, he says, the "ill-intentioned meetings now being held in Iran can only result in damage to both religion and the state" (pp. 44–45). Presumably the clerical political networks with a radical cast that had then been established had continued to meet into 1894, aiming at further whittling down Nasir al-Din Shah's absolutism. Shaikh al-Ra'is was no friend of absolutism, and later played a major role in the constitutional revolution. The message that the threat of European intervention was a more pressing problem than absolutism and that religious leaders should withdraw from politics and support the indigenous monarch against his external enemies had also been enunciated by Shaikh al-Ra'is's spiritual guide, the Baha'i leader 'Abd al-Baha, in the latter's *Treatise on Leadership* (*Risalih-'i Siyasiyyih*), which circulated in manuscript and then was published in Bombay in 1896.[40] This sort of Prussian nationalist emphasis on building a strong state before pursuing "lesser" goals such as democracy was also characteristic for most of his political career of Sayyid Jamal al-Din al-Afghani, Shaikh al-Ra'is's collaborator in the Istanbul Pan-Islamic circle. By the early 1890s, however, Sayyid Jamal al-Din appears to have begun considering the removal of Nasir al-Din Shah more important than any other consideration, and this difference may have given rise to the rumors that the two had fallen out. That is, the very clerical networks of opposition to Nasir al-Din Shah here condemned by Shaikh al-Ra'is were nurtured by the letters and newspapers associated with Aqa Khan Kirman, Sayyid Jamal al-Din, and some of the other Istanbul Iranians most deeply involved in the Pan-Islamic project.[41] This difference in emphasis, between those who saw

Pan-Islam as a way of weakening the shah, and those who saw it as a way of strengthening Muslim "national" identity without rendering the national state so feeble as to become vulnerable to imperial takeover, opened a crucial breach in the ranks of the Istanbul Iranian circle that helped doom their efforts.

Shaikh al-Ra'is argues that the Muslim clergy must exert themselves to establish *sulh-i 'umumi* (universal peace) within the realm of Islam. (Again, this is a millenarian Baha'i technical term evoking faith in the coming of a new age where war and conflict will subside and harmony will prevail among the peoples of various religions.) He criticizes the Shiites who excite the emotions of their common co-religionists by spreading pamphlets around Mecca and the shrine cities of Iraq "speaking of liberty and freedom." Implying that this movement was to some extent British-inspired, he says bitterly, "They imagine that in the shade of such infidel liberty they will be free to practice their religion without dissimulation." He counters that the Shiite shrines of Najaf and Karbala were embellished at the initiative of a *Muslim* state and insists that were Westerners to rule over Arabia and Iraq, "They would implement the 'liberty' of building churches and taverns and of turning the Kaabah into a house of iniquity." He calls for the Shiite clergy of Ottoman Iraq to support the sultan, and expresses the hope that the door for audiences for them with him will be opened (*Ittihad al-Islam,* pp. 45–47).

He explains that the Ottoman and Iranian sovereigns are regarded differently by their two monarchs. Shaikh al-Ra'is says that the Ottoman state was "constrained by circumstances to accept a foreign law," but argues that this beneficial code can now be cast in a different form and clothed in Islamic law. That is, like most Iranian notables he disapproved of the limited secularization of law under the Ottoman Tanzimat or reforms, and hoped a way could be found not so much as to jettison the new codes but to find Muslim jurisprudential grounds for them. He applauds Abdülhamid II's attempt to revive the caliphate and to advance the interests of Islam, as well as to restore unity to the Muslim world (pp. 48–50).

In contrast, he says, Iran's leadership situation is quite different owing to the doctrines of Shiism. There, the spiritual and the temporal do not overlap. Spiritual leadership is in the hands of the Muslim jurisprudents, and civil leadership lies with the monarchy. He remarks that Muslim subjects give their taxes to the civil treasury under threat of force, while they donate religious taxes to the great jurisprudents voluntarily. "The King of the Shi'ites," he admits, "cannot give himself out as the Imam of the Muslims or as being owed their allegiance." Thus, whenever the two institutions of religion and state come into conflict, severe difficulties result.

He proposes that in order to deal with religion-state conflict a special office be established in the Iranian government, so as to bring together the conflicting ideas of the good-intentioned on both sides. He complains of those heedless government officials who have no conception of the material benefits of religion and who wish to render the state completely autonomous from Islamic Law, taking Peter the Great and Charles XII as their models. The well-wishers of religion, he says, counter that strengthening it will strengthen the state and will allow it to avoid wasting its time on personal matters and minutiae (since the latter can be forwarded to the Shiite jurisprudents). He also notes the anti-imperialist argument for appealing to Islam, insofar as the latter's nativism insures that were the foreigner to attempt to intervene in a Muslim state, a great commotion will ensue (this is, of course, the argument of Sayyid Jamal al-Din) (pp. 50–52).

Formulating his ideal for the duocephalous power structure in Iran, he wrote, "I believe that the leaders of religion must aid the Iranian monarchy." He characterizes the leading Shiite clergyman of the time (Mirza Hasan Shirazi, with whom he had studied) as being the "general deputy" of the absent twelfth imam, and says he must "endorse the outward sovereign state of the Shi'ites." Urging the acquiescence of theocratic Shiites in the Qajar monarchy, he gives the example of David, who, despite being a prophet, said, "send to us a king" (Quran, Sura Baqarah, 246). It is necessary, he urges, that the clergy be included in government consultations, and that the two branches of religious experts and state ministers both be respected and coexist harmoniously. Given, he says, that the shah of Iran is intelligent and enlightened, many believed that he could with only a slight effort revivify the state and the people (or religion) of his country.

He concludes by calling upon the great religious leaders in the shrine cities of Arab Iraq to form a religious association called "The Advancement of Islam" (Taraqqi-yi Islam), and employ it to revive the people throughout Iran. He underlines that it would pose no threat to the state and have nothing to do with state goals. It would also work with the Muslim subjects of foreign states such as India and the Caucasus, and would send abroad Muslim missionaries. He laments that while Europeans have paid a great deal of attention to mission, Muslims have lagged behind in this regard, so that the "simple souls" in Africa, India, and China might well become Christians even though their natural inclination would have been toward Islam.

Obviously, citing the headquarters of this society for the Advancement of Islam in the shrine cities made it an Ottoman affair, and while it might have offered some support to the Shiites of Bukhara, Lucknow, and Baku had it been formed, the idea of the shah allowing such an organization free rein to operate in Iran seems as far-fetched as the prospect of a Sunni ruler like Abdülhamid II lending any support to Shiite missionizing of Africans and Indians. The letters that the Iranian committee on Pan-Islam in Istanbul wrote to the Shiite clergy in 1894 urging loyalty to the Pan-Islamic caliphate of Abdülhamid so enraged Nasir al-Din Shah by appearing to poach on his territory that a rupture in Iranian-Ottoman relations was threatened. The Ottomans backed off somewhat, and the Iranian dimension of the Pan-Islamic project was thenceforth downplayed or entirely forsaken by Ottoman diplomats and statesmen, even though individual Iranians in Istanbul on the sultan's payroll, such as Sayyid Jamal al-Din, continued to attempt to gain influence with the Shiite clergy and to work against Nasir al-Din Shah.[42] Despite the sultan-caliph's willingness to attempt to appeal to Shiites for their loyalty, the sultan's officials increasingly pursued a strongly Sunni policy that even involved attempts to combat Shiism in Ottoman Iraq, as Selim Deringil has shown.[43] Shaikh al-Ra'is's book, finished in the Persian Gulf near Muscat early in 1895 and published shortly thereafter in Bombay, appeared around the time the entire project had begun more or less to collapse. Meanwhile, the assassination of Nasir al-Din Shah in 1896 and the involvement of the assassin in the network of Aqa Khan Kirmani and Sayyid Jamal al-Din al-Afghani led to the Ottoman deportation and execution in Tabriz of several members of the old Iranian Pan-Islamist working group. Sayyid Jamal al-Din, though not deported, lived the last year or so of his life under heavy surveillance in Istanbul. Shaikh al-Ra'is settled in Shiraz for some years as a moderate reformer before ultimately emerging as the poet laureate of the constitutional revolution in Iran, 1905–1911.

It seems apparent that the Iranian dimension of Pan-Islam remained undeveloped for a number of reasons. First, as Shaikh al-Ra'is notes, Nasir al-Din Shah did have a great deal of influence among the Shiites, despite not being a religious leader per se. He resisted losing that influence to the sultan-caliph, whom the Pan-Islamists wanted even Shiite Muslims to recognize as a spiritual leader. For Abdülhamid to hope to improve relations with Iran in the sphere of civil diplomacy for the purposes of an Ottoman-Iranian alliance against European imperialism, while at the same time seeking to undermine the loyalty of Shiites to the shah and bring them under his spiritual influence, was wholly unrealistic. Genuine Pan-Islam would have required the sultan to put away Sunni prejudices and adopt a genuinely pluralist approach to religion in the Ottoman Empire rather than coding the Iraqi Shiites as a priori disloyal and objects of conversion. The whole project of Pan-Islam as a fostering of spiritual loyalty to the caliph was in fact heavily imbricated in Sunni triumphalism and Sunni missionizing, so that it was bound to raise alarm among the Shiites of Iraq. That the latter could have been convinced to turn spiritually to a man who honored the early caliphs 'Umar and 'Uthman, whom the Twelver Shiites tended to excoriate, was in any case unlikely. For them to turn toward a man who headed the alternative branch of Islam and was sultan of a government that discriminated against them on religious grounds was just as fantastic.

A second set of contradictions involved the sultan's use of progressive intellectuals to promote his Pan-Islamic ideals. These were willing, on pragmatic grounds, to support the Ottoman sultan despite their general suspicion of autocracy and their general admiration for parliamentarism. This support stemmed from their greater fear of European imperialism. But none of them was willing wholeheartedly to support Nasir al-Din Shah, in part because the tobacco monopoly had convinced them that he was himself soft on imperial encroachments and therefore an unreliable partner in any union for the purpose of making a stand against the British and Russians. The idea of uniting conservative and progressive intellectuals under allegiance to the sultan-caliph of the Ottomans, then, collapsed in the face of the progressives' inability to stomach the shah.

In his essay Shaikh al-Ra'is attempted to deal with all these contradictions. He made the case for the superiority of Islam over other religions. He admitted a need for reform away from Greek-inspired scholasticism and for the education of women, but defended the death penalty in Islam. He pointed out that monotheists have a duty to unite with one another against pagans, and that how much more do Muslims of various branches need to band together in the face of European colonial conquests of the lands of Muslims. He attempted to convince Shiites to cease cursing the early caliphs, and Sunnis to look upon Shiism as a legitimate branch of Islam rather than an execrable heresy. He called all to an allegiance to Sultan Abdülhamid, and ridiculed any hopes the more progressive Shiites in Iraq might have entertained that British rule would give them greater liberty of religious conscience than did the Ottomans. He also called for Shiites to stand behind Nasir al-Din Shah and to cease intriguing against him, lest they inadvertently so weaken Iran as to invite foreign occupation. He attempted to discourage the notion of the illegitimacy of monarchy in Shiite thought (where sovereignty theoretically lies with the absent twelfth imam and so civil governments are denied legitimacy).

The real-world contradictions in the enterprise overwhelmed it. By the mid-1890s relations between Abdülhamid and Nasir al-Din Shah were at a nadir. Even Shaikh al-Ra'is's treatise contained many instances of dissimulation. A man who could privately write back from Bombay of British India as a land of freedom and liberty was not being entirely honest when he criticized the pro-British Shiite *mujtahid*s of Ottoman Iraq. A man who could express his "passionate love" of Sayyid Jamal al-Din was hardly likely to have been sincere in condemning the networks of enlightened intellectuals working against Nasir al-Din Shah in Iran. A man who could see even Ram as a symbol of divine unity, when in India, was not a very convincing crusader for Islamic triumphalism. Despite being a Qajar he had fallen out with the shah. He disliked tyranny, and could see the virtues of British-style liberty, but he hated the idea of European, Christian domination of the Middle East. These contradictions in his identity allowed him to seek a resolution in Pan-Islam, which was anti-imperialist, ecumenical, and potentially progressive, though it did entail working closely with the autocratic Abdülhamid. In the end, however, this project proved too flimsy an umbrella under which to unite the multiplicities of Shaikh al-Ra'is's various identities.

Notes

1. Erving Goffman, *The Presentation of Self in Everyday Life* (New York: Doubleday, 1959); Greg Smith (ed.), *Erving Goffman and Social Organization: Studies in a Sociological Legacy* (London: Routledge, 1999).

2. Anja Pistor-Hatam, *Iran und die Reformbewegung im Osmanischen Reich* (Berlin: Klaus Schwarz Verlag, 1992).

3. For the 'Urabi revolt, see Juan R. I. Cole, *Colonialism and Revolution in the Middle East: Social and Cultural Origins of Egypt's 'Urabi Movement* (Princeton, N.J.: Princeton University Press, 1993).

4. Juan R. I. Cole, *Modernity and the Millennium: The Genesis of the Baha'i Faith in the Nineteenth-Century Middle East* (New York: Columbia University Press, 1998); Peter Smith, *The Babi and Baha'i Religions: From Messianic Shi'ism to a World Religion* (Cambridge, UK: Cambridge University Press, 1987).

5. Ibrahim Safa'i, *Asnad-i Naw-Yaftih* (Tehran: Chap-i Sharq, 1970), p. 119; Cole, *Colonialism*, p. 27.

6. Jacob Landau, *The Politics of Pan-Islam,* rev. ed. (Oxford: Oxford University Press, 1994), pp. 57–58, cf. pp. 9–72.

7. Cezmi Eraslan, *II. Abdülhamid ve Islam Birligi* (Istanbul: Ötüken, 1992), pp. 303–314.

8. Mehrdad Kia, "Pan-Islamism in Late Nineteenth-Century Iran," *Middle Eastern Studies* 2 (1996): 32–39; Homa Nategh, "Mirza Aqa Khan, Sayyed Jamal al-Din et Malkom Khan à Istanbul (1860-1897)," in Thierry Zarcone and Fariba Zarinebaf (eds.), *Les iraniens d'Istanbul* (Paris: Institut Français de recherches en Iran, 1993), pp. 45–60.

9. Anja Pistor-Hatam, "The Persian Newspaper *Akhtar* as a Transmitter of Ottoman Political Ideas," in Zarcone and Zarinebaf (eds.), *Les iraniens d'Istanbul*, pp. 141–147; Orhan Kologlu, "Un journal persan d'Istanbul: *Akhtar*," in ibid., pp. 133–140.

10. Abu al-Hasan Mirza Shaikh al-Ra'is Qajar, *Muntakhab-i Nafis*, 2 vols. in 1 (Tehran: Mahmudi, 1960 [Bombay 1896]), pp. 117–123.

11. Ibid.

12. Meir Litvak, *Shi'i Scholars of Nineteenth Century Iraq* (Cambridge, UK: Cambridge University Press, 1998), p. 166.

13. Shaikh al-Ra'is, *Muntakhab*, p. 15.

14. Ibid., pp. 110–117; this meeting was covered in *Akhtar* and the coverage is quoted by Rahim Ra'isniya, *Iran va 'Uthmani dar Astanih-'i Qarn-i Bistum*, 3 vols. (Teheran: Azadih, 1995), Vol. II, pp. 749–750.

15. Johann Strauss, "La présence diplomatique iranniene à Istanbul et dans les

provinces de l'empire ottoman (1848–1908)," in Zarcone and Zarinebaf (eds.), *Les iraniens d'Istanbul*, pp. 11–32, esp. 19–20; Khan Malik Sasani, *Yadbudha-yi Sifarat-i Istanbul* (Tehran: Firdawsi, 1966), pp. 255–264.

16. Ra'isniya, *Iran va 'Uthmani dar Astanih-'i Qarn-i Bistum*, Vol. II, pp. 749–750.

17. Ibid., p. 754.

18. Litvak, *Shi'i Scholars*, pp. 172–173.

19. Shaul Bakhash, *Iran: Monarchy, Bureaucracy and Reform Under the Qajars: 1858–1896* (London: Ithaca Press, 1978), pp. 331–332.

20. Shaikh al-Ra'is, *Muntakhab*, pp. 16–21; reports in *Akhtar* covering his return to Istanbul are quoted in Ra'isniya, *Iran va 'Uthmani*, Vol. II, p. 757.

21. Nikki Keddie, *Sayyid Jamal al-Din "al-Afghani:" A Political Biography* (Berkeley: University of California Press, 1972), pp. 377–378; Hujjat al-Islam Judaki, "Asnadi dar barih-'i Sayyid Jamal al-Din Asadabadi," *Tarikh-i Mu'asir-i Iran* 7 (1995): 276–290.

22. Abdülhamid II in Thierry Zarcone, "La situation du chi'isme à Istanbul au XIXe et au début du Xxe siècle," in Zarcone and Zarinebaf (eds.), *Les iraniens d'Istanbul*, p. 106.

23. Selim Deringil, "The Struggle Against Shiism in Hamidian Iraq: A Study in Ottoman Counter-Propaganda." *Die Welt des Islams* 30 (1990): 45–62; this quote on pp. 49–50.

24. Ibid., pp. 58–59.

25. Ibid., pp. 54–55.

26. Ibid., p. 53.

27. Ibid., p. 51.

28. Ibid., pp. 50, 51–52.

29. Nikki R. Keddie, "Religion and Irreligion in Early Iranian Nationalism," *Comparative Studies in Society and History* 4 (1962): 265–295.

30. Keddie, *Sayyid Jamal al-Din*, pp. 374–377.

31. Shaikh al-Ra'is in Ra'isniya, *Iran va 'Uthmani*, Vol. II, p. 207.

32. Hamid Algar, *Mirza Malkum Khan* (Berkeley: University of California Press, 1973); Kia, "Pan-Islamism," pp. 36–37.

33. Algar, *Malkum Khan*, p. 43.

34. 'Aziz Allah Sulaymani, *Masabih-i Hidayat*, 9 vols. (Tehran: Baha'i Publishing Trust, 1948–1977), Vol. VII, p. 431.

35. 'Abd al-Hamid Ishraq-Khavari, "Hayrat-i Qajar: Abu al-Hasan Mirza mulaqqab bih Shaikh al-Ra'is," *Ahang-i Badi'* 5 (1948): 239–242, 260–263, 282–286, 321–334, 350–354, 374–378, 397–401; this point on p. 332.

36. Shaikh al-Ra'is/Burhan al-Din Balkhi, in Judaki, "Asnadi," p. 288.

37. Tafrashi, "Shaikh al-Ra'is," p. 65.

38. Judaki, "Asnadi," p. 288.

39. Abu al-Hasan Mirza Shaikh al-Ra'is, *Ittihad-i Islam*, ed. Sadiq Sajjadi (Tehran: Naqsh-i Jahan, 1984 [1895]).

40. 'Abdu'l-Baha 'Abbas Nuri, *Risalih-'i Siyasiyyih* (Tehran: Muhammad Labib, 1933). Available online at: http://h-net2.msu.edu/~bahai/areprint/vol2/siyasi.htm; see Juan R. I. Cole, "'Abdu'l-Baha's *Treatise on Leadership*: Text, Translation, Commentary," *Translations of Shaikhi, Babi, and Baha'i Texts* 2, no. 2 (May 1998). Available online at: http://h-net2.msu.edu/~bahai/trans/vol2/absiyasi.htm.

41. Nategh, "Mirza Aqa Khan," pp. 58–59.

42. Ibid.

43. Deringil, "The Struggle Against Shi'ism."

Part 4

Constructing Identities, Defining Nations

11

Recruitment for the "Victorious Soldiers of Muhammad" in the Arab Provinces, 1826–1828

Hakan Erdem

In 1888 an Ottoman gentleman, Mehmed Arif Bey, wrote an account of his personal reminiscences of the fateful 1877–1878 war with the Russian Empire. Mehmed Arif Bey was, at the time of writing, secretary to the Ottoman high commissioner in Egypt, Ahmed Muhtar Pasha. He had served the same pasha in a similar capacity during the late war. Mehmed Arif Bey was an ardent Ottoman-Turkish nationalist who wrote in near total freedom in Egypt, away from the censorship of Istanbul. He bitterly complained of the way in which things were run in the empire. For him, of all the nationalities of the Ottoman Empire, only the Turks shouldered the burden of the empire's defense.

> Due to our short-sightedness and indecisiveness the defence of the homeland (*vatan*) and the protection of the candle of Islam from adverse winds became the job of, at the best, twelve million Turkish speakers despite the fact that different nationalities such as the Albanians, Kurds, and Arabs, not to mention the Christians, comprise the subjects of our state. The homeland had very limited benefits from the non–Turkish-speaking Ottoman nationalities from the national and religious points. Once upon a time even the Wallachians and Serbs were among the soldiers of the Ottoman armies. The State of Russia recruits soldiers from among a population of one hundred million whereas we are compelled to defend our existence against this enormous northern colossus (*o heykel-i azim-i şimali*) with only the soldiers who could be provided by the ten-to-twelve million strong community of Turkish speakers.[1]

Mehmed Arif Bey was clearly at a loss to understand why the defense of the empire should only be trusted to the Turkish speakers. Observations similar to his would eventually play a big part in the evolution of the

Turkish nationalist discourses over the years and help in shaping self-image and the image of the Turks.

To do justice to Mehmed Arif Bey, it should be noted that his observations found echoes in the writings of contemporary foreign observers. Reading such texts, one gets a picture of the Ottoman army in which the Turks played the dominant role as regular soldiers, and the non-Turkish Muslims a negligible secondary part in the shape of *başıbozuk*s (the famous or infamous irregular soldiers).[2] Modern scholars, too, take it for granted that the bulk of the Ottoman regular army in the reform period was made up of Turks. The picture is quite a clear, if an incomplete, one: The regular army was mainly recruited from Anatolian Turks, and non-Turkish Muslims served—if they did at all—as irregulars. Millions of Muslims lived in areas not subject to conscription, namely, in "Istanbul, Crete, part of Albania, Kurdistan, most of eastern Asia Minor, Bosnia, and the Arab tribal areas of Syria and Iraq," and one could add in the Hijaz, Yemen, and Tripoli. However, the regular army could still be "supplemented with an indefinite number of irregular forces (Kurds, Arabs, and Circassians)."[3] This is, of course, a generalization. Istanbul, for instance, contributed heavily to the formation of the very first regiments of the Asakir-i Mansure in the immediate aftermath of the abolition of the janissary army. There also had been many attempts in the period between 1826 and 1914 to extend conscription. Some such attempts were successful. Arabs fought in the regular army against the Russians in the war of 1877–1878 or for that matter against the British on the Gallipoli front in World War I. Not all Kurds or Circassians were irregulars, and ultimately the unthinkable did also happen, as Christian subjects were conscripted by the Young Turks. However, the picture essentially survives. The regular Ottoman army remains heavily associated with the Turks. For example, writing on Middle Eastern army modernization, Malcolm E. Yapp remarks, "The 1914 Ottoman population has been estimated at 25 million, of whom about 10 million are classified as Turks. These bore the greatest burden."[4]

The question to be asked is, of course: Why did the Turks come to play such a role as far as the regular Ottoman army of the nineteenth century was concerned? To adopt or revert to the contemporary Western perception that the Ottoman Empire was all along the Turkish Empire per se and it was only natural to see the Turks bearing the burden would be definitely an oversimplification that erases the important nuances of a rich historical experience. Yapp, in the article quoted above, provides some clues by arguing that the new army was politically and, ultimately, militarily more reliable.[5] Can we push this a little further and say that this implicitly means that the non-Turkish Muslims were excluded from the regular army on the grounds that they were not politically or militarily reliable? Do we have any proof of such exclusion on the part of the central Ottoman state? To find some answers to the immediate questions posed, one needs to look at the foundation of the new regular army of the Ottoman Empire in its two major reincarnations, the Nizam-ı Cedid and the Asakir-i Mansure, the latter surviving and creating a historical continuum down to our own day.

The foundation and formative years of the Asakir-i Mansure are somehow glossed over in Ottoman historiography. The whole project is perceived mainly as one further necessary step in military modernization that brought about a European-like army that had European-like uniforms and weapons and trained like the European armies did. At best, it is perceived as paving the way toward a more thorough Westernization in social or political spheres by replacing that main block of opposition, the janissaries. A monographic study dedicated to the Asakir-i Mansure is long overdue. Some work was done on the officer corps, internal organization, and training of the new army, but little is known about its ethnic composition, the soldiers at the level of private, or for that matter, the role of the new army in the evolution or invention of a new Ottoman identity.[6] I somehow have my doubts that the founding of the Asakir-i Mansure was simply a new chapter in the long military annals of the Ottoman Empire. It went much deeper than that. As far as I am concerned, the final and successful launching of the regular army with the creation of the Asakir-i Mansure, rather than the better-known reforms of the ensuing Tanzimat period, was the clearest expression in the Ottoman Empire of the idea of breaking with the past. After much deliberation and a colossal setback in the shape of the destruction of the Nizam-ı Cedid army, the Ottoman center brought itself to accepting the idea of conscription and, what is more important, made it palatable to its Turkish-speaking peasant population. The genie of conscription was out of the bottle.

Tackling the question of determining the role of Mehmed Ali Pasha's army in the development of Egyptian nationalism, Khaled Fahmy came to the conclusions that Mehmed Ali had had no national project in mind, that the fellahs had not derived any pride from their association with the army, and that the role played by his army was, therefore, only an indirect one:

> Nevertheless, the army did unwittingly contribute to the rise of Egyptian nationalism by homogenizing the experience of tens of thousands of Egyptians over a period that exceeds twenty years by instilling in them the feeling of hatred of the "Ottomans" and thus helped in their collective "imagination" of the nation. This creation of the "other" that wars are singularly successful at doing was operational in Mehmed Ali's army not in directing the men's sentiments of animosity against the army of the Greek rebels, or the Wahhabi brigands, let alone the army of the Ottoman sultan, but against their own Turkish-speaking officers. These feelings of animosity towards the "Ottoman" eventually came to fruition two or three generations later when the frustrated leaders of these *fellah*-soldiers, the middle-ranking, Arabic-speaking officers, broke out in open rebellion together

with other disgruntled members of Egyptian society against Turco-Circassian domination.[7]

When we raise a similar question concerning the role of the Asakir-i Mansure regular-conscript army in the development of Ottoman-Turkish nationalism, we certainly are on shakier ground, as the Ottoman case does not offer us such outlets as cited above. This is not to say that the Ottoman conscripts were without resentment for their officers or for the Ottoman government. However, such resentment could not be built around such an ethnic rift existing in the army, conducive to the development of a national sentiment, as was the case with the Egyptian army. If there was an ethnic rift to speak of, this was not between officers and men but rather between the army as a whole and the non-Turkish provinces of the empire, whether they were inhabited by Muslims or non-Muslims. The implications of such an ethnic division are clear enough. A regular Ottoman army that did not or could not incorporate non-Turkish Muslims into its ranks would be increasingly perceived as a foreign army of occupation and would strengthen the anti-Ottoman/Turkish sentiments of non-Turkish provincials when it was used to pacify such provinces. Similarly, the "Turks" who bore the greatest burden of the defense of the empire would have come to view the internal and external others very much in the same light, and, as one could claim, they would tend to create their own reactive nationalist sentiment against the enemy from within or without. Given the centrality of the army in all modern, nation-state–building societies, one could argue that the sentiments of the ethnic group that dominated the army would ultimately evolve into the official nationalism of that specific ethnic group by easily overshadowing other nationalisms. This is in no way to say that ethnic groups, let alone nations themselves, are primordial or permanently existing bodies from time immemorial. They themselves are historical constructs assignable to a certain time, and they are in a permanent state of change induced by a multiplicity of factors, not the least by the state they found or the army they dominate.

When Sultan Mahmud II simultaneously destroyed the janissaries and declared the foundation of a new army—the Asakir-i Mansurey-i Muhammediye—on 15 June 1826, the idea of a regular army in the Western mold was more than thirty years old. In fact, one such army, the Nizam-ı Cedid, was actually launched in 1792 and was well on its course to supplant the janissary army until its own abolition in 1807, which came mainly as a result of janissary and ulema opposition. Taking the advice of his grand vizier, Koca Yusuf Pasha, Sultan Selim III decided to systematically exploit a hitherto rarely used source—namely, the Muslim-Turkish peasantry of Anatolia and Rumelia—to form the Nizam-ı Cedid army. For one student of Ottoman modernization, Niyazi Berkes, this "was the nearest idea to the establishment of a national army."[8] As he points out, "[F]or the first time in Ottoman history most of the privates of these regiments were Turkish peasants recruited from Anatolia."[9] Indeed, the bulk of the Nizam-ı Cedid recruits came mainly from central Anatolia. Reading documents of the Nizam-ı Cedid period, one gets the impression that the Turks were markedly preferred as soldiers over other ethnic groups in the empire. Although there is nothing to suggest in such documents that non-Turks were technically barred from joining the army, they resonate with a very strong bias in favor of the Turks. It seems that the reputation of the Turks as soldiers among Ottoman field commanders and bureaucrats survived the abolition of the Nizam-ı Cedid army unscathed. We have many contemporary testimonies in writing indicating such a preference. This strong pro-Turkish bias can be said to have reached new heights in the decade before the establishment of the Asakir-i Mansure, especially during the initial stages of the Greek war of independence.

This is not the place to discuss the reasons behind the Ottoman commanders' love affair with the Turks. Suffice it to say that the Turks came to be seen as a disciplined, loyal group of people who did their best on the battlefields as opposed to the salaried troops of other ethnic origins. One common strand in the reports or letters of field commanders is to urge the center to be provided with troops of the *Türk uşağı* (Turkish lads) rather than unreliable or disloyal, salaried, say, Albanian troops. It should be noted in this context that the letters of the "Egyptian" İbrahim Pasha during the Morean campaign to his father, Mehmed Ali, urging him to send *evlad-ı Türk* (Turkish officers) to replace his officer losses,[10] were not exceptional at all. They were in full agreement with similar demands made by the Ottoman commanders. Thus, the question of their own role in all this aside, it can be asserted that the Turks long before the launching of the Asakir-i Mansure emerged as the most preferred and reliable ethnic group in the Ottoman Empire as far as military matters were concerned. Do we have any evidence that this continued to have been the case after the new conscript army was established? Any answer in the affirmative would help much to explain the state of things described above, namely, that the regular army relied mainly on the Turks.

To start with, there is nothing in the *kanunname*s (sultanic law codices) and *ferman*s (imperial edicts) on the new army to suggest that non-Turks were not eligible to the Asakir-i Mansure. One could have thought that such a discriminatory attitude would not be formally voiced or written into the body of the law of the empire. Such indeed might have been the case as far as the ethnicity of the conscripts was concerned. However, we have a discriminatory stipulation of another, yet similar, kind openly voiced in the imperial *kanunname* of Asakir-i Mansurey-i Muhammediye. There is enough evidence to suggest that Sultan Mahmud's distrust of converts to

Islam, in a most un-Islamic way, knew no bounds. The sultan legitimized his massacre of the janissaries partially in a logic that would be anathema to the Ottomans of a century ago. Clearly, under the influence of the ideas of such staunch opponents of the janissaries as Köse Kethüda Mustafa Reşid Efendi,[11] the abolitionary *ferman* maintained that

> bodies of infidels were discovered among the executed. They had the sign of the infidels' cross as well as the mark of the 75th [one of the janissary regiments H.E.] tattooed to their arms. People from various ethnic roots/backgrounds (*ecnas-ı muhtelife*) intermingled with them. Hence, they always had Christian spies disguised as Muslims among themselves. Whenever it was requested from them to expel and clear such spies they kept ignoring such pleas and [advice].[12]

Thus, converts emerged as one group of people who were not to be trusted, and as such their services for the new army were to be declined. What is amazing from our point of view is that this discriminatory attitude found a most clear expression in the text of the *kanunname* of the Victorious Soldiers. There Mahmud explicitly states that *mühtedi* (converts) should not be conscripted into his new army.[13] We also have evidence that the stipulation was carried into practice. For example, in September and October 1827, Mahmud gave orders to Mehmed Said Galip Pasha, the governor general of Erzurum, to recruit strong bachelors of peasant stock for the Asakir-i Mansure but reminded him that they were not to be converts.[14] Such a state of affairs presents a break with Ottoman practices of the past. Associating the converts with the janissary army of the past, Mahmud seems to have been moved by a desire not to "repeat the mistakes of the previous Ottoman rulers." The implications are clear: The sultan was unwilling to believe the sincerity of the converts and other forces that religion can be suspected to have been at play. On a different occasion, it was Mahmud and his grand vizier who approached the conversion of a Greek notable to Islam with extreme skepticism, saying, "[W]e cannot trust their embracing of Islam at such times" (*bunların bu aralık kabul-ü İslam etmelerine itimad olunamaz*).[15] Needless to say, conversion is all that counts to erase the difference between a Muslim and a non-Muslim; and nobody, including the sultan, had any right to doubt it. Times were different indeed.

We also have evidence of distrust on the part of the central Ottoman government (or its agents) shown to the Muslims of much longer standing, despite what the very name of the new army, namely, the Victorious Soldiers of Muhammad, implied. Scrutinizing the sultan's policy vis-à-vis non-Turkish Muslims is crucial to understand the whole edifice of a centralized empire he was seeking to create. In this context, the cases of two

Arab provinces of the empire, Damascus and Aleppo, are particularly illuminating.

Shortly after the abolition of the janissary army, the Ottoman government began to make new inroads into centralization. To achieve this goal, it had to physically tighten its control over the provinces, if somewhat at the cost of upsetting previous balances. In the eyes of the rulers of the Ottoman Empire, the old world order of the late eighteenth and early nineteenth centuries simply came to be synonymous with chaos or disorder. The chief tool available to the center was its new standing army, the Asakir-i Mansure, which was launched in Istanbul, at the center. As far as Mahmud and his advisers were concerned, the shortest and surest way to achieve centralization was to extend the new army to the provinces. In late 1826 and early 1827, the Ottoman government wanted to "correct" things in the southern province of Damascus. A former grand vizier, Hacı Salih Pasha, who had been to Damascus twice, once as *mütesellim* (deputy governor) and once as governor, was appointed governor general of the province. It is fairly certain that a great deal of correspondence did take place between the center and the Damascus province in this episode of centralization. However, I could locate in the archives only a group of three documents, an extremely detailed and long report by Hacı Salih to the grand vizier, Selim Sırrı Pasha, and two shorter but more confidentially written letters by the *vali* (governor general) to his agent in Istanbul, Necib Efendi. Together with the minutes by the grand vizier and the sultan, it is this group of documents that provides the basis for my reconstruction of what took place.

The task of Hacı Salih was indeed a colossal one. He was expected to "bring the province of Şam under control" (*Şam eyaletinin dahi taht-ı rabıtaya idhali*). Falling back on his previous experience, the *vali* was fully aware of the difficulties. As he explained to the grand vizier, law and order ceased to function in the province for a number of years, due to lack of protection. The *urban* (nomadic Arabs) had begun to molest the inhabitants of the towns and villages with the results that production and tax receipts declined, and famines and food shortages became the order of the day. The governors general of Damascus, for their part, had begun to ask for help from the central government to fulfill their duties, chief among them to organize the pilgrimage caravan. The pasha observed that thanks to the sultan "all administrative regulations" (*bilcümle nizamat-ı mülkiye,* read Tanzimat before Tanzimat) were now being ordered. Therefore, he hoped that his province, too, would benefit from these reforms. The molestations of the *urban* would be ended. Production and tax receipts would increase. The state would reap great benefits (*canib-i Devlet-i Aliye'ye dahi menafi-i külliye hasıl olacağı*) after the deduction of the expenses for the *hac* (annual pilgrimage to Mecca) service. It seems that Hacı Salih on a previous occasion, perhaps when he was still in Istanbul, promised to "administer the pilgrimage without help, to protect and revitalize the villages, and to recruit a regiment of *Asakir-i Mansure* with the surplus money."[16]

This was certainly music to the ears of Mahmud and his men. However, they had their reservations as to its feasibility, as it was not clear at all how all this could be achieved. Hacı Salih was, in fact, promising good government without changing much. As he saw it, the Asakir-i Mansure would be an outcome or side product of government policies in Damascus; it would not be used to implement them. Not persuaded, the Ottoman government put the question to the *kilar emini* (chief of the larder), Mehmed Ağa, who was the official responsible for the provisioning of the pilgrimage caravan and, at the time, in Istanbul. Mehmed Ağa was very forthcoming and did not mince his words. It was impossible to achieve anything with the existing soldiers in Damascus, as they were very friendly with the *urban*. They had to be replaced with new soldiers. However, settled Arabs were not suitable for recruitment as they valued their lives much, and there were not enough numbers of so-called Turkish lads in Damascus. Therefore, the new soldiers had to be recruited from among the Turks of Anatolia. The old soldiers should be dismissed and sent to their provinces as the new ones arrived (*tertib olunacak asker Türk uşağından tahrir olunmak ve bu asker yerleştiği gibi eski takımların memleketlerine tard ve tebidleri tedbirine bakılmak lazım geleceği*). A troop of 3,000 Asakir-i Mansure, that is, two regiments, would suffice to maintain law and order in the province. One of the regiments had to be cavalry, the other infantry. If the governor general positioned 1,000 soldiers in Hawran, 1,000 in Hama and Homs, and keep the last 1,000 in his own retinue, the province would be rendered prosperous in a very short time. As for the financial side, the *kilar emini* was of the opinion that the current military expenditure of the Damascus province would suffice to cover the expenses of these two regiments. At present, of the total expenses of the province—worth 10,000 kise—6,000 kise went to the pay of the existing soldiers. This was as good as squandering this money for nothing. Every three soldiers taken to the Hijaz were regarded as having one *tezkire* (ration slip) entitling them to have a specified quantity of provisions. There were 450 such ration slips. By the time the pilgrimage caravan reached Mecca, only one soldier from each group of three remained with the caravan. Even the remaining ones would try to cheat by giving their military headgear to the pilgrims. This was because the soldiers who had to be employed in Damascus were from Urfa or Bızınlıs, or were other Kurds and tribal people (*Urfalı ve Bızınlı ve sair aşayir ve Ekrad taifesinden*) who had already been settled in the province of Damascus for some years. Like the destroyed janissaries (*Yeniçeri taifey-i makhuresi*), they had come to own property there through means of illegitimate force.[17]

The *kilar emini*'s views, no doubt to the annoyance of Salih Pasha, carried the day in Istanbul. We do not have the text of the exact instructions to the pasha, and this is somewhat important in the light of an unfolding controversy between him and the center. However, an attempt can be made to reconstruct them, as he reiterated them to his *kapukethüdası* (agent of the *vali*) in a letter he wrote in February 1827. The pasha's instructions looked fairly straightforward. The sultan's wish was to install the Asakir-i Muhammediye in Damascus as well. The old soldiers were to be expelled. As it was impossible to recruit Turkish soldiers in Damascus, and as the Arabs did not make good soldiers, the new soldiers were to be recruited from Anatolia, one of the regiments from Sivas, the other from Adana. The pasha also claimed to have received orders to recruit a third regiment locally in Damascus. Even on the surface of it, this last point looks very suspect, as the pasha himself freely repeats here and elsewhere the sultan's wish to expel the old soldiers bag and baggage! The decision to attend the pilgrimage in person or send a capable deputy was left to Salih Pasha by the grand vizier. Writing to his agent in Istanbul the pasha told him that without knowing the state of the Hijaz road he could not make a decision yet.[18]

Almost a month later the pasha was still using the same argument to gain time or perhaps to obstruct the imperial orders, and that with good reason, too. The *vali* continued to receive orders from the center urging him to make up his mind and to progress as planned. His fresh instructions urged him to take extra caution not to recruit Kurds in Sivas and Adana (*Sivas ve Adana'da yazılacak süvari ve piyade askerin içinde ekrad taifesinden bir ferd bulunmamasına ihtimam ve dikkat olunmak*). Salih Pasha's troubles were truly insurmountable. Despite his subservient and evasive attitude vis-à-vis the capital, he could not help voicing his concerns about the plan. He claimed that there was a motley group of 15,000 people in Damascus who up until that time provided escort service to the pilgrimage caravan. He was not positive at all whether it would be possible to expel these people by relying on only two regiments of Asakir-i Mansure![19] His two small solutions were simple procrastination and, as we are shortly to see, to launch the Asakir-i Mansure locally.

In his letter to Kapukethüdası Necib Efendi, Salih Pasha was much more frank and down to earth. He could also be absolutely sure that the contents of his letter, or even better the letter itself, would catch the eye of the sultan. Freed from the strict bureaucratic formalities, he disclosed that he expected soldiers from Adana, the nearer of the Anatolian provinces, not to arrive in Damascus before a period of six months expired. In the intervening period, the *urban,* who could not be paid their *hüvve,* or *khuwwa* (tax/tribute payable to the nomads), by the peasantry, would attack the villages. The existing soldiers of Damascus, who fraternized with the *urban* as if they were relatives or tribesmen (*hısım ve kabile misüllü ülfet edüp*), would do nothing to protect the villagers. Therefore, it was essential that a regiment of foot and half a regiment of cavalry Asakir-i Mansure soldiers from Istanbul, in their full equipment, should reach Damascus before the Id al-Adha festival. Only after he got rid of the undisciplined troops of Damascus, and after receiving disciplined, trained regular troops (*başı bağlı muntazam ve muallem asker*), the *vali* told the *kapukethüdası* he could protect the "poor subjects" and revitalize the Hawran.[20]

As to the launching of the Asakir-i Mansure locally, it seems that Salih Pasha was violating his instructions. He wrote to the grand vizier that he appointed two worthy persons captain, clothing them in great coats and issuing them *şubaras* (a kind of headgear used by the Asakir-i Mansure before the adoption of the fez), instructing them to recruit "Turkish lads, not the Kurds" (*Ekrad taifesinden olunmayarak Türk uşağından*) who volunteered for service in the Asakir-i Mansure ranks. He admitted that he met with little success, as the soldiers of Damascus were used to receiving 110 kuruş per person, a sum originally intended for three soldiers, for doing nothing. He was of the opinion that when the soldiers of Sivas and Adana reached Damascus, the local soldiers would be compelled to register, and those who would not would be sent away.[21] Selim Sırrı Pasha, the grand vizier, heavily criticized Salih Pasha's action in his *telhis* (report) to the sultan. He expressed surprise at the immediate launching of the Asakir-i Mansure in Damascus, the more so in the absence of approval by the center to recruit local soldiers (*bahusus yerliden tahriri tensib olunmamış iken*). He also observed that it was impossible to send him any trained soldiers from Istanbul, as 5,000 or 6,000 Asakir-i Mansure troops were already serving in the provinces at the time. Moreover, the *vali* was demanding fully trained and equipped soldiers whose half-a-year's salaries were to be paid by Istanbul. The grand vizier suggested that the conscripts from Sivas and Adana should be sent to Damascus in their old clothes, in batches of 150 to 200, without being formed into full regiments. There, the *vali* should organize them as he saw fit. Similarly, the horses for cavalry should be procured locally in Damascus. Arms and other equipment should be bought by the Damascus treasury from foreign dealers. All Istanbul could do was to issue instructions to the governors general of Adana and Sivas and send military trainers to Damascus. For locally recruiting Asakir-i Mansure, the *vali* had to be reprimanded in the following words:

> You also write that you began to enroll soldiers from among the old soldiers of Şam. As indicated to you previously these people are just like the abolished Janissaries. They are addicted to a number of irregularities and are especially accustomed to receive salaries of 110 kuruş. It is highly unlikely that these soldiers will be brought under discipline and order. It is also highly unlikely to employ them in return for monthly salaries of 20

kuruş. You should desist from registering them. If you have some other compelling reason to do so it remains unclear as you did not write the truth to us.[22]

Mahmud II for his part approved the grand vizier's instructions to the governor of Damascus, saying laconically, "I do not know why he recruits [soldiers] from the locals when we have written to him on everything and issued him instructions." He gave orders that the military trainers should be sent from the troops of Hüsrev Pasha, since the gardeners did not fully master the new training.[23]

Toward the end of 1827 the center made another attempt to extend the Asakir-i Mansure in Syria. On 30 August 1827, another former grand vizier, Mehmed Emin Rauf Pasha, was appointed governor general of Aleppo.[24] While he was still in Kıreli, in Anatolia, on his way to his province, Rauf Pasha received orders to recruit Asakir-i Mansure soldiers and employ them instead of *tüfenkci*s (musketeers) and *delil*s (guides, pioneers) in Aleppo. The *tüfenkci*s, *sekban*s (musketeers or later riflemen), and *delil*s were paid soldiers recruited from Anatolia. In praise of the center's decision, Rauf Pasha wrote to his *kapukethüdası* in Istanbul that the *sekban*s and *delil*s were soldiers who frowned upon the idea of even serving in Rumelia, let alone serving in other provinces. If two out of ten among the *sekban*s worked hard, the rest were a useless crowd. The *delil*s were worse. Therefore, it was very appropriate to dismiss them and organize the Asakir-i Mansure. He promised to do his best when he reached Aleppo. However, he cautiously added that he required at least a month's time to get to know the people of Aleppo before he initiated recruitment there. He asked the *kapukethüdası* to intercede with the Sublime Porte on his behalf, as it was certain that he would lag behind other governors who had received similar orders.[25]

Two months later, Rauf Pasha was in an altogether different mood. His orders were to locally recruit two battalions, and he begun to enroll soldiers for the first battalion. On a previous occasion he had written to the grand vizier that a regiment of the new troops should be recruited from the Karaman province and the *sancak*s (Ottoman administrative units) of Teke and Hamid and sent to Aleppo, since the local people "did not deserve to be recruited as Asakir-i Mansure" (*bunlar Asakir-i Mansure tahririne şayeste olamayacağından*). Only then he would prepare a list of Ottoman soldiers in his retinue (*maiyeti çakeranemde olan Osmanlu askeri*) and begin to enroll for the second battalion. All troops were to be financed by the Aleppo province. On that occasion, the commander-in-chief (*serasker*) opined that it was impossible to send any troops to Aleppo, as more than enough soldiers had been recruited from the province of Karaman and the *sancak*s of Teke and Hamid. Therefore, the *vali* was ordered to proceed with the recruitment of the second battalion from among the young, strong, bachelors belonging to the "good families"(*şürefa/ashraf*—that is, purported descendants of the prophet Muhammad) of Aleppo. This second battalion was to be replaced by another and sent somewhere else after its soldiers were properly trained. Rauf Pasha had a long catalog of complaints against this first battalion, which was meant to be permanently stationed in Aleppo. According to him, the soldiers who were attracted by the fancy uniforms were losing all their enthusiasm after they were brought under discipline. In fact, "the majority, perhaps all of the people of Aleppo" were "still relishing the taste of their previous freedom" (*evvel ki serbestliklerinin lezzeti elyevm damaklarında olup*). Compelled by their innate nature (*ber muktezay-ı cibilliyet*), they provoked and deceived each other to commit many a crime. The recruited soldiers went to the non-Muslim households and persecuted them with demands of wine, *arak* (alcoholic drink with aniseed), or money. They did not pay the shopkeepers for the food they obtained. While casually enumerating the undisciplined acts of the soldiers, the pasha let the center know that he also thwarted a conspiracy against the state. The soldiers, he wrote, always mixed and fraternized with mischievous, conspiratorial people. He had received spy reports that in a coffeehouse Ahmed, son of Kasab Canberuş, and his friend Kasab Ebu Merbuş told some soldiers that if need be they should "form a society" (*cemiyet ederek*) and that they themselves were ready to give help. Acting swiftly, the *vali* raided their house that night and arrested them together with six Mansure soldiers.

As Ahmed was a known conspirator, he was executed in the morning between Şeyh Bekir and Şeyh Barak. As for the soldiers, they were put behind bars after their uniforms were taken back, and they were severely beaten. For the pasha, so long as they remained in their own country it would be impossible to trust the soldiers and to expect either loyalty or good service for the Sublime State from them (*vatanlarında oldukça bunlardan layıkıyla emniyet caiz ve Devlet-i Âliye işine yarayacak hidmet ve sadakat memul olmadığı*). On the other hand, as they displayed so little willingness to enroll for service in their country, they could only be forcibly recruited to be sent elsewhere. For the moment, their numbers were still small, and they could be controlled by the *sekban*s in Şeyh Barak. However, if their numbers increased, they would have to be stationed in inns in the town. This would make it more difficult to prevent them from molesting *ashab-ı suk* (shopkeepers) and the *reaya* (tax-paying subjects). One last, and bewildering, problem as far as the *vali* was concerned, was their training. The infantry instructor from the capital knew a little Turkish, so they did not have much of a problem with him. However, the cavalry instructor did not know any Turkish at all. The privates did not understand Turkish either (*süvari muallimi hiç Türkı lisan bilmediğinden ve asker dahi*

Türkçe anlamadığından). The instructor talked to his own translator in "Frankish." His translator talked to the Arabic translator in Turkish. The Arabic translator talked to the privates in Arabic! As a result, training was a bit sluggish. Rauf Pasha insisted on being sent a trained body of troops together with their officers. These soldiers would be stationed in the castle and at the gates to properly secure Aleppo. Only then could the mercenary soldiers be dismissed or sent elsewhere.[26]

The grand vizier once more consulted the *serasker* on the issue. The *serasker* admitted that in light of the arguments of Rauf Pasha, recruiting soldiers from Aleppo was somewhat objectionable. However, he maintained his earlier position and left it to the grand vizier to decide to send the Anatolians to Aleppo.[27] The grand vizier, for his part, came to the conclusion that both the *vali* and the *serasker* had a point. He suggested that the whole project should be "dropped and postponed for the time being" (*şimdilik bu maddenin terk ve tehiri*).[28] Sultan Mahmud gave his consent to the postponement of the attempt until a more suitable time and ordered the return of the military instructors to Istanbul. For a man whose armies were at the time fighting in the Greek war of independence, which was seen by the Ottomans as nothing but a result of the activities of secret societies, and for a man who daily received reports from the Balkans that this or that Albanian chief was in correspondence with the Greek leaders, Mahmud was remarkably nonchalant about Rauf Pasha's conspiracy story.

> Why did not Rauf Paşa think on this matter before? It is strange that after all this time elapsed he shows the problematic sides of this issue now. . . . The people of Aleppo are bad-tempered and conspiratorial-minded (*haşin ve müfsid ademler*) but the said governor lacks quick wits. He is overpowered by his paranoia. It is obvious that things took the turn they did because of his laxity. Undisciplined people do not improve simply with the passage of time. Of course they need pressure. Such paranoid considerations prevented and still prevent many jobs from being undertaken at the right time.[29]

Such is the story of the center's two attempts to extend the regular army in two Arab provinces. There are obvious dissimilarities, and also some parallels, between the two cases. It appears that the central government and the *vali*s played diametrically opposed roles in each of the cases. In Damascus it was the governor who wanted, despite the categorical orders of the center, to employ at least some of the local troops as Asakir-i Mansure, perhaps to absorb the social and economic waves of the intended military transformation. In Aleppo it was the center that initially ordered the local recruitment of the Asakir-i Mansure troops in the face of the growing and eventually successful resistance of the governor.

In Damascus the association of the Asakir-i Mansure with ethnic Turks presented relatively few problems. When he launched his own regiment in Damascus, the governor took great lengths to assure Istanbul that he was, in fact, implementing the *ferman* of the sultan by recruiting Turks only. The fact that Istanbul did not approve of his recruiting local *Türk uşağı* might be taken as an indication that ethnic concerns did not play a part in the center's decisions. It is true that the center's main concern was to get rid of local troops associated with the janissaries, in return for conscript Asakir-i Mansure. However, one is left wondering why there should not be any Kurds among the Anatolians, or for that matter why the local Arabs should not be conscripted as regular soldiers. Previously, different ethnic groups dominated different military groups in Syria.[30] Karl Barbir suggests that "it was the strong sense of *'asabiyya* (feeling of social solidarity) rather than ethnic differences that appears to have given each group its identity."[31] Without entering into a discussion about what constitutes ethnicity, consanguinity seems to be only one and not necessarily the most important factor. One can argue that the converse was also true, namely, that the social solidarity of the military groups was created and bolstered by their ethnic-regional roots.[32] On one hand, the Ottoman government thought in this vein when it attempted to prevent the recruitment of the Kurds into Asakir-i Mansure troops earmarked for the Damascus province. On the other hand, the government did not apply the same kind of logic as far as the *Türk uşağı* were concerned. It may be that the different ethnic groups controlled specialized military groups in Damascus for a long period of time, and the government was now throwing its weight behind one of them to the exclusion of others. This was a classical, textbook example of using an ethnic preference and as such it was important. Especially so, if this was part of an empire-wide pattern, as I would like to argue. One is, indeed, left wondering on what basis people were classified as Turks or Kurds when they were recruited for the new army, whether in Damascus or in Anatolia. More important is the question of how people reacted to such a policy.

The case of Aleppo is more complicated. Here, too, the main concern of the government was to get rid of the mercenary troops. However, the central government ordered the *vali* to recruit Asakir-i Mansure troops from among the *şürefa/ashraf* and peasants instead of sending conscripts from Anatolia. As pointed out by Rafeq, Aleppo was one place where the *ashraf* played a major political role. They were engaged in "deadly struggles" with the janissaries, the culmination of which came with a massacre by the janissaries in 1798.[33] The fact that the *ashraf* were historical rivals of the janissaries should have made them politically reliable in the eyes of the central government that had abolished the janissary army at the center only a year or so before. As for the "peasants," in the absence of more data it is impossible to be more precise about their identity, or rather about what the government meant by peasants. They very well might have been the Arabic-speaking peasants of the immediate hinterland of Aleppo. In this case, they must have been regarded as an "uncorrupted" group of people who were not part and parcel of the local military system until that point. As the northern *sancak*s of the Aleppo vilayet were well within Anatolia, it is also possible that by peasants, the center meant people of that northern area. In fact, in Rauf Pasha's dispatch there is reference to a group of 100 soldiers who were asked from Antakya and Kilis to complete the recruitment of the first battalion in Aleppo. Only half did show up and thought that they were to serve as salaried troops, no doubt as the case had been on many a previous occasion. Rauf Pasha's orders were clear: He was to form two battalions of *ashraf* and peasant soldiers in Aleppo. How much he succeeded in enticing the *ashraf* to serve as conscript privates in the regular army is only to be guessed. However, from the pasha's remark that the majority of the conscripts, and especially the peasants, arrived in a state of nakedness (*geldiklerinde ekseri çıplak ve kurevîsinin cümlesi donsuz*), it can be deduced that he largely recruited poor people. Even then, he managed to recruit only 322 soldiers, well below the prescribed 500 for the first battalion.[34]

Rauf Pasha himself never used the term "*Türk uşağı*" when he wanted soldiers from Anatolia. On the other hand, he made an open reference to "Ottoman soldiers" in distinguishing soldiers from Anatolia from the locals. Regardless of the terminology he used, however, we can be pretty sure that what Rauf Pasha meant was the same group of soldiers referred to as *Türk uşağı* in so many other documents. He carefully named the Anatolian regions from which soldiers could be recruited. The reason for this specific preference can only be guessed at. It is just possible that Rauf Pasha was influenced by the *sekban*s who originally came from these areas. Regardless of what he thought about the *sekban*s and *delil*s in the first place, the *vali* certainly relied on them to control or, as he put it, to "counterbalance" the Arab soldiers. It is also possible that Rauf Pasha did not want to antagonize the center-right from the start but left it to time. In either case, Rauf Pasha's opposition to the recruitment of the locals as regular soldiers was substantial. What is more important, the center, that is, the *serasker*, the grand vizier, and the sultan himself gave him credit on the difficulty or impossibility of recruiting soldiers locally in Aleppo. This requires the existence of a similar mind or that of shared stereotypes among the Istanbul-centered Ottoman officialdom. In his dispatch to Istanbul, Rauf Pasha was unsparing in his views on the locals. He wrote that the *şürefa* and the non-*şürefa* of Aleppo were equals when it came to hatching plots![35] Istanbul did not criticize or reprimand Rauf Pasha for expressing such sharp views, rather the problem in its eyes was that he did not let the center know the state of affairs in Aleppo beforehand!

Why did the center order the recruitment of the locals in the first place then, especially against the background of its policies in the neighboring province of Damascus? It might be that the reason cited by officials at the center, namely, overexploitation of the Anatolian regions for the recruitment of soldiers, forced the Ottoman government to try its luck with the locals in Aleppo. If such was the case, Aleppo was one of the very first examples of the attempts to extend conscription beyond Anatolia and Rumelia. Needless to say, Aleppo was only a qualified success. In fact, Ottoman efforts to extend the regular army in these two Arab provinces could not be of a more sustained nature, as Syria would be occupied for a decade by İbrahim Pasha of Egypt, from 1831. However, in spite of these meager beginnings, we have evidence that Asakir-i Mansure troops from Aleppo and Damascus were around until the Egyptian occupation. We also have evidence that the prejudices of the Ottoman commanders against the southern troops continued unabated. In January 1829, for example, during yet another war with Russia, Salih Pasha, the commander-in-chief of the Ottoman armies in the east, wrote a detailed dispatch to Istanbul asking the capital not to send troops from Damascus and Aleppo to the front, as they were not suitable for service there. The pasha suggested that the two Arab provinces could send *bedeliye* (substitution money) instead of soldiers.[36]

To sum up, in 1827–1828 the Ottoman government made two successive attempts to tighten its control over two important Syrian provinces, Aleppo and Damascus. From this episode we learn that Anatolian Turks, rather than local troops, were ideally preferred by the Ottoman center and Ottoman provincial administration alike. This seems to be part and parcel of an empire-wide pattern most probably shaped by Ottoman experiences, mainly in the Balkans. There is indeed enough evidence to suggest that ethnic Turks of the empire were preferred, for reasons to be discussed elsewhere, over any other ethnic group as far as the regular army was concerned. Even a short perusal of the Ottoman-archive catalog of documents on the Asakir-i Mansure suggests that the overwhelming majority of conscripts came from what is increasingly referred to as the heartlands of the Ottoman Empire, populated by the ethnic Turks, rather than from the outlying areas.[37] It might be argued that the Turks have always formed the backbone of the Ottoman armies ever since the Ottoman government enrolled the services of the *sekban*s and the *levent*s (also musketeers or later riflemen) in response to the European military revolution of the sixteenth century. Such an approach would certainly underestimate the role of the Albanian or Kurdish mercenaries on the eve of the founding of the regular army. Little place was reserved for the salaried mercenaries in Mahmud's new army, regardless of their ethnicity, but it seems that only one ethnic group, the Turks, made the necessary transformation and came to dominate it. This was, no doubt, a result of the dialogue between the deliberate policies of the center and the reactions of the provincials.

Notes

1. Mehmed Arif Bey, *Başımıza Gelenler* (Cairo: Maarif Matbaasi, 1321/1903–1904), pp. 57–58, 157.

2. J. Baker, *Turkey in Europe* (London: Cassel Petter & Galpin, 1877), pp. 304–305.

3. Malcolm. E. Yapp, "The Modernization of Middle Eastern Armies in the Nineteenth Century: A Comparative View," in V. J. Parry and M. E. Yapp (eds.), *War, Technology, and Society in the Middle East* (London: Oxford University Press, 1975), pp. 347, 351.

4. Ibid., p. 353.

5. Ibid., p. 347.

6. See, for example, Musa Çadırcı, "Renovations in the Ottoman Army (1792–1869)," *Revue Internationale d'Histoire Militaire* 67 (1988): 87–102; A. Levy, "The Officer Corps in Sultan Mahmud II's New Ottoman Army, 1826–39," *International Journal of Middle East Studies* 2 (1971): 21–39; Mübahat S. Kütükoğlu, "Asakir-i Mansure-i Muhammediyye Kıyafeti ve Malzemesinin Temini Meselesi," *Doğumunun 100.Yılında Atatürk'e Armağan* (Istanbul: Istanbul Üniversitesi Edebiyat Fakültesi Yayınları, 1981), pp. 519–605; Necati Tarcan, "Tanzimat ve Ordu," in *Tanzimat* (Ankara: Milli Eğitim Bakanlığı Yayınları, 1940), pp. 129–136.

7. Khaled Fahmy, *All the Pasha's Men: Mehmed Ali, His Army, and the Making of Modern Egypt* (Cambridge, UK: Cambridge University Press, 1997), p. 268.

8. Niyazi Berkes, *Türkiye'de Çağdaşlaşma* (Istanbul: Doğu-Batı Yayınları, 1978), p. 89.

9. Ibid., p. 95.

10. Fahmy, *All the Pasha's Men*, p. 247.

11. Köse Kethüda Mustafa Reşid was one of the leading figures behind the Nizam-ı Cedid. He penned a treatise against the janissaries in 1807. The treatise, otherwise known as the *Koca Sekbanbaşı Layihası,* is named *Hülasātu'l-Kelām fi Reddi'l-Avām*. The archival copy of the treatise is full of invective against the janissaries in general and against the converts in particular. See BA/Hatt-ı Hümayun/48106-A, 1222/1807.

12. BA/Hatt-ı Hümayun/48106, 1241/1826; see also BA/Hatt-ı Hümayun/51356-C, 1241/1826.

13. BA/Hatt-ı Hümayun/48112, Gurre Zilhicce 1241/7.7.1826.

14. BA/Cevdet/Askeri/97157/Rebiyülevvel 1243/September–October 1827.

15. BA/Hatt-ı Hümayun/28473/1237/1821–1822.

16. BA/Hatt-ı Hümayun/21164, Hacı Salih to Selim Sırrı, 13 Şaban 1242–12.3.1827.

17. Ibid., and BA/Hatt-ı Hümayun/ 21145, Hacı Salih to Necib Efendi, 13 Şaban 1242–12.3.1827.

18. BA/Hatt-ı Hümayun/ 21154-A, Salih Pasha to Necib Efendi, 27 Receb 1842/24.2.1827.

19. BA/Hatt-ı Hümayun/ 21164, Salih Pasha to Selim Sırrı Paşa, 13 Şaban 1242–12.3.1827.

20. BA/Hatt-ı Hümayun, 21145, Salih to Necib Efendi, 13 Şaban 1242–12.3.1827.

21. BA/Hatt-ı Hümayun/ 21164, Salih Pasha to Selim Sırrı Pasha, 13 Şaban 1242–12.3.1827.

22. Ibid. Telhis.

23. Ibid. Hat (imperial writing).

24. Mehmed Süreyya, *Sicill-i Osmani,* N. Akbayar (ed.), Vol. IV (Istanbul: Tarih Vakfi, 1996), pp. iv, 1361–1362.

25. BA/Hatt-ı Hümayun/44297, Gurre Rebiyülevvel 1243/ 22.9.1827.

26. BA/Hatt-ı Hümayun/ 43502, Rauf Pasha to Selim Sırrı Pasha, 5 Cemaziyelevvel 1243–24.11.1827.

27. BA/Hatt-ı Hümayun/43502-A, Serasker to Selim Sırrı Pasha, n.d.

28. BA/Hatt-i Hümayun/43502, Telhis.

29. BA/Hatt-ı Hümayun/43502, Hat.

30. Abdul Karim Rafeq, "The Local Forces in Syria in the Seventeenth and Eighteenth Centuries," in Parry and Yapp (eds.), *War, Technology*, pp. 283 ff.

31. K. Barbir, *Ottoman Rule in Damascus, 1708–1758* (Princeton, N.J.: Princeton University Press, 1980), p. 96.

32. For *cins* solidarity, see Metin Kunt, "Ethnic-Regional (*cins*) Solidarity in the Seventeenth Century Ottoman Establishment," *International Journal of Middle East Studies* 5 (1974): 233–239.

33. Rafeq, *The Local Forces,* pp. 280–281, 306.

34. BA/Hatt-ı Hümayun/43502.

35. Ibid.

36. BA/Hatt-ı Hümayun/43820, 16 Receb 1244–16.1.1829.

37. BA/Bāb-ı Defterī/Asakir-i Mansure Defter Kataloğu (D.ASM).

12

The Politics of History and Memory: A Multidimensional Analysis of the Lausanne Peace Conference, 1922–1923

Fatma Müge Göçek

"A nation which loses awareness of its past gradually loses its self," states Milan Kundera.[1] Nations indeed sustain and reproduce themselves by remembering significant historical events of their past, developing official narratives around them, and celebrating them on every occasion. Yet these historical events can also challenge the legitimacy of the nations if oppositional narratives start to be voiced by some and embraced by others. The politics of history and memory thus prove to be a double-edged sword for nations; it can either bolster and sustain an interpretation of the past or oppose and destroy it. Understanding how and why certain interpretations of historical events dominate over others at certain periods and over time has been a continuing challenge for scholars. While history has focused on the nature of the historical documentation employed by each interpretation, historical sociology has placed more emphasis on the societal context, especially on the existing power relations in producing the outcome. With these issues in mind, this chapter studies one such significant historical event in the history of the emergence of the Turkish nation-state, the 1922–1923 Lausanne peace conference. Internationally, the conference marks the first official recognition of the Ankara government as the only legitimate representative of the Turkish people. Nationally, it is also at the conference that the legal principles on which the Turkish republic that was subsequently declared on 29 October 1923 began to take shape.

The interpretations of what the Lausanne conference has meant to the Turkish nation also become highly contentious as a consequence of its significance. "Lausanne is the site where [the Turkish] nation made all the major world powers acknowledge, recognize and sign her independence warrant . . . the only one of its kind that brought to the Turkish nation everything she wanted and fought for [at the War of Independence]," declares Hikmet Şölen,[2] a schoolteacher of the new republic, in a lecture commemorating the sixteenth anniversary of the signing of the treaty; his statement reflects the official interpretation of this historical event. "What Lausanne brought was a small Turkey with unnatural borders, a Turkey devoid of all character and distinction, deprived of economic resources, surrounded by a Greek strategic circle through the islands," argues Kadir Mısıroğlu, a much-imprisoned Islamist lawyer and amateur historian, in a frequently censored three-volume analysis of the Lausanne conference; his declaration in turn represents one of the many critiques of the official interpretation.[3]

A critical analysis of the historical documentation employed by these two contradictory interpretations reveals probably the only common characteristic between them: Both build their arguments extensively on memoirs and biographies, which complicate historical analysis in general and empirical verification in particular. The archival documentation is still largely closed to public investigation. The official publications are unhelpful for critical analysis. How then should one analyze the Lausanne conference, given this problematic relationship of history and memory and given the inadequacy of historiographical techniques?

In this chapter, I propose a multidimensional approach, one that focuses both on the construction of the historical event in the past and its reconstruction in the present, and one that resolves the issue of the politics of memory by situating both the event and its reconstruction in the larger societal context. Bringing together disparate periods and social spaces enables one to recognize the social patterns in the historical event that create meanings. And it is specifically these meanings that suggest why one interpretation of the event prevails over another.

When applied to the historical event of the Lausanne conference, such an approach first concentrates on the construction of the event itself in Lausanne and then its contextualization in Ankara. This application highlights the issue of democratic leadership and opposition in the Turkish nation-state formation as underlying the historical interpretations of that period. Next, the approach moves to the reconstruction of the event in contemporary Turkey and then locates the larger societal context within which disparate secularist and Islamist narratives develop. This connection reveals, in turn, that the issue still remains one of democratic leadership and opposition; yet it is now further complicated by imagined associations that extend beyond the boundaries of the Turkish nation-state. In summary, the multidimensional approach comprises two stages where time and space intersect to produce and reproduce the historical event: (1) The construction stage focuses exclusively on the meanings underlying the historical event of the Lausanne conference in one time period, 1922–1923, across two separate spaces, Lausanne and Ankara; and (2) the reconstruction stage highlights how these meanings are reinterpreted in the present across two distinct social spaces, one secular and the other Islamist.

Elements of the New Approach to Middle Eastern History

The proposed combination of disparate time periods and spaces within one analytical framework follows from a considerable body of literature that epistemologically problematizes the divide between the past and the present. Some scholars question the origin of historical knowledge and argue, following Benedetto Croce's famous phrase, "[A]ll history is contemporary history,"[4] that it is not possible to know the past other than through its interpretation in the present.[5] The method through which historical knowledge is acquired further complicates the problem of the divide between the past and present for, as John Lukacs states, the "antiquated ideal of complete 'objectivity' is not only impossible but, in many ways, deceiving."[6] The scholar located in the present analyzing the historical knowledge unwittingly brings into his or her endeavor the epistemological framework of the present. For instance, Barry Schwartz studies the United States to reveal how, at specific time periods and contexts, the Gettysburg Address acquires a sequence of meanings that either heightens its popularity or leads to its virtual seclusion.[7]

Given the malleability and permeability of the boundaries of time and space, one's point of departure for historical analysis can no longer be totally monolithic and consistent but needs to provide space, in both the past and the present, for the incomplete, disparate, and inappropriate fragments of the historical event. If indeed there are multiple locations of historical knowledge, why are they often not readily apparent in the contemporary narratives of historical events? The answer lies in the major societal force that dominates the epistemological framework of our contemporary world: nationalism. Nation-states produce and reproduce themselves through an imagined unity and coherence, one that necessarily has to downplay the complexity of historical memory and causality. Events start to follow one another linearly and in progression; the conception of time becomes hegemonic and therefore unquestioned as the historical gets conflated with the national. The temporal hegemony extends to establishing control over historical actors: The dominant ideology attempts to "rhetorically fix national identities to legitimate its monopoly";[8] it makes claims on territories, peoples, and cultures for all of its history. Recently, David

McCrone has articulated how nationalism creatively remaps the past for it to appear as consistently progressing to the present form of the nation-state:

> The "past" is a wonderful source of legitimacy for those who would change the present for a new future. . . . The "narrative" of the nation is told and retold through national histories, literatures, the media and popular culture, which together provide a set of stories, images, landscapes, scenarios, historical events, national symbols and rituals. Through these stories national identity is presented as primordial, essential, unified and continuous.[9]

The legitimacy acquired through possessing the past strengthens nationalism but also exposes it to attack. Each social group within the nation attempts to locate and therefore legitimate its place within the official historiography by remembering and reinterpreting the past. As history and historical documentation become so crucial to a social group's sense of identity, the evidence itself becomes the focus of struggle, enhancing the national presence of some groups and obscuring that of others.

It is in this context that memoirs and biographies become very significant, as they present unauthorized remembrances of the past; they often allude to discrepancies in official narratives, to the messy, Janus-faced quality of historical knowledge. The instability of memory also allows a variety of interpretations, one that often destabilizes the official narrative. As James Scott points out:

> [E]very subordinate group creates, out of its ordeal, a "hidden transcript" that represents a critique of power spoken behind the back of the dominant. The powerful, for their part, also develop a hidden transcript representing the practices and claims of their rule that cannot be openly avowed. A comparison of the hidden transcript of the weak with that of the powerful and of *both* hidden transcripts to the public transcript of power relations offers a substantially new way of understanding resistance to domination.[10]

Alternate narratives undermine the domination of the public transcript and present, in turn, a self-portrait of dominant elites that naturalizes their power and conceals their weaknesses. Scott further notes that "the greater the disparity in power between dominant and subordinate and the more arbitrarily it is exercised, the more the public transcript of subordinates will take on a stereotyped, ritualistic cast. In other words, the more menacing the power, the thicker the mask."[11] Indeed, the alternate narratives start to espouse conspiracy theories and other far-fetched explanations of historical events. This chapter, informed by these theoretical insights, attempts to develop a new approach to a historical event of the Middle East, the Treaty of Lausanne.

The Historical Event as Constructed in Lausanne

The conference occurred within the following political context: The defeat of the Ottoman Empire in World War I and the subsequent Allied occupation of the empire by England, France, and Italy started the Turkish war of independence in Anatolia, which was organized and directed by a renegade Turkish government in Ankara that politically separated itself from the Istanbul government of the Ottoman sultan. The eventual victory of the Turkish army against the Greeks, who had helped the Allied powers occupy Anatolia, and the increasing tensions in Europe in the aftermath of World War I led the Allied powers to sign an armistice with the Turkish government and then summon a peace conference in Lausanne. Even though the members of the conference were England, France, Italy, and the Ankara government, England set the agenda. The Allies presumed that their recognition of the Ankara government through inviting them to Lausanne to participate was an honor and privilege in and of itself; they intended the conference to be the medium through which they would dictate the terms under which the Ankara government was established as a state. The Ankara government had a very different vantage point, however. Having won the war of independence, it perceived of the convening of the Lausanne conference as a political testimony to its military victory; the conference, for it, was thus going to be the site where the new Turkish nation-state established itself on its own terms within the world political order.

The primary issues, in the order they were taken up at the conference, were the partitioning of Western Thrace and Mosul, the control of the Bosphorus and Dardanelle Straits, the future location of the Greek patriarchate in Istanbul, and war reparations and legal and economic capitulations.[12] The conference started in Lausanne on 21 November 1922 and was interrupted on 4 February 1923, when the sides failed to reach agreement over the issue of the abolition of capitulations, especially legal ones.[13] The second stage of the conference started on 23 April 1923, and the Lausanne Treaty was finally signed on 23 July 1923. The Allied powers in general and Lord Curzon in particular had expected the treaty to be signed within a couple of weeks; they did not anticipate the perseverance of the Turkish delegation in defending its own terms or the resistance of the Ankara government to accepting the Allied proposals.

The main historical actors of the Lausanne conference who shaped the narrative of the historical event by leaving various accounts of it were as follows: Lord Curzon, the foreign minister of England, who headed the British delegation, which also included Sir Horace Rumbold, the British high commissioner to Constantinople; and Harold Nicolson, foreign service representative. The Turkish delegation was officially headed by İsmet Pasha, a general in the war of independence and a close friend of Mustafa

Kemal, the rising military leader of the war and the subsequent political leader of the Ankara government; the associate delegate was Rıza Nur, the Turkish minister of health and the political choice of the opponents of Mustafa Kemal in the Turkish assembly. The U.S. delegation, which attended the conference as observers, was headed by diplomats Richard Washburn Child and Joseph Grew. Another interesting account is that of Mevhibe Hanım, the wife of İsmet Pasha who accompanied her husband during the second stage of the negotiations.

Comparative Accounts on the Event

The synchronic reading of these multiple historical accounts provides the parameters of the culture of the conference, namely, the concerns of each delegation, their stands on certain issues, and their views of one another. These dynamics also signal certain silences about the conference, things unsaid but nevertheless significant: The mode of information flow within and among the delegations, both through the employment of technological means such as the telegraph, and through the use of informal networks such as dinner parties, often helped each issue under discussion at the conference. Another silence concerns gender—women who attended the conference with their husbands, or women to whom the husbands wrote their accounts in the form of copious letters, are not taken into consideration.

The accounts of Lord Curzon and Sir Horace Rumbold are either in the form of reports to London or letters to their spouses with no discernible difference in formality among them. They reveal that the British regarded themselves above all the others at the conference (especially the Turks), expected to determine all the terms of the conference, and failed to understand the nature of the new political animal called nationalism, dismissing it, in the case of the Turks, as obstinacy. In his correspondence, Lord Curzon seems concerned, more than the immediate conference, about how his performance might affect his chances of becoming the prime minister and how he could sustain Allied unity especially in affairs relating to Germany.[14] His views on the conference mostly take the form of complaints about the various delegations, especially the Turks, and also reveal an occasional unease about the possibility of renewed conflict if the negotiations fail. Curzon, while "being the last man to wish to do a good turn to the Turks," wanted "to achieve something like peace in Anatolia" and was willing for that purpose to recognize a limited presence to Turks in Europe. Curzon's views of other delegations cover a wide spectrum of complaints ranging from the observation that the discussions with the Turks are nothing but "wrangle, wrangle, wrangle," that the French colleagues are disgusting as they "fawned upon İsmet Pasha like old roues courting some youthful courtesan," and that the Americans are "childlike."[15]

Sir Rumbold's accounts of the conference revolve around how aptly Curzon handled matters. His view of other delegations was disparaging of the Turks and, to a certain degree, of the Americans. He starts off by stating that "a swollen-headed Turk is a dreadful person to deal with and . . . the Kemalist regime . . . is inspired by blind chauvinism, hates all foreigners and is against foreign intervention."[16] During the conference, he finds the Turkish head delegate İsmet "irritating, tiresome . . . afflicted with deafness which, added to his limited intelligence, makes it a work of almost superhuman difficulty to get him to understand any argument at all,"[17] "the extraction of a concession from him was like pulling out an old molar,"[18] and notes that the Turkish delegate Rıza Nur "had no pretensions to being a gentleman and easily lost his temper."[19] In general, he has "never run up against such a lot of pig-headed, stupid, irritating people" in his life.[20] "There are times I wish I could," he adds, "plunge the whole Turkish delegation . . . whose methods were those of the bazaar . . . into the lake and have done with it."[21]

The memoirs of İsmet Pasha and Rıza Nur, and the telegraph reports to Ankara represent the medium through which one can infer the Turkish delegation's perception of the conference; there is no indication of letter writing. All the correspondence constantly acknowledges that the Turkish delegation has the most at stake at the conference as they are there to secure a new Turkish state. The Turkish delegation is also the one most closely monitored. The delegation's detailed reports on the negotiations are promptly sent back to Ankara to the assembly, which discusses them, and sends back its response to each issue by telegraph. During the delay in the response, when the delegates have to use their own initiative, İsmet and Nur often end up opposing one another because they represent different segments of the national assembly. As a consequence, unlike the other delegation members, the accounts of the Turkish delegates refer much more to domestic politics and also to one another.

İsmet Pasha makes the transition from being a general to the Turkish foreign minister and head delegate at the Lausanne conference upon Mustafa Kemal's request.[22] In his accounts of the conference, İsmet painstakingly describes the process through which he was selected as the head delegate and the procedure he followed in reporting to the national assembly in an attempt to dispel the impression that Mustafa Kemal imposed his own choice on the assembly. İsmet is also very sharp and forthright in his accounts, admitting time and again his inexperience in diplomatic matters, particularly in how he "states things too directly in press interviews,"[23] and, how, as an amateur diplomat and a soldier, he presents his opinion in too concise and dry a manner.[24] Because of his past experiences, he refers to diplomacy and civilian life through military terminology, perceiving the Lausanne conference as another war, "one for which the Turkish delegation mobilized for and worked 24 hours around the clock."[25] İsmet's civilian bearing is not very impressive, however; he seems to have preferred to remain a soldier, feeling uncomfortable in civilian clothing and etiquette, which he had to learn from the Turkish representative in France. Among the delegates, İsmet comments the most on Curzon, describing him as "a large and handsome man, one who loved showing off talking with the gestures of an orator and charming everyone around him."[26] He also reads Curzon's intentions well and is particularly aware of "Curzon's tactic of giving priority in the negotiations to the Allied interests and leaving all the issues important to the Turks for later."[27]

While İsmet became a leading statesman in Turkey after the Lausanne conference, Rıza Nur and others who had been in opposition in the national assembly were gradually marginalized and embittered. As a consequence, Nur's lengthy account of the Lausanne conference is very critical of the performance of İsmet as the head of the Turkish delegation.[28] Nur states that while İsmet uses up all his time at the conference writing reports to Ankara in general, and separately to Mustafa Kemal in particular, Nur spends long, sleepless nights preparing the Turkish responses to issues that İsmet then reads at sessions as if they were his own. That this assessment is colored by competition becomes evident, however, as Nur also mentions that when the Turkish delegation takes walks and boat rides during the weekends and race among themselves, Nur constantly tries to beat İsmet and no one else.[29] Unlike the accounts of any other delegate that, at most, delicately mention the presence of wives or family at the conference, Nur also devotes a whole section of his memoirs to İsmet's wife.[30] He proceeds to describe how, unlike Nur's rich, learned, cosmopolitan wife, İsmet's wife knows no French, has trouble mixing with men, and faints under pressure; she also has only two outfits and no significant jewelry. Still, Nur states that she is "pure, a true Muslim who prays five times a day and very honorable."

In relation to issues negotiated at the conference, Nur does indeed seem to make correct judgments on some but then fails rather seriously on others. He interprets the British stand on Mosul better than İsmet does when he argues that the British would not go to war over Mosul, and the Turks should, therefore, try hard to get it back from them. On another issue, during the discussions of Turkish debt payments, Celal Bayar, an adviser to the Turkish delegation who would later become the president of the republic, alerts Nur that the debts need to be paid not in gold bullion but in currency. Nur immediately acts upon the advice and eventually saves the treasury vast amounts. Neither İsmet nor the other financial consultants had been aware of this option.[31]

The U.S. accounts by Grew and Child, both career diplomats, also survive in the form of memoirs based on diaries kept during the conference, as well as in letters written to family members. The observer status of the U.S. delegation, unlike others who have to concentrate on their negotiation, enables the Americans to spend time analyzing the conference in utmost detail.[32] Contrary to British depictions, the U.S. delegates are extremely professional, astute, and sharp in their observations. Their accounts confirm the arrogance of the British delegation and sympathize with the difficult position of the Turkish one.

Child describes İsmet as "absurdly small, deaf, in poor health, with a face which has in it suffering, anxiety, slyness and sweetness. He is bent over the table reading statements haltingly in curious French. In private he indulges in long silences and suddenly changes the topic."[33] The contrast between İsmet's statements and Curzon's replies is as strong as "that between a Greek temple and a dish of scrambled eggs."[34] Yet even though Curzon's "brilliant, ordered forensic displays are totally lost on İsmet," he is "as good a bargainer as I have ever seen. . . . His policy is one of exhausting, of laying siege, of attrition."[35] İsmet indeed has "a complex mentality blanketed under the veneer of extreme simplicity. To Curzon he appears as an ignorant and rough little man who at moments when Curzon wants him to yield something becomes inexpressive or merely reiterates some sentence he has said a dozen times before . . . creating in Curzon a kind of tempest inner rage and a sense of his total lack of power to proceed." Even though Curzon thinks this comes from İsmet's stupidity, Child is certain that "when his mind ceases to function openly it is functioning marvelously within. . . . İsmet knows the value of simple stupidity."[36] İsmet also can entertain and have fun; when he invites the U.S. delegation to a Turkish dinner for about eighty people, he asks them to remain behind and then "ordered green chartreuse and proceeded to drink to our healths in one glass after another with a speed and regularity which I have never seen equalled. Between glasses he slapped his knee, lay back and laughed most heartily at absolutely nothing and then grasped our hands in both his and remarked what a wonderful life it was."[37] Curzon, according to the Americans' accounts, speaks to the Turks "as a schoolmaster, who liking his own highly developed command of language, talks to children."[38] During the final meeting of the conference, İsmet receives "the treatment which would make the third degree in a Harlem police station seem like a club dinner. He had deep circles around his eyes, his hair was standing on end, and he looked completely worn out, but still holding his ground manfully in spite of all assaults."[39]

Unlike the British, the U.S. delegation is able to grasp the most significant fact of the conference, that the Turks have national aspirations that are beyond negotiation. Child takes note "of the Turkish nation entering a new era of enthusiasm, of the feel of youth and of self-confidence."[40] Grew recalls how Curzon, at a private dinner, describes "some of his talks with İsmet," where he tells İsmet "how he reminds [Curzon] of a music box that plays the same old tune day after day, that of sovereignty, sovereignty, sovereignty."[41] Grew then reflects on how Curzon "seemed to have no understanding of the Turkish national aspirations . . . did no good to the causes of the Allies by browbeating İsmet as if the latter had been one of his 'natives' in India."[42] Grew concludes that Curzon could accomplish more by being less clever, less derisive, and more respectful.

Silences: Power Relations Exposed

Any account of a historical event holds a combination of silences that are often unique to it.[43] Within the Lausanne conference, three silences stand out to affect the course of the negotiations. The most significant silence concerns the control of information by the Allied powers in general, and Britain in particular. The British do not acknowledge anywhere that they interrupted and deciphered all of the wired correspondence between Lausanne and Ankara, which gave them an incredible edge in the negotiations, and the Turks a high level of anxiety about being spied on. The information control also extended to the use of informal networks among the delegates of Western powers to share information and attain a better grasp on the issues under negotiation. The second silence pertains to the significance of diplomatic skills in the outcome of the conference. Among the participating delegations, only the Turkish one was not led by career diplomats; the Western diplomatic dexterity when combined by its lack in the Turkish delegation seems to have influenced the outcome of the conference as well. The third silence concerns the role gender plays in documenting the historical event of the Lausanne conference. A significant amount of the information left by the British and U.S. delegates on the Lausanne proceedings came from the letters written to the wives, mothers, and mothers- and sisters-in-law, who then preserved them—a task rarely acknowledged in historiography.

The Turkish delegation communicated with Ankara through telegraphs, whereby about fifteen were sent each way every day, as well as through the slower method of letters.[44] There were two channels of wired communication available to the Turks. One, called the "Eastern" line, ran over the Mediterranean sea to the East to Asia and was under the control of the British; the other, named the "Köstence" line, went over land through

Romania and the city of Köstence to Istanbul and was under the authority of the French.[45] The Turks in Lausanne preferred the Eastern line because it worked better than the Köstence one; even then, communication was very difficult and often interrupted. Especially in the second stage of the negotiations, Martin Gilbert notes that Rumbold's work was made easier because "the British intelligence had succeeded in intercepting İsmet's instructions from Angora"; Rumbold stated that "this information we obtained at the psychological moments from secret sources were invaluable to us, and put us in a position of a man who is playing Bridge and knows the cards in his adversary's hand."[46] One correspondence from Mustafa Kemal stating that enclosed was a new code because the British had broken the previous one, and another one from the Turkish prime minister recommending the use of the other line, indicates that Turks perhaps suspected some interference but were not at all aware that all of their codes had been broken by the British. Their access to this correspondence also gave the British a competitive edge over the other Western powers for they were able to find out about who communicated what to the Turks without their knowledge. The Turkish delegation, in the meanwhile, lost trust in each other as they suspected one another of spying for Britain; they were also accused by the powers they communicated and negotiated with for promptly leaking information.

The British, French, and U.S. delegates to the Lausanne conference were mostly diplomats who knew one another from previous assignments; they had already established connections and networks that could be utilized in acquiring intelligence. For instance, Nicolson bluntly stated that the British delegation felt "a greater community of sympathy . . . relations of complete confidence and personal friendship" with the French delegation than they would ever have with the Turks.[47] Similarly the U.S. delegation interacted with the British one socially and informally; Joseph Grew "took tea with Sir Horace [and Lady Rumbold]," with whom he had been a colleague in Cairo and Berlin and then had corresponded regularly.[48] Curzon also received gifts on his birthday in January from the U.S. delegates and their wives.[49] The Turkish delegation was largely left out of this network. As most of the delegation constituted people with limited diplomatic experience, their chances of having met the Western delegates in previous assignments were close to nil. Even though there were experienced Ottoman diplomats who could have been recruited by Ankara to serve in Lausanne, the national assembly was concerned that these people would undermine its interests.

The Western delegations in general, and Curzon and Grew in particular, were also seasoned diplomats who quickly established control over events, often forcing the Turkish delegation to present its case before revealing where the three powers, Great Britain, France, and Italy, stand on the issue. Unlike the members of other delegations, neither İsmet nor Nur were trained diplomats; they had between them two experiences in diplomacy. İsmet had previously arbitrated the armistice with the Allied powers, and Nur the border agreement with the Soviet Union. İsmet also "spoke bad French haltingly and with the indistinct enunciation of a deaf man, frequently searching for his words or consulting his notes."[50] He was not used to the stress of diplomacy, either; when the Americans tried to get more concessions from the Turkish delegation to unsuccessfully avoid the interruption of the conference, he "kept rubbing his forehead as if almost dazed . . . saying in Turkish 'my heart is squeezing me,' and kept going next door to consult with his experts, staying three minutes, and returning as if he had not seen them at all."[51] One should note, however, that sending someone like İsmet to represent Ankara also upset diplomatic protocol as İsmet challenged the power relations rather than working within them as a diplomat would do, thereby throwing everyone off balance.

The wives of the members of the delegations are especially significant in generating and sustaining communication networks through which one accesses information about the Lausanne conference. The letters written by the British and U.S. delegates to various female relatives especially convey their personal observations and assessments, which they are often loath to include in their official reports. In addition, the wives also employ informal networks to attain information on matters that would be of use to their husbands, especially in advancing their careers, gathering intelligence especially on appointments, scandals, and slights. For instance, the spouses of Lord Curzon and Sir Horace Rumbold constantly report on who they saw and dined with, what was discussed about political and diplomatic figures they know in common, and what was hinted about their husbands' professional performance.[52] The social occasions such as teas, dinners, and excursions also helped women exchange information with one another. The wives often mimic their husbands' attitudes on matters and also carry on their husbands' fights for them, slighting the wives of those who have been dismissive of their husbands. The few Turkish women in the delegation did not participate in these social events thereby missing a social network.

The Lausanne conference is unique in that there exists, in addition to the British and U.S. correspondence with female relatives, an account by Mevhibe Hanım, wife of İsmet, who attended the second stage of the conference. Her memoirs exist as recounted by her daughter and granddaughter after her death "so that her son and all Turkish children could get a chance to know her."[53] After getting to know Lausanne during the first stage of the conference talks, İsmet then asked Mustafa Kemal's opinion about taking Mevhibe to Lausanne for the second stage. The two men decided that it would be "a very good idea for a young woman to improve herself through seeing the world."[54] The surviving letters written daily by Mevhibe to her mother and mother-in-law describing her trip make up the only such documents from the Turkish delegation. In them, Mevhibe remarked on the wives of the members of the Turkish delegation she associated with, especially Nur's wife, İffet, with whom she became good friends, as the two took the car allocated to İsmet and went shopping and sightseeing. İffet was "flippant, liked to joke and talk"; she complained about her husband, Rıza Nur, who was "difficult and irritable, [which made her] try to forget their domestic troubles by turning her attention to the outside world."[55] İsmet was also involved with his wife's comfort and was attentive to her needs; he immediately employed a French language teacher for her, but she objected because the teacher was male, a decision she later very much regretted.[56] Mevhibe was aware of all the issues being discussed at the conference, probably through her husband who shared information with her. Mevhibe recounted how Nur, though hardworking, was rash and also impatient with İsmet for being too cautious. The peace treaty was signed, she recounted, at the end of long negotiations during which İsmet stayed up until morning several days in a row.[57]

The Lausanne Conference as Construed in Ankara

The Lausanne negotiations helped articulate the disparate visions of what the emerging Turkish nation-state ought to be. As the debates on this issue continued both among İsmet and Nur in Lausanne and among the national assembly members in Ankara who followed the Lausanne proceedings very closely, it became evident that there was a lot of disagreement, especially in relation to the role of the Ottoman sultan in the new nation-state. While Mustafa Kemal's majority group at the assembly advocated a state form that minimized this role, the minority opposition in general wanted to preserve the Ottoman heritage in a stronger political form. Before the Lausanne conference, when the Allied powers indicated that they were planning to invite to the conference representatives from both the Istanbul and Ankara governments, the national assembly quickly declared that it did not recognize the government of the sultan, thereby indirectly revoking his dynasty's right to rule (*saltanat*).[58] They did, however, continue to recognize his symbolic powers as caliph, namely the *hilafet,* the office of the leader of the Muslim world. Hence the Lausanne conference propelled the national assembly to make decisions even before it started.

During the discussions in Ankara of the Lausanne conference negotiations, the form of the new nation-state became clearer. The debates over the issue of the abolition of the legal capitulations were especially significant in this respect. The Allied powers argued that they needed to retain their own court systems in Turkey because the domestic law was based on

Islamic legal premises and therefore inapplicable to Westerners. In the process of defending their legal sovereignty, the national assembly agreed to reform and secularize the Turkish judicial system after "modern" Western principles. This decision freed the judiciary from the control of the Ottoman sultan and also undermined his authority as the caliph. The negotiations over Turkey's geographical boundaries, the position of its minorities, and the location of the patriarchate forced the national assembly to deliberate what constituted Turkish identity and sovereignty. These long sessions of deliberation also revealed that the representatives in general and the majority group in particular had limited tolerance for political difference. After the interruption of the Lausanne conference in February, the political opposition was subdued first through the murder of Ali Şükrü, the informal leader of the opposition group, and then through the holding of new elections that altered the composition of the assembly by significantly reducing the size of the opposition. After the signing of the treaty, the assembly speedily designated Ankara as the capital, declared the form of government a republic, and later abolished the caliphate.

It is also at this juncture that oppositional accounts of the Turkish nation-state formation started to emerge. Mustafa Kemal gave a long speech on the history of the creation of the Turkish republic, which then formed the core of the official national narrative on all historical events, including the Lausanne conference. The long 1927 speech was delivered in the first person singular at a party congress where Kemal personally read the speech over six days, for a total of thirty-six hours and thirty-one minutes.[59] He hailed particularly İsmet the hero of the conference for forcing the Allied powers to recognize the new Turkish state in its own terms. Yet oppositional accounts also started to appear. The main criticism of the oppositional narratives was the undemocratic process of Turkish nation-state formation, specifically concerning the issue of who was vested with how much power at whose expense.

Unlike the group of Mustafa Kemal that argued these issues were being negotiated democratically, the opposition claimed that Kemal and his formerly soldier friends were taking too many liberties with democratic representation. Among these, the accounts of close comrades-in-arms of Kemal during the war of independence were especially forceful. They claimed that they had been replaced in Kemal's regard by others who had surrounded him not, as his comrades did, as equals, but rather as his subordinates. These former friends all thought that Kemal had assumed too much power, that the transition of his friends from the military to the national assembly worked against the separation of powers, and that political opposition in the republic was not sufficiently tolerated. The memoirs of Rauf as recounted by Kandemir, and of Ali Fuat and Nur, spelled out the main criticisms of the Turkish nation-state formation process led by Kemal. For instance, Ali

Fuat, a former comrade-in-arms of Kemal, recounted in his memoirs that there was a prevailing sentiment among the opposition group in the assembly that "İsmet had lost at the negotiations what had been won on the battlefields through many hardships."[60] Rauf's recollections were actually recorded by a friend who stated that they undertook this endeavor because Orbay had been very upset by the way history was retold.[61] The main theme running through the recollection was how Kemal's retinue constantly worked to alienate him from his old friends. Also, Rıza Nur provides in his memoirs a very engaging, literally page-by-page critique of the long speech of Mustafa Kemal,[62] especially commenting on how Kemal took total credit for starting the independence movement, overlooked the spontaneous mobilization that was occurring throughout the empire, and also discussed all the issues with them, gathered their ideas, and then presented them to the world as his own.[63]

The Contemporary Reconstruction of the Lausanne Conference

The constraints in the contemporary reconstruction of the Lausanne conference in particular and the history of the Turkish republic in general are succinctly summarized by Erik Zürcher's comments on the historiography of the Turkish independence movement. He notes that there is an "enormous attention devoted to the subject by the authorities and the continuous stream of publications [are] nearly all of the restatements of thoroughly 'orthodox' Kemalist positions," and that "no really scholarly biography exists of the man who dominates the history of modern Turkey to such an extent."[64] The reasons for this state of affairs include "lack of interest in political history, an uncritical belief in the Kemalist truth, or the obvious attraction of studying the epic story of the rise of the Turkish phoenix rather than the maneuvering of— sometimes—rather shady characters, [and] also from a lack of accessible sources and therefore a lack of opportunity to check and/or revise the established version."[65]

Since the main archival collections are closed for the period after 1914 or open to only those who do not challenge the accepted historical version, memoirs and autobiographies are therefore the only sources that provide "facts and opinions which differ considerably from Mustafa Kemal's version and the Turkish standard history based on it."[66] The writing of a critical biography of Kemal is also not helped, he adds, by the existence of Article 1 of Law 5816, which reads: "[A]nyone attacking or insulting the memory of Atatürk shall be punished with one to three years imprisonment."[67]

Memoirs and biographies therefore dictate the politics of memory in the contemporary period, as Kemal's account of the Lausanne conference in his long speech becomes the master narrative reproduced and championed by the secularists, and the oppositional memoirs form the basis for the alternate interpretations of the Lausanne Treaty by the Islamists. Yet the Islamists co-opt these oppositional memoirs with a twist; because the responsibility of the allegedly wrong paths taken by the Turkish republic cannot, by law, be blamed on Kemal and his close circle, the agency is subverted instead to anti-Semitic conspiracy theories: Islamists suspect dark Western forces outside the republic pulling the strings of the secularists within, with the intention to destroy Turkey.

The official narrative on the Lausanne Treaty identifies it as the most significant historical and legal document of the Turkish republic, which internationally recognized, for the first time, the republic's sovereignty. The anniversaries of the treaty are therefore celebrated religiously, and the ensuing speeches are often immediately published. Among such publications is İsmet's own 1973 recollection of the event on its fiftieth anniversary; İsmet is known and respected at this point as a famous general, a friend of Kemal, and an important statesman and prime minister of Turkey. His recollection is then reprinted on the conference's seventieth anniversary.[68] İsmet reiterates the official historical narrative and the central role given to Kemal describing how he single-handedly "convened the Erzurum and Sivas congresses and led the war of independence." He thus downplays the role of all other participants who were mostly marginalized or eliminated from Turkish political life, with the exception of a few like İsmet, who himself barely survived through his unswerving loyalty, which was sorely tested during the last years of Kemal's life.

The occasion of the fiftieth anniversary of Lausanne is also celebrated with another publication, which commences to reiterate in the foreword the official rhetoric of the Lausanne Treaty.[69] It states specifically that the treaty documented Turkey's unity and independence internationally and that İsmet Pasha demonstrated his "immortal political personality, fine and keen diplomacy as well as his tough and bold representation of the Turkish cause whenever necessary." It then presents essays on various legal dimensions of the treaty, including two essays on İnönü as the "hero of the Lausanne conference." Similarly, the seventieth anniversary of the Lausanne Treaty is commemorated by an international conference sponsored by the İsmet İnönü Foundation, where scholars again assessed the significance of the treaty in official terms and again avoided acknowledging the criticisms.[70] Other accounts reiterating the official viewpoint include Burhan Cahit,[71] Suphi Nuri,[72] and Hayri Ürgüblü.[73] Another favorable work on İnönü traces his life events with minimal criticism.[74]

Neither the official narrative nor those addressing the criticisms raised about it address the question of why such alternate explanations continue to surface and persist through the decades in spite of stringent legal sanctions. Abdurrahman Dilipak's introduction to Nur's recently republished memoirs starts to explain why there is such a need to challenge the official history and explanations, declaring that "the exaggerated, mythologized, surreal forms of official Turkish history can no longer bear the heavy load of the demands of societal change."[75] After stating that he does not in any way support Nur's claims, Dilipak argues that his memoirs nevertheless are important "in capturing the truth." He then points out the inadequate amount of knowledge and documentation available on other historical events and hopes memoirs like this one would force the state to release the pertinent documents. Hence the lack of critical thinking on republican history, coupled with the plethora of censorship on available documents, are his main concerns. This position reiterates, in an interesting way, the main issues raised by the opposition in the national assembly in the 1920s, namely, the lack of tolerance toward criticism and opposite views.

One Islamist employs Nur's memoirs to develop a conspiracy theory about the emergence of the secular nation-state.[76] His narrative traces the beginning of the end of the Ottoman Empire to the 1898 Zionist congress in Zurich to attain some land in Palestine for the Jews; the conspiracy starts there and sets out to destroy the moral fabric of all societies that stand in the way of Zionist ambitions, including the Ottoman Empire. In a subsection entitled "Did we win or lose at Lausanne?" the author criticizes that the Lausanne Treaty "has been frozen, turned into a taboo, the secrets of which have never been deciphered, and its text has never been critically analyzed."[77] He identifies the giving up of the oil-rich Mosul province as the most significant compromise, "the singular cause for the shortness of breath . . . the fountainhead of the economic disorder, mental and social problems . . . we all suffer as a nation."[78]

The most significant account criticizing the Lausanne Treaty is the three-volume work of Mısıroğlu with the apt title *Lausanne: Victory or Complete Defeat?*, where his answer obviously supports the latter option. The author's foreword presents the alternative narrative and its construction in its fullest:

> There have only been three reprints of this work in 28 years because political authorities do not grant the ideas that have been expressed in it the right to live. As a consequence, rather than disappearing, these ideas lead to the emergence of an "underworld" . . . where many have reprinted and distributed our work clandestinely. . . . That "war is fraudulent" is a true hadith. One should not condone such a behavior today in this world and especially in our country when one cannot deny the presence of at least a cold war between faith and blasphemy (*iman ve küfür*). Actually we ourselves had used a similar reasoning twenty years ago and resorted to a legal trick to present our work to the public in spite of severe Kemalism.[79]

The next page has a quotation from Ali Şükrü, to whom the volumes are dedicated, stating, "[T]he accusers are history and the homeland." The narrative starts with the emergence of Islam as a religion and moves from the seventh century to the Lausanne Treaty in twenty-eight pages when the author states that "Lausanne marks Turkey's unconditional surrender to the West."[80] The whole narrative of the independence war is also turned on its head as the Ottoman sultan and his retinue emerge as the good side to the treachery of the Kemalists who were also British agents.[81] The Misak-ı Milli (National Pact) was not formulated by the National Assembly in Ankara, he contends, but instead by the last Ottoman Assembly in Istanbul. The Ottoman sultan supported and financed Kemal's attempts in Anatolia, attempts filled with many mistakes that have since been covered up. The most significant accusation is that Kemal wanted to be the caliph himself but had a sudden change of heart when he could not garner internal support and also made a pact with the British, through the mediation of Haim Nahum, that Turkey would be given a peace treaty in return for the abolition of the caliphate.

The documentation of these claims consists mostly of oblique references to memoirs, especially to that of Rıza Nur, yet the most crucial documents are noted to be "in the safekeeping of the author who cannot legally publish them under existing laws." After a detailed analysis of Turkey's losses, the author lists six "causes of these dramatic losses," all of which allude to the shortcomings of İsmet Pasha, as being inexperienced in diplomacy, lacking the necessary linguistic skills, failing to ask the opinions of his experts due to his dictatorial nature, suffering from his physical disability of deafness, not being a true believer in the independence movement, and having the unfortunate trait of extreme suspicious nature and cowardice. Under other reasons that ensue are those working against the Turks, such as Haim Nahum and the Jewish convert Cavid Bey and others. Mısıroğlu concludes by emphasizing the spiritual losses of Lausanne. In order not to end up in prison, he argues, "the kind of mentality that confiscated the first volume even though the events depicted there were much less contested, would definitely not tolerate the 'naked truth' on issues such as the caliphate contained in this volume."[82]

Conclusion

Significant historical events acquire or lose power across time. In the context of Turkish history, the Lausanne conference seems to be one such event; it was debated during its inception in 1922–1923 and is still widely disputed today. This chapter analyzed the politics of memory around the Lausanne conference through a multidimensional analysis that focused synchronically on the historical event as it acquired contradictory meanings and interpretations first in Lausanne and in Ankara in 1922–1923 and then in contemporary Turkey.

Memoirs and biographies reveal most fully the spectrum of meanings that emerge around the conference. The contextual analyses of both time periods reveal nation-state formation and political representation as the most significant factors instigating the politics of memory. Both Kemal's group and his opposition generate alternate accounts on the effect of the Lausanne conference; while one party sees it as a venue to achieve secularized modernity, the other one notes its mode of undemocratic Westernization. These stands have been co-opted by the secularists and Islamists in the contemporary period. While the secularists valorize and idolize the Lausanne Treaty and celebrate the secular, modern, and democratic republic it created, the Islamists draw on the oppositional memoirs and, because of the legal liability of criticizing Kemal's performance, generate anti-Semitic conspiracy theories that find fault not with domestic enemies but with foreign ones.

Notes

1. Milan Kundera, *The Book of Laughter and Forgetting* (New York: Penguin, 1980), p. 235.
2. Hikmet Şölen, *Lozan Hakkında bir Konferans* (Aydın: CHP Basımevi, 1939), pp. 3, 20.
3. Kadir Mısıroğlu, *Lozan: Zafer mi Hezimet mi?* 3 vols. (Istanbul: Sebil, 1992), Vol. I, p. 5.
4. Benedetto Croce, *History: Its Theory and Practice* (New York: Russell and Russell, 1960).
5. E. H. Carr, *What Is History?* (London: Macmillan, 1961); R. G. Collingwood, *The Idea of History* (Oxford: Clarendon Press, 1946).
6. John Lukacs, *Historical Consciousness: The Remembered Past* (New Brunswick, N.J.: Transaction, 1994), p. 324.
7. Barry Schwartz, "Rereading the Gettysburg Address: Social Change and Collective Memory," *Qualitative Sociology* 19 (1996): 395.
8. Jonathan Boyarin, "Space, Time, and the Politics of Memory," in Jonathan Boyarin (ed.), *Remapping Memory: Politics of Time and Space* (Minneapolis: University of Minnesota Press, 1994), p. 16.
9. David McCrone, "Inventing the Past: History and Nationalism," in David McCrone (ed.), *The Sociology of Nationalism: Tomorrow's Ancestors* (London: Routledge, 1998), p. 52.
10. James C. Scott, *Domination and the Arts of Resistance: Hidden Transcripts* (New Haven, Conn.: Yale University Press, 1990), p. xii.
11. Ibid., p. 3.
12. Curzon maneuvered to assume the chairmanship of the conference and then organized and timed the agenda such that "the subjects in which Turks were in a weak position should be taken first." See Harold Nicolson, *Curzon: The Last*

Phase 1919–1925 (London: Constable; Boston: Houghton Mifflin, 1934), p. 292.

13. Ernest Hemingway, who covered the Lausanne conference for the *Toronto Star*, states that the sessions of the conference were held "in the Chateau de Ouchy which is so ugly that it makes the Odd Fellows' Hall of Petoskey, Michigan, look like the Parthenon." See Ernest Hemingway, "Mussolini, Europe's Prize Bluffer," in W. White (ed.), *Dateline: Toronto: The Complete Toronto Dispatches, 1920–1924* (New York: Charles Scribner's Sons, 1985), pp. 253–259.

14. Nicolson, *Curzon*, p. 284.

15. David Gilmour, *Curzon* (London: John Murray, 1994), p. 532.

16. Martin Gilbert, *Sir Horace Rumbold: Portrait of a Diplomat, 1869–1941* (London: Heinemann, 1973), p. 277.

17. Ibid., p. 291.

18. Ibid., p. 296.

19. Ibid., p. 282.

20. Ibid., p. 283.

21. Ibid., p. 292.

22. İsmet Pasha states in his memoirs that while representing the national assembly at the Mudanya armistice, he reported the negotiations to Kemal every night by telegram and then applied the *talimat* (orders) he received. See İsmet İnönü, *Hatıralar*, 2 kitap (Ankara: Bilgi, 1987), pp. 32–33. This working relationship, which proved successful, probably convinced Kemal to consider İsmet for the Lausanne negotiations.

23. Ibid., p. 54.

24. Ibid., p. 87.

25. Ibid., p. 114.

26. Ibid., p. 75.

27. Ibid., p. 74. Indeed, after having secured Britain's interests, Curzon lets the French and Turkish delegations share the blame of interrupting the conference over the negotiation of the capitulations, which were much more important to the French and the Turks than the British.

28. Rıza Nur, *Hayat ve Hatıratım*, 3 vols. (Istanbul: İşaret, 1992), Vol. II, pp. 119–161, 179–453.

29. Ibid., p. 411.

30. Ibid., pp. 412–414.

31. İsmet Bozdağ, *Bir Çağın Perde Arkası* (Istanbul: Kervan, n.d.), pp. 26–29.

32. Joseph Grew states that Child "regards the conference as a game of poker, takes no statement on its face value, assumes, in the case of others, that words are a convenient means of disguising their thoughts, and studies the expressions of the other delegates at the conference table in order to read their minds exactly as he would at a game of poker." Joseph C. Grew, *The Turbulent Era: A Diplomatic Record of Forty Years, 1904–45* (Boston: Houghton Mifflin, 1952), p. 503.

33. Richard Washburn Child, *A Diplomat Looks at Europe* (New York: Duffield and Company, 1925), p. 96.

34. Ibid., p. 118.

35. Ibid., p. 96.

36. Ibid., p. 95.

37. Grew, *The Turbulent Era*, p. 539. This depiction vastly differs from the one presented in Refik Halid's *Çankaya*, where İsmet rarely participates in Mustafa Kemal's long dinner parties involving a lot of drinking.

38. Child, *A Diplomat Looks*, p. 91.

39. Grew, *The Turbulent Era*, p. 584.
40. Child, *A Diplomat Looks*, p. 82.
41. Grew, *The Turbulent Era*, p. 525.
42. Ibid., pp. 553–554.
43. Michel-Rolph Trouillot, *Silencing the Past: Power and the Production of History* (Boston: Beacon Press, 1995); Robert Berkhofer, Jr., *Beyond the Great Story: History as Text and Discourse* (Cambridge, UK: Belknap Press, 1995).
44. Bilal Şimşir, *Lozan Telgrafları,* Vol. II (Ankara: TTK, 1994), p. xii.
45. Ibid., p. xvii.
46. Gilbert, *Sir Horace Rumbold*, p. 28.
47. Nicolson, *Curzon*, p. 286.
48. Grew, *The Turbulent Era*, p. 486.
49. Nicolson, *Curzon*, p. 326.
50. Grew, *The Turbulent Era*, p. 512.
51. Ibid., pp. 553–554.
52. Leonard Mosley, *The Glorious Fault: The Life of Lord Curzon* (New York: Harcourt, Brace, and Company, 1960), p. 286; Gilbert, *Sir Horace Rumbold*, pp. 255, 278–279.
53. Gülsün Bilgehan, *Mevhibe* (Ankara: Bilgi, 1995), p. 6.
54. Ibid., p. 109.
55. Ibid., p. 122.
56. Ibid., p. 124.
57. Ibid., pp. 135–136.
58. İnönü, *Hatıralar*, p. 47.
59. Gazi Mustafa Kemal Atatürk, Vol. II: *Nutuk-Söylev: 1920–1927* (Ankara: TTK, 1989).
60. Ali Fuat Cebesoy, *General Ali Fuat Cebesoy'un Siyasi Hatıraları* (Istanbul: Vatan, 1957), p. 300.
61. Feridun Kandemir, *Söyledikleri ve Söylemedikleri ile Rauf Orbay* (Istanbul: Sinan, 1965), p. 19.
62. Namely, Nur, *Hayat*, Vol. III, pp. 26, 52–53, 165, 183, 212, 230, 274, 285, 307.
63. Ibid., p. 48.
64. Erik Jan Zürcher, *Political Opposition in the Early Turkish Republic: The Progressive Republican Party* (Leiden: E. J. Brill, 1991), pp. 2, 4.
65. Ibid., p. 5; see also Erik Jan Zürcher, *The Unionist Factor: The Rise of the Committee of Union and Progress in the Turkish National Movement* (Leiden: E. J. Brill, 1984), p. 24.
66. Zürcher, *Political Opposition*, p. 8; see also Zürcher, *The Unionist Factor*, pp. 24–25.
67. Zürcher, *The Unionist Factor,* p. 29.
68. İsmet İnönü, *İstiklal Savaşı ve Lozan* (Ankara: Atatürk Araştırma Merkezi, 1993).
69. *Lozan'ın 50.yılına armağan*. Studies in Commemoration of the Lausanne Peace Treaty on Its 50th Anniversary (Istanbul: Fakülteler Matbaası, 1978), p. v.
70. İnönü Vakfı, *70.yılında Lozan Barış Antlaşması: Uluslararası seminer, 1993* (Ankara: Ajanstürk, 1994).
71. Burhan Cahit, *Mudanya Lozan Ankara* (Istanbul: Kanaat, 1933).
72. Suphi Nuri, *Sevres ve Lausanne* (Istanbul: Arkadaş, 1934).
73. Hayri Ürgüblü, *Lozan* (Ankara, 1936).
74. Metin Heper, *İsmet İnönü* (Leiden: E. J. Brill, 1998).

75. Nur, *Hayat*, Vol. III, p. 17.
76. Bozkurt Avşar, *Bir Muhalifin Portresi: Dr. Rıza Nur* (Istanbul: Belgesee, 1992).
77. Ibid., p. 90.
78. Ibid., p. 91.
79. Mısıroğlu, *Lozan*, Vol. I, pp. 13–16.
80. Ibid., p. 94.
81. Ibid., pp. 95–210.
82. Ibid., Vol. III, p. 9.

13

Arab Society in Mandatory Palestine: The Half-Full Glass?

Rashid Khalidi

Comparing the Incomparable

In examining developments in Palestine during the British Mandate period, comparisons are frequently made between Palestinian Arab society and the *yishuv*, the burgeoning Jewish community. Such comparisons encompass social, economic, and cultural affairs and can be found in the social-scientific literature and in historical accounts, as well as in popular treatments of both societies and of the conflict between them.[1] The reasons for making such comparisons between the two communities are obvious: Until 1948, they shared the country and were in competition with one another, and in that year one completely vanquished and established its hegemony over the other in terms of population, control of land, and much else.

Such comparisons are clearly necessary for understanding the outcome of the conflict between what ultimately became two separate societies and polities. They are necessary even though comparisons of this sort may be quite misleading because they de-emphasize crucial external factors such as foreign political and economic support and operate as if these two protagonists were alone in the ring, whereas one was strongly supported externally, and the other was nearly bereft of external support. In fact, comparisons between the two societies are particularly important for understanding what happened and why during the crucial period that witnessed a growing disparity in power between them in favor of the *yishuv*, beginning in the 1930s. At the outset of that decade, the Jewish population of Palestine came to 17.8 percent of the total. By its end, spurred by the arrival of tens of thousands of refugees annually from Nazism in Europe, the country's Jewish population totaled nearly 31 percent.

Given that both sides were acutely aware that the outcome of the struggle between them depended in large measure on controlling the country's demography, far-sighted Zionist leaders such as David Ben Gurion realized that these growing numbers provided the critical demographic mass that in time would finally make it possible to dominate the country. Such an outcome was impossible to foresee when the numbers of Jews as a proportion of the total population actually declined in the late 1920s.[2] Equally important, during the 1930s, the Jewish sector of the economy came to have the larger share of the country's national income: By 1936, that part of the economy of Palestine controlled by Jews was already bigger than that belonging to the Arabs, and the disparity between them would only increase as time went on.[3]

Such comparisons also have utility for purposes other than comprehending the course of the conflict between the two communities, including understanding some aspects of each side's respective economic and social development. However, these comparisons are less useful for other purposes, for reasons that are often ignored. Three factors of incommensurability between the two societies ought to strike the informed observer. The first is the marked differences between them in terms of investment and, in particular, capital inflow per capita. According to Zeev Sternhell, during the 1920s "the annual inflow of Jewish capital was on average 41.5 percent larger than the Jewish net domestic product (NDP) . . . its ratio to NDP did not fall below 33 percent in any of the pre–World War II years and was kept at about 15 percent in all but one year since 1941."[4] By one calculation, the contributions of American Jews alone to the Zionist project by 1948 totaled well over $375 million,[5] or five times the average national income of the Jewish sector of the economy in the 1930s. Combined with wide disparities between the Arab and Jewish sectors in human capital—notably in literacy,[6] education,[7] and technical training, in all of which the Arab sector suffered serious deficiencies—it can be imagined what an advantage such a phenomenally high ratio of capital investment per capita gave to the *yishuv* by comparison with Palestinian Arab society. Put simply, the result of these considerable capital inflows and related disparities was that on a per capita basis, in relative terms one society was exceedingly rich and the other quite poor. Thus in 1936, per capita national income in the Jewish sector was £P44 (44 Palestinian pounds); in the Arab sector it was £P17. By 1948 these disparities had grown even greater.[8]

The second factor of incommensurability is that the *yishuv* was always overwhelmingly urban (notwithstanding the emphasis that Zionist ideology and propaganda placed on rural settlement and on an almost mystical connection with the land) and was principally concentrated in the Jaffa-Haifa coastal region and Jerusalem, while Palestinian society was predominantly rural. Even at the end of the mandate, by which time a significant shift of

Arabs from country to city had taken place, Palestinian society was still overwhelmingly rural—32.7 percent lived in cities and large towns, in contrast with the Jewish population, which was 76.2 percent urban.[9] The related disparities in terms of occupation were also great: While only 13 percent of the Jewish population was dependent on agriculture, about half of the Arab population was.[10] In terms of communications, mobilization, indoctrination, and many other factors, this concentration of the Jewish population proved to be an advantage, as it was strategically during the fighting of 1948 when the small *yishuv* benefited from being on interior lines, first against the Palestinians and later against the Arab armies.

The third factor is the essentially European nature of Zionist ideology and of all the major political currents within the *yishuv*. This contrasted with the more diverse range of local, Arab, Islamic, European, and other sources for the political trends found within Palestinian Arab society, which in this respect was very similar to other parts of the Greater Syria region. As Zeev Sternhell and others have convincingly shown, in the development of national identity and of "ethnic religious and cultural particularity," Israel was "not dissimilar to other states in Central and Eastern Europe."[11] Moreover, the great majority of the population of the *yishuv* in effect constituted a self-selecting sample, united by the Zionist ideology that had brought most of them to Palestine. The overwhelmingly non-Zionist majority of Jews leaving Eastern Europe in the late nineteenth and early twentieth centuries had avoided Palestine, with most preferring the United States as a destination. Most of those Jews who came to Palestine, at least before the horrors of the Nazi persecutions, had done so because they wanted to and because they shared in the ideology and aspirations of the *yishuv*. This winnowing-out process made for a Jewish society in Palestine that was remarkably homogeneous at this early stage, at least in ideological terms.

By contrast, I have argued at length in an earlier study that the overlapping identities of Palestinians that emerged during approximately the same period as did modern Zionism included elements of Ottoman, Arab, Islamic, Christian, local Palestinian, and European ideologies and thought.[12] While a certain synthesis of these elements eventually emerged, Palestinian politics nevertheless remained ideologically less homogeneous than that within the *yishuv*. The differences between the kinds of influences on Zionism and Palestinian nationalism could not be more obvious than in the realm of ideology, although both were ostensibly national movements. With these ideological and political differences and the profound social and economic dissimilarities in which they were rooted came great disparities in types of political formations and organizational capabilities, which reflected themselves in practice in a variety of ways.

There are many other differences between the two societies that could be cited as reasons why comparison between them should only be undertaken with great care and with due regard for the specificity of each. They include factors like the very different class structures and social formations of each, with one an entirely new society drawn primarily from the Jewish communities of Europe, with important Oriental Jewish admixtures, and the other a society quite similar in most respects to those of the surrounding Arab countries. These socioeconomic differences in turn produced greater income disparities on the Arab side by comparison with the relatively egalitarian *yishuv*.[13] Another difference was the contrast between the ethnic make-up of the two societies. On the one hand, there was the diverse *yishuv*, consisting mainly of immigrants from dozens of countries (who only came to share a single vernacular language after they arrived in Palestine), and on the other hand, there was the generally quite homogeneous ethnic and linguistic composition of Palestinian society.

For a clearer understanding of Palestinian Arab society per se, however, more fruitful and more meaningful comparisons can be made between it and the societies of neighboring Arab countries like Lebanon, Syria, and Jordan, and even with much larger and more distant ones like Egypt and Iraq. Here again the reasons should be obvious. Over at least the preceding few centuries, Palestine had always been intimately linked economically, administratively, and in social terms to the surrounding regions, and in particular to the other parts of Greater Syria. The state of development of its economy, its social structure and patterns of land tenure, and the political and ideological trends that affected it were all broadly similar to those in neighboring Arab countries, particularly those immediately adjacent to it to the north and east. For purposes of meaningful comparison with Palestine in such domains, these are clearly the countries to examine.

One reason why such comparisons with neighboring Arab societies are particularly useful is that it is often argued that Palestinian society before 1948 was incomplete or distinctively flawed in some fashion and that this was part of the explanation for its rapid collapse in 1948 during the climactic conflict with the *yishuv*. The unspoken implication is that the Palestinians did not have the preconditions for a successful national effort and therefore were doomed to lose in a conflict with a Jewish society that clearly did have these preconditions. Leaving aside the question of precisely why the Palestinians were so overmatched in 1948 (which will be touched on briefly in the next section), it is worth looking at the degree to which Palestinian society had developed before 1948 by comparison with its much more similar Arab neighbors. That it had not developed to the same degree as the Jewish society with which it uneasily shared the country should be obvious. We have already seen to what extent this was the case in terms of a number of key economic and social indicators. The consequence of this disparity in terms of the capacity of the two polities for social, political, and ultimately military mobilization should be equally obvious.

The degree of economic and social advancement of the *yishuv* indicated a capacity for generating considerable state power, a capacity that was fully realized in 1948 and afterward. Small though the Jewish population of Palestine was, by early 1948 the *yishuv* already contained within it many of the institutions characteristic of a fully developed society. These included notably a completely formed state bureaucracy and army, both of which were far beyond the embryonic stage and indeed were fully ready to be born in 1948. It is clear that Palestinian society had not developed in a similar fashion and was able to generate neither a state structure nor an army to match those of the *yishuv*, with disastrous consequences for its capabilities for social and other forms of mobilization when the crisis of 1948 broke.

By contrast, the Arab countries around Palestine, which received their independence before Israel did, possessed complex governmental structures with many of the features of an independent state, including military forces, well before they won their freedom from their French and British colonial masters. Although Palestinian society was in this respect highly dissimilar to other Arab societies, it is worth comparing them in the social, economic, and cultural spheres, as well as in terms of the institutions of what is fashionable today to call "civil society." Perhaps such a comparison can help us to understand why Palestinian society was less successful than other, otherwise similar, Arab societies in meeting the challenges of the conclusion of the mandatory period. Before doing that, however, let us briefly examine what happened to Palestinian Arab society in the debacle of 1948 and review some of the conventional explanations for these events.

Reasons for the Defeats of 1948

At the beginning of 1948, the Arabs constituted an absolute majority of the population of Palestine and were a majority in fifteen of the country's sixteen subdistricts.[14] Beyond this, they owned nearly 90 percent of the country's privately owned land.[15] In a period of a few months, from April until October, more than half of the nearly 1.4 million Palestinian Arabs became refugees, and the Palestinians who had remained within the new state of Israel (which now controlled 77 percent of the entire country) had been reduced to a small minority. Jordan and Egypt administered the remaining 23 percent of Palestine, but under whichever regime they now lived, the Palestinians were largely dispossessed of their property and had no control over most aspects of their lives. In a few months, this large Arab majority—which constituted over two-thirds of the population of the country—had been decisively defeated by a Jewish minority, which was less than half its size.

The degree of harm done to Palestinian society in 1948 is hard to convey, even via such stark descriptions. But that harm was more than just a matter of a majority of the population becoming refugees. Beyond this, Jaffa and Haifa, the two cities with the largest Arab populations, and which throughout the mandate period were the most dynamic centers of Arab economic and cultural life, had been conquered, most of their population dispersed, and their property taken over. The same thing had happened to the cities and towns of Lydda, Ramle, Acre, Safad, Tiberias, Beisan, and Bir Sabe'. Together, these centers included about half of the Palestinian urban population of the country, which totaled over 400,000 people.[16] Of the over 500 Arab villages in the country, more than 400 had been subjugated, their populations were driven out or fled in terror, their land was confiscated by the victors, and they were forbidden to return.[17] These were massive and long-lasting changes: In the 77 percent of Palestine that was taken over to become Israel, the end result of this process was the creation of a sizable Jewish majority. The basic demographic and property contours created by this seismic event are still extant to this day.

What were the causes for this debacle, in which Palestinian society, urban and later rural, crumbled with a rapidity that astonished even its Zionist opponents and that has been inscribed in Palestinian memory as *al-Nakba* (the catastrophe)?[18] The traditional Israeli narrative of these events ascribed responsibility entirely to the Arabs, whose leaders are said to have told their followers to flee.[19] Since the late 1980s, Israeli scholars using newly opened Israeli and British archives have shown these assertions to be baseless.[20] In some cases they reprised or substantiated arguments made by earlier writers such as Walid Khalidi and Erskine Childers,[21] confirming the falseness of claims that Arab leaders told the Palestinians to flee, with newly accessible evidence from the Israeli and Western archives.

Important though the work of these Israeli scholars was, their focus was largely on Israeli actions and, to a lesser extent, on those of the British, and they drew their conclusions primarily from Israeli, British, and U.S. sources. Only secondarily did they focus on the actions and motivations of the Arab states and the Palestinians. In explaining the reasons for the actions of the Palestinians, beyond the effect of Zionist actions and those of the great powers, these Israeli writers have tended to stress the weakness of Arab social and political cohesion and the flight of the Arab upper and middle classes before the fighting reached its height.[22]

Most Arab accounts of what happened in 1948 have tended to describe the Palestinians as having been overwhelmed by superior force. The stress in these accounts is on the strength of the Zionist forces, the complicity with them of the withdrawing British army, and the support for them of the United States and the USSR. Other accounts stress the complicity with Israel of Transjordan, which fielded by far the most powerful Arab army in Palestine, the military weakness of the Arab states, and the debilitating internecine divisions among them. Yet others underscore the willingness of Zionist factions to resort to ruthless terrorist attacks on civilians, notably at Deir Yasin, and the bombardment of heavily populated urban areas, especially Jaffa and Haifa.[23]

It is outside the scope of this chapter to analyze the specific military or diplomatic causes of the Palestinian debacle and the accompanying Zionist victory of 1948. Nevertheless, even if we ignore the proximate causes of these climactic events, we are left with the hard question of why Palestinian society crumbled so rapidly and why hundreds of thousands of people fled their homes in that year. With the exception of a few Palestinian historians who have touched on some of the reasons for the Palestinians' failures in this period,[24] such questions have tended to get relatively little attention in Palestinian and Arab historiography. As we have seen, this has generally focused on the external causes for defeat, rather than examining the internal dynamics of Palestinian society.

To provide a fuller and more profound explanation of why Palestinian society fell apart so rapidly in 1948, it is necessary to focus on events well before that date, and notably on the impact of a series of failures that culminated in the disastrous outcome for the Palestinians of the revolt of 1936–1939 and the long-lasting effects of these failures on Palestinian society and politics. It is necessary to examine as well the underlying reasons for the striking lack of organization, cohesion, and unanimity in the Palestinian polity in the years preceding 1948, particularly in view of the marked contrast with the improving situation of the *yishuv* in the same period.

There can be little question that Palestinian society was deeply divided internally in the decades before 1948 and that these divisions contributed to the debacle of that year. However, it is futile to try to explain the collapse of that society in 1948 by means of a simplistic analysis comparing Palestinian society to the highly cohesive and unified *yishuv*, concluding with a circular reasoning process that relates Palestinian political failures to the relative social backwardness of Palestinian society. Instead, what is necessary is a comprehensive analysis that would isolate some of the causes for Palestinian political failures, essentially by comparing the task they faced to that faced by other Arab national movements at about the same time and in the same region. Thereafter, this analysis would go on to compare Palestinian society to other Arab societies. We will make an attempt to do some of these things in the next section.

On the political level, such a comprehensive approach would take into account the fact that the Palestinian Arabs were in the unusual situation of a new polity emerging without being allowed any of the attributes of stateness. In one respect, the Palestinians were unlike the *yishuv* under the leadership of the Zionist movement, unlike the peoples of Egypt, Iraq, Syria,

Lebanon, and Jordan, and indeed unlike the peoples in most other colonial and semicolonial domains in the Middle East and North Africa in the interwar years. Specifically, they had no international sanction for their identity, no accepted and agreed context within which their putative nationhood and independence could express itself, and no access to any of the levers of state power. The contrast with the situation of other Arab countries is illustrative: By 1946, Yemen, Saudi Arabia, Egypt, Iraq, Syria, Lebanon, and Transjordan were already independent states, while Morocco, Tunisia, and most of the Gulf shaikhdoms were protectorates of different forms nominally under their own indigenous governments. Although the former colonial powers retained military bases even in most of the nominally independent states, all had accepted indigenous state structures.

This outcome was largely a result of the fact that the terms of all the other mandates, and the positions of the colonial powers in most other Arab countries (the notable exceptions being Libya and Algeria), were predicated on the assumption that there existed in each case a people in being or in emergence with the eventual right to independence and statehood. In the case of the Zionists in Palestine, this was explicitly recognized in the terms of the British Mandate for Palestine, which reprised the wording of the Balfour Declaration in speaking of a "Jewish people" with a right to a "national home." The Palestinians were both explicitly and by omission denied the same recognition: The mandate for Palestine, as promulgated by the League of Nations on 24 July 1922, mentioned their "civil and religious rights" but *not* their political or national ones or their existence as a people. The Palestinian Arabs as such in fact are mentioned in neither the declaration nor the mandate.

The governmental system set up in Palestine by the British to execute the terms of the mandate reflected the basic ideas of these documents. The Palestinian Arabs were in consequence given neither access to control of the mandate government nor the right to build up their own powerful autonomous parastate structure, as the Zionists were with the Jewish Agency. Even later British attempts to redress this imbalance, such as different proposals for a legislative assembly or for an Arab agency, were fatally compromised by the requirement that the Arabs accept the terms of the mandate, which enshrined their inferior status by comparison with that of the Jews. In other words, the Palestinian Arabs were not accorded the right of national self-determination and accepted status, as were the Jews of Palestine (and as the other mandates promised the peoples of Syria, Lebanon, Iraq, and Transjordan). Instead, they were to be allowed to share with the Jews in some of the functions of government but unlike them were to do so not by right laid down in the documents defining the mandate but on sufferance, as it were.

These are not insignificant matters in assessing the failures of the

Palestinians. They meant that they did not have the uncontested neutral and universally accepted forum/entity that a state or a parastate provides to a polity. In the case of the *yishuv* and the other countries under the mandate system, such a forum proved invaluable as an axis around which the polity could coalesce, or as a focus for its action, even if complete control over it was denied by the colonial power. Instead of such a state forum, what the Palestinian Arabs had were religious leaderships, authorized, encouraged, legitimated, and subsidized by the British. Indeed these leaderships were often very much in the nature of an "invented tradition," as described by Eric Hobsbawm and Terence Ranger.[25] Thus, the British created the entirely new post of "Grand Mufti of Palestine." There previously had been a mufti of Jerusalem, an important post in the past but one both limited in terms of geographical scope and authority and, in the Ottoman and every other Islamic system, clearly subordinate in power and prestige to that of the *qadi* (judge) of Jerusalem. Similarly, in keeping with their vision of a Palestine composed of three religious groups (only one of which, the Jews, had national rights and status) the British created the Supreme Muslim Council. This was an entirely new body that was entrusted with the *waqf* (charitable trust) revenues that had formerly gone to the Ottoman state, and which were later supplemented by direct British subventions.[26] Into these powerful positions, the British placed one man, Hajj Amin al-Husayni, who served them exceedingly well for the succeeding decade and a half, until 1937 when he felt obliged to align himself with a popular rebellion against his former British masters. Hajj Amin, whose brother and three generations of his family before him had held the post of "Hanafi Mufti of Jerusalem," was appointed to the post ahead of other apparently more qualified, and older, candidates. In doing so, the British were gambling that this young radical, only recently pardoned for his nationalist activities, would serve British interests by maintaining calm in return for his elevation to the post. Despite constant Zionist complaints about him, this gamble paid off for the British until the mid-1930s, when the mufti could no longer contain popular passions.[27]

In explaining the lack of political cohesion of the Palestinians, especially in the crucial decade of the 1930s and afterward, the lack of access to the mechanisms of state or any other recognized central forum does not, of course, explain everything, important though it is in understanding differences between the Palestinian polity and both the *yishuv* and national movements in other Arab states. There were important social and personal factors as well, which must be factored into any explanation of why the Palestinians failed so abjectly on the political and military levels in the decade prior to 1948. Fascinating though such an explanation may be, we must leave this matter in order to explore briefly the ways in which Palestinian society compared with other Arab societies at this time. Such a comparison will provide us with the background against which such an explanation of proximate causes for what happened in Palestine in the years leading up to 1948 must be considered.[28]

What Can Be Compared

An attempt to compare Palestinian and some other Arab societies in the interwar period must confront the fact that the data for the former is much more extensive than for the latter. This is partly because the Palestinian Arabs were part of a country dominated by a larger Jewish economy and an increasingly powerful *yishuv* that had governmental capabilities nearly on a European level, including the power to collect voluminous data.[29] By contrast, in spite of European colonial rule in various forms, the level of data collection in the other Arab countries was lower. The only partial exception was Egypt, whose asymmetrically developed economy was in some respects highly advanced,[30] and where the collection of statistics had advanced in keeping with the importance of Egyptian agriculture to the world economy.[31]

It is nevertheless possible to make illuminating comparisons between Palestine and its Middle Eastern neighbors in a number of areas, one being literacy. Here Palestine was clearly in advance of some other countries. Thus, the literacy of Muslim males over the age of seven in Palestine, Egypt, and Turkey was 25.1 percent, 20.3 percent, and 17.4 percent, respectively, at about the same time.[32] Given the existence in both Palestine and Egypt of a large number of Christians, who had higher literacy rates, the overall literacy rates of these two countries compared even more favorably with those in Turkey than these figures would indicate. The abysmally low rates of female literacy (only 3.3 percent of Muslim females in Palestine were literate in 1931) brought down the overall totals for all three countries. As late as 1947, in spite of massive efforts to expand and improve education in the interim, only 22.8 percent of all Egyptian adults were literate,[33] a figure matched by Palestinian adults sixteen years earlier in 1931.[34] In Syria and Lebanon, male literacy rates were higher than in other countries of the region—in 1932, Syria's was 32 percent and that of Lebanon 53 percent.[35]

Another area where comparison is useful is education. We have seen that in Palestine by 1947 nearly half the Arab school-age population was enrolled in schools. In that year, 147,000 of an estimated Arab school-age population of 330,000 (or 44.5 percent) were being educated in government and private schools, with 103,000 in the former and the rest in the latter.[36] While these figures may seem modest by recent standards, they represent a significant improvement in little over two decades: Just over 20 percent of

Arab school-age children were in schools in 1922–1923. And in the towns in 1945–1946, 85 percent of boys and 65 percent of girls were in school. The problem was in the countryside, where only 65 percent of boys and 10 percent of girls were in school, a problem caused, in part, because only 432 of about 800 villages had schools.[37] It is nevertheless striking that by the end of the mandate period, a majority of Arab boys in both city and countryside, and of Arab girls in the cities, were in school.

In Egypt, there was a major expansion of the educational system in the same period, during which education became a national issue, in view of the reluctance of the British since the time of Lord Cromer to allow expenditure on education. School enrollment went from 324,000 in 1913 to 942,000 in 1932, but even with further expansion by education-minded national governments, by the end of World War II, Egypt's schools were able to accommodate only well under half of the school-age population.[38] The educational situation in Syria compared even more unfavorably with that in Palestine. In 1938 there were 58,867 students in 472 state schools in Syria, while in Palestine 402 state schools had 49,400 Arab pupils.[39] The Syrian numbers compare very poorly with those in Palestine, given that the Arab population of Palestine was less than half that of Syria. These figures also do not reflect the proportionately larger number of Palestinians than Syrians in foreign and missionary schools.

In a realm related to those of literacy and education, namely, the press, Palestine also compared favorably with its neighbors. Although there are no reliable circulation figures for any Middle Eastern country for this period, the press grew and expanded in direct relation to the expansion of literacy and education. In spite of its relatively small population, Palestine supported a remarkable number of newspapers and other periodicals. Many of these publications were ephemeral or had a restricted number of readers, though the audience for a newspaper was often larger than might be imagined and often considerably higher than the number of subscribers, as newspapers were commonly read out loud in homes, coffee-shops, and other private and public gathering places.

The number of newspapers and periodicals established in Palestine from World War I to the end of the mandate was striking—200, with forty-eight founded until 1929, eighty-five in the 1930s, and sixty-seven to 1948.[40] By way of contrast, in Syria during the same years of the mandate, only ninety titles appeared.[41] The number of papers published in both Egypt and Lebanon was certainly greater than the totals for Palestine, and the quality was often higher, due to the large market of the former and the sophisticated level of the journalism in both Cairo and Beirut. Even before 1914, Beirut and Cairo had become the preeminent centers for Arabic-language journalism. In Beirut and other parts of what was to become Lebanon, 143 periodicals had been founded by 1914.[42] Nevertheless, the

Palestinian press generally compared quite favorably with that in most other Arab countries in this period, as any reader of *Filastin* or *al-Karmil* during this period could attest.[43]

The last set of figures that can be provided are economic statistics. Unfortunately, it is difficult to make good comparisons here, since the nature of the existing figures is so different, and often incommensurate, where data exists at all. For Egypt, where the best statistics exist outside of Palestine, estimates of national income for the late 1930s range from £E168–200 million (168–200 million Egyptian pounds),[44] while we have seen that the national income of Palestine for 1936 was £P33 million, of which the Arab sector produced £P16 million. This amounted to a national income per capita for the Arabs of Palestine of about £P17.4, as against a range of £E10.5–12.5 per capita for Egypt in 1937, at a time when Egypt's population was 13.8 million.

Although reliable national income estimates for other Arab countries are hard to come by, there is one other set of figures that might provide a yardstick for comparison—the government revenue and expenditure. The only trick here is to estimate what share of the revenue and expenditure of the British mandatory government in Palestine should be allocated to each community. This was a vexed issue during the mandate, with the relatively wealthy *yishuv* claiming that they provided a disproportionate share of revenue, while the Arabs (who did not enjoy either the parastate services of the Jewish Agency or the *yishuv*'s lavish capital inflows) benefited from a disproportionate share of expenditures. These numbers are nevertheless of some comparative utility, even with all these caveats.

Government revenue in Palestine grew from £P2.45 million in 1930–1931 to £P4.64 million in 1936–1937, and to £P8.9 million in 1942–1943.[45] Expenditure in the same years totaled £P2.56, 6.07, and 10.25 million. Even if one assumes that more than half of both revenue and expenditure should be allocated to the Jewish sector of the population, the contrast is striking with countries like Iraq, Syria, and Lebanon, whose populations were respectively triple, double, and the same size as that of Arab Palestine. Iraq's revenues were ID (Iraq dinar) 3.84, ID6.02, and ID12 million and its expenditures ID3.83, ID7.15, and ID11.23 in the same three years. Syrian government revenues and expenditures were much smaller: Converted into sterling, the former amounted to £1.24, £1.13, and £2.49 million with the latter in similar ranges. Lebanon's government was even smaller; its revenue and expenditure was about half that of Syria.

These numbers relate a period of just over a decade when overall the Arab sector of the economy produced about half of Palestine's national income (though its share was much larger than that of the Jewish sector at the beginning and somewhat smaller at the end). During that time, the Palestinian government raised far more money per capita from, and spent far more money per capita on, its Arab population than did that of Iraq. Moreover, in absolute terms it raised and spent more than those of Syria and Lebanon by multiples ranging from two to ten over these eleven years.

The size of government may be less likely to be considered an index of progress today than it once was, and it is certainly no measure of what is usually understood by the term "civil society." In the Palestinian case this is particularly true, given that from 22 percent to 33 percent of expenditure during these years was on "security,"[46] which in the late 1930s, in particular, meant the forcible suppression of the Arab majority in the interest of the Jewish minority. Nevertheless, when these figures on the money raised and spent by government are taken together with the figures cited above on national income, on the press, education, and literacy, a clear picture emerges. This is of a Palestinian society and economy that were certainly as fully developed as those of any other neighboring Arab country in the same era. A myriad of subjective observations about the relative general prosperity of Palestinian Arab society, or the high standard of Palestinian journalism, or the excellent quality of the Palestinian educational system, as visitors from other Arab countries perceived them, support such quantitatively derived conclusions for all the flaws in the figures available.

None of this conclusively explains what happened to Palestinian society in 1948. It should, however, help to dispose of the canard that this was in some measure a less than complete society, or one that was irremediably mired in social backwardness. Palestinian society was certainly overmatched by the European standards (and truly exceptional levels of capital investments per capita) of the *yishuv* in a variety of economic, social, and organizational realms. Nonetheless, it was manifestly as advanced as any other in the region, and considerably more so than several. As I have tried to show elsewhere,[47] by the early years of the mandate the Palestinians had already developed a modern national consciousness that had taken hold among important segments of the population. Nevertheless, as the climactic decade of the 1930s went on, in spite of the remarkable effort embodied in their revolt of 1936–1939, the Palestinians certainly fell short of the high standards of political cohesion and advanced political organization exhibited by the Zionist movement.

During this critical decade, the *yishuv* managed to surmount successfully the grave challenges posed by the flood of Jewish immigrants to Palestine fleeing the Nazis, the Palestinian revolt of 1936–1939, and the shock of the 1939 White Paper that limited British support for Zionism. For reasons that must remain beyond the scope of this chapter, the Palestinians did not succeed in surmounting the related challenges they faced during this decade from Britain, Zionism, and internal Palestinian and inter-Arab divisions.

What this chapter has hopefully shown is that, these failures notwithstanding, Palestinian society before 1948 was in comparative terms relatively coherent and reasonably developed in some respects. What the Palestinians lacked, in other words, was neither a sense of identity nor a vibrant civil society. What they apparently did lack, however, was the capacity for social and political mobilization and the support for this process that a state or parastate structures would have provided. The search for an explanation for their lack of political cohesion and advanced political and military organization must therefore be directed elsewhere, perhaps toward some of the political questions touched on in the preceding section.[48] What this chapter has attempted to show is that by the standards of its time and place, Palestinian society could be seen as at least a half-full glass, even as by the demanding standards of comparison, competition, and conflict with the *yishuv*, it may have appeared even less than half empty.

Notes

1. For one of many examples of this tendency to make such comparisons, see J. C. Hurewitz, *The Struggle for Palestine*, 2nd ed. (New York: Schocken, 1976), Chapters 2–4.

2. Walid Khalidi, *From Haven to Conquest: Readings in Zionism and the Palestine Problem Until 1948*, 2nd printing (Washington, D.C.: Institute for Palestine Studies, 1987), Appendix I, pp. 842–843. The increase in the Jewish population during the 1930s is particularly striking in view of its decline as a proportion of the total population from 1926 to 1929, from 18.4 percent to 17.7 percent. See Barbara Smith, *The Roots of Separatism in Palestine: British Economic Policy, 1920–1929* (Syracuse, N.Y.: Syracuse University Press, 1993), Table 3, p. 65.

3. Robert Nathan, Oscar Gass, and Daniel Creamer, *Palestine: Problem and Promise: An Economic Study* (Washington, D.C.: Public Affairs Press, 1946), Table 1, p. 148.

4. Zeev Sternhell, *The Founding Myths of Israel* (Princeton, N.J.: Princeton University Press, 1998), p. 217.

5. W. Khalidi, *Haven*, Appendix V, pp. 851–852.

6. According to the 1931 census, only about 22 percent of Palestinian Arabs were literate, as against 86 percent of Jews; extrapolated from table in Nathan, Gass, and Creamer, *Palestine*, p. 142, and from Jewish Agency for Palestine, Economic Research Institute, *Statistical Handbook of Middle Eastern Countries: Palestine, Cyprus, Egypt, Iraq, the Lebanon, Syria, Transjordan, Turkey* (Jerusalem: Jewish Agency, 1945), Table 9, p. 6

7. By the end of the mandate, 44.5 percent of school-age Arab children were in school (A. L. Tibawi, *Arab Education in Mandatory Palestine: A Study of Three Decades of British Administration* [London: Luzac, 1956], tables, pp. 270–271), while virtually the entire Jewish school-age population received schooling.

8. Roger Owen, "Economic Development in Mandatory Palestine," in George Abed (ed.), *The Palestinian Economy: Studies in Development Under Prolonged Occupation* (London: Routledge, 1988), Table 2.6, p. 26.

9. Jewish Agency, *Statistical Handbook,* Table 4, p. 3. The figures are based on a 1942 estimate.

10. The figures for the Jewish population are from ibid., Table 8, p. 6, and are

a Jewish Agency estimate dating from 1943; those for the Arab population are from the 1931 census, cited in Said Himadeh (ed.), *Economic Organization of Palestine* (Beirut: American University of Beirut, 1938), Table XVII, p. 34. Typically, there is more and better data for the Jewish than for the Arab population of Palestine.

11. Sternhell, *Founding Myths*, p. 14.

12. Rashid Khalidi, *Palestinian Identity: The Construction of Modern National Consciousness* (New York: Columbia University Press, 1997).

13. Sternhell, *Founding Myths*, shows that the egalitarian rhetoric of Zionism was not always reflected in practice, pp. 282 ff.

14. The only subdistrict that had a Jewish majority was Jaffa, where Tel Aviv was located. The most comprehensive study of population in Palestine, Justin McCarthy, *The Population of Palestine: Population Statistics of the Late Ottoman Period and the Mandate* (New York: Columbia University Press, 1990), table, p. 37, indicates that the Arab population of Palestine was 1,339,773 in 1946 and the Jewish population 602,586. Both had grown larger by 1948. Population by subdistrict is cited in the report of the UN General Assembly committee to consider the UN Special Committee on Palestine minority report, 11 November 1947, cited in W. Khalidi, *Haven*, p. 678, map, p. 671.

15. W. Khalidi, *Haven,* p. 680, map, p. 673, gives UN figures, based on British Mandate statistics. According to them, in 1946 Jews owned 10.6 percent of the privately owned land in Palestine, and Arabs owned almost all of the rest.

16. According to the last British estimates, cited in McCarthy, *Population*, table, p. 163, the Arab urban population of the country in 1944 amounted to over 408,000 people. About 199,000 of them lived in these cities and towns, the vast majority of whom were forced to flee their homes in 1948, as were about 30,000 Arab inhabitants of the western part of Jerusalem.

17. The most careful work on the topic is Walid Khalidi (ed.), *All That Remains: The Palestinian Villages Occupied and Depopulated by Israel in 1948* (Washington, D.C.: Institute for Palestine Studies, 1992), which enumerates 418 such villages.

18. This is the title of the seminal work by Qustantin Zurayq, *Ma'na al-Nakba* [The meaning of the catastrophe] (Beirut: Dar al-'Ilm lil-Malayin, 1948) [translated as *The Meaning of the Disaster* by R. Bayley Winder (Beirut: Khayat, 1956)]. Zurayq was a Princeton-trained historian of Damascene origin who served as a Syrian minister, acting president of the American University of Beirut, president of the Syrian University, and chairman of the board of trustees of the Institute for Palestine Studies.

19. It was Ben Gurion himself who gave canonical form to these allegations in a 1961 speech, as is pointed out by Ilan Pappé in *The Making of the Arab-Israeli Conflict, 1947–1951* (London: I. B. Tauris, 1994), pp. 88–89.

20. Benny Morris, *The Birth of the Palestinian Refugee Problem 1947–1949* (Cambridge, UK: Cambridge University Press, 1987); Tom Segev, *1949: The First Israelis* (New York: Free Press, 1986); Simha Flapan, *The Birth of Israel: Myths and Realities* (New York: Pantheon, 1987); and Avi Shlaim, *Collusion Across the Jordan* (New York: Columbia University Press, 1988), all contributed to this refutation, as did Ilan Pappé, in *The Making*.

21. Walid Khalidi, "Plan *Dalet:* The Zionist Master Plan for the Conquest of Palestine," *Middle East Forum* 37, no. 9 (November 1961): 22–28; "The Fall of Haifa," *Middle East Forum* 35, no. 10 (December 1959): 22–32; "Why Did the Palestinians Leave?" *Middle East Forum* 34, no. 6 (July 1959): 21–24, 35; Erskine Childers, "The Other Exodus," *The Spectator*, no. 6933 (12 May 1961): 672–675,

and "The Wordless Wish: From Citizens to Refugees," in Ibrahim Abu Lughod (ed.), *The Transformation of Palestine* (Evanston, Ill.: Northwestern University Press, 1971), pp. 165–202. W. Khalidi's "Plan *Dalet*" article, together with the fascinating 1961 correspondence about it and Childers's work, and a number of appendices, is reproduced in *The Journal of Palestine Studies* 18, no. 1 (Autumn 1988): 4–70.

22. See, for example, Morris, *The Birth*, pp. 128–131.

23. See, for example, Ghassan Kanafani, *Thawrat 1936 fi Filastin: Khalfiyyat wa tafasil wa tahlil* (Beirut: Popular Front for the Liberation of Palestine, 1974); A.W. Kayyali, *Palestine: A Modern History* (London: Croom Helm, 1978); Naji 'Allush, *al-Muqawama al-'Arabiyya fi Filastin* (Beirut: Dar al-Tali'a, 1968). Walid Khalidi, drawing on his years of research into the topic, has published a study in Arabic of the fighting of 1948, *Khamsuna 'aman 'ala taqsim Filastin (1947–1997)* (Beirut: Dar al-Nahar, 1998). It is a sequel to another volume on the partition plan.

24. These include Issa Khalaf, *Arab Factionalism and Social Disintegration, 1939–1948* (Albany: State University of New York Press, 1991); Philip Mattar, *The Mufti of Jerusalem: Al-Hajj Amin al-Husayni and the Palestinian National Movement* (New York: Columbia University Press, 1988); and R. Khalidi, *Palestinian Identity*.

25. Eric Hobsbawm and Terence Ranger (eds.), *The Invention of Tradition*, Canto ed. (Cambridge, UK: Cambridge University Press, 1992).

26. For more details, see the illuminating University of Chicago Department of Near Eastern Languages and Civilizations dissertation (defended May 1998) by Weldon Matthews, "The Arab Istiqlal Party in Palestine, 1927–1934."

27. The best study of the mufti's career is Philip Mattar, *Mufti of Jerusalem*. How the mufti helped the British curb Palestinian radicalism is thoroughly explored by Matthews's thesis, "The Arab Istiqlal Party."

28. For a more complete analysis of this topic, see R. Khalidi, "The Palestinians and 1948: The Underlying Causes of Failure," in Avi Shlaim and Eugene Rogan (eds.), *Rewriting the Palestine War: 1948 and the History of the Arab-Israeli Conflict* (Cambridge, UK: Cambridge University Press, 2001), pp. 12–36.

29. For an illustration of the truth of this observation, it is necessary only to examine the detailed tables of Zionist statistics reproduced in McCarthy, *Population*, pp. 217–235, and the extraordinary compendium produced by the Jewish Agency's Economic Research Institute, *Statistical Handbook*.

30. The classical study is by Charles Issawi, "Asymmetrical Development and Transport in Egypt, 1800–1914," in William Polk and Richard Chambers (eds.), *The Beginnings of Modernization in the Middle East* (Chicago: University of Chicago Press, 1968), pp. 383–400.

31. See the "Introduction" to Roger Owen, *Cotton and the Egyptian Economy, 1820–1914: A Study in Trade and Development* (Oxford: Oxford University Press, 1969), pp. xxiv–xxv, for details on the improvement in the collection of statistics in Egypt in the latter part of the nineteenth century.

32. The dates were 1931, 1927, and 1927, respectively: Nathan, Gass and Creamer, *Palestine*, p. 142.

33. John Waterbury, *The Egypt of Nasser and Sadat*, Table 3.6, p. 44.

34. Extrapolated from 1931 census figures in Jewish Agency, *Statistical Handbook*, Table 9, p. 6.

35. Charles Issawi, *The Fertile Crescent, 1800–1914: A Documentary*

Economic History (Oxford: Oxford University Press, 1988), p. 30. Issawi does not specify, but it is clear from the context that these are male rather than overall literacy rates.

36. These figures are derived from tables on pp. 270–271 of A. L. Tibawi, *Arab Education* (those for school-age population and government school enrollment are for 1947–1948; the last available figures for private schools are for 1945–1946). See Ylana Miller, *Government and Society in Rural Palestine1920–1948* (Austin: University of Texas Press, 1985), pp. 90–118, for an excellent account of the spread of education in rural areas, generally at the instigation of the rural population and notwithstanding the obstacles often placed in their way by the British.

37. Miller, *Government and Society in Mandatory Palestine*, p. 98, citing the Palestine Government Department of Education *Annual Report, 1945–46.*

38. Charles Issawi, *Egypt at Mid-Century: An Economic Survey* (Oxford: Oxford University Press, 1954), p. 67.

39. A. L. Tibawi, *A Modern History of Syria, Including Lebanon and Palestine* (London: Macmillan, 1969), p. 357.

40. Yusuf Khuri (ed.), *al-Sihafa al-'arabiyya fi Filastin, 1876–1948* (Beirut: Institute for Palestine Studies, 1976). These figures include periodicals reopened under different names after being closed by the authorities.

41. Derek Hopwood, *Syria 1945–1986: Politics and Society* (London: Unwin Hyman, 1988), p. 165.

42. Charles Issawi, *The Middle East Economy: Decline and Recovery* (Princeton, N.J.: Markus Weiner, 1995), p. 137.

43. For more details on the Palestinian press, see R. Khalidi, *Palestinian Identity*, and R. Khalidi, "Anti-Zionism, Arabism, and Palestinian Identity: 'Isa al-'Isa and *Filastin*," forthcoming in S. Seikaly (ed.), *Political Identity in the Arab East in the Twentieth Century* (Beirut: American University of Beirut Press).

44. Issawi, *Egypt*, p. 83. During the period in question, Egyptian and Palestinian pounds and Iraqi dinars were linked to sterling (the Egyptian pound was worth slightly more).

45. The figures in this and the following paragraphs are drawn from Jewish Agency, *Statistical Handbook*, Table 40, p. 26 (Palestine); Table 37, p. 94 (Iraq); and Table 27, p. 111 (Syria and Lebanon).

46. Ibid., Table 40, p. 26.

47. R. Khalidi, *Palestinian Identity.*

48. Although this problem is briefly addressed in the final chapter of ibid., attempts to find a fuller explanation are made in Rashid Khalidi, "Anti-Zionism," and Rashid Khalidi, "The Palestinians and 1948."

14

Manly Men on a National Stage (and the Women Who Make Them Stars)

Walter Armbrust

> My father told me that on the day I was born our house was surrounded by English soldiers because they knew that a huge demonstration would be organized from there. When I came into the world my father chose the name Farid after the immortal leader Muhammad Farid who was exiled for his nationalist positions.[1]

The occasion for the above quote was the imminent release of Egyptian actor Farid Shauqi's highly patriotic 1957 film *Port Said*.[2] At that point Shauqi was roughly one decade into a film career that would span fifty years and unaware that by the end of the 1950s he would already have appeared in his most critically successful and, arguably, most popular films. To his dying day the image of Shauqi, the forthright nationalist, can be readily confirmed by anyone familiar with his films, regardless of their opinion on his acting abilities or on the value of his life's work.

Shauqi did not evoke nationalism iconographically. That kind of representation is more commonly associated with women,[3] whereas men, on the whole, were given more active roles in the representational economy. In any case, Shauqi was an actor, and actors are enmeshed in too great a variety of narratives to "stand" for the nation in the same way as the figure of Marianne in France, for example, or even statues of famous men in virtually any nation-state. Shauqi was an active participant in representation, but he was also a commercial product. Furthermore, by the mid-1950s Shauqi had emerged as a star who embodied a national ideal tailored to working-class notions of masculinity. Character actors and roles become conventionalized, but stars are polysemous by nature because they have public identities outside of their roles. Shauqi's capacity to represent a national ideal linked to a masculine ideal was therefore formed through the inherently unstable and fluid vehicles of commerce and stardom.

Although for social actors nationalism operates through cultural and historical certainties, contemporary students of nationalism do not take these certainties for granted but rather focus on how they are constructed. As Michael Herzfeld puts it, the "apparent fixities" of nationalism are "the products of the very things they deny: *action*, *agency*, and *use*."[4] An analysis of how Shauqi's constantly reformulated identity was marketed to his public therefore offers a highly advantageous perspective on the process of national identity formation. Furthermore, Shauqi became a meaningful public figure through social and technological processes widely utilized throughout the latter half of the twentieth century. His image was a product of both mass media marketing and personal effort, and it often took on contrasting or even contradictory effects.

Discontinuities in Shauqi's representation created "the possibility of conflict as significant and productive in itself, as an open-ended series of dialectics that might have produced different resolutions for different groups of people."[5] Social dialectics can be seen in many sites of cultural production and must be understood in historical context.[6] A crucial aspect of Shauqi's historical context is that he was as much a mass-produced product as a cultural symbol. Consumers of mass culture can never be understood as standardized, homogenized, "mass people";[7] therefore, the key to understanding Shauqi (and many other comparable figures) is to acknowledge that his narratives were marketed in association with advertising, and more important, that the line between the two is often unclear. The ambiguity between Shauqi the product and Shauqi the public figure adds further complexity to the "productive conflicts" (to paraphrase Marilyn Booth) evoked by Shauqi in his polysemous representations of nationalism. All of these ambiguities revolve around the ways that Shauqi was gendered. The machismo of the patriotic Shauqi quoted in this chapter's epigraph was far from the whole story.

The Gender of Nationalist Representation

It is rare for nationalist discourse to ignore women, but it is equally true that nationalist narratives construct men as socially dominant. Perhaps for this reason recurrent images of "the nation as woman" are striking and have received quite a bit of attention in literature on gender in the Middle East and elsewhere. For example, Beth Baron argues that in the late nineteenth and early twentieth centuries, various manifestations of women were not just a potential strategy of representation but were actually the favored iconic embodiment of Egyptian nationalism.[8] Afsaneh Najmabadi notes that Iranian nationalists represented the homeland as a female body,[9] and in doing so, they followed a practice widespread in many nations.[10] Booth shows how Jeanne d'Arc narratives were ambivalently inscribed in Egyptian women's magazines from the early twentieth century such that Jeanne could symbolize active opposition to colonial rule, peasant authenticity, or an example of gentle femininity suitable for the woman's role in domestic life, if not of the actualization of domesticity.[11]

All of these authors focus on the use of female imagery to represent nations. However, if Shauqi is to be properly understood, then the gendering of nationalist representation must be examined in wider focus. One must be careful not to assume that women were polysemous symbols of the nation amenable to multiple registers of meaning according to class, historical context, and other contingencies whereas men were simply men—an undifferentiated brotherhood of nationalists. On the contrary, masculinity is as socially constructed as femininity. Consequently, "focusing on masculinity should not be seen as a shift away from feminist projects, but rather as a complementary endeavour, indeed one that is organically linked."[12]

Shauqi's masculine representation of nationalism fits into a pre-established pattern. Baron notes that symbolic representations of the nation overwhelmingly took female form and that male figures such as *Misri effendi* (Egyptian effendi) and *ibn al-balad*[13] were less pervasive. But by the mid-1940s, *ibn al-balad*—shown in the popular magazine *al-Ithnayn*[14] as a wizened figure in peasant clothing rather than in the urban tarbush worn by *Misri effendi* in the 1920s[15]—was clearly used to represent the nation in many cartoons by Muhammad Rakha (see Figures 14.1 and 14.2).

In these cartoons, the nation is represented by a man, but the style is metonymic rather than metaphoric; *ibn al-balad* is "the average citizen" as Baron suggested in the case of the outmoded *Misri effendi* of the 1920s,[16] but in this case he is the part that stands for the whole rather than one object standing for another. Both styles of representations could be combined in a single cartoon. In Figure 14.3 the Egypt/Sudan Siamese twins are given national labels, but they are mute representations.

The male representative of the nation—a peasant *ibn al-balad*—is more active and articulate than his female counterpart. He gets to comment; they merely appear. This gendered nationalist representation was consonant with most local practice, which assigned more active public roles to men than women. But the rise of Shauqi to stardom suggests greater complexities in the confluence of gender and national identity.

The Rise of Shauqi

Shauqi was born around 1919 and died on 28 July 1998, after a long and prolific career. He entered his profession in 1938 as an amateur stage actor and joined the fledgling High Institute for Acting under the auspices of the

Figure 14.1
"President Roosevelt announced that every family would get a respectable home after the war." Ibn al-Balad, "I want one of those." He points to a modern villa labeled "Complete independence." *Al-Ithnayn* 501 (17 January 1944), p. 7. By Muhammad Rakha.

Ministry of Social Affairs in 1946. By 1947 he began to appear in films.[17] Until 1952 Shauqi was entirely restricted to secondary roles, almost always as the villain in a seemingly endless chain of melodramas. But he never saw playing the villain as his calling.[18] His writing suggests aspirations to high art, but by the time he attained stardom in the mid-1950s he was known strictly as a popular—even populist—figure. Some of Shauqi's breakthrough roles called for him to be manly, irresistible to women, and to triumph over any adversity. Such roles resonate easily with the defense of feminine honor, and in the 1950s, when Egypt was newly independent, it was a short step from defending the honor of women to defending the honor of the nation. But Shauqi did not simply become a heartthrob. Rather he made a conscious appeal to lower-class sensibilities, becoming, at a certain point in his career, the self-proclaimed *malik al-tirsu*—"king of the cheap seats."

Shauqi's he-men were not copies from John Wayne stories or of any other variant of tough guys in the U.S. cinema. It is, of course, true that many Egyptian films are patterned on U.S. films, but the degree to which

Figure 14.2
Ibn al-Balad, "The tram is more expensive; food is more expensive; fabric is more expensive. But I'm the same as I was!" *Al-Ithnayn* 510 (20 March 1944), p. 1. By Muhammad Rakha.

Figure 14.3
"Siamese Twins (Egypt and Sudan joined at the hip)." Ibn al-Balad, "Can those two be separated?" Doctor, "Yes, but both of them will die." *Al-Ithnayn* 523 (3 July 1944), p. 4. By Muhammad Rakha.

Egyptian films are intentional copies of foreign models, as opposed to adaptations, is routinely overstated,[19] and the capacity of Hollywood to adapt stories from virtually anywhere is understated. Shauqi fashioned his persona to fit both his own self-image and the times in which he rose to prominence. His image was only partly a product of the roles he played in films. The other factors that produced the king of the cheap seats were first, his ability to gain control of some aspects of the production of his own films and, second, the auxiliary media through which his image was elaborated, particularly fan magazines. The element in Shauqi's life that ties these two things together—his success in gaining control over production, and the elaborating imagery of the fan magazines—is, paradoxically, a woman. The crucial element in constructing the preeminent he-man of the Egyptian cinema in the 1950s was, as we shall see, his tie to a woman.

Farid Shauqi, king of the cheap seats and some-time nationalist icon, is not necessarily the Farid Shauqi who comes most readily to mind for Egyptian cinema fans. "King of the cheap seats" was Shauqi's own preferred designation and the title of his 1978 autobiography. However, a perhaps more common nickname for Shauqi is *wahsh al-shasha* (beast of the screen). Shauqi's bread-and-butter role was not the masterful he-man defending feminine and national virtue but the villain—and usually not a redeemable villain forced to do wrong by circumstances or social ills but rather a crude thug, petty hood, lounge lizard, blackmailer, or drug smuggler. Early in his film career he sometimes juggled three or four of these roles (all in different studios, but all dastardly) at the same time.[20]

Shauqi was one of the most prolific actors in the history of Egyptian cinema. One Egyptian director (not a Shauqi fan) told me grudgingly that "at least Shauqi always stayed in the market." This was an understatement. He is credited with having appeared in 275 films.[21] Mahmud Qasim and Ya'qub Wahbi count 331 films for Mahmud al-Miligi, a career character actor who also played villains. By their count nobody else is close.

Hoda Sultan

Shauqi became a star first through his ability to gain control of at least some parts of the production process and, second, through the elaborating imagery of fan magazines. Both were linked to his relationship with Hoda Sultan, his second wife (he married three times), with whom he appeared in many of his best films.

When Sultan and Shauqi married in 1951, Shauqi was at the height of his "beast of the screen" days. Critics were unimpressed. One article pithily dismissed him: "The critics thought he would rise quickly. But in less than one year he started taking villain roles. Farid Shauqi developed. He became famous. He got rich. He got fat. He married Hoda Sultan."[22] Of course at the time this article was written, the larger picture of Shauqi's career was unclear. But by 1957 he had begun to expand on his repetitive villain roles. His marriage to Hoda Sultan was an important step in this process.

Many of Shauqi's villain roles made him appear tough or threatening, but his roles rarely made him into an endearing or even redeemable character. Even so, these films could be notable. Perhaps his signature villain role occurs in *Hamido,*[23] in which Shauqi plays a fisherman/drug smuggler who impregnates his girlfriend (played by Sultan). Instead of making her an honest woman, he takes her for a boat ride and throws her over the side.

Too physically imposing to be a comedian, unable to sing, and already typecast, trying to make himself into a strong masculine figure was perhaps the most obvious strategy for Shauqi to follow. The cultural milieu in which he defined his manliness is often described in academic literature on the Middle East as part of an "honor" complex. Men and women conceive of themselves in a relationship of complementarity: The honor of men and their kin groups is inherently linked to the sexual shame of women. Men occupy a public realm in which honor is "projected," while women are part of a familial "sacred realm" that must be protected.[24] Although the analytical usefulness of the honor/shame complex has been both criticized and elaborated from a number of perspectives,[25] the value of assertive male honor "covering" female vulnerability was (and still is) relevant to Shauqi's audience. That such a value was expressed differently in various social milieus, and by men and women, does not detract from its general recognizability.[26] Honor (and sometimes, particularly in his early career, its absence) was therefore a trope in his masculine film narratives. But in the larger context of Shauqi's public image—in both cinema and print media—his career was part of a reorganization of the patriarchal gender hierarchy to which literature on honor refers.

When Shauqi married Sultan in 1951, the effect on his public image was contradictory. For one thing, Sultan was simply a more valuable commercial property because she could both act and sing (see Figure 14.4). From the 1930s until the end of the 1960s, singers consistently commanded the highest fees in the Egyptian film business. Sultan began her film career at the same time as Shauqi, in 1947, and appeared in far fewer films. But from the beginning she was given better roles. By the mid-1950s she was somewhere near the top of both the singing and the acting professions. A 1957 article in *al-Kawakib* estimated the earning power of the stars on a per-hour basis.[27] One needn't assume the estimates were completely accurate, but if one takes the article as a rough opinion of the relative worth of the stars, a Hoda Sultan, at £E16 per hour, was worth roughly twice a Farid Shauqi, who appeared somewhere near the bottom of the chart, at £E8 per hour.[28]

Of course money was not the whole story. Shauqi made more films than Sultan, who appeared in seventy over the course of her career.[29] However, films were not her only venue. She also gave concerts, made recordings, and presumably was given air time on the radio. By the time of their marriage, both Shauqi and Sultan augmented their income with live theater. Sultan might also have had access to publicity advertising.[30]

Controlling Production

In 1951, when they married, Hoda Sultan was a potential problem for Shauqi. How could a physically imposing actor like himself—a figure unsuited to comedy and with no singing abilities—create a positive screen persona? As the colonial era ended, there was clearly an opportunity for an actor who could cater to the working class. Earlier male stars in the

Figure 14.4
Hoda Sultan. The text notes that she had already become a notable singer and that she entered the film business as a star. *Al-Kawakib* 21 (October 1950), p. 26.

Egyptian cinema had tended to be dapper and more oriented to the bourgeois technocratic class than to the working class.[31] Masculine personae in the 1930s and 1940s were typified by such actors as Anwar Wagdi or Yusuf Wahbi, both of whom could be (and often were) plausibly shown wearing smoking jackets and living in large villas. The time was ripe for the emergence of a figure more tailored to the working class. But how convincing would a working-class figure be if he were seen as being under his wife's thumb?

One way Shauqi used the unequal commercial balance between himself and Sultan to his advantage was to move into writing and producing his own films. His autobiographies never say outright that he was able to do this because of having access to Hoda Sultan's money. It might have simply been a matter of Sultan's star power. Nonetheless, Shauqi did not start writing film scripts until the production company formed by him and Hoda Sultan started producing them. Their company was called Aflam al-'Ahd al-Gadid, New Era Films. The difference between Shauqi's earlier work as a villain and the films that he produced and often wrote was immediately obvious. Their first effort, in 1952, was *Boss Hasan*,[32] which remains a classic of the Egyptian cinema (see Figure 14.5).

Shauqi plays a worker from the lower-class neighborhood of Bulaq who gets seduced by a decadent, rich woman from the elite neighborhood of Zamalek. Sultan plays his faithful wife from the old neighborhood. Shauqi's character is morally weak and naive, but redeemable. By the end of the film he sits passively in the rich woman's car as she runs over his own son (who makes a miraculous recovery). Sultan magnanimously accepts her husband's return (Figure 14.6) but not until the rich woman has been killed, thereby freeing Shauqi's character from the spell cast by her money and corrupt ways.

Shauqi became known for producing a kind of cinematic realism—which, like the novel,[33] tends to be congenial to nationalism.[34] Shauqi later turned to overtly nationalist themes, but before he ever made a stridently nationalist film he redefined himself over a period of five years, never completely abandoning his bread-and-butter villain roles yet steadily augmenting them with alternative images, usually of his own production. In many of these he still played the heavy. Perhaps his most memorable villain role was *Hamido,* made in 1953, which Shauqi wrote himself, and which he and Sultan produced (Figure 14.7).

Shauqi's character in the film was completely reprehensible, but *Hamido* was an interesting production for its time and was credited as a significant portrayal of the dangers of narcotics. Another social issue film from this period was *They Made Me a Criminal*[35] in 1954, based on the James Cagney vehicle *Angels with Dirty Faces*. Then in 1957 Shauqi produced and starred in a film written by Nagib Mahfuz that became paradigmatic of the way lower-class traditional society was imagined. This was *The Tough Guy,*[36] in which Shauqi plays a rough-hewn character from the countryside—a beefy he-man compared to the sly peasant *ibn al-balad* of Muhammad Rakha's 1940s cartoons. Shauqi's peasant tough guy comes to the Rod al-Farag vegetable market in Cairo, which is plagued by a domineering merchant who fixes prices to nobody's advantage but himself and some powerful backers from high society. He temporarily replaces the king of the vegetable market but eventually is forced to return to his proper station.

Figure 14.5
Advertisement for *Boss Hasan* (1952). Hoda Sultan is the only figure shown in photographic detail. Shauqi appears slightly above her to the right, completely undistinguished from the rest of the cast, even though he was the film's protagonist and its most developed character. *Al-Kawakib* 47 (24 June 1952), p. 29.

Figure 14.6
Photograph from a news item listing films currently playing in local theaters. It shows Sultan, Shauqi, and their son reunited in working-class Bulaq after Shauqi's flirtation with upper-class corruption in Zamalek. The caption reads, "*Boss Hasan*, Egyptian Musical." More evidence that the film was marketed through Sultan, even though it was overwhelmingly Shauqi's vehicle. *Al-Kawakib* 47 (24 June 1952), p. 44.

Figure 14.7
Advertisement for *Hamido* (1953). One year after *Boss Hasan*, Shauqi gets top billing in the advertisement. The woman overshadowing Shauqi is Hoda Sultan. *Al-Kawakib* 121 (24 November 1954), p. 27.

Films such as these were one way that Shauqi fashioned a new image for himself.[37] It was an image that articulated with discourses targeting "undesirable" behavior, particularly of the lower class, for censure. But in Shauqi's hands, social reform was packaged with an image that depended fundamentally on the portrayal of virile masculinity. Shauqi could not have achieved prominence without Hoda Sultan, but gaining a measure of control over his productions through his partnership with Sultan was still only part of what made Shauqi significant. As an emergent star it was inevitable that Shauqi's image would be constructed by both film narratives and the elaborating imagery of fan magazines. These were also crucially tied to Sultan.

Shauqi as Partner and Guardian

Hoda Sultan's popularity as a singer gave her considerable power, but it did not make her autonomous, for her singing was a family vocation, and she came into the business after her brother, Muhammad Fauzi, who like Sultan, was a highly successful singer and film actor.[38] According to Shauqi, Fauzi was unhappy at the idea of his sister entering show business, but anxieties about family honor were eased by his recognition of Shauqi's suitability as her guardian.[39] It has often been noted that the brother-sister relationship is crucial to the construction of honor in Middle Eastern societies.[40] Anthropologist Suad Joseph argues that the real foundation of patriarchy in Arab society comes not from the relationship of children to their parents but to the socialization of brothers and sisters, in which siblings of the opposite sex learn their sexual roles by "rehearsing" for each other. Consequently, a great deal of family honor is tied to a brother's relationship to his sister: It is often the brother who has primary responsibility for disciplining a woman who is perceived to have offended family honor.[41]

Joseph makes her argument in the context of Lebanese refugee camps, and one cannot automatically assume a perfect correspondence between the social significance of brother-sister relations in 1990s Lebanon and 1950s Cairo. However, brother-sister relationships in Egypt are a point of tension, and the way Shauqi describes his role in mediating between Sultan and Fauzi is quite reminiscent of the general outlines of Joseph's ethnography. It therefore comes as no surprise that in public Shauqi went to great lengths to present himself as close to Muhammad Fauzi and willing to assume the role of being his sister's guardian. As Shauqi put it, "Muhammad Fauzi began to feel at ease because his sister was now living a stable and honorable life with an artist and colleague that he knew would protect her and distance her from the errors and dangers that could befall a woman living alone, particularly when she was a beautiful woman to whom all the wolfish men in the artistic milieu aspired."[42]

Shauqi's life with Sultan was a constant subject of fan magazines, and it appears that Shauqi participated willingly in making Sultan's private life public. Many of these articles emphasized the difficulties that Shauqi had in reconciling his wife's highly public life with his own masculine honor.[43] Such emphases can be read as an extension of their film narratives, consistent with the presumptions that filmmakers made about the sensibilities of Shauqi's lower-class audiences. But on the whole, fan magazine representations of their marriage suggested more than mere protectiveness. Shauqi played the strict husband but also pointedly signaled his willingness to treat his wife as an equal. Sultan was complicit (at least in public) in Shauqi's public balancing act between the strict male guardian of honor and the magnanimous business-partner husband. In one article, she related a story in which Shauqi went out with some journalists and forgot to come home. She yells at him furiously, and he tries to sweet talk her to no avail. She goes to her sister's house for the day. Shauqi eventually gets her to return by calling her "in his capacity as the producer Farid Shauqi," telling her that he has a role for her to play and he'll pay whatever she wants. The role is of a wife—his wife—hosting a Lebanese distributor for dinner. Initially she refuses, but when she thinks of the money they will lose she calls back and "takes the role." Eventually she decides she wants to apologize to him, and while acting, her "role" starts to blur the line between acting and reality: "I surprised Farid. He thought I was acting a role, but not living it. Indeed, he only realized that I'd forgiven him after we'd said goodbye to our guest, after which he started once again to try to appease me!"[44]

This article is typical of many sketches from the married life of Shauqi and Sultan, which were resolved not in favor of Shauqi's offended masculinity but in the interests of business. In the fan magazines, the bourgeois companionate marriage always won out over Shauqi's "Eastern" sense of honor. Whether or not the stories were real, they served as an extension of the actors' screen personas. This elaboration of personality outside film texts is one of the things that makes a star—which Shauqi was clearly becoming by the mid-1950s—different from an actor.

Contrary to the tough, lower-class image of his many gangster films, Shauqi often presented himself in print as stable, modern, and middle class. One installment of his 1957 memoirs was accompanied by a photograph of him and Sultan happily piling wedding presents on a mattress. The caption read, "Farid Shauqi and Hoda Sultan working together to set up their happy home in the beginning of their marriage."[45] The cooperative domesticated man in the photo makes an obvious contrast to the rogues' gallery of characters he played on the screen and, more important, to the more positive lower-class characters played by Shauqi in his ascent to stardom. An article about Hoda's life story early in her career even reverses the violent stereotype of Shauqi's screen roles, showing her pretending to choke him (Figure 14.8).

وفي عام ١٩٥١ خفق قلبي بالحب .. فاحببت « فريد » وتزوجته

Figure 14.8
Sultan and Shauqi reverse roles as she pretends to choke Shauqi, who appears in a very genteel smoking jacket that is quite out of place for a screen tough-guy. The text has Sultan saying, "In 1951 my heart throbbed with love . . . for Farid Shauqi." *Al-Kawakib* 21 (October 1950), p. 26.

In his later autobiography, Shauqi told elaborate stories of how well he cared for Sultan's daughter by one of her earlier husbands.[46] This was no retrospective memory tailored for an audience with changed sensibilities, for in the 1950s he made every effort to let the public know that he was more than willing to care for Sultan's daughter by another man.[47] When telling of his and Sultan's courtship, he describes writing her a love letter and then waiting by the phone like a vulnerable teenager.[48] Many of his not-so-tough images were associated with his relationship to Sultan, but Sultan was not his only device for showing a gentle nature. In an article titled "Terror on the Set" ("Ru'b al-blatoh"), he describes shooting a gangster scene calling for him and another actor to threaten each other with guns. Each becomes nervous because they've just seen a play in which the plot revolves around a murder committed on stage in a play where real bullets were used instead of blanks. He begins this story by saying, "Don't believe that I'm a villain, as all the directors and writers and producers want to cast me. Don't think that I'm a bloody murderer. I kill only on the screen—in real life I'm afraid of my shadow."[49]

Port Said

By 1957 Shauqi, the tough guy, "afraid of his shadow," had emerged as a star. In that same year, the patriot began to emerge. Shauqi was by no means unique in his efforts to associate himself with the politics of the Free Officer regime. Fan magazines are replete with images and articles showing that entertainers, artists, and intellectuals were solidly on the side of a populist government. No doubt the degree of sincerity in this material varied, and in later years some were remembered for their nationalism more than others.

The 1956 Suez War, Gamal Abdul Nasser's moment of glory, was Shauqi's chance to make a great leap from his "beast of the screen" persona to a completely different image: Farid Shauqi, defender of the nation. The breakthrough film for this version of Shauqi was *Port Said*, made less than a year after the war. Shauqi's memoir describes infiltrating into the city before the conflict was over with a film crew dressed as fishermen.[50] Allegedly it was Nasser himself who called on Shauqi to make the film, and the project was one of the first large-scale experiments in government-subsidized filmmaking in Egypt. *Port Said* was not "the" film of the revolution—that honor belongs to *My Heart's Return*,[51] which was directed the same year as *Port Said* by the same director, 'Izz al-Din Zulfiqar. But *Port Said* signaled Shauqi's arrival to stardom. Shauqi the patriot was not a great departure from the persona developed in fan magazines throughout the decade, but it was an image obviously at odds with the homicidal drug dealers and petty thieves portrayed in so many of his films.

Like virtually all Egyptian war films, *Port Said* was unabashedly patriotic (see Figures 14.9 and 14.10).[52] The film opened to the strains of the song "*Allahu akbar fauqa kayd al-mu'tadi*" (God is above the plots of aggressors), a stirring march composed to commemorate the victory over the tripartite aggression.[53] Sultan plays a blind, and hence vulnerable, citizen of Port Said. Shauqi defends her honor and, by extension, that of the nation. Shauqi's character in the film was simply superhuman.

Port Said demonstrated Shauqi's star status, but it was also probably the beginning of his artistic decline. With few exceptions he rarely appeared in films after 1960 that were artistically memorable or even as commercially successful as those of his rather more ambitious 1950s rise to stardom. Stardom achieved appears to have made Shauqi gravitate to more obvious and stereotypical films. Perhaps Shauqi's long decline was foreshadowed by the critical reception of *Port Said*. For critics, no films could be nationalistic enough. *Port Said* was criticized for concentrating too much on individual stories and not enough on the big picture. Egyptian defenders were shown shooting at the sky, but no dead English paratroopers were shown hitting the ground. A rape scene was harshly criticized on the

Figure 14.9
An advertisement for *Port Said* (1957) reads, "A great leap forward for the Egyptian film, achieved by Farid Shauqi. . . . First Egyptian film about the brutal aggression. . . . A true depiction of the events that took place in Port Said during the aggression." The three soldiers bayoneting the French, British, and Israeli flags are modeled by Shauqi.

مشهد من فيلم « بور سعيد » يمثل اهل المدينة الباسلة وهم يقاومون
الغزاة . ان نورى السعيد لم يرض عن الفيلم فمنع عرضه في العراق

Figure 14.10
A publicity still from *Port Said* (1957). Shauqi stands in the forefront on the right. The caption reads, "A scene from *Port Said* depicting the people of the fearless city opposing the invasion. Nuri al-Sa'id [leader of Iraq] was unhappy with the film and banned it in Iraq." *Al-Kawakib* 368 (19 August 1958), p. 8.

grounds that the woman's fiancé was visibly crushed rather than consumed by revenge.[54]

In the end Shauqi's nationalism was a significant part of his legacy, but ultimately not through his nationalist films. His importance lies rather in his contribution to building Egypt's version of modern bourgeois masculinity, which was integral to national identity. Ironically he did this in the slip zone between his tough screen roles and the surprisingly gentle personality elaborated in fan magazines. The most important image of Shauqi therefore was not the invincible soldier of *Port Said* or the dashing leading man (Figure 14.11) but the sensitive husband of Hoda Sultan, who sought to be known as a modern family man.

Conclusion

Film scholar John Ellis defines a star as "a performer in a particular medium whose figure enters into subsidiary forms of circulation, and then feeds back into future performances."[55] The subsidiary fan-magazine images of Shauqi were ambivalent—always oscillating between images that emphasized his violent screen roles and others that softened him and made him look tame. Disjunctions between screen image and subsidiary elaboration create a combination of distance and closeness—from glamorous, larger-than-life screen personality to the "girl (or boy) next door." Jackie Stacey suggests that the instability of the star image creates pleasure in filmgoers. Since the star image is never fixed, it can potentially appeal to a range of pleasure-producing effects, including emulation, identification, and admiration.[56] The differentiation of off-screen and on-screen personalities is a common attribute of stardom in general: "The star's . . . intertextuality is not simply an extension of the star's meaning, but is the only meaning that the star ever has. In other words, the star's image cannot exist or be known outside this shifting series of texts."[57]

The conventions that produced this simultaneous effect of nearness and distance were imported from U.S. fan magazines and reworked in an Egyptian context. The U.S. model helps us to understand how the Egyptian analog functioned. Steven Cohan, writing on masculinity in the U.S. cinema, notes that efforts to produce an identity between the screen persona and the off-screen image of actors was common in the 1950s.[58] The dominant paradigm at that time was to construct men as essential beings, no different on the screen than they were in real life. Women, by contrast, were constructed in a performative manner—as a shifting series of masquerades. One of the goals of Cohan's book is to show the many ways that masculinity was also a product of performance. Shauqi's ongoing elaboration of

Figure 14.11
Shauqi in blackface as the mythic hero 'Antar Ibn Shaddad in *'Antar Ibn Shaddad* in 1959 (the movie was not released until 1961). The woman is Kuka, an actress who specialized in Bedouin or Upper Egyptian roles. *Al-Jil* 409 (16 November 1959), p. 29.

public personality was obviously as contrived as that of any U.S. movie star.

One essential ingredient to understanding how the masquerade was constructed, and to what end, was the audience to whom the images were addressed. In the case of the U.S. counterparts to *al-Kawakib* (my main printed source for this essay), it was almost exclusively women. In the long-running (since 1911) magazine *Photoplay*, which Cohan uses extensively in his analysis, almost every product advertised was oriented to female readers. These included bras and stockings, feminine hygiene, toiletries, and of course clothes: all products for women. Femininity itself was represented as a product of artifice structured by consumption. U.S. fan magazines contained a substantial amount of male cheesecake: men for display; men as sexual objects. A feature on Tony Curtis, for example, shows a wholesome happily married man at home with his wife (Janet Leigh, who of course was a fantasy object herself). This is similar to the way Shauqi was presented with Hoda Sultan. However, the text describes Curtis as Marilyn Monroe might have been described in her heyday: "He stands 5 feet, 11 inches and weighs 158 pounds. He has a 4-inch chest expansion and a 28-inch waist. He enjoys boxing and wrestling, but does not like to ride horseback."[59] By contrast *al-Kawakib* featured endless photographs and drawings of bodies (more female than male) but never anything quite so empirically salacious.

There were similarities between *al-Kawakib*'s presentation of gendered stardom and that of *Photoplay*, but there were also differences. As previously mentioned, the magazine attempted to include in its repertory serious analysis of the film industry and often extremely negative reviews of films, along with marketing and representational conventions that were essentially adapted from U.S. fan magazines. In a similar vein, the advertising was much more ambivalent—and far less plentiful—than that of *Photoplay*. In *al-Kawakib* products designed for the consumption of women were featured regularly, as they were in *Photoplay*, but *al-Kawakib* featured far more advertising that was probably aimed at men: Healthtex men's underwear, Bata men's shoes, Magnetophone reel-to-reel tape recorders, Muska cameras, Atkinson's men's cologne, and Phillips radios are a few examples. The advertisements do not constitute proof that the audience was, in fact, composed of any particular ratio of men to women. But the relative balance in *al-Kawakib* on gendered consumption suggests at least that the producers of the magazine either were not sure who was buying the product, or that they believed their audience was mixed.

Shauqi, the tough-guy villain and, as the decade wore on, heroic defender of honor, was presented in films as a physically imposing specimen of manhood, but he was never marketed like Tony Curtis—as a "hunk." This was partly because his image was ostensibly oriented toward "popular" audiences for whom auto mechanics, porters, fishermen, and by the end of the decade, stalwart soldiers were the intended ideals of identification. Class considerations are important in the creation of Shauqi's image, but class alone, like psychoanalytic theories of desire that purportedly explain the marketing strategies of films and fan magazines, is insufficient to explain how Shauqi's masculinity was constructed. Perhaps in the end the paradoxical nature of Shauqi's masculinity is itself part of the explanation. As a star he was bound to be a malleable figure, as stars are, by nature, composed of ordinary and extraordinary elements synthesized by a single figure.[60] In the case of Shauqi, the man featured in *al-Kawakib*, unlike that of film narratives, was an honorable gentleman who could balance an image of manliness with a highly publicized marriage to a woman who made more money than he did, who was essential to his ability to gain some control of the roles in which he was cast, and therefore to his stardom.

The paradox is surely sharpened by the fact that for a substantial portion of Shauqi's audience the "exceptional nature" of Shauqi's image must have been differently construed than in the U.S. star model upon which his stardom was patterned. Shauqi's films—particularly if the often-proclaimed lower-class appeal of his films was more than just stereotype—were shown to audiences for whom the "ordinary" activities of couples in bourgeois domestic situations were, at a minimum, novel, and quite possibly went beyond mere novelty to a much more problematic association with imposed alien customs. This was an audience for which (in the case of male spectators) the idea of a sister going to the cinema in any company but that of a male family member was unacceptable. Consequently the "ordinary" for many filmgoers in the cheap seats, to whom Shauqi's characters were supposed to appeal, may well have been Shauqi's pointed and publicly proclaimed assurances that he could protect Hoda Sultan's honor and therefore the honor of her brother, Muhammad Fauzi. This kind of idealized image was what Ellis calls an "invitation to cinema," the point of which was to form one element of an "impossible paradox" combining the ordinary and the extraordinary.[61] This was constructed differently in Egypt than it was in the United States. One element of difference lay in relation to gender norms distinct from U.S. society. The many ostensibly intimate glimpses published in fan magazines of Shauqi and Sultan as happy partners (or sometimes as genially disputing partners) were quite at odds with the experiences of large segments of the audience. The "extraordinary" for Ellis consists of the figure who is "removed from the life of mere mortals, has rarified and magnified emotions, is separate from the world of the potential film viewer."[62] Shauqi and Sultan, however, as the happy couple *in the pub-*

lic eye—an impossibility in older forms of gender discourse—were not so much larger than life as they were utterly unrecognizable as a familiar image of the couple next door.

Most star studies assume that stars and the popular films in which they operate inherently promote conservatism.[63] However, in the context of Egyptian cinema, it may pay to look at conservatism more flexibly. A masculinity defined in relation to control of women's sexuality was the conservative social background of Shauqi's work in the cinema. Shauqi often fit comfortably within the parameters of this kind of masculinity. Paradoxically this was what made him a potent figure in restructuring gender norms through mass media. It made him compelling to his audience at a certain historical juncture. But the image he and Sultan promoted in fan magazines subsidiary to their screen roles, yet integral to their public personas, was of a kind of companionate marriage at odds with gender relations typical of "traditional" society. The latter image was one that both Arab and Western feminists, as well as modernists of many different political leanings, might well favor. Ultimately such labels as "conservative" or "progressive" cannot do justice to the complexity of figures such as Shauqi. A tough guy on the surface, he was nonetheless a figure of creative ambiguity.

Notes

1. Farid Shauqi, "Mudhakkirat Farid Shauqi" (Memoirs of Farid Shauqi), *al-Kawakib* 299 (23 April 1957): 16.

2. *Bur Sa'id*, 'Izz al-Din Zulfiqar (Cairo: Aflam al-'Ahd al-Gadid, 1957).

3. There is extensive literature on feminine iconography of collective identity. Some examples are Maurice Agulhon, *Marianne into Battle: Republican Imagery and Symbolism in France, 1789–1880*, trans. by Janet Lloyd (Cambridge, UK: Cambridge University Press, 1981); Michael Cameron Amin, "Selling and Saving 'Mother Iran': Gender and the Iranian Press in the 1940s," *International Journal of Middle East Studies* 33 (2001): 335–361; Beth Baron, "Nationalist Iconography: Egypt as a Woman," in Israel Jankowski and James P. Gershoni (eds.), *Rethinking Nationalism in the Arab Middle East* (New York: Columbia University Press, 1997), pp. 105–124; Marilyn Booth, "The Egyptian Lives of Jeanne d'Arc," in Lila Abu-Lughod (ed.), *Remaking Women: Feminism and Modernity in the Middle East* (Princeton, N.J.: Princeton University Press, 1998), pp. 171–211; Eric Hobsbawm, "Man and Woman in Social Iconography," *History Workshop* 6 (1978): 121–138; and Afsaneh Najmabadi, "The Erotic *Vaṭan* [homeland] as Beloved and Mother: To Love, to Possess, and to Protect," *Comparative Studies in Society and History* 39 (1997): 442–467. See also Elizabeth Thompson on the construction of gendered citizenship in colonial Syria; representation is only a small part of the analysis, but the book features a representation of Lebanon that consists of a seated Marianne-like figure guarded by a standing nude man holding a large sword. Thompson, *Colonial Citizens: Republican Rights, Paternal Privilege, and Gender*

in French Syria and Lebanon (New York: Columbia University Press, 2000), cover, pp. 247–248. All of these scholars note that while icons of collective identity often (perhaps typically) were female, the main ideological agenda was patriarchal.

4. Michael Herzfeld, *Cultural Intimacy: Social Poetics in the Nation-State* (New York: Routledge, 1997), p. 165 (emphasis in the original).

5. Booth, "Egyptian Lives," p. 175.

6. Booth encourages "close attention to specific historically grounded discourses of the time" (ibid., p. 174) to understand the ambiguities posed by "famous women" biographies. Her point (and mine) in making an issue of ambiguities is not that the readings enabled by a given text are so open as to be indecipherable, but that an emphasis on productive ambivalences may in fact enable a better appreciation of how a text was read.

7. Some of the influential voices in the shift away from the tendency to view mass production in the cultural sphere as a simple replacement of small-scale local cultures by a homogenizing industrialized culture (or a "culture industry" as scholars associated with the Frankfurt school would have it) are Arjun Appadurai (ed.), *The Social Life of Things: Commodities in Cultural Perspective* (Cambridge, UK: Cambridge University Press, 1986); Jean Baudrillard, *The Mirror of Production*, trans. by M. Poster (St. Louis: Telos Press, 1975); Pierre Bourdieu, *Distinction: A Social Critique of the Judgement of Taste*, trans. by Richard Nice (Cambridge: Harvard University Press, 1984); Daniel Miller, *Modernity, an Ethnographic Approach: Dualism and Mass Consumption in Trinidad* (Oxford: Berg, 1994); and Daniel Miller (ed.), *Acknowledging Consumption: A Review of New Studies* (New York: Routledge, 1995). The approaches these authors take to consumption in mass societies are by no means unified. All of them endeavor to explain the operations of power through material culture, as would earlier styles of analysis predicated on a radical disjuncture between industrialized and preindustrial societies (and other types of binary oppositions now viewed as, at best, local distinctions to be understood as socially constructed and, at worst, colonial impositions). All start from the assumption that the relation of people to material culture is fundamentally social and always subject to local conditions, even in an environment of rationalized mass production.

8. Baron, "Nationalist Iconography," p. 122.

9. Najmabadi, "The Erotic *Vaṭan.*"

10. Andrew Parker et al. (eds.), *Nationalisms and Sexualities* (New York: Routledge, 1992).

11. Booth, "Egyptian Lives." The ideal of domesticity evoked by Jeanne d'Arc was by no means "traditional"; rather, it was a modernist recasting of gender complementarity resembling European bourgeois ideals of domesticity (particularly of the Victorian era—see John Tosh, *A Man's Place: Masculinity and the Middle-Class Home in Victorian England* [New Haven, Conn.: Yale University Press, 1999]), but not reducible to them. For similar analyses of the same phenomenon in a Middle Eastern context, see also Omnia Shakry, "Schooled Mothers and Structured Play: Child Rearing in Turn-of-the-Century Egypt," in Abu-Lughod, *Remaking Women*, pp. 126–170; and Afsaneh Najmabadi, "Crafting an Educated Housewife in Iran," in Abu-Lughod, *Remaking Women,* pp. 91–125.

The similarities to Victorian ideals evident in Egyptian discourse were perhaps not coincidental. Victorian backstage theatrical narratives often bore a striking resemblance to plotlines of Egyptian backstage musical films beginning in the 1940s (Roberta Dougherty, "Dance and the Dancer in Egyptian Film," paper presented at the Middle East Studies Association, Chicago, Illinois, 1998). Backstage musicals conspicuously addressed the issue of how women's respectability could be reconciled with the public (and disreputable) profession of acting. Thus, they are relevant to the Jeanne d'Arc narratives analyzed by Booth, which also grappled with the dynamic of public versus domestic roles for women. If Egyptian filmmakers were familiar with theatrical antecedents to these backstage musical films (which was certainly often the case for many other Egyptian films), then it is entirely possible that Victorian ideals had been part of the Egyptian cultural milieu for some time—that they entered social circulation in Egypt along with the Jeanne d'Arc narratives.

12. Emma Sinclair-Webb, "Preface," in Mai Ghoussoub and Emma Sinclair-Webb (eds.), *Imagined Masculinities: Male Identity and Culture in the Modern Middle East* (London: Saqi Books, 2000), p. 8. On masculinity, see also Michael Herzfeld, *The Poetics of Manhood: Contest and Identity in a Cretan Mountain Village* (Princeton, N.J.: Princeton University Press, 1985). He writes on a social milieu close to the Middle East, though he questions the utility of calling "honor and shame" a Mediterranean phenomenon. "Honor," of course, has long been an anthropological preoccupation in analyses of Middle Eastern gender systems, and largely from a masculine perspective. Pierre Bourdieu's "The Sentiment of Honour in Kabyle Society," in John Peristiany (ed.), *Honour and Shame: The Values of Mediterranean Society* (London: Weidenfeld and Nicolson, 1965) is a classic of the literature. For a critical review, see Rosemary Coombe, "Barren Ground: Re-Conceiving Honour and Shame in the Field of Mediterranean Ethnography," *Anthropologica* 32 (1990): 221–238. Lila Abu-Lughod, *Veiled Sentiments: Honor and Poetry in a Bedouin Society* (Berkeley: University of California Press, 1986) and Anne Meneley, *Tournaments of Value: Sociability and Hierarchy in a Yemeni Town* (Toronto: University of Toronto Press, 1996) look at how women achieve the supposedly "male" prerogative of honor. Most of the honor literature focuses on rural or nonsedentary societies, but Sawsan el-Messiri's *Ibn al-Balad: A Concept of Egyptian Identity* (Leiden: Brill, 1978) examines masculine identity in an urban context. Marc Schade-Poulson, *Men and Popular Music in Algeria: The Social Significance of Raï* (Austin: University of Texas Press, 1999) focuses on masculinity in the context of musical performance and media.

13. These were mobile terms of appellation that were deployed in a contrastive discourse of social types in modern Egyptian society. *Effendi,* originally a Turkish term of respect, became associated with petty bureaucrats by the late nineteenth century. As the twentieth century wore on, the term became increasingly archaic and could be used in a joking or satiric sense (bureaucrats were designated by more prosaic terms such as *muwazzaf*). *Ibn al-balad* had a more complex history. As a social label, it tended to have lower-class urban connotations (Messiri, *Ibn al-Balad*). As a term of self-appellation, it essentially meant "one of us." Depending on context, *balad* could refer to a collectivity as narrow as a village or as wide as the nation. The slippage between the sociological sense of the term and its self-ascriptive sense makes the term highly evocative but impossible to pin down. It works rather like the slang term "Bubba" in the United States. "Bubba" is a Southern "good ol' boy"—a "redneck" if one is using the term sociologically. But during national political elections everyone becomes a "Bubba" (e.g., in the 1992 election when the blue-blooded George Bush senior endeavored to be seen consuming pork rinds).

14. In 1947 *al-Ithnayn*, a lavishly illustrated variety magazine with a heavy emphasis on show business, was estimated by the British Foreign Office to have a weekly circulation of 120,000. Ami Ayalon, *The Press in the Arab Middle East: A History* (Oxford: Oxford University Press, 1995), p. 150. According to the available

circulation figures compiled by Ayalon, this was far more than any of the magazine's rivals.

15. Both the Egyptian terms (*Misri effendi* and *ibn al-balad*—actually "Bubba," too) referred to notions of authenticity, though what these notions were tied to changed historically. For more on *ibn al-balad,* see Walter Armbrust, *Mass Culture and Modernism in Egypt* (Cambridge, UK: Cambridge University Press, 1996), Marilyn Booth, *Bayram al-Tunisi's Egypt: Social Criticism and Narrative Strategy* (Exeter: Published for the Middle East Centre, St. Antony's College, Oxford, by Ithaca Press, 1990), and Messiri, *Ibn al-Balad*. On *bint al-balad*, the female analog of *ibn al-balad*, see Evelyn Early, *Baladi Women of Cairo: Playing with an Egg and a Stone* (Boulder, Colo.: Lynne Rienner Publishers, 1993).

16. Baron, "Nationalist Iconography," pp. 115–116.

17. A more complete account of Shauqi's rise to stardom appears in Walter Armbrust, "Farid Shauqi: Tough Guy, Family Man, Cinema Star," in Ghoussoub and Sinclair-Webb, *Imagined Masculinities*, pp. 199–226.

18. Farid Shauqi, *Malik al-tirsu* (King of the cheap seats) (Cairo: Maktabat Ruz al-Yusuf, 1978), pp. 91–92.

19. The dismissal of Egyptian cinema on grounds of inauthenticity is on its last legs. It would be fair to say that viewing superficially Westernized phenomena in Egypt and other non-Western societies as part of a complex local reality has entered the academic mainstream through broad movements in academia such as postcolonial studies, the study of transregional movements, and the introduction of popular culture as an acceptable academic topic. Previously such phenomena as Shauqi's adaptation of putatively Western forms in his films were dismissed as evidence of corruption or inauthenticity. Such dismissal is no longer to be taken seriously.

20. Shauqi, "Mudhakkirat," *al-Kawakib* 303, p. 5.

21. Mahmud Qasim and Ya'qubWahbi (eds.), *Mausu'at al-mumaththil fi al-sinima al-misriyya, 1927–1997* (Encyclopedia of the actor in the Egyptian cinema, 1927–1997) (Cairo: Dar al-Amin. 1997).

22. "Kanu . . . thumma asbahu," *al-Kawakib* 283 (1 January 1957): 72.

23. *Hamido,* directed by Niyazi Mustafa (Cairo: Wahid Farid, 1953).

24. Bourdieu, "The Sentiment of Honour."

25. Coombe, "Barren Ground."

26. Key attributes of honor have even been incorporated into ideologies of national citizenship, glossed as "paternalism" (Thompson, *Colonial Citizens*).

27. "Nujumuna: Kam yataqaduna fi al-sa'a?" (Our stars: How much do they earn in an hour?), *al-Kawakib* 284 (8 January 1957): 54–55.

28. The top earner was singer Farid al-Atrash at £E100 per hour. Layla Murad, the next-highest-earning star, made £E50 per hour. Abd al-Halim Hafiz, then a rising star, joined Fatin Hamama, the only nonsinger in the top four spots, at £E41. Hoda Sultan, at £E16 per hour, was tied with several others for the tenth-highest-paid star.

29. Qasim and Wahbi, *Mausu'at al-mumaththil.*

30. For more elaboration on advertising in fan magazines and how it contrasts with the U.S. models from which it was derived, see Armbrust, "Farid Shauqi."

31. The shift in cartoon imagery representing the nation as a man foreshadowed 1950s possibilities for recasting male stars in a working class register. As previously mentioned, in the 1930s the male image of the nation was *Misri effendi*—a man in tarbush in an office. By the mid-1940s, he was a peasant identified as *ibn al-balad* (see Figures 14.1–14.3). But Muhammad Rakha's colonial Ibn al-Balad was a

wizened wisecracker. The postcolonial lower-class characters portrayed by Shauqi were beefy, vigorous, and usually not peasants.

32. *Al-Usta Hasan,* directed by Salah Abu Sayf (Cairo: Salah Abu Sayf, 1952). Shauqi says in his later autobiography (*Malik al-tirsu*, p.151) that he produced the film. In 1957 he mentioned in *al-Kawakib* that he produced the film not as a New Age Films work but as a production by "*aflam Farid Shauqi wa Hoda Sultan*"; Shauqi, "Mudhakkirat," *al-Kawakib* 302, pp. 16–17, 37. However, the titles of the video copy say that the producer was director Salah Abu Sayf, as does *The Encyclopedia of Arab Cinema* (Mona al-Bindari, Mahmud Qasim and Ya'qub Wahbi, *Mausu'at al-aflam al-'Arabiyya* [Cairo: Bayt al-Ma'rifa, 1994]).

33. Benedict Anderson, *Imagined Communities: Reflections on the Origin and Spread of Nationalism* (New York: Verso, 1991), pp. 29–40.

34. It should be noted that Shauqi's realism was never as widely acknowledged as that of Salah Abu Sayf, for whom *Boss Hasan* was also a breakthrough film.

35. *Ga'aluni mugriman,* directed by Atif Salim (Cairo: Farid Shauqi, 1954).

36. *Al-Futuwwa,* directed by Salah Abu Sayf (Cairo: Aflam al-'Ahd al-Gadid, 1957).

37. Shauqi made many films in the 1950s—important and otherwise. A Farid Shauqi filmography can be found in Qasim and Wahbi, *Mausu'at al-mumaththil.* For more detailed information on the films themselves, see Bindari et al., *Mausu'at al-aflam.*

38. For comparison, see Virginia Danielson, *The Voice of Egypt: Umm Kulthum, Arabic Song, and Egyptian Society in the Twentieth Century* (Chicago: University of Chicago Press, 1997) on how Umm Kulthum built a phenomenal singing career together with a reputation for sexual modesty.

39. Shauqi, *Malik al-tirsu*, p. 147.

40. For example, Hilma Granqvist, *Marriage Conditions in a Palestinian Village*, Part I. *Commentationes Humanarum Litterarum,* Vol. III, No. 8 (Helsingfors: Societas Scientiarum Fennica, 1931); Michael Meeker, "Meaning and Society in the Near East: Examples from the Black Sea Turks and the Levantine Arabs (II)," *International Journal of Middle East Studies* 7 (1976): 383–422.

41. Suad Joseph, "Brother/Sister Relationships: Connectivity, Love, and Power in the Reproduction of Patriarchy in Lebanon," *American Ethnologist* 21 (1994): 50–73.

42. Shauqi, *Malik al-tirsu*, p. 151.

43. See Shauqi, "Mudhakkirat," *al-Kawakib* 303, which is more fully described in Armbrust, "Farid Shauqi."

44. Hoda Sultan, "Zauga lil-igar" (Wife for rent), *al-Kawakib* 314 (6 August 1957): 38.

45. Shauqi, "Mudhakkirat," *al-Kawakib* 303.

46. Shauqi, *Malik al-tirsu*, p. 152.

47. Shauqi, "Mudhakkirat," *al-Kawakib* 304, pp. 30–31.

48. "Mudhakkirat," *al-Kawakib* 303, 304.

49. *Al-Kawakib* 294 (19 March 1957): 39.

50. Shauqi, *Malik al-tirsu*, p. 165.

51. *Radd qalbi,* directed by 'Izz al-Din Zulfiqar (Cairo: Asiya, 1957).

52. As yet there have been no Egyptian antiwar films. It is also true that war films in general are a minor genre in Egyptian cinema. All told, out of approximately 3,000 films there are perhaps twenty that make wars their major focus.

53. The song was written by 'Abd Allah Shams al-Din. In 1969 it was adapted as Libya's national anthem.

54. *Al-Kawakib* 313 (30 July 1957): 22.

55. John Ellis, *Visible Fictions: Cinema, Television, Video* (Boston: Routledge and Kegan Paul, 1982), p. 91.

56. Jackie Stacey, *Star Gazing: Hollywood Cinema and Female Spectatorship* (New York: Routledge, 1994), pp. 130–175.

57. Paul McDonald, "Star Studies," in Joanne Hollows and Mark Jancovich (eds.), *Approaches to Popular Film* (New York: Manchester University Press, 1995), p. 83.

58. Steve Cohan, *Masked Men: Masculinity and the Movies in the Fifties* (Bloomington: Indiana University Press,1997).

59. Alan Macdonald, "Tony Stole a Trolley!" *Motion Picture and Television Magazine* (August 1953): 32.

60. Ellis, *Visible Fictions*, 95.

61. Ibid., p. 97.

62. Ibid.

63. McDonald, "Star Studies," p. 80.

Part 5

Conclusion

15

The Return of the Concrete?

Israel Gershoni & Ursula Woköck

In 1991, Albert Hourani put forward an agenda for the study of the Middle East.[1] Thoroughly reviewing the profession and mapping out major trends and paradigms dominant within it, Hourani was convinced that "[n]ow we are in the age of 'social history.'" For him, this history was "the study of economic relationships and the deep structures of society, and of changes in them, within a framework of ideas derived from Marxism, or from the historians of the Annales school, or from a mixture of the two." The gist of this sort of history is "a study of the relationships between power and wealth, how each of them affects the other." In spite of his sympathy for a social history thus defined (especially for the Annales paradigm of collective *mentalités*), and what appeared to him as the beginning of its constructive impact on Middle Eastern studies, Hourani felt a certain discomfort with the possibility of such a history's potential hegemony. He saw in it a dangerous tendency "to reduce the lives of individual human beings to movements of classes or other collectivities." He argued for the need to reassert "human consciousness" and "the minds of individuals" and reintroduce them into social history. He insisted on bringing "truth" back to the agenda of the study of the history of the Middle East: "If the ideas of Power and Wealth can be organizing principles of historical thought, so too can Truth," he wrote. In other words, Hourani was attempting to transmit a message that there is—paraphrasing William H. Sewell—more to life than the relentless pursuit of wealth, status, and power.[2]

The map Hourani drew, although unquestionably a faithful reflection of the ongoing development of Middle Eastern studies, was not entirely up to date with regard to the historical discipline in general. In 1991, such "social history" (for many, "new social history") was suffering a serious decline in face of the aggressive intrusion of "the cultural turn," or "the linguistic turn," which gave a tremendous lift to cultural studies and its various subdisciplines. The "new cultural history" and, alongside it, the "new intellectual history," emerged as the dominant schools in the study of history and, more generally, in the field of humanities.[3] What came to be known as "culturalism" offered a more fashionable and more attractive paradigm. As Richard Biernacki noted, "[T]he new cultural history took shape in the 1980s as an upstart critique of the established social, economic, and demographic histories," eclipsing the social history that had been dominant in the 1960s and the 1970s.[4]

Historians' enthusiasm for Annales's structure and *mentalités* now paved the way for an almost obsessive fascination with discourse, meaning, representation, narrative, and fiction, as well as the interaction between power and discursive and symbolic systems along the lines of Michel Foucault (and Edward Said). The confidence in the social explanation was undermined; old, scientific, explanatory paradigms collapsed; and these developments reinforced "the general displacement of the social in favor of culture viewed as linguistic and representational. Social categories were to be imagined, not as preceding consciousness culture or language but as depending upon them. Social categories only came into being through their expressions or representations."[5] Historians' interest now became focused on sign rather than class; on the symbolic or cultural capital more than the economic or financial capital; on interpretation rather than explanation; on representation more than reality; on text more than context; and on meaning more than experience. Structural-material histories were replaced by discursive-fictional histories, by "stories in history."[6] Even on the more practical level, historians' concerns were focused on the study of cultural practices more than on classes, social structures, or the economic-social praxis. Culture was perceived as a symbolic, linguistic, and representational system, clearly bounded and highly integrated, an object open for multidimensional interpretations and investigations.[7]

Nevertheless, approximately a decade after this dramatic shift, another change took place. We are now confronting the beginning of "beyond the cultural turn." As Victoria E. Bonnell and Lynn Hunt have demonstrated, the culturalist paradigm, although not completely exhausted, is in dire need of profound re-examination. The term "culture" has become problematized; the status of culture and the frames of its definition are being seriously questioned. In the culturalist approach, limitations have been exposed, and weaknesses and "thorny problems" have been recognized. Increasingly more methodological as well as epistemological dilemmas have been pointed out.[8] True, this self-criticism does not overshadow the satisfaction derived from the substantial contribution provided by the cultural turn, which was "most successful in overturning the tried-and-true materialist metaphors about base and superstructure (in classical Marxism) or first-economic, second-social, and third-political and cultural levels (in the French Annales school of history)."[9] In spite of this noteworthy accomplishment, however, there remained a fundamental unease. At the center of the puzzle was a feeling that almost everything had become cultural, that culture was everywhere, and under the shadow of the culturalist paradigm, our ability for causal explanation "takes a back seat, if it has a seat at all."[10] In a similar formulation, "the cultural turn threatened to efface all reference to social context or causes and offered no particular standard of judgment to replace the seemingly more rigorous and systematic approaches that had predominated [social history] during the 1960s and 1970s. Detached from their previous assumptions, cultural methods no longer seemed to have any foundation."[11]

Although the rethinking of culturalism has yet to reach an alternative paradigm or a definitive new agenda, it has radiated some of the tiredness of culturalism, narrativism, discursivism, and deconstructionism. It somehow points to a new commitment—first subvertive and now seemingly a consensus—to return to the concrete, the real, the empirical, and the explanatory. This is an effort to recover "concrete activities," to view culture more as a practice or agency than as a coherent, highly integrated system of symbols and meanings. It strives to trace the performative aspect of culture, rather than the simply expressive. It assumes that culture is a more diffused, decentered, and loosely integrated entity, constantly contested and undergoing changes. This is a call to study the "real" aspects of material culture, the place in which culture "takes concrete form, and those concrete forms make cultural codes most explicit." Work along these lines promises to "draw our attention to the material ways in which culture becomes part of everyday social experience and therefore becomes susceptible to change."[12]

Obviously, this is neither a simplistic nor nostalgic return to class or structure in the previous sense in which these two realities were examined, free from culture or consciousness. The linguistic turn seems to have liberated us once and for all from the illusion of sterile science and clean, pure investigation. As Hayden White put it, after the linguistic turn, it was no longer possible to produce a science of society "that is not contaminated with ideological preconceptions."[13] The theories and insights of the culturalist paradigm and the stimulation that culturalism brought to the historical discipline will and should remain. The discursive definition of culture, the narrative as providing "a link between culture as a system and culture as a practice,"[14] and the crucial importance of paying attention to the study of forms of cultural representation of social reality are all indispensable legacies. It appears that, for the historian, even more so than for the sociologist, anthropologist, or literary critic, this self-critique mood brought about by "beyond the cultural turn" is good news. It may be music to historians' ears to find that it insists on defending the autonomy of a well-defined discipline, as preconditioned for interdisciplinary projects: "[I]nterdisciplinarity can only work if there are, in fact, disciplinary differences. Thus, a renewed emphasis on disciplinary difference, or 'redisciplinarization,' seems to be in order."[15] Moreover, it calls for causal explanation, rigorous empirical investigation of case studies, in which the evidence is carefully gathered and comparisons are employed to ensure generalizations.

Although Hourani did not see, and could not foresee, these rapid changes of fashions and trends in the intellectual environment, it seems that his suggestion to find a functional balance between power, wealth, and truth in the study of history in general, and in the study of the Middle East in particular, has again become relevant in the age of rethinking culturalism. Interestingly enough, one can find some similarity between the mood underlying the "beyond the cultural turn"—to restore a sense "of social embeddedness, without reducing everything to its social determinants"[16]—and Hourani's agenda. The need to bring back the real, the concrete, and the empirical to the cultural picture, namely, to return the social and the economic to the discursive, the representational, and the narrativisitic, reflects a strategy imbued in Hourani's program. Indeed, beyond the new cultural history and the cultural turn, it is time to establish a balance between the cultural and the social and to re-examine, in more equal and less patronizing modes, the relations between them. Gone is the assumption that economic-social infrastructures exclusively determine culture and cultural discourse, and, by the same token, gone is the clinging to the presupposition that language exclusively constitutes social reality and that the latter entirely depends upon its cultural representation. Like Hourani, Bonnell and Hunt present a complex picture within which social reality and the representation of social reality exist not only in tension and conflict but also through interreactions, mutual feedbacks, negotiation, and dialogue. Culture is irreducible, but so, too, are society and politics. Each of them is interdependent and interrelated but also autonomous and independent. The historian is called upon to trace the complex relational processes and dynamics between all these realms of human thought and activity.

The chapters included in this volume are located at this intersection. Each of them, in its own approach, deals with interactions and mutual feedbacks between power, wealth, and truth. They attempt to find a better balance between representation and reality, between meaning and experience, and between text and context. Beyond this, they express a commitment to bring about a new thinking, or new perspective, to particular case studies. And this, through solid historical research, empirical evidence, emphasis on the representational without giving up the explanatory, and by going from specific case studies to broader comparisons and generalizations. In other words, each of these studies tries to redirect its subject matter to new avenues, suggesting new possibilities.

The contributions here can be clustered around four main themes: (1) challenging the simplistic dichotomy between modern and premodern/traditional; (2) rethinking the specific relation between the concrete and its location in the regional/global context, by focusing on the aspects of social embeddedness; (3) reconsidering prevailing views on cultural-intellectual history by readjusting the level of inquiry for concrete case studies; and (4) expanding our perspectives on nationalism, with particular emphasis on the formation of national identities.

The modernization theme was hinged on a rather rigid dichotomy between the modern and the traditional. Right from the outset it was met by serious criticism of the essentialist, undynamic concept of the traditional and/or premodern. The studies included here carry that criticism further by questioning the very rigidity of the dichotomy. On the basis of concrete case studies, it is argued that modern interpretive frameworks as, for example, that of political economy, may be used for understanding traditional Ottoman monetary policies; that the traditional Islamic legal system had the inherent potential for reform geared toward modern developments and that it was actually realized (until European intervention intersected); and that practices (of army recruitment) fostering the modern perceptions of nationalism emerged out of prenationalist and, in that sense, premodern local Ottoman developments.

Another set of contributions attempts to rethink the specific relation between the concrete and its location in the regional/global context, by emphasizing the issue of social embeddedness. All of them argue for the critical importance of the concrete historical case study. Thus, the approach of micro-history investigating the ritual murder trial in Damascus in 1840 leads into the framework of French colonial policies in the Middle East; Qajar paintings are not only situated within the context of their intended viewers but also within that of Iranian-European cultural power relations. In two contributions, the understanding of processes of globalization are shown to require a specific local focus—once biographically approaching a central figure in the interaction between the local and the global, and once bringing back in the concept of class (within the territorial state). Two other contributions put the emphasis on the readjustment of potential frames of reference: relocating ideas, in this case two competing Turkish national narratives, into their sociopolitical contexts, as well as a society, namely, Palestinian society, from the comparative context of the Zionist *yishuv* (burgeoning Jewish community in Palestine) only, to a wider, regional one, in particular that of Greater Syria.

A third set of chapters can be read as an attempt to reconsider commonly held approaches to intellectual-cultural history. With regard to Middle Eastern societies, intellectual history has tended to focus on the elite stratum, and thus was more often than not caught in the modernization paradigm. Four contributions here demonstrate alternative venues for the study of intellectual history that promise a more complex understanding of cultural-ideational developments. Thus, the concrete focus in one chapter is put on "lost voices" and social practices of wider social strata in pre-1914 Egypt. This theme is further illustrated in another chapter. The latter specifically investigates texts relating to the issues of family and slavery, which are situated in the contexts of both British colonial rule and Egyptian-Sudanese relations. The recovery of another lost voice in the Ottoman context is able to retrieve the hitherto neglected Iranian dimension of Pan-Islam. Last, but not least, the study of Egyptian cinema and the popular culture surrounding it is able to add major insights to our understanding of the formation of national identity.

A fourth common theme is nationalism. Three chapters contribute to our understanding how nation within a territorial state became thinkable. In the nineteenth century, it was actually the recruitment practices of the new Ottoman army that provided a basis to perceive of national identities in non-Ottoman terms; and at the turn of the century, an early wave of globalization can be shown to trigger the emergence of an Egyptian state perspective. At the same time, novel social practices play a crucial role in the process in which the idea of nation disseminates to wider social strata. In a later period, the cultural-social environment of the cinema provides an arena for the formation of national identity on the popular, nonelite level. A historic event that is of constitutive importance for the way in which the nation is imagined is under study in two other chapters. Until today, the accounts of the Lausanne conference have provided the Turkish national discourse with two competing narratives. By contrast, the outcome of the events of 1948 often entailed a Palestinian narrative that took the Zionist *yishuv* as its only comparative framework—although, as is shown above, this is not the only or even most fruitful option.

The contributions assembled in this volume neither pretend to be the last word on, nor to offer any sense of closure of, persistent issues concerning our profession. Rather, they suggest new approaches and new perspectives on specific areas and case studies in particular times and places. They attempt to reassess and revise established, commonplace concepts and paradigms. They are well aware, however, that many areas and issues remain to be investigated. Their findings are often suggestive, rather than definitive, hoping to open new doors and offer fresh insights to our understanding of chapters in the history of the modern Middle East.

Notes

1. Albert Hourani, "How Should We Write the History of the Middle East?" *International Journal of Middle East Studies* 23 (1991): 134–135, in particular.

2. William H. Sewell, Jr., "The Concept(s) of Culture," in Victoria E. Bonnell and Lynn Hunt (eds.), *Beyond the Cultural Turn* (Berkeley: University of California Press, 1999), p. 36.

3. For example, see Lynn Hunt (ed.), *The New Cultural History* (Berkeley: University of California Press, 1989).

4. Richard Biernacki, "Method and Metaphor After the New Cultural History," in Bonnell and Hunt, *Beyond the Cultural Turn*, p. 62.

5. Victoria E. Bonnell and Lynn Hunt, "Introduction," in Bonnell and Hunt, *Beyond the Cultural Turn*, p. 9.

6. See Sarah Maza, "Stories in History: Cultural Narratives in Recent Works in European History," a review essay, *American Historical Review* 101 (1996): 1493–1515.

7. Early theoretical and intellectual sources for this new cultural turn and cultural history can be found already in the 1970s, especially in the works of French poststructuralists such as Jacques Derrida, Michel Foucault, and Roland Barthes, the symbolic anthropology of Clifford Geertz, the sociology of culture of Pierre Bourdieu, and the metahistorical narrativism of Hayden White. See, for example, Clifford Geertz, *The Interpretation of Cultures* (New York: Basic Books, 1973); Hayden White, *Metahistory: The Historical Imagination in Nineteenth-Century Europe* (Baltimore: Johns Hopkins University Press, 1973); Hayden White, *Tropics of Discourse: Essays in Cultural Criticism* (Baltimore: Johns Hopkins University Press, 1978); and Pierre Bourdieu, *The Field of Cultural Production*, edited and with an introduction by Randal Johnson (New York: Columbia University Press, 1993). Bourdieu originally wrote the articles that appear in this volume in the 1970s and 1980s. Obviously, from the 1970s, literary criticism theories also had a major impact on the new cultural and intellectual histories. See, for example, John Higham and Paul K. Conkin (eds.), *New Directions in American Intellectual History* (Baltimore: Johns Hopkins University Press, 1979); Dominick LaCapra and Steven L. Kaplan (eds.), *Modern European Intellectual History: Reappraisals and New Perspectives* (Ithaca: Cornell University Press, 1982); Dominick LaCapra, *History and Criticism* (Ithaca: Cornell University Press, 1985); John E. Toews, "Intellectual History After the Linguistic Turn: The Autonomy of Meaning and the Irreducibility of Experience," *American Historical Review* 92 (1987): 879–907; Hayden White, *The Content of the Form: Narrative Discourse and Historical Representation* (Baltimore: Johns Hopkins University Press, 1987); James Tully (ed.), *Meaning and Context: Quentin Skinner and his Critics* (Oxford: Polity Press, 1988); Peter Novick, *That Noble Dream: The "Objectivity Question" and the American Historical Profession* (Cambridge, UK: Cambridge University Press, 1988); Hunt, *The New Cultural History*; Dominick LaCapra, *Soundings in Critical Theory* (Ithaca: Cornell University Press, 1989); David Harlan, "Intellectual History and the Return of Literature," *AHR* Forum, *American Historical Review* 94 (1989): 581–609; David A. Hollinger, "The Return of the Prodigal: The Persistence of Historical Knowing," *American Historical Research Review* 94 (1989): 610–621; and Joyce Appleby, Lynn Hunt, and Margaret Jacob, *Telling the Truth About History* (New York: W. W. Norton, 1994). Also see Itamar Even-Zohar, the special issue on "Polysystem Studies," *Poetics Today* 11, no. 1 (Spring 1990).

8. In particular, see the illuminating introduction in Hunt and Bonnell, *Beyond the Cultural Turn*.

9. Ibid., "Introduction," p. 26.

10. Ibid., p. 11.

11. Ibid., pp. 9–10.

12. Ibid., p. 11. Also see Sewell, "The Concept(s) of Culture," pp. 35–61.

13. Hayden White, "Afterword," in Bonnell and Hunt, *Beyond the Cultural Turn*, p. 316.

14. Bonnell and Hunt, "Introduction," p. 17.

15. Ibid., p. 14.

16. Ibid., p. 26.

Glossary

amradkhānah: brothel of young male prostitutes
arak: an alcoholic drink with aniseed
başıbozuks: irregular soldiers
bedeliye: substitution money
diwan: the court of the provincial governor
effendiyya: gentlemanly class in Egypt, mostly Turco-Circassian, considered petty bureaucrats by the late nineteenth century. In the twentieth century, the term refers to members of the educated middle class; the members of this group can not only be identified as such, but they also see themselves as members of this group (a social group in and for itself).
ferman: an imperial edict
hac: annual pilgrimage to Mecca
hijri: Muslim calendar (calculating years after the *hijra*)
hilafet: office of the leader of the Muslim world
hüvve (khuwwa): "brotherhood"; euphemism for the tribute paid by the settled people to the nomads in Arabia
iftā': act of issuing fatwas by the jurisconsult (mufti)
ijāzas: certificates
'ilm: knowledge
kanunname: sultanic law codices
levents: musket-bearing mercenaries hired from Anatolia
madhhab: school
mashāyikh al-madhhab: *mujtahid*s of the school (*madhhab*) belonging to generations after the founding scholars
mawlid al-nabi: the Prophet's birthday

mujtahid: jurisprudent, highly qualified jurist
mütesellim: deputy governor who ruled a province on behalf of a governor
naṣṣ: text
pasha/Pasha: rank in Ottoman hierarchy
qadi: judge
qaḥbah'khānah: houses of (women) prostitution
qasida: a poem following an ancient Arabic structure, which is a rigid triparite one
qiyās: method of legal interference
rājiḥ: sound or preponderant
reaya: tax-paying subjects
salam: contract that involves the ordering of (usually fungible) goods to be delivered in the future for a price paid in the present
sancak: Ottoman administrative unit
sekbans: musket-bearing mercenaries
serasker: commander-in-chief
şürefa: purported descendants of the Prophet (Turkish)
takhrīj: legal interference
talaba: students at a religious institution of learning
tanẓīmāt: reform period
'ulamā [Arabic], ulema [Turkish]: Muslim scholars
urban: nomadic or tribal Arabs
vakıf [Turkish]: pious endowment/charitable trust
vali: Ottoman governor general of a province
vatan [Turkish], *vaṭan* [Arabic]: homeland
waqf [Arabic]: pious endowment/charitable trust

Bibliography

Abdel-Khalek, Gouda, "Looking Outside or Turning NW? On the Meaning and External Dimension of Egypt's Infitah, 1971–1980," *Social Problems* 28 (1981): 394–409.

'Abdu'l-Baha 'Abbas Nuri, *Risalih-'i Siyasiyyih* (Tehran: Muhammad Labib, 1933).

Abu-Lughod, Lila, *Veiled Sentiments: Honor and Poetry in a Bedouin Society* (Berkeley: University of California Press, 1986).

Abu-Lughod, Lila (ed.), *Remaking Women: Feminism and Modernity in the Middle East* (Princeton, N.J.: Princeton University Press, 1998).

Abu-Manneh, Butrus, "The Islamic Roots of the Gülhane Rescript," *Die Welt des Islams* 34 (1994): 173–203.

Aceldama (Cagliari: Stab. Tip. G. Dessi, 1896).

'Adli, Huwayda, *al-'Ummal wa'l-siyyasa: al-dawr al-siyyasi li'l-haraka al-'ummaliyya fi misr min 1952–1981* (Cairo: al-Ahali, 1993).

Agulhon, Maurice, *Marianne into Battle: Republican Imagery and Symbolism in France, 1789–1880,* trans. by Janet Lloyd (Cambridge, UK: Cambridge University Press, 1981).

Ahmad, Feroz, *The Making of Modern Turkey* (London: Routledge, 1993).

Alexander, Michael Christopher, "Between Accommodation and Confrontation: State, Labor, and Development in Algeria and Tunisia," Ph.D. dissertation, Duke University, 1996.

———, "State, Labor and the New Global Economy in Tunisia," in Dirk Vandewalle (ed.), *North Africa: Development and Reform in a Changing Global Economy* (New York: St. Martin's Press, 1996), pp. 177–202.

Algar, Hamid, *Mirza Malkum Khan* (Berkeley: University of California Press, 1973).

'Allush, Naji, *al-Muqawama al-'Arabiyya fi Filastin* (Beirut: Dar al-Tali'a, 1968).

al-Amidi, Sayf al-Dīn al-Āmidī, *al-Ihkām fī Uṣūl al-Aḥkām,* 3 vols. (Cairo: Maṭba'at 'Alī Ṣubayḥ wa-Awlādihi, 1387/1968).

Amin, Galal A., *Egypt's Economic Predicament: A Study in the Interaction of External Pressure, Political Folly, and Social Tension in Egypt, 1960–1990* (Leiden: E. J. Brill, 1995).

Amin, Michael Cameron, "Selling and Saving 'Mother Iran': Gender and the Iranian Press in the 1940s," *International Journal of Middle East Studies* 33 (2001): 335–361.

Anderson, Benedict, *Imagined Communities: Reflections on the Origin and Spread of Nationalism* (New York: Verso, 1991).

Appadurai, Arjun (ed.), *The Social Life of Things: Commodities in Cultural Perspective* (Cambridge, UK: Cambridge University Press, 1986).

Appleby, Joyce, Lynn Hunt, and Margaret Jacob, *Telling the Truth About History* (New York: W. W. Norton, 1994).

Arat, Zehra, *Deconstructing Images of the Turkish Woman* (Basingstoke: Macmillan, 1998).

Arif Bey, Mehmed, *Başımıza Gelenler* (Cairo: Maarif Matbassi, 1321/1903–1904).

Armbrust, Walter, "Farid Shauqi: Tough Guy, Family Man, Cinema Star," in Mai Ghoussoub and Emma Sinclair-Webb (eds.), *Imagined Masculinities: Male Identity and Culture in the Modern Middle East* (London: Saqi Books, 2000), pp. 199–226.

———, *Mass Culture and Modernism in Egypt* (Cambridge, UK: Cambridge University Press, 1996).

Atatürk, Gazi Mustafa Kemal, *Nutuk-Söylev*. Vol. II: *1920–1927* (Ankara: TTK, 1989).

Avery, Peter, Gavin Hambly, and Charles Melville (eds.), *The Cambridge History of Iran*, Vol. VII (Cambridge, UK: Cambridge University Press, 1991).

Avşar, Bozkurt, *Bir Muhalifin Portresi: Dr. Rıza Nur* (Istanbul: Belgesee, 1992).

Ayalon, Ami, *The Press in the Arab Middle East: A History* (Oxford: Oxford University Press, 1995).

Badron, Margot, *Feminists, Islam, and Nation* (Princeton, N.J.: Princeton University Press, 1995).

Bairoch, Paul, "Globalisation, Myths and Realities," in R. Boyer and D. Drache (eds.), *States Against Markers: The Limits of Globalisation* (London: Routledge 1996), pp. 173–192.

al-Baji, Aba al-Walid, *Kitab al-Hudud fi al-Usul* (Beirut and Homs: Mu'assasat al-Zu'bi, 1392/1973).

Baker, J., *Turkey in Europe* (London: Cassel Petter & Galpin, 1877).

Baker, Sir Samuel W., *Ismailia: A Narrative of the Expedition to Central Africa for the Suppression of the Slave Trade* (London: Macmillan and Company, 1879).

Bakhash, Shaul, *Iran: Monarchy, Bureaucracy and Reform Under the Qajars: 1858–1896* (London: Ithaca Press, 1978).

Baklanoff, A., *al-Tabaqa al-'amila fi misr al-mu'asira* (Damascus: Markaz al-Abhath wa'l-Dirasat al-Ishtirakiyya fi al-'Alam al-'Arabi, 1988).

Bal, Mieke, *Reading "Rembrandt": Beyond the Word-Image Opposition* (Cambridge, UK: Cambridge University Press, 1991).

Baring, Evelyn, "Recent Events in India," *The Nineteenth Century* 14 (October 1883): 587–588.

———, *Modern Egypt*, 2. vols (New York: The Macmillan Company, 1908).

Baring, Maurice, *The Puppet Show of Memory* (London: Cassel, 1987).

Baron, Beth, "Nationalist Iconography: Egypt as a Woman," in James Jankowski and Israel Gershoni (eds.), *Rethinking Nationalism in the Arab Middle East* (New York: Columbia University Press, 1997), pp. 105–124.

———, *The Women's Awakening in Egypt* (New Haven, Conn.: Yale University Press, 1994).

———, "The Construction of National Honour in Egypt," *Gender and History* 5 (1993): 244–255.

———, "Mothers, Morality, and Nationalism in Pre-1919 Egypt," in Rashid Khalidi et al. (eds.), *The Origins of Arab Nationalism* (New York: Columbia University Press, 1991), pp. 271–288.

Baudrillard, Jean, *The Mirror of Production,* trans. by M. Poster (St. Louis: Telos Press, 1975).

Beinin, Joel, "Will the Real Egyptian Working Class Please Stand Up?" in Zachary Lockman (ed.), *Workers and Working Classes in the Middle East* (Albany: State University of New York Press, 1994), pp. 247–270.

Berenson, Edward, *The Trial of Madame Caillaux* (Berkeley: University of California Press, 1992).

Berkes, Niyazi, *Türkiye'de Çağdaşlaşma* (Istanbul: Doğu-Batı Yayınları, 1978).

Berkhofer, Robert, Jr., *Beyond the Great Story: History as Text and Discourse* (Cambridge: Belknap Press, 1995).

Berlin, Isaiah, *Against the Current* (New York: Penguin Books, 1982).

Berman, Art, *From the New Criticism to Deconstruction: The Reception of Structuralism and Post-Structuralism* (Urbana: University of Illinois Press, 1988).

Berque, Jacques, *Egypt: Imperialism and Revolution* (London: Faber and Faber, 1972).

Bianchi, Robert, *Unruly Corporatism: Associational Life in Twentieth-Century Egypt* (New York: Oxford University Press, 1989).

———, "The Corporatization of the Egyptian Labor Movement," *Middle East Journal* 40 (1986): 429–444.

———, *Interest Groups and Political Development in Turkey* (Princeton. N.J.: Princeton University Press, 1984).

Biernacki, Richard, "Method and Metaphor After the New Cultural History," in Victoria E. Bonnell and Lynn Hunt (eds.), *Beyond the Cultural Turn* (Berkeley: University of California Press, 1999), pp. 62–92.

Bilgehan, Gülsün, *Mevhibe* (Ankara: Bilgi, 1995).

al-Bindari, Mona, Mahmud Qasim, and Ya'qub Wahbi, *Mausu'at al-aflam al-'Arabiyya* (Cairo: Bayt al-Ma'rifa, 1994).

al-Bīṭār, 'Abd al-Razzāq, *Ḥulyat al-Bashr fī Tārīkh al-Qarn al-Thālith 'Ashar*, ed. M. B. Bīṭār, 3 vols. (Damascus: Maṭbū'āt al-Majma' al-'Ilmī al-'Arabī, 1963).

Bonnell, Victoria E., and Lynn Hunt, "Introduction," in Victoria E. Bonnell and Lynn Hunt (eds.), *Beyond the Cultural Turn* (Berkeley: University of California Press, 1999), pp. 1–32.

Bonnell, Victoria E., and Lynn Hunt (eds.), *Beyond the Cultural Turn* (Berkeley: University of California Press, 1999).

Booth, Marilyn, "The Egyptian Lives of Jeanne d'Arc," in Lila Abu-Lughod (ed.), *Remaking Women: Feminism and Modernity in the Middle East* (Princeton, N.J.: Princeton University Press, 1998), pp. 171–211.

———, *Bayram al-Tunisi's Egypt: Social Criticism and Narrative Strategy* (Exeter: Published for the Middle East Centre, St. Antony's College, Oxford, by Ithaca Press, 1990).

Bordo, Michael D., "Money, Deflation, and Seigniorage in the Fifteenth Century," *Journal of Monetary Economics* 18 (1986): 337–346.

Bourdieu, Pierre, *The Field of Cultural Production*, edited and with an introduction by Randal Johnson (New York: Columbia University Press, 1993).

———, *Distinction: A Social Critique of the Judgement of Taste,* trans. by Richard Nice (Cambridge: Harvard University Press, 1984).
———, "The Sentiment of Honour in Kabyle Society," in John Peristiany (ed.), *Honour and Shame: The Values of Mediterranean Society* (London: Weidenfeld and Nicolson, 1965).
Boyarin, Jonathan, "Space, Time, and the Politics of Memory," in Jonathan Boyarin (ed.), *Remapping Memory: Politics of Time and Space* (Minneapolis: University of Minnesota Press, 1994), pp. 1–37.
Bozdağ, İsmet, *Bir Çağın Perde Arkası* (Istanbul: Kervan, n.d.).
Braudel, Fernand, *Civilization and Capitalism, 15th–18th Century,* Vol. III: *The Perspective of the World* (New York: Harper and Row Publishers, 1984).
Brenner, Robert, *Turbulence in the World Economy* (London: Verso, 1999).
Brockelmann, Carl, *Geschichte der arabischen Literatur*, 2 vols. (Leiden: E. J. Brill, 1943–1949); 3 supplements (Leiden: E. J. Brill, 1937–1942).
Burke, Edmund, III (ed.), *Struggle and Survival in the Modern Middle East* (London: I. B. Tauris, 1993).
Çadırcı, Musa, "Renovations in the Ottoman Army (1792–1869)," *Revue Internationale d'Histoire Militaire* 67 (1988): 87–102.
Cahit, Burhan, *Mudanya Lozan Ankara* (Istanbul: Kanaat, 1933).
Carr, E. H., *What Is History?* (London: Macmillan, 1961).
Cebesoy, Ali Fuat, *General Ali Fuat Cebesoy'un Siyasi Hatıraları* (Istanbul: Vatan, 1957).
Cezar, Yavuz, *Osmanlı Maliyesinde Bunalım ve Değişim Dönemi: XVIII. yy.dan Tanzimat'a Mali Tarih* (Istanbul: Alan Yayıncılık, 1986).
Cezmi Eraslan, *II. Abdülhamid ve Islam Birligi* (Istanbul: Ötüken, 1992).
Chartier, Roger, *Cultural History: Between Practices and Representations* (Cambridge, UK: Polity Press, 1988).
———, *The Cultural Uses of Print in Early Modern France* (Princeton, N.J.: Princeton University Press, 1987).
Child, Richard Washburn, *A Diplomat Looks at Europe* (New York: Duffield and Company, 1925).
Childers, Erskine, "The Wordless Wish: From Citizens to Refugees," in Ibrahim Abu-Lughod (ed.), *The Transformation of Palestine* (Evanston, Ill.: Northwestern University Press, 1971), pp. 165–202.
———, "The Other Exodus," *The Spectator*, no. 6933 (12 May 1961): 672–675.
Cipolla, Carlo M., "Currency Depreciation in Medieval Europe," *Economic History Review* 15 (1963): 413–422.
Cohan, Steven, *Masked Men: Masculinity and the Movies in the Fifties* (Bloomington: Indiana University Press, 1997).
Cohen, David, "La circulation monétaire entre les Principautés Roumaines et les terres Bulgares (1840–1878)," *Bulgarian Historical Review* 4, no. 2 (1976): 55–71.
Cole, Juan R. I., *Modernity and the Millennium: The Genesis of the Baha'i Faith in the Nineteenth-Century Middle East* (New York: Columbia University Press, 1998).
———, "'Abdu'l-Baha's *Treatise on Leadership*: Text, Translation, Commentary," *Translations of Shaykhi, Babi, and Baha'i Texts* 2, no. 2 (May 1998).
———, *Colonialism and Revolution in the Middle East: Social and Cultural Origins of Egypt's 'Urabi Movement* (Princeton, N.J.: Princeton University Press, 1993).
Collingwood, R. G., *The Idea of History* (Oxford: Clarendon Press, 1946).

Collins, Jeffrey G., *The Egyptian Elite Under Cromer, 1882–1907* (Berlin: Klaus Schwarz Verlag, 1984).

Coombe, Rosemary, "Barren Ground: Re-Conceiving Honour and Shame in the Field of Mediterranean Ethnography," *Anthropologica* 32 (1990): 221–238.

Cooper, Mark N., *The Transformation of Egypt* (Baltimore: Johns Hopkins University Press, 1982).

Croce, Benedetto, *History: Its Theory and Practice* (New York: Russell and Russell, 1960).

Cuno, Kenneth, *The Pasha's Peasants: Land, Society, and Economy in Lower Egypt, 1740–1858* (Cambridge, UK: Cambridge University Press, 1992).

da Mondovi, Giambattista, *Relazione del Padre Tomaso da Calangiano di Sardegna missionario apostolico cappuccino. Il processo verbale diretto contro gli Ebrei di Damasco nel'anno 1840* (Marseille, 1850).

Danielson, Virginia, *The Voice of Egypt: Umm Kulthum, Arabic Song, and Egyptian Society in the Twentieth Century* (Chicago: University of Chicago Press, 1997).

Davis, Natalie Zemon, *The Return of Martin Guerre* (Cambridge: Harvard University Press, 1983).

Daws, Madiha, "Al-'Amiyya al-misriyya 'inda 'Abdallah al-Nadim," *Buhuth nadwah al-ihtifal bi-dhikry maruur ma'itah 'am 'ala wafaa' 'Abdallah al-Nadim* (Cairo: Al-Majlis al-'Ala lil-Thaqafah, 1997).

Deringil, Selim, "The Struggle Against Shiism in Hamidian Iraq: A Study in Ottoman Counter-Propaganda," *Die Welt des Islams* 30 (1990): 45–62.

Derrida, Jacques, *Of Grammatology,* trans. by Gayatri Chakrvorty Spivak (Baltimore: Johns Hopkins University Press, 1976).

Diba, Layla S., "Early Qajar Period: 1785–1834," in Layla S. Diba and Maryam Ekhtiar (eds.), *Royal Persian Paintings: The Qajar Epoch 1785–1925* (London: Brooklyn Museum of Arts in association with I. B. Tauris, 1998), pp. 169–171.

———, "Persian Painting in the Eighteenth Century: Tradition and Transmission," in *Muqarnas*, Vol. VI, ed. Oleg Grabar (Leiden: E. J. Brill, 1989), pp. 147–160.

Diba, Layla S., and Maryam Ekhtiar (eds.), *Royal Persian Paintings: The Qajar Epoch 1785–1925* (London: Brooklyn Museum of Arts in association with I. B. Tauris, 1998).

Driault, Jean, *L'assassinat du Père Thomas et le Talmud* (Paris: Edition de la Vieille France, 1922).

du Velay, A., *Essai sur l'Histoire Financière de la Turquie* (Paris: Arthur Rousseau, 1903).

Dundes, Alan (ed.), *The Blood Libel Legend: A Case Book in Anti-Semitic Folklore* (Madison: University of Wisconsin Press, 1991).

Early, Evelyn, *Baladi Women of Cairo: Playing with an Egg and a Stone* (Boulder, Colo.: Lynne Rienner Publishers, 1993).

Ekhtiar, Maryam, "The Qajar Visual Aesthetic: Highlights from the Brooklyn Museum Collection," *Orientations* (July 1989): 46–53.

Ellis, John, *Visible Fictions: Cinema, Television, Video* (Boston: Routledge and Kegan Paul, 1982).

Even-Zohar, Itamar, "Polysystem Studies," *Poetics Today* 11, no. 1 (Spring 1990).

Fahmy, Khaled, *All the Pasha's Men: Mehmed Ali, His Army, and the Making of Modern Egypt* (Cambridge, UK: Cambridge University Press, 1997).

Falk, S. J., *Qajar Paintings: Persian Oil Paintings of the 18th and 19th Centuries* (London: Faber and Faber Ltd., in association with Sotheby Parke-Bernet, 1972).

Faris, Habib Effendi, *Sarakh al-Bari* (Cairo: H. Faris, 1891).

Faroqhi, Suraiya, *Coping with the State, Political Conflict, and Crime in the Ottoman Economy, 1550–1720* (Istanbul: ISIS Press, 1995).
———, "Rural Society in Anatolia and the Balkans During the Sixteenth Century," *Turcica* 9 (1977):161–196, and 11 (1979):103–153.
———, "Sixteenth-Century Periodic Markets in Various Anatolian Sancaks," *Journal of the Economic and Social History of the Orient* 22 (1979): 32–80.
———, "The Early History of Balkan Fairs," *Südost-Forschungen* 37 (1978): 50–68.
Febvre, Lucien, *Philippe II et Franche-Comté* (Paris: Université de Paris, 1911).
Felski, Rita, *The Gender of Modernity* (Cambridge: Harvard University Press, 1995).
Fenina, Abdelhamid, "Les Monnaies de la Régence de Tunis sous les Husaynides, Études de Numismatiques et d'Histoire Monétaire (1705–1891)" (Thèse de Doctorat, Nouveau Régime, Université de Paris-Sorbonne, 1993).
Ferguson, Niall, *The World's Banker: The History of the House of Rothschild* (London: Weidenfeld and Nicolson, 1998).
Ferrier, Ronald W., *The Arts of Persia* (New Haven, Conn.: Yale University Press, 1989).
Ferrier, Ronald W. (trans. and ed.), *A Journey to Persia: Jean Chardin's Portrait of a Seventeenth-Century Empire* (London: I. B. Tauris, 1996).
Flapan, Simha, *The Birth of Israel: Myths and Realities* (New York: Pantheon, 1987).
Frankel, Jonathan, *The Damascus Affair* (Cambridge, UK: Cambridge University Press, 1997).
Galib, İsmail, *Takvim-i Meskukat-ı Osmaniye* (Istanbul, H. 1307/1889–1890).
Gallagher, Nancy Elizabeth, *Approaches to the History of the Middle East: Interviews with Leading Middle East Historians* (Reading, UK: Ithaca Press, 1994).
Garmrūdī, Mīrzā Fattāḥ Khān, *Safarnāmah*, ed. Fatḥ al-Dīn Fattāḥī (N.p., 1969).
Geertz, Clifford, *The Interpretation of Cultures* (New York: Basic Books, 1973).
Genç, Mehmet, "Esham," in *Islam Ansiklopedisi*, Vol. XI (Istanbul: Diyanet Vakfı, 1995), pp. 376–380.
Gershoni, Israel, and Ehud R. Toledano, "Editors' Introduction," *Poetics Today* 14 (1993): 241–245, special issue on *Cultural Processes in Muslim and Arab Societies.*
Gershoni, Israel, and Ehud R. Toledano (eds.), *Cultural Processes in Muslim and Arab Societies,* special issues of *Poetics Today* 14, no. 3 (1993) and 15, no. 2 (1994).
Gershoni, Israel, and James P. Jankowski, *Egypt, Islam, and the Arabs: The Search for Egyptian Nationhood, 1900–1930* (Oxford: Oxford University Press, 1986).
Ghoussoub, Mai, and Emma Sinclair-Webb (eds.), *Imagined Masculinities: Male Identity and Culture in the Modern Middle East* (London: Saqi Books, 2000).
Gilbert, Felix, *Machiavelli and Gucciardini: Politics and History in Sixteenth-Century Florence* (Princeton, N.J.: Princton University Press, 1965).
Gilbert, Martin, *Sir Horace Rumbold: Portrait of a Diplomat, 1869–1941* (London: Heinemann, 1973).
Gilmour, David, *Curzon* (London: John Murray, 1994).
Ginzburg, Carlo, *Clues, Myths, and the Historical Method* (Baltimore: Johns Hopkins University Press, 1989).
———, *The Cheese and the Worms: The Cosmos of a Sixteenth-Century Miller* (London: Routledge and Kegan Paul, 1980).

Goffman, Erving, *The Presentation of Self in Everyday Life* (New York: Doubleday, 1959).
Goldberg, Ellis J., *Tinker, Tailor, and Textile Worker: Class and Politics in Egypt, 1930–1954* (Berkeley: University of California Press, 1986).
Granqvist, Hilma, *Marriage Conditions in a Palestinian Village.* Part I. *Commentationes Humanarum Litterarum,* Vol. 3, No. 8 (Helsingfors: Societas Scientiarum Fennica, 1931).
Grew, Joseph C., *The Turbulent Era: A Diplomatic Record of Forty Years, 1904–45* (Boston: Houghton Mifflin, 1952).
Grunwald, Kurt, "'Windsor-Cassel'—the Last Court Jew," *Leo Baeck Institute Year Book* 14 (1969): 119–161.
Hafez, Sabry, *The Genesis of Arabic Narrative Discourse* (London: Saqi Press, 1993).
Hallaq, Wael B., *Authority, Continuity, and Change in Islamic Law* (forthcoming).
———, *A History of Islamic Legal Theories* (Cambridge, UK: Cambridge University Press, 1997).
———, "From *Fatwa*s to *Furu*': Growth and Change in Islamic Substantive Law," *Islamic Law and Society* 1 (1994): 29–65.
———, "On the Authoritativeness of Sunni Consensus," *International Journal of Middle East Studies* 18 (1986): 427–454.
al-Hamawi, Ahmad, *Sharh al-Ashbah*, printed with Ibn Nujaym's *Ashbah.*
Hansen, Bent, *The Political Economy of Poverty, Equity, and Growth: Egypt and Turkey* (Oxford: Oxford University Press, 1991).
Harlan, David, "Intellectual History and the Return of Literature," *American Historical Review* 94 (1989): 581–609.
al-Ḥaṣkafī (al-'Alā'ī), 'Alā' al-Dīn Muḥammad 'Alī, *al-Durr al-Mukhtār*, printed with Ibn 'Ābidīn's *Ḥāshiyat Radd al-Muḥtār*, 8 vols. (repr.: Beirut: Dār al-Fikr, 1399/1979).
Hemingway, Ernest, "Mussolini, Europe's Prize Bluffer," in W. White (ed.), *Dateline: Toronto: The Complete Toronto Dispatches, 1920–1924* (New York: Charles Scribner's Sons, 1985), pp. 253–259.
Henriques, Ursula, "Who Killed Father Thomas?" in V. D. Lipman (ed.), *Sir Moses Montefiore—A Symposium* (Oxford: Oxford Centre for Postgraduate Hebrew Studies and Jewish Historical Society of England, 1982).
Heper, Metin, *İsmet İnönü* (Leiden: E. J. Brill, 1998).
Herzfeld, Michael, *Cultural Intimacy: Social Poetics in the Nation-State* (New York: Routledge, 1997).
———, *The Poetics of Manhood: Contest and Identity in a Cretan Mountain Village* (Princeton, N.J.: Princeton University Press, 1985).
Hexter, J. H., *Doing History* (Bloomington: Indiana University Press, 1971).
Heyd, Uriel, "Ritual Murder Accusations in 15th- and 16th-Century Turkey," *Sefunot* 5 (1961): 135–150.
Higham, John, and Paul K. Conkin (eds.), *New Directions in American Intellectual History* (Baltimore: Johns Hopkins University Press, 1979).
Hill, Christopher, *Intellectual Origins of the English Revolution* (Oxford: Clarendon Press, 1965).
Hill, Christopher (ed.), H. N. Brailsford, *Levellers and the English Revolution* (London: Cresset Press, 1961).
Himadeh, Said (ed.), *Economic Organization of Palestine* (Beirut: American University of Beirut, 1938).

Hirst, Paul, and Graeme Thompson, *Globalisation in Question* (Cambridge, UK: Polity Press, 1996).
Hobsbawm, Eric, "Man and Woman in Social Iconography," *History Workshop* 6 (1978): 121–138.
Hobsbawm, Eric, and Terence Ranger (eds.), *The Invention of Tradition*, Canto ed. (Cambridge, UK: Cambridge University Press, 1992).
Hollinger, David A., "How Wide the Circle of the 'We'? American Intellectuals and the Problem of the Ethnos Since World War II," *American Historical Review* 98 (1993): 317–337.
———, "The Return of the Prodigal: The Persistence of Historical Knowing," *American Historical Review* 94 (1989): 610–621.
Hopwood, Derek, *Syria 1945–1986: Politics and Society* (London: Unwin Hyman, 1988).
Hourani, Albert, "How Should We Write the History of the Middle East?" *International Journal of Middle East Studies* 23 (1991): 125–136.
———, *Arabic Thought in the Liberal Age* (Oxford: Oxford University Press, 1962; Cambridge, UK: Cambridge University Press, 1983).
Hourani, Albert, Philip S. Khoury, and Mary C. Wilson (eds.), *The Modern Middle East: A Reader* (London: I. B.Tauris, 1993).
Hsia, Ronnie Po-Chia, *The Myth of Ritual Murder: Jews and Magic in Reformation Germany* (New Haven, Conn.: Yale University Press, 1988).
Hunt, Lynn (ed.), *The New Cultural History* (Berkeley: University of California Press, 1989).
Hurewitz, J. C., *The Struggle for Palestine*, 2nd ed. (New York: Schocken, 1976).
Hyamson, A. M., "The Damascus Affair—1840," *Transactions of the Jewish Historical Society of England* 16 (1952): 47–71.
Ibn 'Ābidīn, *Hashiyat Radd al-Muhtar*, 8 vols. (repr.: Beirut: Dar al-Fikr, 1399/1979).
———, *Nashr al-'Urf fī Binā' Ba'ḍ al-Aḥkām 'alā al-'Urf*, in *Majmū'at Rasā'il Ibn 'Ābidīn* (N.p., 1970).
———, *Sharḥ al-Risāla al-Musammā bi-'Uqūd Rasm al-Muftī*, in *Majmū'at Rasā'il Ibn 'Ābidīn*, 2 vols. (N.p., n.d.).
———, *Tanbīh al-Ruqūd 'alā Masā'il al-Nuqūd*, in *Majmū'at Rasā'il Ibn 'Ābidīn*, 2 vols. (N.p., n.d.), pp. 58–67.
Ibn al-Ḥājib, Jamāl al-Dīn, *Muntahā al-Wuṣūl wal-Amal fī 'Ilmayy al-Uṣūl wal-Jadal*, ed. M. Badr al-Dīn al-Na'sānī (Cairo: Maṭba'at al-Sa'āda, 1326/1908).
Ibn al-Ṣalāḥ, 'Uthmān b. 'Abd al-Raḥmān, *Adab al-Muftī wal-Mustaftī*, ed. Muwaffaq 'Abd al-Qādir (Beirut: 'Ālam al-Kutub, 1986).
Ibn Manẓūr, Jamāl al-Dīn, *Lisān al-'Arab*, 15 vols. (repr.: Beirut: Dār Ṣādir,1972).
Ibn Māza, 'Umar Ibn 'Abd al-'Azīz al-Ḥusām al-Shahīd, *Sharḥ Adab al-Qāḍī*, ed. Abū al-Wafā' al-Afghānī and M. al-Hāshimī (Beirut: Dār al-Kutub al-'Ilmiyya, 1414/1994).
Ibn Nujaym, Zayn al-Dīn, *al-Ashbāh wal-Naẓā'ir* (Calcutta: al-Matba'a al-Ta'līmiyya, 1260/1844).
Ibn Qudāma, Muwaffaq al-Dīn, *Rawḍat al-Nāẓir wa-Junnat al-Munāẓir*, ed. Sayf al-Dīn al-Kātib (Beirut: Dār al-Kitāb al-'Arabī, 1401/1981).
Ibn Quṭlūbughā, Zayn al-Dīn, *Tāj al-Tarājim fī Ṭabaqāt al-Ḥanafiyya* (Baghdad: Maṭba'at al-Muthannā, 1962).
İnalcık, Halil, *The Middle East and the Balkans Under the Ottoman Empire: Essays on Economy and Society* (Bloomington: Indiana University Turkish Studies and Turkish Ministry of Culture Joint Series, 1993).

———, "Osmanlı İdare, Sosyal ve Ekonomik Tarihiyle İlgili Belgeler: Bursa Kadı Sicillerinden Seçmeler," *Türk Tarih Kurumu, Belgeler* 14 (1981): 1–91.
İnönü, İsmet, *İstiklal Savaşı ve Lozan* (Ankara: Atatürk Araştırma Merkezi, 1993).
———, *Hatıralar*, 2 kitap (Ankara: Bilgi, 1987).
İnönü Vakfı, *70.yılında Lozan Barış Antlaşması: uluslararası seminer, 1993* (Ankara: Ajanstürk, 1994).
Ishraq-Khavari, 'Abd al-Hamid, "Hayrat-i Qajar: Abu al-Hasan Mirza mulaqqab bih Shaykh al-Ra'is," *Ahang-i Badi'* 5 (1948): 239–242, 260–263, 282–286, 321–334, 350–354, 374–378, 397–401.
Ismael, Jacqueline S., and Earl L. Sullivan (eds.), *The Contemporary Study of the Arab World* (Edmonton: University of Alberta Press, 1991).
Ismael, Tareq Y. (ed.), *Middle East Studies: International Perspectives on the State of the Art* (New York: Praeger, 1990).
Issawi, Charles, *The Middle East Economy: Decline and Recovery* (Princeton, N.J.: Markus Weiner, 1995).
———, *The Fertile Crescent, 1800–1914: A Documentary Economic History* (Oxford: Oxford University Press, 1988).
———, *The Economic History of Turkey, 1800–1914* (Chicago: University of Chicago Press, 1980).
———, "Asymmetrical Development and Transport in Egypt, 1800–1914," in William Polk and Richard Chambers (eds.), *The Beginnings of Modernization in the Middle East* (Chicago: University of Chicago Press, 1968), pp. 383–400.
———, *Egypt at Mid-Century: An Economic Survey* (Oxford: Oxford University Press, 1954).
Jankowski, James, and Israel Gershoni (eds.), *Rethinking Nationalism in the Arab Middle East* (New York: Columbia University Press, 1997).
Jennings, R. C., "Loans and Credit in Early 17th-Century Ottoman Judicial Records," *Journal of the Economic and Social History of the Orient* 16 (1973): 168–216.
Jewish Agency for Palestine, Economic Research Institute, *Statistical Handbook of Middle Eastern Countries: Palestine, Cyprus, Egypt, Iraq, the Lebanon, Syria, Transjordan, Turkey* (Jerusalem: Jewish Agency, 1945).
Jīdī, 'Umar, *al-'Urf wal-'Amal fī al-Madhhab al-Mālikī* (Rabat: Maṭba'at Faḍāla, 1982).
Johansen, Baber, "Coutumes locales et coutumes universelles," *Annales Islamologiques* 27 (1993): 29–35.
Joseph, Suad, "Brother/Sister Relationships: Connectivity, Love, and Power in the Reproduction of Patriarchy in Lebanon," *American Ethnologist* 21 (1994): 50–73.
Judaki, Hujjat al-Islam, "Asnadi dar barih-'i Sayyid Jamal al-Din Asadabadi," *Tarikh-i Mu'asir-i Iran* 7 (1995): 276–290.
al-Jundi, Anwar, *'Abd al-'Aziz Jawish: min ruwwad al-tarbiyya w'al-sahafa w'al-ijtima'* (Cairo, al-Dar al-Misriyya lil-Ta'lif wal-Tarjama, 1965).
Kanafani, Ghassan, *Thawrat 1936 fi Filastin: Khalfiyyat wa tafasil wa tahlil* (Beirut: Popular Front for the Liberation of Palestine, 1974).
Kandemir, Feridun, *Söyledikleri ve Söylemedikleri ile Rauf Orbay* (İstanbul: Sinan, 1965).
"Kanu . . . thumma asbahu," *al-Kawakib* 283 (1 January 1957): 72.
Kara, Metin, "The Workers as a Class Were Defeated," *Merip Reports,* no. 121 (February 1984): 21–27.
Kayyali, A.W., *Palestine: A Modern History* (London: Croom Helm, 1978).

Kazgan, Haydar, "İkinci Sultan Mahmut devrinde enflasyon ve darphane amiri Kazaz Artin," *Toplum ve Bilim* 11 (1980): 115–130.
Keddie, Nikki R., *Sayyid Jamal al-Din "al-Afghani": A Political Biography* (Berkeley: University of California Press, 1972).
———, "Religion and Irreligion in Early Iranian Nationalism," *Comparative Studies in Society and History* 4 (1962): 265–295.
Kelekyan, Diran, "Kazaz Artin," *Tarihi Osmani Encümeni Mecmuası*, 26 and 27 (June and August H. 330/1912).
Keppel, George, *Personal Narrative of a Journey from India to England . . . in the Year 1824* (London: Henry Colburn, 1827).
Ker Porter, Sir Robert, "At the Court of Fath Ali Shah," in B. W. Robinson and Gianni Guadalupi (eds.), *Qajar: Court Paintings in Persia* (Milan: Franco Maria Ricci, 1990), pp. 53–207.
Kerr, Malcolm, *Islamic Reform: The Political and Legal Theories of Muḥammad 'Abduh and Rashıd Riḍā* (Berkeley: University of California Press, 1966).
Khalaf, Issa, *Arab Factionalism and Social Disintegration, 1939–1948* (Albany: State University of New York Press, 1991).
Khalidi, Rashid, "Anti-Zionism, Arabism, and Palestinian Identity: 'Isa al-'Isa and *Filastin*," in S. Seikaly (ed.), *Political Identity in the Arab East in the Twentieth Century* (Beirut: American University of Beirut Press, forthcoming).
———, "The Palestinians and 1948: The Underlying Causes of Failure," in Avi Shlaim and Eugene Rogan (eds.), *Rewriting the Palestine War: 1948 and the History of the Arab-Israeli Conflict* (Cambridge, UK: Cambridge University Press, 2001), pp. 12–36.
———, *Palestinian Identity: The Construction of Modern National Consciousness* (New York: Columbia University Press, 1997).
Khalidi, Rashid, et al. (eds.), *The Origins of Arab Nationalism* (New York: Columbia University Press, 1991).
Khalidi, Walid, *Khamsuna 'aman 'ala taqsim Filastin (1947–1997)* (Beirut: Dar al-Nahar, 1998).
———, "Plan *Dalet* Revisited," *Journal of Palestine Studies* 18 (Autumn 1988): 4–70.
———, *From Haven to Conquest: Readings in Zionism and the Palestine Problem Until 1948*, 2nd printing (Washington, D.C.: Institute for Palestine Studies, 1987).
———, "Plan *Dalet*: The Zionist Master Plan for the Conquest of Palestine," *Middle East Forum* 37, no. 9 (November 1961): 22–28.
———, "The Fall of Haifa," *Middle East Forum* 35, no. 10 (December 1959): 22–32.
———, "Why Did the Palestinians Leave?" *Middle East Forum* 34, no. 6 (July 1959): 21–24, 35.
Khalidi, Walid (ed.), *All That Remains: The Palestinian Villages Occupied and Depopulated by Israel in 1948* (Washington, D.C.: Institute for Palestine Studies, 1992).
Khalīfa, Ḥājjī, *Kashf al-Ẓunūn 'an Asāmī al-Kutub wal-Funūn*, 2 vols. (Istanbul: Maṭba'at Wakālat al-Ma'ārif al-Jalīla, 1941–1943).
Khuri, Yusuf (ed.), *al-Sihafa al-'arabiyya fi Filastin, 1876–1948* (Beirut: Institute for Palestine Studies, 1976).
Kia, Mehrdad, "Pan-Islamism in Late Nineteenth-Century Iran," *Middle Eastern Studies* 2 (1996): 30–52.
Kienle, Eberhard, "More Than a Response to Islamism: The Political

Deliberalization of Egypt in the 1990s," *Middle East Journal* 52 (1998): 219–235.
King, Stephen J., "The Politics of Market Reform in Rural Tunisia," Ph.D. dissertation, Princeton University, Princeton, N.J., 1997.
Kocaer, Remzi, *Osmanlı Altın Paraları* (Istanbul: Güzel Sanatlar Matbaası, 1967).
Kologlu, Orhan, "Un journal persan d'Istanbul: *Akhtar*," in Thierry Zarcone and Fariba Zarinebaf (eds.), *Les iraniens d'Istanbul* (Paris: Institut Français de recherches en Iran, 1993), pp. 133–140.
Korayem, Karima, "Structural Adjustment, Stabilization Policies, and the Poor in Egypt," *Cairo Papers in Social Science* 18, no. 4 (Winter 1995–1996).
Koury, George, "The Province of Damascus," Ph.D. dissertation, University of Michigan, 1970.
Krause, Chester L., and Clifford Mishler, with Colin R. Bruce II, *Standard Catalog of World Coins,* 21st ed. (Iola, Wisc.: Krause Publications, 1994).
Kundera, Milan, *The Book of Laughter and Forgetting* (New York: Penguin, 1980).
Kunt, Metin, "Ethnic-Regional (*cins*) Solidarity in the Seventeenth Century Ottoman Establishment," *International Journal of Middle East Studies* 5 (1974): 233–239.
Kütükoğlu, Mübahat S., "Asakir-i Mansure-i Muhammediyye Kıyafeti ve Malzemesinin Temini Meselesi," *Doğumunun 100.Yılında Atatürk'e Armağan* (Istanbul: Istanbul Üniversitesi Edebiyat Fakültesi Yayınları, 1981), pp. 519–605.
LaCapra, Dominick, *Soundings in Critical Theory* (Ithaca, N.Y.: Cornell University Press, 1989).
———, *History and Criticism* (Ithaca, N.Y.: Cornell University Press, 1985).
LaCapra, Dominick, and Steven L. Kaplan (eds.), *Modern European Intellectual History: Reappraisals and New Perspectives* (Ithaca, N.Y.: Cornell University Press, 1982).
Landau, Jacob, *The Politics of Pan-Islam*, rev. ed. (Oxford: Oxford University Press, 1994).
———, "Ritual Murder Accusations and Persecutions of Jews in 19th-Century Egypt," *Sefunot* 5 (1961): 415–460.
Landes, David, *Bankers and Pashas: International Finance and Economic Imperialism in Egypt* (London: Heinemann, 1958).
Langmuir, Gavin, *Towards a Definition of Antisemitism* (Berkeley: University of California Press, 1990).
Laurent, Achille, *Relation historique des affaires de Syrie depuis 1840 jusqu'en 1842*, Vols. I and II (Paris: Gaume Frères, 1846).
Layard, Sir Henry, *Early Adventures in Persia, Susiana, and Babylonia* (London: John Murray, 1887).
Lazreg, Marnia, *The Eloquence of Silence* (New York: Routledge, 1994).
Levy, A., "The Officer Corps in Sultan Mahmud II's New Ottoman Army, 1826–39," *International Journal of Middle East Studies* 2 (1971): 21–39.
Libson, Gideon, "On the Development of Custom as a Source of Law in Islamic Law," *Islamic Law and Society* 4 (1997): 131–155.
Litvak, Meir, *Shi'i Scholars of Nineteenth-Century Iraq* (Cambridge, UK: Cambridge University Press, 1998).
Loewenstein, L. H., *Damascia* (Rodelheim: J. Lehrberger, 1841).
Lozan'ın 50.yılına armağan. Studies in Commemoration of the Lausanne Peace Treaty on Its 50th Anniversary (İstanbul: Fakülteler Matbaası, 1978).
Lukacs, John, *Historical Consciousness: The Remembered Past* (New Brunswick, N.J.: Transaction, 1994).

Macdonald, Alan, "Tony Stole a Trolley!" *Motion Picture and Television Magazine* (August 1953): 32–33, 73.

Makdisi, Ussama, *The Culture of Sectarianism* (Berkeley: University of California Press, 2000).

Mandaville, J. E., "Usurious Piety: The Cash Waqf Controversy in the Ottoman Empire," *International Journal of Middle East Studies* 10 (1979): 295–304.

Mardam Bey, Khalīl, *A'yān al-Qarn al-Thālith 'Ashar fī al-Fikr wal-Siyāsa wal-Ijtimā'* (Beirut: Mu'assasat al-Risāla, 1977).

al-Marghīnānī, Burhān al-Dīn, *al-Hidāya: Sharḥ Bidāyat al-Mubtadī*, 4 vols. (Cairo: Muṣṭafā Bābī al-Ḥalabī, 1400/1980).

Margulies, Ronnie, and Ergin Yıldızoğlu, "Trade Unions and Turkey's Working Class," *Merip Reports,* no. 121 (February 1984): 15–20, 31.

Marlowe, John, *Cromer in Egypt* (London: Elek Books, 1970).

Mattar, Philip, *The Mufti of Jerusalem: Al-Hajj Amin al-Husayni and the Palestinian National Movement* (New York: Columbia University Press, 1988).

Matthews, Weldon, "The Arab Istiqlal Party in Palestine, 1927–1934," Ph.D. thesis, University of Chicago, 1998.

Maza, Sarah, "Stories in History: Cultural Narratives in Recent Works in European History," a review essay, *American Historical Review* 101 (1996): 1493–1515.

McCrone, David, "Inventing the Past: History and Nationalism," in D. McCrone (ed.), *The Sociology of Nationalism: Tomorrow's Ancestors* (London: Routledge, 1998), pp. 44–63.

McCarthy, Justin, *The Population of Palestine: Population Statistics of the Late Ottoman Period and the Mandate* (New York: Columbia University Press, 1990).

McClintock, Anne, *Imperial Leather: Race, Gender, and Sexuality in the Colonial Contest* (New York: Routledge, 1995).

McDonald, Paul, "Star Studies," in Joanne Hollows and Mark Jancovich (eds.), *Approaches to Popular Film* (New York: Manchester University Press, 1995), pp. 79–97.

Meeker, Michael, "Meaning and Society in the Near East: Examples from the Black Sea Turks and the Levantine Arabs (II)," *International Journal of Middle East Studies* 7 (1976): 383–422.

Mellini, Peter, *Sir Eldon Gorst: The Overshadowed Proconsul* (Stanford, Calif.: Hoover Institute Press, 1977).

Meneley, Anne, *Tournaments of Value: Sociability and Hierarchy in a Yemeni Town* (Toronto: University of Toronto Press, 1996).

el-Messiri, Sawsan, *Ibn al-Balad: A Concept of Egyptian Identity* (Leiden: E. J. Brill, 1978).

Metcalf, Thomas R., "Ideologies of the Raj," in *The New Cambridge History of India*, Vol. 3, No. 4 (Cambridge, UK: Cambridge University Press, 1994).

Miles, Margaret R., *Image as Insight: Visual Understanding in Western Christianity and Secular Culture* (Boston: Beacon Press, 1985).

Miller, Daniel, *Modernity, an Ethnographic Approach: Dualism and Mass Consumption in Trinidad* (Oxford: Berg, 1994).

——— (ed.), *Acknowledging Consumption: A Review of New Studies* (New York: Routledge, 1995).

Miller, Ylana, *Government and Society in Rural Palestine1920–1948* (Austin: University of Texas Press, 1985).

Mishaqa, Mikhayil, *Murder, Mayhem, Pillage, and Plunder: The History of*

Lebanon in the 18th and 19th Centuries, trans. Wheeler Thackston (Albany: State University of New York Press, 1988).
Mısıroğlu, Kadir, *Lozan: Zafer mi Hezimet mi?* 3 vols. (Istanbul: Sebil, 1992).
Miskimin, Harry A., *Money and Power in Fifteenth-Century France* (New Haven, Conn.: Yale University Press, 1984).
Mitchell, Timothy, *Colonising Egypt* (Cambridge, UK: Cambridge University Press, 1988).
Morier, James, *A Journey Through Persia, Armenia, and Asia Minor, to Constantinople, in the Years 1808 and 1809* (London: Longman et al., 1812).
Morris, Benny, *The Birth of the Palestinian Refugee Problem 1947–1949* (Cambridge, UK: Cambridge University Press, 1987).
Mosley, Leonard, *The Glorious Fault: The Life of Lord Curzon* (New York: Harcourt, Brace, and Company, 1960).
Motomura, Akira, "The Best and Worst of Currencies: Seigniorage and Currency Policy in Spain, 1597–1650," *The Journal of Economic History* 54 (1994): 104–127.
Moulton, Edward L., *Lord Northrook's Indian Administration 1872–1876* (London: Asia Publishing House, 1968).
Mu'īn, Muhammad, *Farhang-i Fārsī* (Tehran: Amīr Kabīr, 1985).
al-Mudarri, Muhammad, *Mashayikh Balkh min al-Hanafiyya*, 2 vols. (Baghdad: Wizarat al-Awqaf. Silsilat al-Kutub al-Haditha, 1979).
Murad, Nicolas, *Notice historique sur l'origine de la nation maronite et sur ses rapports avec la France, sur la nation druze et sur les diverses population du mont liban* (Paris: Librairie d'Adrien le Clere et Cie., 1844).
al-Mūṣilī, 'Abd Allāh b. Mawdūd, *al-Ikhtiyār li-Ta'līl al-Mukhtār*, ed. Maḥmūd Abū Daqīqa, 5 vols. (Beirut: Dār al-Kutub al-'Ilmiyya, n.d.).
Na'īsa, Yūsuf, *Mujtama' Madīnat Dimashq*, 2 vols. (Damascus: Ṭlās, 1986).
al-Nadim, 'Abdallah, *Al-A'daad al-Kamila li majallat al-Ustaadh*, Vol. I (Cairo: Al-Hi'yyat al-'amma lil-kitaab, 1994).
Naff, Thomas (ed.), *Paths to the Middle East: Ten Scholars Look Back* (Albany: State University of New York Press, 1993).
Naim, C. M., "The Theme of Homosexual (Pederastic) Love in Pre-Modern Urdu Poetry," in Muhammad Umar Memon (ed.), *Studies in the Urdu Gazal and Prose Fiction* (Madison: University of Wisconsin, 1979), pp. 120–142.
Najmabadi, Afsaneh, *Women with Moustaches and Men without Beards: Gender and Sexual Anxieties of Iranian Modernity* (forthcoming).
———, "Gendered Transformations: Beauty, Love, and Sexuality in Qajar Iran," *Journal of Iranian Studies* (forthcoming).
———, "Crafting an Educated Housewife in Iran," in Lila Abu-Lughod (ed.), *Remaking Women: Feminism and Modernity in the Middle East* (Princeton, N.J.: Princeton University Press, 1998), pp. 91–125.
———, "Reading for Gender Through Qajar Art," in Layla S. Diba and Maryam Ekhtiar (eds.), *Royal Persian Paintings: The Qajar Epoch 1785–1925* (London: Brooklyn Museum of Arts in association with I. B.Tauris, 1998), pp. 76–89.
———, "The Erotic *Vaṭan* [homeland] as Beloved and Mother: To Love, to Possess, and to Protect," *Comparative Studies in Society and History* 39 (1997): 442–467.
———, "*Zanhā-yi millat:* Women or Wives of the Nation," *Iranian Studies* 26 (1993): 51–71.
Nategh, Homa, "Mirza Aqa Khan, Sayyed Jamal al-Din et Malkom Khan à Istanbul

(1860–1897)," in Thierry Zarcone and Fariba Zarinebaf (eds.), *Les iraniens d'Istanbul* (Paris: Institut Français de recherches en Iran, 1993), pp. 45–60.
Nathan, Robert, Oscar Gass, and Daniel Creamer, *Palestine: Problem and Promise: An Economic Study* (Washington, D.C.: Public Affairs Press, 1946).
Nelson, Joan, "Overview: The Politics of Long-Haul Reform," in Joan Nelson (ed.), *Fragile Coalitions: The Politics of Economic Adjustment* (Washington, D.C.: Overseas Development Corporation, 1989), pp. 3–26.
Niblock, Tim, "International and Domestic Factors in the Economic Liberalization Process in Arab Countries," in Tim Niblock and Emma Murphy (eds.), *Economic and Political Liberalization in the Middle East* (London: British Academic Press, 1993), pp. 55–87.
Nicolson, Harold, *Curzon: The Last Phase 1919–1925* (London: Constable; Boston: Hughton Mifflin, 1934).
Nochlin, Linda, *Women, Art, and Power and Other Essays* (New York: Harper and Row, 1988).
Novick, Peter, *That Noble Dream: The "Objectivity Question" and the American Historical Profession* (Cambridge, UK: Cambridge University Press, 1988).
Nubar Pasha, *Mémoires de Nubar Pasha* (with Introduction and Notes by Mirrit Butros Ghali) (Beirut: Librairie du Liban, 1983).
"Nujumuna: Kam yataqaduna fi al-sa'a?" (Our stars: How much do they earn in an hour?) *al-Kawakib* 284 (8 January 1957): 54–55.
Nur, Rıza, *Hayat ve Hatıratım*, 3 vols. (Istanbul: İşaret, 1992).
Nuri, Suphi, *Sevres ve Lausanne* (Istanbul: Arkadaş, 1934).
O'Donnell, Guillermo, "Reflections on the Patterns of Change in the Bureaucratic-Authoritarian State," *Latin American Research Review* 12 (1978): 3–38.
Ölçer, Çüneyt, *Sultan II. Mahmud Zamanında Darp Edilen Osmanlı Madeni Paraları* (Istanbul: Yenilik Basımevi, 1970).
Ortner, Sherry B., "Theory in Anthropology Since the Sixties," *Comparative Studies in Society and History* 26 (1984): 126–166.
Owen, Roger, "Economic Development in Mandatory Palestine," in George Abed (ed.), *The Palestinian Economy: Studies in Development Under Prolonged Occupation* (London: Routledge, 1988), pp. 13–36.
———, *The Middle East in the World Economy, 1800–1914* (London: Methuen, 1981).
———, *Cotton and the Egyptian Economy, 1820–1914: A Study in Trade and Development* (Oxford: Oxford University Press, 1969).
Paidar, Parvin, *Women and the Political Process in Twentieth-Century Iran* (Cambridge, UK: Cambridge University Press).
Pamuk, Şevket, *Five Hundred Years of Prices and Wages in Istanbul and Other Ottoman Cities, 1469–1998* (Ankara: Turkey State Institute of Statistics, Historical Statistics Series, forthcoming).
———, *A Monetary History of the Ottoman Empire* (Cambridge, UK: Cambridge University Press, 1999).
———, "In the Absence of Domestic Currency: Debased European Coinage in the Seventeenth-Century Ottoman Empire," *The Journal of Economic History* 57 (1997): 345–366.
Pappé, Ilan, *The Making of the Arab-Israeli Conflict, 1947–1951* (London: I. B. Tauris, 1994).
Paret, Rudi, "Istiḥsān and Istiṣlāḥ," *Shorter Encyclopaedia of Islam* (Leiden: E. J. Brill, 1974), pp. 184–186.

Parfitt, Tudor, "'The Year of the Pride of Israel': Montefiore and the Damascus Blood Libel of 1840," in Sonia and V. D. Lipman (eds.), *The Century of Moses Montefiore* (Oxford: Publication for the Littman Library of Jewish Civilisation in association with the Jewish Historical Society of England by Oxford University Press, 1985).

Parker, Andrew, et al. (eds.), *Nationalisms and Sexualities* (New York: Routledge, 1992).

Parry, V. J., and M. E. Yapp (eds.), *War, Technology, and Society in the Middle East* (London: Oxford University Press, 1975).

Pfeifer, Karen, "How Tunisia, Morocco, Jordan, and Even Egypt Became IMF 'Success Stories' in the 1990s," *Middle East Reports,* no. 210 (Spring 1999): 23–27.

———, "Between Rocks and Hard Choices: International Finance and Economic Adjustment in North Africa," in Dirk Vandewalle (ed.), *North Africa: Development and Reform in a Changing Global Economy* (New York: St. Martin's Press, 1996), pp. 25–63.

Pierce, Leslie, *The Imperial Harem* (Oxford: Oxford University Press, 1993).

Pieritz, G.W., *Persecution of the Jews at Damascus* (London: London Society for Promoting Christianity Amonst the Jews, 1840).

Pistor-Hatam, Anja, "The Persian Newspaper *Akhtar* as a Transmitter of Ottoman Political Ideas," in Thierry Zarcone and Fariba Zarinebaf (eds.), *Les iraniens d'Istanbul* (Paris: Institut Français de recherches en Iran, 1993), pp. 141–147.

———, *Iran und die Reformbewegung im Osmanischen Reich* (Berlin: Klaus Schwarz Verlag, 1992).

Pollock, Griselda, *Vision and Difference: Femininity, Feminism, and Histories of Art* (London: Routledge, 1988).

Posener, S., *Adolphe Crémieux: A Biography* (Philadelphia: Jewish Publication Society of America, 1940).

Posusney, Marsha Pripstein, *Labor and the State in Egypt: Workers, Unions, and Economic Restructuring, 1952–1996* (New York: Columbia University Press, 1997).

Qāḍīkhān, Fakhr al-Dīn Ḥasan b. Manṣūr al-Ūzajandī, *Fatāwā Qāḍīkhān*, printed on the margins of *al-Fatāwā al-Hindiyya*, Vols. I–III (repr.: Beirut: Dār Iḥyā' al-Turāth al-'Arabī, 1400/1980).

Qasim, Mahmud, and Ya'qub Wahbi (eds.), *Mausu'at al-mumaththil fi al-sinima al-misriyya, 1927–1997* (Encyclopedia of the actor in the Egyptian cinema, 1927–1997) (Cairo: Dar al-Amin, 1997).

al-Qudūrī, Aḥmad b. Muḥammad b. Ja'far, *Mukhtaṣar* (Beirut: Dār al-Kutub al-'Ilmiyya, 1997).

al-Qurashī, Abū al-Wafā' Muḥammad, *al-Jawāhir al-Muḍī'a*, 2 vols. (Haydarabad: Maṭba'at Majlis Dā'irat al-Ma'ārif al-Niẓāmiyya, 1332/1913).

Ra'isniya, Rahim, *Iran va 'Uthmani dar Astanih-'i Qarn-i Bistum*, 3 vols. (Tehran: Azadih, 1995).

Radwan, Samir, Vali Jamal, and Ajit Ghose, *Tunisia: Rural Labour and Structural Transformation* (London: Routledge, 1991).

al-Rafi'i, 'Abd al-Rahman, *Muhammad Farid: ramz al-ikhlas w'al-tadhiyya* (Cairo: Maktab al-Nahda al-Misriyya, 1948).

———, *Mustafa Kamil: ba'ith al-haraka al-wataniyya* (Cairo: Maktab al-Nahda al-Misriyya, 1939).

al-Rāzī, Fakhr al-Dīn, *al-Maḥṣūl fī 'Ilm Uṣūl al-Fiqh*, 2 vols. (Beirut: Dār al-Kutub al-'Ilmiyya, 1408/1988).
Richards, Alan, and John Waterbury, *A Political Economy of the Middle East*, 2nd ed. (Boulder, Colo.: Westview Press, 1996).
———, *A Political Economy of the Middle East: State, Class, and Economic Development* (Boulder, Colo.: Westview Press, 1990).
Roberson, Barbara Allen, "Judicial Reform and the Expansion of International Society: The Case of Egypt," Ph.D. dissertation, London School of Economics and Political Science, 1998.
Rorty, Richard, *Objectivity, Relativism and Truth* (Cambridge, UK: Cambridge University Press, 1991).
Rose, Jacqueline, "Edward Said Talks to Jacqueline Rose," in Paul A. Bové (ed.), *Edward Said and the Work of the Critic: Speaking Truth to Power* (Durham, N.C.: Duke University Press, 2000), pp. 9–30.
Roy, Delwin A., "Egyptian Emigrant Labor: Domestic Consequences," *Middle Eastern Studies* 22 (1991): 551–582.
Rustum, Asad, *Materials for a Corpus of Arabic Documents Relating to the History of Syria Under Mehemet Ali Pasha*, Vol. V (Beirut: American Press, 1933).
Safa'i, Ibrahim, *Asnad-i Naw-Yaftih* (Tehran: Chap-i Sharq, 1970).
Saḥḥāfbāshī, Ibrāhīm, Safarnāmah-'i Ibrāhīm Saḥḥāfbāshī Ṭiḥrānī, ed. Muḥammad Mushīrī (Tehran: Shirkat-i mu'allifān va mutarjimān-i Irān, 1978).
Şahiner, Araks, "The Sarrafs of Istanbul: Financiers of the Empire," M.A. thesis, Department of History, Boğaziçi University, 1995.
al-Sarakhsī, Shams al-A'imma, *al-Mabsūṭ,* 30 vols. (Cairo: Maṭba'at al-Sa'āda, 1906–1912).
Sasani, Khan Malik, *Yadbudha-yi Sifarat-i Istanbul* (Tehran: Firdawsi, 1966).
Sass, Benjamin, "The Silver and Billon Coins Minted at Constantinople Under Sultan Mahmud II (1223–1255 H.)," *The American Numismatic Society Notes* 18 (1972): 167–175.
Saul, Samir, *La France et l'Egypte de 1882 à 1914: Intérêts économiques et implications politiques* (Paris: Ministère de l'Economie, des Finances et de l'Industrie, 1997).
Schade-Poulsen, Marc, *Men and Popular Music in Algeria: The Social Significance of Raï* (Austin: University of Texas Press, 1999).
Schwartz, Barry, "Rereading the Gettysburg Address: Social Change and Collective Memory," *Qualitative Sociology* 19 (1996): 395–422.
Scott, James C., *Domination and the Arts of Resistance: Hidden Transcripts* (New Haven, Conn.: Yale University Press, 1990).
Scott, Joan Wallach, "Women's History," in Peter Burke (ed.), *New Perspectives on Historical Writing* (Cambridge, UK: Polity Press, 1991), pp. 42–66.
———, *Gender and the Politics of History* (New York: Columbia University Press, 1988).
Segev, Tom, *1949: The First Israelis* (New York: Free Press, 1986).
Semmel, Bernard, *The Liberal Ideal and the Demon of Empire: Theories of Imperialism from Adam Smith to Lenin* (Baltimore: Johns Hopkins University Press, 1993).
Sewell, William H., Jr., "The Concept(s) of Culture," in Victoria E. Bonnell and Lynn Hunt (eds.), *Beyond the Cultural Turn* (Berkeley: University of California Press, 1999), pp. 35–61.
Shafei, Omar, "Workers, Trade Unions, and the State in Egypt: 1984–1989," *Cairo Papers in Social Science* 18, no. 2 (Summer 1995).

Shafik, Ahmed, "L'Esclavage au point de vue musulmane," *Bulletin de la Société de Géographie de l'Egypte* 5 (1892): 465.
Shahidian, Hammed, "Dushvārīhā-yi nigārish-i tārīkh-i zanān dar Irān," *Iran Nameh* 12, no. 1 (Winter 1994): 81–128.
Shaikh al-Ra'is Qajar, Abu al-Hasan Mirza, *Muntakhab-i Nafis*,. 2 vols. in 1 (Tehran: Mahmudi, 1960 [Bombay, 1896]).
———, *Ittihad-i Islam*, ed. Sadiq Sajjadi (Tehran: Naqsh-i Jahan, 1984 [1895]).
Shakry, Omnia, "Schooled Mothers and Structured Play: Child Rearing in Turn-of-the-Century Egypt," in Lila Abu-Lughod (ed.), *Remaking Women: Feminism and Modernity in the Middle East* (Princeton, N.J.: Princeton University Press, 1998), pp. 126–170.
Shapiro, Susan E., "A Matter of Discipline: Reading for Gender in Jewish Philosophy," in Miriam Peskowitz and Laura Levitt (eds.), *Judaism Since Gender* (New York: Routledge, 1997), pp. 158–173.
Sharabi, Hisham (ed.), *Theory, Politics, and the Arab World: Critical Responses* (New York: Routledge, 1990).
Sharḥ al-Majalla, 2 vols. (repr.: Beirut: Dār al-Kutub al-'Ilmiyya, 1923).
al-Shāṭibī, Abū Isḥāq Ibrāhīm, *al-Muwāfaqāt fī Uṣūl al-Aḥkām*, 4 vols. (Cairo: Maṭba'at al-Madanī, 1969).
Shauqi, Farid, *Malik al-tirsu* (King of the cheap seats) (Cairo: Maktabat Ruz al-Yusuf, 1978).
———, "Mudhakkirat Farid Shauqi" (Memoirs of Farid Shauqi), *al-Kawakib* 299 (23 April 1957): 16–17, 36; 302 (14 May 1957): 16–17, 37; 303 (21 May 1957): 5; 304 (28 May 1957): 30–31.
———, "Ru'b al-blatoh," *al-Kawakib* 294 (19 March 1957): 39.
Shaw, Stanford J., and Ezel Kuran Shaw, *History of the Ottoman Empire and Modern Turkey*, Vol. II, *1809–1975* (London: Cambridge University Press, 1977).
Shlaim, Avi, *Collusion Across the Jordan* (New York: Columbia University Press, 1988).
Shreve Simpson, Marianna, with contributions by Massumeh Farhad, *Sultan Ibrahim Mirza's Haft Awrang: A Princely Manuscript from Sixteenth-Century Iran* (Washington, D.C., and New Haven, Conn.: Freer Gallery of Art and Yale University Press, 1997).
Şimşir, Bilal, *Lozan Telgrafları*. Vol. 2 (Ankara: TTK, 1994).
Sinclair-Webb, Emma, "Preface," in Mai Ghoussoub and Emma Sinclair-Webb (eds.), *Imagined Masculinities: Male Identity and Culture in the Modern Middle East* (London: Saqi Books, 2000).
Skidelsky, Robert, *John Maynard Keynes: Hopes Betrayed, 1883–1920* (London: Macmillan, 1983).
———, *John Maynard Keynes: The Economist as Saviour, 1920–1937* (London: Macmillan, 1992).
Smith, Barbara, *The Roots of Separatism in Palestine: British Economic Policy, 1920–1929* (Syracuse, N.Y.: Syracuse University Press, 1993).
Smith, Greg (ed.), *Erving Goffman and Social Organization: Studies in a Sociological Legacy* (London: Routledge, 1999).
Smith, Peter, *The Babi and Baha'i Religions: From Messianic Shi'ism to a World Religion* (Cambridge, UK: Cambridge University Press, 1987).
Şölen, Hikmet, *Lozan Hakkında bir Konferans* (Aydın: CHP Basımevi, 1939).
Sonbol, Amira (ed.), *The Last Khedive of Egypt: Memoirs of Abbas Hilmi II* (Reading, UK: Ithaca, 1998).

Sourdel, D., "*Ghulām*," in *Encyclopaedia of Islam,* Vol. II (Leiden: E. J. Brill, 1965), pp. 1079–1091.
Speke, John Hanning, *Journal of the Discovery of the Source of the Nile* (Mineola, N.Y.: Dover Publications, 1996).
Sprachman, Paul, "*Le beau garçon sans merci:* The Homoerotic Tale in Arabic and Persian," in J. W. Wright, Jr., and Everett K. Rowson (eds.), *Homoeroticism in Classical Arabic Literature* (New York: Columbia University Press, 1997), pp. 192–209.
Stacey, Jackie, *Star Gazing: Hollywood Cinema and Female Spectatorship* (New York: Routledge, 1994).
Sternhell, Zeev, *The Founding Myths of Israel* (Princeton, N.J.: Princeton University Press, 1998).
Stock, Brian, *Listening for the Text: On the Uses of the Past* (Baltimore: Johns Hopkins University Press, 1990).
———, *The Implication of Literacy: Written Language and Models of Interpretation in the Eleventh and Twelfth Centuries* (Princeton, N.J.: Princeton University Press, 1983).
Stone, Lawrence, "The Revival of Narrative: Reflections on a New Old History," *Past and Present* 85 (1979): 3–24.
———, *Crisis of the Aristocracy 1558–1641* (Oxford: Clarendon Press, 1965).
Strachey, Lytton, *Eminent Victorians: Cardinal Manning, Dr. Arnold, Florence Nightingale, General Gordon* (New York: Random House, 1918).
Strauss, Johann, "La présence diplomatique iranniene à Istanbul et dans les provinces de l'empire ottoman (1848–1908)," in Thierry Zarcone and Fariba Zarinebaf (eds.), *Les iraniens d'Istanbul* (Paris: Institut Français de recherches en Iran, 1993), pp. 11–32.
Strouse, Jean, *Morgan: American Financier* (New York: Random House, 1999).
al-Subkī, Tāj al-Dīn, *Ṭabaqāt al-Shāfiʿiyya al-Kubrā*, 6 vols. (Beirut: Dār al-Maʿrifa, 1906).
Sulaymani, ʿAziz Allah, *Masabih-i Hidayat*, 9 vols. (Tehran: Baha'i Publishing Trust, 1948–1977).
Sultan, Hoda, "Zauga lil-igar," *al-Kawakib* 314 (6 August 1957): 38.
Sultan, Jem, *Coins of the Ottoman Empire and the Turkish Republic: A Detailed Catalogue of the Jem Sultan Collection*, 2 vols. (Thousand Oaks, Calif.: B&R Publishers, 1977).
Süreyya, Mehmed, *Sicill-i Osmanī*, N. Akbayar (ed.). Vol. IV (Istanbul: Tarih Vakfī, 1996).
Sussman, Nathan, "Debasements, Royal Revenues, and Inflation in France During the Hundred Years' War, 1415–1422," *The Journal of Economic History* 53 (1993): 44–70.
al-Suyūṭī, Jalāl al-Dīn, *al-Ashbāh wal-Naẓāʾir fī Qawāʿid wa-Furūʿ Fiqh al-Shāfiʿiyya* (Beirut: Dār al-Kutub al-ʿIlmiyya, 1399/1979).
Tancoigne, M., *A Narrative of a Journal into Persia and Residence at Teheran* (London: printed for William Wright, by W. Shackell, 1820).
Tarcan, Necati, "Tanzimat ve Ordu," in *Tanzimat* (Ankara: Milli Eğitim Bakanlığı Yayınları, 1940), pp. 129–136.
Tavakoli-Targhi, Mohammad, "Refashioning Iran: Language and Culture During the Constitutional Revolution," *Iranian Studies* 23 (1990): 77–101.
———, "The Formation of Two Revolutionary Discourses in Modern Iran: The

Constitutional Revolution of 1905–1906 and the Islamic Revolution of 1978–1979," Ph. D. disseration, University of Chicago, 1988.
Thane, Pat, "Financiers and the British State: The Case of Sir Ernest Cassel," *Business History* 28, no. 1 (January 1986): 80–99.
The St. Petersburg Muraqqa (Milano: Leonardo arte, 1996).
Thompson, E. P., *Romantics: England in the Revolutionary Age* (New York: New Press, 1997).
———, "The Moral Economy of the British Crowd in the Eighteenth Century," *Past and Present* 50 (1971): 76–135.
Thompson, Elizabeth, *Colonial Citizens: Republican Rights, Paternal Privilege, and Gender in French Syria and Lebanon* (New York: Columbia University Press, 2000).
Tibawi, A. L., *A Modern History of Syria, Including Lebanon and Palestine* (London: Macmillan, 1969).
———, *Arab Education in Mandatory Palestine: A Study of Three Decades of British Administration* (London: Luzac, 1956).
Tignor, Robert, *Modernization and British Colonial Rule in Modern Egypt, 1882–1914* (Princeton, N.J.: Princeton University Press, 1966).
Tilly, Charles, "Food Supply and Public Order in Modern Europe," in C. Tilly (ed.), *The Formation of Nation States in Western Europe* (Princeton, N.J.: Princeton University Press, 1975), pp. 35–151.
Tlas, Mustafa, *Fatir Sahyun* (Damascus: Tlasdar, 1987).
Toews, John E., "Intellectual History After the Linguistic Turn: The Autonomy of Meaning and the Irreducibility of Experience," *American Historical Review* 92 (1987): 879–907.
Toledano, Ehud, *Slavery and Abolition in the Ottoman Middle East* (Seattle: University of Washington Press, 1998).
———, *The Ottoman Slave Trade and Its Suppression: 1840–1890* (Princeton, N.J.: Princeton University Press, 1982).
Tosh, John, *A Man's Place: Masculinity and the Middle-Class Home in Victorian England* (New Haven, Conn.: Yale University Press, 1999).
Trouillot, Michel-Rolph, *Silencing the Past: Power and the Production of History* (Boston: Beacon Press, 1995).
Troutt Powell, Eve, *A Different Shade of Colonialism: Egypt, Great Britain, and the Mastery of the Sudan* (Berkeley: University of California Press, forthcoming).
Tucker, Judith, *Women in Nineteenth-Century Egypt* (Cambridge, UK: Cambridge University Press, 1985).
Tully, James (ed.), *Meaning and Context: Quentin Skinner and His Critics* (Oxford: Polity Press, 1988).
Turkey, State Institute of Statistics, *Türkiye Istatistik Yıllığı* (Istanbul: Prime Minister's Office, 1973–1995).
Ürgüblü, Hayri, *Lozan* (Ankara, 1936).
Vandewalle, Dirk, "From the New State to the New Era: Toward a Second Republic in Tunisia," *Middle East Journal* 42 (1988): 602–620.
——— (ed.), *North Africa: Development and Reform in a Changing Global Economy* (New York: St. Martin's Press, 1996).
Walden, Bello, with Shea Cunningham and Bill Rau, *Dark Victory: The United States, Structural Adjustment, and Global Poverty* (London: Pluto Press, 1994).
Waterbury, John, "Export-Led Growth and the Center-Right Coalition in Turkey," in

Tevfik F. Nas and Mehmed Odekon (eds.), *Economics and Politics of Turkish Liberalization* (Bethlehem, Penn.: Lehigh University Press, 1992).
———, *The Egypt of Nasser and Sadat: The Political Economy of Two Regimes* (Princeton, N.J.: Princeton University Press, 1983).
Wehr, Hans, *A Dictionary of Modern Written Arabic*, ed. J. Milton Cowan (Ithaca, N.Y.: Cornell University Press, 1966).
Wensinck, A. J. [Ch. Pellat], "*Ḥūr*," in *Encyclopaedia of Islam,* Vol. III (Leiden: E. J. Brill, 1971), pp. 581–582.
White, Hayden, "Afterword," in Victoria E. Bonnell and Lynn Hunt (eds.), *Beyond the Cultural Turn* (Berkeley: University of California Press, 1999), pp. 315–324.
———, *The Content of the Form: Narrative Discourse and Historical Representation* (Baltimore: Johns Hopkins University Press, 1987).
———, *Tropics of Discourse: Essays in Cultural Criticism* (Baltimore: Johns Hopkins University Press, 1978).
———, *Metahistory: The Historical Imagination in Nineteenth-Century Europe* (Baltimore: Johns Hopkins University Press, 1973).
Willis, Michael, *The Islamist Challenge in Algeria: A Political History* (New York: New York University Press, 1996).
Wittgenstein, Ludwig, *Tractatus Logico-Philosophicus* (London: Routledge and Kegan Paul, 1933).
World Bank, *Will Arab Workers Prosper or Be Left Out in the Twenty-First Century? Regional Perspectives on World Development Report 1995* (Washington, D.C.: The World Bank, 1995).
———, *World Development Report 1991: The Challenge of Development* (Washington, D.C.: The World Bank, 1991).
Wright, J. W., Jr., and Everett K. Rowson (eds.), *Homoeroticism in Classical Arabic Literature* (New York: Columbia University Press, 1997).
Yapp, Malcolm E., "The Modernization of Middle Eastern Armies in the Nineteenth Century: A Comparative View," in M. V. Parry and M. E. Yapp (eds.), *War, Technology, and Society in the Middle East* (London: Oxford University Press, 1975), pp. 330–366.
Yeşılada, Birol A., and Mahır Fısunoğlu, "Assessing the January 24, 1980 Economic Stabilization Program in Turkey," in Henri J. Barkey (ed.), *The Politics of Economic Reform in the Middle East* (New York: St. Martin's Press, 1992).
Yeldan, A. Erinç, "The Economic Structure of Power Under Turkish Structural Adjustment: Prices, Growth and Accumulation," in Fikret Şenses (ed.), *Recent Industrialization Experience of Turkey in a Global Context* (Westport, Conn.: Greenwood Press, 1994), pp. 74–90.
Zarcone, Thierry, "La situation du chi'isme à Istanbul au XIXe et au début du XXe siècle," in Thierry Zarcone and Fariba Zarinebaf (eds.), *Les iraniens d'Istanbul* (Paris: Institut Français de recherches en Iran, 1993), pp. 97–111.
Zarcone, Thierry, and Fariba Zarinebaf (eds.), *Les iraniens d'Istanbul* (Paris: Institut Français de recherches en Iran, 1993).
Zilfi, Madeline C., "The *Ilmiye* Registers and the Ottoman *Medrese* System Prior to the Tanzimat," in *Contributions à l'histoire économique et sociale de l'Empire ottoman* (Leuven: Éditions Peeters, 1983), pp. 309–327.
al-Ziriklī, Khayr al-Dīn, *al-A'lām.* 8 vols. (Beirut: Dār al-'Ilm lil-Malāyīn, 1980). Vol. 3.
Zubaida, Sami, *Islam, the People and the State: Political Ideas and Movements in the Middle East* (London: I. B. Tauris, 1993).

Zurayq, Qustantin, *Ma'na al-Nakba* (Beirut: Dar al-'Ilm lil-Malayin, 1948); translated as *The Meaning of the Disaster* by R. Bayley Winder (Beirut: Khayat, 1956).

Zürcher, Erik Jan, *Political Opposition in the Early Turkish Republic: The Progressive Republican Party* (Leiden: E. J. Brill, 1991).

———, *The Unionist Factor: The Rise of the Committee of Union and Progress in the Turkish National Movement* (Leiden: E. J. Brill, 1984).

The Contributors

Walter Armbrust is the Albert Hourani Fellow of St. Antony's College at Oxford University. He is the author of *Mass Culture and Modernism in Egypt* (Cambridge University Press, 1996), and editor of *Mass Mediations: New Approaches to Popular Culture in the Middle East and Beyond* (University of California Press, 2000). Currently Dr. Armbrust is working on a cultural history of Egyptian cinema.

Joel Beinin is professor of Middle East history at Stanford University. During 2001–2002 he served as president of the Middle East Studies Association of North America. His most recent book is *Workers and Peasants in the Modern Middle East* (Cambridge University Press, 2001).

Juan R. I. Cole is professor of Middle Eastern and South Asian history at the University of Michigan and editor of the *International Journal of Middle East Studies*. His publications include *Roots of North Indian Shi'ism in Iran and Iraq* (University of California Press, 1988); *Colonialism and Revolution in the Middle East* (Princeton University Press, 1993); and *Modernity and the Millennium* (Columbia University Press, 1998).

Hakan Erdem teaches in the Department of History at Boğaziçi University, Istanbul. His publications include *Slavery and Its Demise in the Ottoman Empire, 1800–1909* (Macmillan, 1996). He is currently engaged in research on the reign and reforms of Mahmud II.

Israel Gershoni is a professor in the Department of Middle Eastern and

African History, Tel Aviv University. His latest publications include *Light in the Shade: Egypt and Fascism, 1922–1937* (Tel Aviv: Am Oved, 1999) [in Hebrew]; (coedited with Haggai Erlich) *The Nile: Histories, Cultures, Myths* (Lynne Rienner Publishers, 2000); and (coedited with Yaakov Elman) *Transmitting Jewish Traditions: Orality, Textuality and Cultural Diffusion* (Yale University Press, 2000).

Fatma Müge Göçek is an associate professor of sociology and women's studies at the University of Michigan. This article is the first product of her new project on silences in Turkish history.

Wael B. Hallaq is full professor of Islamic law at the Institute of Islamic Studies, McGill University. He has written over fifty articles and several books on Islamic legal theory, law, and logic. His latest book is titled *Authority, Continuity and Change in Islamic Law* (Cambridge University Press, 2001). He is now editing an eight-volume series published by Cambridge University Press under the title *Themes in Islamic Law*. Professor Hallaq is also the author of the first volume of this series, *The Origins and Early Evolution of Islamic Law and Jurisprudence*, now in progress.

Rashid Khalidi is professor of Middle East history and director of the Center for International Studies at the University of Chicago. He is the author of *Palestinian Identity: The Construction of Modern National Consciousness* (Columbia University Press, 1997); *British Policy Towards Syria and Palestine, 1906–1914* (Ithaca Press, 1980); and *Under Siege: PLO Decision-making During the 1982 War* (Columbia University Press, 1986).

Zachary Lockman teaches modern Middle East history at New York University. He is the author of *Comrades and Enemies: Arab and Jewish Workers in Palestine, 1906–1948* (University of California Press, 1996), and (with Joel Beinin) *Workers on the Nile: Nationalism, Communism, Islam and the Egyptian Working Class, 1882–1954* (Princeton University Press 1987).

Afsaneh Najmabadi is professor of history and of women's studies at Harvard University. Her publications include *The Story of the Daughters of Quchan: Gender and National Memory in Iranian History* (Syracuse University Press, 1998), and *Women with Moustaches and Men without Beards: Gender and Sexual Anxieties of Iranian Modernity* (University of California Press, forthcoming).

Roger Owen is the first A. J. Meyer Professor of Middle East History at Harvard University. He is the author of *The Middle East in the World Economy, 1800–1914* (Methuen, 1981), *State, Power and Politics in the Making of the Middle East* (Routledge, 1992), and (with Şevket Pamuk) *A History of the Middle East Economies in the Twentieth Century* (I. B. Tauris and Harvard University Press, 1998). He is currently at work on a biography of Evelyn Baring, Lord Cromer.

Şevket Pamuk is professor at the Atatürk Institute for Modern Turkish History and in the Department of Economics, Boğaziçi University. He is an economic historian of the Ottoman Empire and Middle East from 1500 to the present. His most recent publications are *A Monetary History of the Ottoman Empire* (Cambridge University Press, 2000) and *A History of the Middle East Economies in the Twentieth Century* (I. B. Tauris and Harvard University Press, 1998, together with Roger Owen).

Eve M. Troutt Powell is an assistant professor at the University of Georgia, where she teaches the history of the modern Middle East. Her book, *A Different Shade of Colonialism: Egypt, Great Britain and the Mastery of the Sudan* (University of California Press), will be published in 2002. She is currently working on a project tracking the lives of African slaves in the Islamic Mediterranean, and has coedited a volume with John Hunwick, *African Slavery in the Middle East and North Africa During the 19th Century* (Markus Wiener Press, 2001).

Mary C. Wilson is professor of history at the University of Massachusetts at Amherst. Her publications include *King Abdullah, Britain and the Making of Jordan* (Cambridge University Press, 1987) and *The Modern Middle East: A Reader* (University of California Press, 1993), edited with Albert Hourani and Philip Khoury.

Ursula Woköck studied law at the Universities of Hamburg, Tübingen, and Freiburg; and later studied history of the Middle East at Tel Aviv University. She is currently working on the history of German Orientalism, mid-nineteenth to mid-twentieth centuries.

INDEX

About the Book

Reflecting cutting-edge scholarship and covering more than two centuries of change, this seminal collection represents key trends in the historiography of the modern Middle East.

The authors each combine a methodological theme with concrete, original research, relating theoretical issues to the actual writing of history. Their topics range from the Israeli-Palestinian conflict to globalization, from well-established historical figures to new actors, from the elite to broader strata of society.

Applying new kinds of methodology—showing new ways of "doing history"—the book serves as a singular guide to current developments in the field.

Israel Gershoni is a professor of Middle Eastern history at Tel Aviv University. His publications include *Egypt, Islam and the Arabs: The Search for Egyptian Nationhood, 1900–1930* and *Redefining the Egyptian Nation, 1930–1945* (both coauthored with James Jankowski), and *The Nile: Histories, Cultures, Myths* (coedited with Haggai Erlich). **Hakan Erdem** is a professor of history at Boğaziçi University in Istanbul. He is the author of *Slavery and Its Demise in the Ottoman Empire*. **Ursula Woköck** teaches in the Department of Middle Eastern and African History at Tel Aviv University.